The Olympic Club
of New Orleans

The Olympic Club of New Orleans

Epicenter of Professional Boxing, 1883–1897

S. Derby Gisclair

McFarland & Company, Inc., Publishers
Jefferson, North Carolina

LIBRARY OF CONGRESS CATALOGUING-IN-PUBLICATION DATA

Names: Gisclair, S. Derby, author.
Title: The Olympic Club of New Orleans : epicenter of professional boxing, 1883–1897 / S. Derby Gisclair.
Description: Jefferson, North Carolina : McFarland & Company, Inc., Publishers, 2018 | Includes bibliographical references and index.
Identifiers: LCCN 2018033362 | ISBN 9781476674452 (softcover : acid free paper) ♾
Subjects: LCSH: Olympic Club (New Orleans, La.)—History. | Boxing—Louisiana—New Orleans—History.
Classification: LCC GV1117 .G57 2018 | DDC 796.8309763/35—dc23
LC record available at https://lccn.loc.gov/2018033362

BRITISH LIBRARY CATALOGUING DATA ARE AVAILABLE

ISBN (print) 978-1-4766-7445-2
ISBN (ebook) 978-1-4766-3305-3

© 2018 S. Derby Gisclair. All rights reserved

No part of this book may be reproduced or transmitted in any form or by any means, electronic or mechanical, including photocopying or recording, or by any information storage and retrieval system, without permission in writing from the publisher.

Front cover image is of a T9 Turkey Red boxing card issued in 1911 by the American Tobacco Company (author collection)

Printed in the United States of America

McFarland & Company, Inc., Publishers
Box 611, Jefferson, North Carolina 28640
www.mcfarlandpub.com

To my wife Claire,
who I am lucky enough to have had
in my corner for the better part of 42 years.
Without her I could never
have been a contender in anything.

Table of Contents

Preface ... 1
Introduction ... 3

One—1883 to 1889 ... 21
Two—1890 ... 39
Three—1891 ... 54
Four—1892 ... 77
Five—1893 ... 111
Six—1894 ... 147
Seven—1895 to 1897 ... 168

Epilogue ... 184
Appendix: The Olympic Club Fight Record ... 189
Chapter Notes ... 192
Bibliography ... 199
Index ... 203

Preface

This book is a journey back to another New Orleans in another century. There is no one alive today who can remember life in 19th-century New Orleans. Fortunately, there are scores of historians and writers whose research and insights have helped me to understand the social and cultural constructs of that era. The formative years of New Orleans were spent scratching out a foothold along the bank of the Mississippi River, followed by wave after wave of immigration from French, Spanish, English colonists alongside Haitian and African slaves and free people of color, and American merchants, traders, and bargemen. The city absorbed this tangle of different cultures and languages, with their different spices and different food, their different customs, and different ways of spending their leisure time. The Central African Bantu word for okra is "gumbo," and that is exactly what New Orleans is—a delicious combination of different peoples mixed together over time that makes New Orleans truly unique.

When Errol Laborde, publisher of *New Orleans Magazine*, told me he would welcome an article on boxing in New Orleans, I jumped at the opportunity to share my love of the sport with my fellow New Orleanians. Reaction to "Lords of the Ring" (*New Orleans Magazine*, December 2013) was somewhat overwhelming. I was invited to speak to groups at universities and historical societies. One surprising realization I had when talking about the history of boxing in New Orleans was that while almost everyone recalled the epic fight between champion John L. Sullivan and challenger James J. Corbett, virtually no one could tell me how this fight came to be staged in New Orleans. And absolutely no one knew where this event took place or that it was actually the third world championship fight to be held at the Olympic Club over three successive days during the Fistic Carnival.

It is not surprising that no one had ever heard of the Olympic Club. It was established in 1883 as a gentlemen's athletic club catering to the city's expanding immigrant population in the Third District just downriver from the Faubourg Marigny, and between 1883 and 1893 its membership grew from 23 to more than 1,100. Members included politicians, bartenders, businessmen, attorneys, physicians representing a diverse cross-section of New Orleans society.

People were also generally unaware that for a brief four-year period between 1890 and 1894 it was the premiere boxing venue in America. This small athletic club hosted 33 regulation matches, nearly 40 percent of which were for world, national, or regional titles and championships. Nor were they aware of the club's massive wooden arena that could accommodate more than 10,000 spectators beneath its retractable roof. The arena also featured electric lights and was wired for both telephone and telegraph for the benefit of the working press from around the country.

There are so many little-known aspects of New Orleans that the history of the Olympic Club immediately struck me as one of those stories that needed to be told. It offers not only vignettes of the history of the city itself, but deals with how ambiguously worded laws, along with a healthy dose of political and police indifference, allowed boxing to occur in New Orleans when it was illegal in almost every other state. But the Olympic Club was not a one-dimensional institution. Its members engaged and competed in gymnastics, swimming, billiards and pool, wrestling, target shooting, baseball, and even chess. They held festive social events every quarter. There were at least two serious attempts to dethrone the Olympic Club, one by the Metropolitan Club and the other by the Crescent City Athletic Club. There was even an attempted murder of the club's president by a disgruntled former employer. But the true story of the Olympic Club revolves around the prizefights and exhibitions they staged and the championship-caliber boxers they attracted.

I would like to gratefully acknowledge my many friends at the Library of Congress, the Historic New Orleans Collection, and the New Orleans Public Library for their assistance in acquiring many of the images that appear in the book and, where applicable, for providing their permission to use these images. I also wish to thank Brian Boyles of the Louisiana Endowment for the Humanities for allowing me to rework portions of articles and essays that I contributed to *Louisiana Cultural Vistas* and their online encyclopedia KnowLouisiana.

Introduction

> Give me your tired, your poor,
> Your huddled masses yearning to breathe free,
> The wretched refuse of your teaming shore.
> Send these, the homeless, tempest-tost to me,
> I lift my lamp beside the golden door.
> —Emma Lazarus, "The New Colossus" (1883)

New Orleans was founded by the French in 1718, surreptitiously ceded by France's King Louis XV through the Treaty of Fontainebleau to his Spanish cousin Carlos I following the French & Indian War in 1762, and ruled by the Spanish from 1763 to 1800 courtesy of the Treaty of Paris. When 80 percent of the city was destroyed by a fire which started in the home of army paymaster José Vicente Nuñez at Chartres and Toulouse streets on Good Friday 1788, it was rebuilt by the Spanish government, which is why the French Quarter prominently features Spanish architecture. New Orleans under the Spanish continued its unfortunate relationship with fire when the city was razed in 1792 and again in 1794 when another devastating fire broke out on Royal Street, consuming more than 200 buildings. New Orleans and the Louisiana territory was eventually returned to France in 1800 and was in turn purchased by the United States in 1803.

Perhaps because New Orleans has defied the odds by being situated in such an improbable and, at the time of its founding, a nearly inaccessible location, the city seems to have an affinity for risk takers, gamblers and aficionados of the sporting life who enjoyed participating in or wagering on all manner of games, events, and entertaining diversions. The resiliency of the city's inhabitants during this first century of change in no way diminishes the basic fact that life in colonial Louisiana was hard. Extremely hard. Given the physical nature of work during this period, most adults probably felt little need to engage in physical activity for recreation. Hunting and fishing were utilitarian pursuits rather than recreational endeavors. Diversions were few and limited to those brief social occasions where music and dancing could make one forget about the grind of daily life. What leisure time there was for adults might be spent reading, playing card games such as whist or cribbage, or enjoying board games such as chess, checkers, backgammon, and dominoes. Theatre, vaudeville, and puppet shows were available on all social levels, from taverns to town squares. Popular songs and ballads typically touched on politics, love, and sports such as boxing, cricket, fencing, and horse racing.

Children in colonial New Orleans, like children almost everywhere, played games such as fox and geese, hare and hounds, hopscotch, hide and seek, leapfrog, marbles, and jacks. The French introduced croquet while the Spanish popularized a counting game called "cuantas naranjas."

There was a wave of immigration that began at the turn of the 19th century following the Haitian Revolution in 1791, continuing through the Louisiana Purchase in 1803, resulting in nearly 90 percent of the new immigrants to the United States from Haiti, Cuba, and elsewhere settling in New Orleans by 1809. While the city's ruling class were predominantly white Creoles of French origin, by the time Louisiana was admitted to the Union in 1812 the city had become 63 percent black between free persons of color and enslaved persons of African descent.[1] The term Creole is derived from the Spanish "crillo," referring to children born in the colonies, not, as is often assumed, to the slaves brought to Louisiana. To be Creole was to be born in New Orleans, so by extension anyone—white or black—or anything—horses, cattle, tomatoes or strawberries—would be termed Creole if it was native to New Orleans and, by extension, South Louisiana.

As one clergyman would later quip, "It is no easy matter to go to heaven by way of New Orleans."[2] Nonetheless, immigrants, religious or otherwise, flocked to New Orleans in an exotic mingling of cultures, languages, habits, and manners that made New Orleans more interesting and sometimes more disturbing with each successive wave of immigration. Throwing such diverse cultures together often resulted in marked differences being at odds with one or more other groups, sometimes resulting in violence and lingering ill will. In 1830, New Orleans absorbed another flood of immigrants, but this time it was an influx of German and Irish settlers that caused the city's population to double. From a population estimated to stand at 76,556 during the War of 1812, which came to its conclusion with the Battle of New Orleans in January of 1815, New Orleans' population exploded to 517,762 by 1850.[3] This patchwork of interlocking puzzle pieces ensured that the city's diverse makeup produced an even broader selection of diversions and entertainment found nowhere else throughout the antebellum South or the remainder of the country.

While most immigrants were slowly assimilated into New Orleans' daily life, there was a growing animosity between the city's Creoles and the Anglo-American outsiders, merchants and businessmen brought downriver from Ohio, Tennessee, and Kentucky. The worst of these Anglos were the keelboaters and bargemen who the city tried to confine to a ten-square block area upriver known as the Swamp. There these crude Anglos would be permitted to drink and fight, activities for which they seemed most suited, until it was time for those who survived to walk back home penniless.

The sporting life in New Orleans was also influenced by the weather. The blistering summer, accompanied by the frequent yellow fever epidemics that often swept through the city, sent a significant number of its residents out of town during the summer months. Citizens and visitors enjoyed themselves outdoors during the fall through spring, but those who could afford to do so took off for the Gulf Coast during the summer months. In a city that appreciated music of all kinds from opera at the New Orleans Opera House on Bourbon Street, to the raucous dance halls and concert saloons in the Swamp or the Tenderloin District, from the brass bands, minstrel shows and concerts at West End or Spanish Fort, to the city's own beloved homegrown musical style, jazz, it was not unusual to hear passersby humming or whistling a popular tune as they made their way to the race track or to a cockfight in one of the small backroom pits on the fringe of the French Quarter. Residents and travelers alike could find some source of amusement at almost any hour of the day, even on Sundays. While other parts of the country observed the Sabbath seriously, Catholic Creoles, as a result of the Spanish and French influence in the development of New Orleans, felt unconstrained by the Puritan inhibitions found in New England and the expanding Midwestern United States. This too only served to widen the rift between the Creoles and the Americans.

Unlike most areas of the country whose middle and upper classes were grappling with the concept of what constituted "acceptable" leisure time pursuits, antebellum New Orleanians generally experienced no such cultural angst. Theirs was a city known for its freewheeling approach to fun. Other parts of the country were free to ponder culturally mandated cures for bodily and psychological stress caused by urbanization, industrialization, and the other by-products of progress, but not New Orleans. Following the Civil War an explosion of interest in athletic pursuits that one could enjoy as a spectator as well as a participant provided the citizens of New Orleans with ample opportunity to enjoy their newly acquired leisure time. It was an era that would produce a populace who would heartily embrace a "work hard and play hard" ethic. America as a whole was feeling its way toward a better life and nowhere was this more evident than in New Orleans.

Without radio or television, the city's dozen or so newspapers chronicled daily life and events, including the evolution of sports. The *Daily Picayune*, the *Times-Democrat*, the *Daily States*, the *City Item* and the *New Orleans Crescent* were the most popular dailies with the French paper *L'Abeille* (*The Bee*), the German paper *Deutsche Zeitung* (*German Gazette*), and the black-owned *Louisianian* rounding out the weekly offerings.[4] The short-lived weekly *Mascot* was one of the most controversial and entertaining newspapers available, often the subject of the news itself rather than just reporting on the news. Initially tucked away between the crime reports, business announcements and advertisements of all stripes were stories about sporting events. As there was no dedicated sports section per se, the reader had to carefully scan each column to find mention of the most recent sporting events. Stories on similar sporting events were scattered throughout the paper—baseball box scores, for instance, might be found on three different pages. Whether this was by design or a function of typesetting stories as they became available is unknown. However, by the latter part of the century the number of stories dealing with sports often overshadowed political events and coverage of Presidential elections.

Column space was dear. In a daily edition that averaged only four pages from 1840 to 1850, slowly expanding to an average of ten pages from 1850 to 1860, and again to 12 pages from 1870 to 1880, editors had to determine which stories qualified for coverage. With national and international news, state and local politics, and business news and advertising taking precedence, stories beyond these topics were not as important. Certainly no one's first thought was to write about sports and leisure activities, but when they did it was in a time before dedicated sports reporters. The newspaper had to rely on the firsthand account of someone who actually attended the sporting event, who took the time to write down what they had seen in detail, and then submit it to the newspaper. With any luck their handwriting was legible and their facts accurate and unbiased. As the public's interest in sports grew, the newspapers would assign a reporter to cover whatever sporting event had sent the paper a free ticket.

New Orleans, as well as the rest of urban America, was experiencing a cultural shift from people who bought their food instead of growing it, who purchased their clothes instead of making them, who rented or bought housing instead of building their own homes. And there was a strong need and enthusiasm for amusement and recreation. Along the way recreation turned into organized sports and became a viable commercial pastime for New Orleanians of all ranks. Prizefighters often served as nationalistic surrogates for the city's social and ethnic groups. The Irish in particular would use boxing and baseball as a way to earn money and gain social recognition in much the same way that African Americans would in the mid–20th century. But in the great gumbo that was New Orleans during the 19th century, Irish, Italian, German, French, Spanish and British immigrants all became Americans standing shoulder to shoulder at sporting events. Their appetite for entertainment was satisfied along with their growing pride that their new country could produce athletes of such strength, courage, and stamina. Organized sports had begun to subtly alter and become an integral part of the warp and woof of New Orleans.

New Orleans has always provided a study in stark contrasts, from staunch Catholic moralism to the ready acceptance of prostitution and gambling. In March of 1857, New Orleans became the first and only American city to license prostitution with the adoption of City Ordinance 3267, which raised more than a few eyebrows while also raising between $75,000 and $100,000 annually for the city's coffers. This social experiment would only last two years, being repealed following a barrage of lawsuits filed by the city's furious madams. Prostitution was actually encouraged during the Union occupation of New Orleans during the Civil War, and was even expanded during Reconstruction by ambitious carpetbaggers who explored every possible form of graft and corruption during their temporary assignment in what they believed to be a true cesspool of sin. Brothels were no longer "back of town," but could increasingly be found near residential and business areas. Indeed, the motivation behind Abner Powell's introduction of "Ladies' Day" in 1887 at New Orleans Pelicans baseball games was not to gain a whole new cadre of fans, but rather to tone down the swearing, drinking, and gambling in the grandstands at Sportsman's Park. As luck would have it, newspaper accounts indicated that many of the ladies in attendance were "working girls" who enjoyed the atmosphere of the grandstand just the way it was. There were, however, enough husbands who brought their wives, respectable ladies who, despite their ignorance of the game, became fully engaged in the action midway through the game.[5]

The latter part of the 19th century was truly the beginning of a leisure time renaissance in New Orleans, but don't believe for a minute that this assertion is based on some whimsical, nostalgic notion of what life was like in New Orleans at the time. Indeed, New Orleans was dark, dirty and a riot of numerous unpleasant aromas; ravaged by periodic fires, frequent floods and swarms of determined mosquitos; beset then as now by hurricanes and plagued by a wide variety of diseases such as yellow fever, cholera and malaria that contributed to a life expectancy of 38 years in 1850,[6] making it by most accounts, the least healthy metropolis in America. The city was constantly draining the swampland that surrounded the city, dislocating everything from alligators to water moccasins, in order to provide additional room for expansion. And despite having a privately-owned water company that pumped water from the Mississippi River—which being unfiltered and muddy would prove to be wholly unsuitable for use in cooking, bathing or any other domestic purpose—it would not be until the end of the 19th century that the city properly addressed its sanitation, sewerage and water issues.[7]

What was Bienville thinking when he laid claim to this paradise for France? The original settlers tasked with clearing land for a new settlement were a sad collection of 80 salt bootleggers, accompanied by an assortment of vagabonds, beggars, thieves, and other casualties of French life fresh from the prisons of France, with a couple of engineers thrown in to oversee the work. From the time these first beleaguered settlers arrived, New Orleans was by and large a very violent place where an argument over a card game or a woman could escalate to bloodshed in a heartbeat and where rival gangs of immigrants would stage their very public feuds. Their favorite gathering place was usually a sot hole squarely on the bottom rung of public houses, the *tapis-franc*, an unsavory brothel masquerading as a tavern, usually run by an ex-convict and frequented by felons and sporting the finest collection of gut-rotting concoctions in and around New Orleans. Visiting merchants traveling to the city by riverboat or railroad were regaled with stories of the exotic and strange pleasures waiting to be discovered in New Orleans. Yet it was difficult not to love New Orleans, in either its poverty or its glamor, both of which could shock or sadden, but which would eventually capture these visitors, boring beneath their skin and taking up residence in their hearts. However, nothing could prepare them for the city's rampant lawlessness and its dysfunctional law enforcement system.

Nonetheless, despite the odds, New Orleans continued to scratch out a foothold on the Mississippi River crescent, continued to grow, continued to absorb a tangle of cultures and religions, and inexplicitly continued to thrive. The rapidly frenetic pace that accompanied the transition from a rural-agrarian society to an urban-industrial society, and which afforded even middle-class workers more leisure time, found New Orleanians beginning to take full advantage of the opportunities available to them. Over the years many pundits have tried to characterize the attitude of New Orleanians in this regard—that they would devote as much, if not more, time to the pursuit of happiness than to their chosen vocations; that amassing wealth was secondary to *joie de vivre*; that New Orleans was a city where tradition overshadowed innovation. In many respects, the pundits would be correct. In the conundrum that is New Orleans it should be remembered that the city had the first opera house in the United States (1796), but was the last major city to build a sewerage system (1899).

Anyone trying to understand New Orleans by scratching the surface would be completely and thoroughly perplexed. No more so than watching the lines of uncertain ladies exiting their carriages, dressed to the nines, hiking up their handmade silk dresses as far as they dared in order to avoid the muddy streets by negotiating an uneven path on gunwale sidewalks formed from the tattered lumber planks recycled from the non-stop flotilla of barges and flatboats. Their ultimate destination was the American Theatre, built by James H. Caldwell in 1822 outside of the French Quarter on Camp Street near Poydras in the newly laid out American Sector. Here on the upriver side of the

French Quarter, across Canal Street, the American immigrants to New Orleans established their own enclave to further distance themselves from the Creoles.

In an effort to insulate themselves even more from the Creoles and the other "gullyfluff," that growing underclass of citizens they deemed to be the immoral and corrupt mudsill of society, the Anglo-American community established a number of exclusive social clubs. Such institutions quickly became a staple of the daily life for the upper-class American elite in New Orleans. The Boston Club, established in 1841, is the third oldest gentlemen's social club in the United States. Among the other well-known social organizations still in operation in New Orleans are the Pickwick Club (1857) and the Louisiana Club (1879). Although these concerns are better known today for their role in staging the myriad public parades and private balls during Mardi Gras season, they originated as a convenient gathering place for gentlemen to relax in the company of their social peers while enjoying a game of cards or chess. The citizens of New Orleans were given a glimpse into this blue-stocking world courtesy of the enterprising publisher of the *Daily Picayune*, Eliza Jane Nicholson, who, under the byline "Pearl Rivers," began chronicling the marriages, parties, and travel plans of the city's elite beginning in 1879 in the society pages of her newspaper.[8] She set the standard for what she believed was respectable, what she believed was acceptable, and therefore what everyone should strive to achieve in their own lives. More often than not this advice was couched in phrases such as "what the better element" was doing, with constant reminders of what was expected of "the best class of people." Understanding one's social milieu was engrained into the New Orleans psyche.

Following the formation of specialty clubs such as the Southern Yacht Club (1849), the Harmony Club (1863), and the French Opera Club (1869), came the organization of the Young Men's Gymnastic Club (1869) which was actually reconstituted from the residual membership of the Young Men's Gymnasium (1857). Later there would be the Chess, Checkers, and Whist Club (1880), the Camera Club (1880), and a wide range of other organizations catering to a diverse population. Each appealed to the specific interests of its members while providing a social aspect to their activities.

The most popular of these newer specialty social clubs were those dedicated to the cultivation of athletics and fitness.

Athletic Clubs

The prevailing attitude towards athletic endeavors was to insist upon a clear and distinct line between amateur and professional athletics. Competing for monetary consideration would not only result in the loss of one's amateur status, but more importantly was also not considered to be the sort of conduct a proper gentleman would engage in. At first blush this seems rather incongruous in a city that openly embraced gambling—from the Louisiana State Lottery to betting on horse racing, cockfights, and other athletic events to frequenting the scores of gambling houses scattered throughout the city. But it was not that money was involved on the periphery, but rather the act of being paid to play a game that initially caused the unfavorable sentiment towards paid athletes.

Beginning prior to the Civil War and continuing thereafter, the formation of sporting organizations nationwide was on the rise with the establishment of the National Association of Base Ball Players (1858), the National Association of Amateur Oarsmen (1872), the National Rifle Club Association (1871), the League of American Wheelmen (1880), the United States Lawn Tennis Association (1881), and the United States Golf Association (1894).

Gymnasiums were among the first purely athletic clubs, and one of the first gymnasiums established in New Orleans was Roper's Gymnasium, Sparring and Fencing Academy which opened on January 22, 1844, at No. 12 St. Charles Street.[9] Extolling the virtues of physical exercise as well as advertising exaggerated claims of medical benefits of exercise such as removing "pains in the breast; also Dyspepsia, and almost any chronic disease." Dyspepsia, in its simplest form, is better known as indigestion. The proprietor, Jim Roper, was an Englishman who came to New Orleans between 1833 and 1838. Despite being quite tall, he initially found work as a jockey, but he was also known for "indulging in the sports of the ring" and for training others to box.

By 1854 Roper moved to larger quarters shared with John Travis' shooting gallery at 9 Perdido Street between Carondelet and St. Charles, on the second floor above The Shades, and advertised it as Roper & Travis's Gymnasium. By 1855 the concern was advertised as Roper's Gymnasium, Pistol Gallery and Chess Room. By 1865 it was known as Roper's Gymnasium and School of Arms, still highlighting boxing and fencing lessons.[10] For nearly 25 years Roper served generations of New Orleanians worried about being "loose in limb, weak in muscle, and hollow in chest." Athletic development was considered a medical necessity to overcome the impact of urbanization and industrialization on a growing middle and upper-class segment of the population also seeking to offset a lifestyle of "amusement, gaiety and dissipation."

Following Roper's death in 1868 came the formation of several gymnasiums, principally the Clerk's Benevolent Association Gymnasium at 107 St. Charles Street (opposite the St. Charles Theatre) and the American Gymnasium at 103 St. Charles Street in the former home of the Normal Gymnasium founded in 1858. The Young Men's Christian Association (Y.M.C.A.) and the Young Men's Gymnastic Club (Y.M.G.C.) would also emerge between 1869 and 1879.

Gymnasiums were generally operated on a subscription basis or a monthly membership plan. This allowed them to accommodate all levels of society. However, following the trend in business both nationally and locally, private clubs were later chartered and reorganized as stock companies, requiring a member to own at least one share of stock in the venture. The intent was to prevent the lower classes from participating, but also to provide the needed capital to acquire and fully furnish a suitable facility. Among the most successful athletic clubs in New Orleans were the Young Men's Gymnastic Club and the Southern Athletic Club (1888), each boasting in excess of a thousand members at their peak. However, the most famous athletic club of them all was the Olympic Club.

The Olympic Club

During its brief tenure (1883–1897) the Olympic Club offered its members a wide variety of diversions and sponsored teams to compete in numerous disparate activities:

- Gymnastics, calisthenics, and general fitness (1883–1897)
- Chess, board games, and card games (1884–1897)
- Swimming (1885–1897)
- Billiards and pool (1885–1897)
- Boxing (1885–1897)
- Wrestling (1885–1897)
- Target shooting (1886–1897)
- Tug of war (1887)
- Baseball (1891–1892)

At one point in 1891 there was a proposal to sponsor a rowing regatta, but nothing lasting ever came of the idea. In 1895 a small group even proposed putting on bull fights,[11] but this too came to nothing. As broad a slate of available activities as the Olympic Club provided its members, there were three that seemed to resonate the most with these vibrant young men—target shooting, billiards, and boxing.

Rifle Clubs

In the early 19th century, it was not altogether unusual to spot someone in New Orleans, like most cities, carrying a rifle or shotgun through the streets. Rifles were commonly used in hunting and for personal defense. Arms and ammunition could be readily purchased in New Orleans at Gossip & Company (1840), Hubbard & Bowers (1844), William Kernaghan's (1852), Fulsom & Company (1866) or Taylor & Churchill (1869) where rifles were offered for sale ranging in price from $10 to $20.[12]

The idea of using a rifle or shotgun for recreation was still something of a novel concept in the early 19th century. Firearms were, after all, utilitarian instruments manufactured for the practical purpose of hunting or self-defense. The thought of firing off 100 to 200 cartridges in competitive target practice was, to most people, just wasting ammunition and probably did not even occur to many Americans. Even those who found themselves drawn into an "affair of honor" stood a better than average chance of surviving the encounter as these duels would frequently not result in fatal wounds. There are numerous published accounts of duels with pistols, muskets, shotguns, and rifles where multiple rounds of fire missed the participants completely.[13] And, as urban settlements became more developed and secure, citizens eventually felt little need to carry a rifle or a shotgun when a small pistol such as a Derringer would serve its owner well at close range in most situations.

Not surprisingly, attitudes evolved as time passed. In 1840 New Orleanians could take part in a Christmas Day turkey shoot at John Dunn's property across the Mississippi River just above the Second Municipal Ferry. For 25 cents per shot you could try your hand at bagging one of 50 gobblers released at a distance of 120 yards.[14] Summertime amusements at resorts along the Gulf Coast also included pistol and rifle shooting.

In the early 1840s the New Orleans Rifle Club was organized and its members frequently competed against one another and periodically engaged in contests with visitors to the city. The club's shooting grounds were located in Algiers.[15] In 1845 a member of the club bested a gentleman from Switzerland at an undisclosed site across the river, possibly at the club's range, each firing 50 shots from the improbable distance of 166 yards. Another such contest was held in February of 1848 between a member of the club and a gentleman from Kentucky at the rope walk along the Melpomene Canal.[16]

As in many things, it was a point of pride among competitive shooters to prove the pedigree and performance of their favorite rifles, and New Orleanians were justifiably proud of the firearms produced locally. Many of the rifles used in these competitive events were manufactured in New Orleans by the firm of Allen & Hille at 89 Magazine Street. After the Civil War, Louis Gerteis continued to produce firearms from his facility at 75 Magazine Street.[17] Other popular brands, those with national and international distribution and recognition, would have included Minie (1847), Sharps (1848), Springfield (1855), Joslyn (1855), J.F. Brown (1860), Henry (1860), Stevens (1864), and Winchester (1866). Popular pistol brands used in New Orleans were Remington (1816), Dean & Adams (1851), Smith & Wesson (1852), and Colt (1855).

When Jim Roper moved his popular gymnasium in 1855 into John Travis' shooting gallery on Perdido Street just off St. Charles Avenue, Travis had earned a national reputation as "the best pistol shot in the world,"[18] and this in a city that was considered by many to be the dueling capital of the United States.[19] Interest was such that by 1857 there were several shooting galleries along St. Charles Avenue between Canal Street and City Hall.[20]

Contributing to the growing popularity of target shooting were the numerous military groups formed that became part of the state militia, such as the Montgomery Guards, the Marion Rifles, and the Louisiana Greys. Each group had their own uniforms and armory and their practice grounds were scattered across the outskirts of the city where they conducted marching drills and target practice.[21] However, as the escalating tone of regional and national militant political rhetoric grew louder and louder, New Orleanians began engaging in target shooting in earnest to better be prepared should the rumored war between the states become a reality.[22] Those living in urban areas who had given any thought to becoming proficient in battle, the ultimate expression of self-defense, honed their skills at these galleries or in the countryside. During the Civil War, Union forces quickly discovered, sometimes fatally, that Southern soldiers were much better sharpshooters than their Northern counterparts. In fact, records indicate that the Union army initially only purchased nine sniper rifles, with only six of those outfitted with telescopic sights,[23] while most Southern units had soldiers who brought their own long rifles.

After the war, organized groups of shooters began to grow as several rifle clubs were formed—the Crescent City Rifle Club (1869), the New Orleans Rifle Club (reformed in 1870), the Behan Rifle Club (1873), the Jackson Rifle Club (1874), and the Washington Artillery Rifle Club (1877). In the decade between 1875 and 1885, the two most prominent and active organizations were the New Orleans Rifle Club and the Crescent City Rifle Club. Their competitions were generally between their own club members, although they periodically challenged each other. They were also occasionally pitted against groups passing through New Orleans such as when Major A.B. Leach and the celebrated Irish national team visited the city 1874.[24] The two clubs shared a common shooting ground known as Frogmoor, located near City Park and the Fair

Grounds, backing up to Bayou St. John.[25] There the Irish shooters quickly discovered that these everyday Americans were far better at long range shooting than even the British national team.

In 1876 there were additional mounds built at Frogmoor at distances of 800, 900, and 1,000 yards which would enhance the existing ranges at 50, 200, and 500 yards. These long-distance ranges not only had individual spotters with telescopes next to each shooter, but were also connected by telegraph from the target mound to the shooter to convey the shooter's results immediately. The clubs also encouraged competition between female shooters, arranging for special oversized targets to accommodate them.[26]

On October 12, 1876, the Crescent City Rifle Club sponsored a novel interstate rifle match which attracted teams from clubs in eight states: Rhode Island, New York, Michigan, Vermont, Connecticut, Wisconsin, Massachusetts, and Louisiana. New York entered four different teams in the competition. Teams were allowed to compete on their respective home ranges overseen by impartial third-party judges, with the resulting scores being transmitted daily to New Orleans by telegraph. The results were tallied and the standings were retransmitted to all of the participating clubs. Contested over a period of several weeks, the tournament was an ambitious and innovative undertaking that drew national attention to the riflemen of New Orleans. The trophy was eventually captured by the Crescent City Rifle Club with a score of 1,507 points,[27] followed by the Amateur Rifle Club of New York City at 1,423 and the Dearborn Rifle Club of Chicago at 1,420. The victorious Crescent City Rifle Club was admirably represented by Dr. George Howe, John K. Renaud, Dudley Selph, R.G. Eyrich, Colonel John Glynn, A.D. Babbitt, Major William Arms, and L.B. DaPonta. It is worth noting that four of the five members of the second place Amateur Team from New York were also members of the American national team that had set a record of 1,577 in international competition at the Creedmoor Range in Long Island, New York.

The Crescent City Rifle Club also sponsored the Scooler Bulls-Eye Trophy, an annual contest sponsored by a local jewelry company. The tournament pitted the most proficient local shooters against one another to tally the most bull's eyes with ten shots from 800 yards, 15 shots from 900 yards, and 20 shots from 1,000 yards.[28] At this distance, and shooting without a scope, the three-inch to five-inch center of the target looked more like a pinhead, attesting to the skill of these shooters. As in most tournaments, shooters competed from various positions—standing, kneeling, and prone being the most common. In 1876 the trophy was captured by Dr. George Howe who narrowly defeated John K. Renaud by the score of 209 to 197. The competition was still being held as late as 1884 on the "prairie back of St. Charles and Marengo."[29]

By 1886 the Louisiana Rifle Club had established their range on Poland Avenue in the city's Third District and organized competition between teams from several social clubs such as the Olympic Club, the Bachemin Club and the Eicke Club.[30] The following year there was a very active rifle club scene in the city, with 17 individual rifle clubs competing in the Louisiana State Rifle League against each other and other clubs throughout the state. The most popular New Orleans rifle clubs were the J.P. Arnoult Rifle Club, the Bachemin Rifle Club, the Commercial Rifle Club, the Eagle Rifle Club, the Eicke Rifle Club, the Endeavor Rifle Club, the Enterprise Rifle Club, the Expectation

Rifle Club, the Lawson Rifle Club, the Louisiana Rifle Club, the Metropolitan Rifle Club, the Olympic Rifle Club, the Orleans Rifle Club, the Pelican Rifle Club, the Southern Rifle Club, the Unexpected Rifle Club, and the Volunteer Rifle Club.

Weather permitting, there were competitive shooting events nearly every weekend. Among the very first events sponsored by the Olympic Club was a rifle tournament.[31] However, it was not at all unusual for someone to belong to the Olympic Club, but compete for one of the other rifle clubs. In due course, many of these rifle clubs consolidated or merged with a broader athletic club. These tournaments would attract non-shooting club members, but were also open to the public free of charge and would often draw anywhere from a few dozen to several hundred spectators. The winning rifle team might take home a modest cash prize, but usually the prize most sought after was a specified number of rifle cartridges. Given that a team might field as many as ten shooters, each of whom would fire off between 45 and 50 shots in each of three rounds of competition, a rifle club could expend from 1,500 to 2,000 cartridges per day. A three-day event could cost each shooter as much as $75 to $100, so winning 5,000 cartridges[32] not only replenished the team's armory, but could also be quite profitable, side wagers notwithstanding.

The average New Orleanian could also witness feats of remarkable sharpshooting by attending Buffalo Bill's touring Wild West Show, which grew from a modest band of 24 performers in a stage show at the St. Charles Theatre during holiday week 1879 into a full blown, raucous outdoor production during their month-long engagement at Oakland Park in 1883 featuring hundreds of performers. During their extended, five month stay in 1885, spectators not only witnessed Buffalo Bill's skill with a rifle, but also that of headliners Annie Oakley and Calamity Jane. For 50 cents, New Orleanians could surround themselves with the romantic notion of settling the West and defeating the savage Indian nations that they had only read about in dime novels.[33] This was a powerful draw to those entrenched in urban environments.

Billiards

The game of billiards was introduced into colonial America and found its way to New Orleans as early as 1723, growing in popularity across all social classes.[34] Billiards was less expensive than bowling or ten pins and was more individualistic. The popularity of the game evolved on two divergent tracks—the first among the upper class and the second among the hoi polloi. Although often looked down upon by many, the city's upper-class citizens would enjoy the game from the comfort of their homes or at their private club while everyone else would have to seek their satisfaction in one of the city's many billiard parlors and pool halls.[35] The rise in popularity was in direct proportion to the rise in the number of companies manufacturing billiard equipment and tables. By 1837 the New Orleans cabinet and furniture manufacturing firm of Barnes & Uhjohn at 85 Bienville Street advertised their inventory of domestically manufactured billiard tables,[36] which could be outfitted with cues and billiard balls from the Golden Comb just around the corner at 70 Chartres Street.

The decline in the number of billiard tables available in taverns, coffee houses, and billiard parlors coincided with the emergence of private social clubs. For instance, the Pelican Club House on Canal and Baronne streets had its entire third floor converted into a single spacious 2,000-square-foot room occupied exclusively by billiard tables.[37] The involvement of the upper class had little or no impact on the development of the game. In a never-ending search for respectability, to many billiards was merely another way of proving one's manhood that did not involve drinking, fighting, or wenching.

When resort hotels along the Gulf Coast from Pass Christian, Mississippi, to Pensacola, Florida, began advertising billiard rooms as part of their amenities, local hoteliers like the St. Louis Hotel and the St. Charles Hotel took notice and began outfitting their properties to keep pace. M.M. Miller opened a spacious billiard hall over the Holt House on Gravier Street just across the street from the St. Charles Hotel.[38] The St. Louis Hotel widely advertised their billiard room, which was attached to the Brunswick sales office and was located in the concourse beneath the hotel. There patrons could select from tables trimmed in rosewood, bird's eye maple, mahogany, birch or oak whose felt-covered playing surface could be either marble, slate or wood.[39] The rebuilt St. Charles Hotel even offered separate billiard rooms for ladies.[40]

In 1857 New Orleans was often described as "one perpetual carnival," but it was not Bourbon Street or the French Quarter that was the focus of all of the excitement. Rather, it was a six block stretch on St. Charles Avenue between Canal Street and City Hall that developed what was a distinct "individuality of character." Indeed, in this six-block stretch there were no fewer than 45 bars ranging from doggeries to guzzle shops. During the day, the area was generally quiet, with the Bank of New Orleans attracting the most attention from the typical coming and going of its customers. After sunset, however, the scene came alive with its diverse mixture of "eating houses, saloons, shooting galleries, billiard rooms, and bowling alleys alongside music halls and theatres."[41]

Proponents of the game extolled its virtues as a cerebral, mathematical pursuit that could be enjoyed all year long by both men and woman. In addition to the "scientific" appeal, having women present at billiard tournaments would temper the language and conduct of the crowd. However, what had once been a casual pastime was becoming increasingly more competitive, principally through the efforts of billiard parlor owners who sponsored these spirited events.[42] On December 4, 1857, a match between two players identified only as "the Algiers Bull" and "the Bayou Lafourche Mule" for $2,500 a side began at an undisclosed French Quarter billiard hall and was anticipated to last for several days.[43] On December 17, 1860, a match began between William Foley of Detroit and William Tobin of California for $500 at the Odd Fellow's Hall—a thousand points up in a four-ball carom game—was also thought to take several days to complete.[44]

Why would it take so long to finish a single billiard match? In most instances, it was the agreed upon point total needed to win the match that accounted for the protracted time period. For instance, in the Foley–Tobin four-ball carom match in 1860, the first player to reach a thousand points won the game and the $500 prize. Four-ball carom was a popular billiards game, played on a standard five foot by ten foot pocketless table with four billiard balls, usually two white, one red and one pink (although there are other color variations). One of the white balls is marked with a red spot to distinguish it as the cue ball. A player scores a single *point* when the shooter's cue ball *caroms* on any two other balls in the same *shot*—with the opponent's cue ball serving as an *object ball* for the shooter. Two points are scored when the shooter caroms on each of the three object balls in a single shot. A carom on only one ball results in no points, and ends the shooter's turn.[45] Thus when played for only a few hours each evening it could easily take two to three days for a player to tally up a thousand points. Shooters didn't mind though because if they were cold one night their fortunes might reverse the next night and keep them in the match. After all, there were hundreds of dollars on the line; this in a time when the average annual income in Louisiana was $300 for a laborer, $550 for a blacksmith.[46]

Like many leisure time pursuits, billiards came under the scrutiny of those whose moral indignation with what they perceived to be blatant idleness. As soon as money became involved, billiards became tarnished and the reputation of those who played the game as well as the blacklegs and sharpers who engaged in gambling on the game suffered as well, at least in the eyes of those trying to raise the principles and standards of the citizens of New Orleans, sparing them the inevitable decline into the bottomless pit of moral turpitude that they believed was overtaking the city. Irrespective of the virtuous attempt to persuade the general populace to reject the game, billiard parlors were scattered across New Orleans, from the hotel billiard rooms to saloons and public billiard parlors to private clubs such as the Louisiana Pelican Club, the Boston Club, and the Olympic Club. And despite the oft-cited distasteful reputation of the game and its seedy players, billiards and pool remained a very popular public and private pastime in New Orleans. Its only rivals were baseball and boxing.

Boxing

Boxing is an easy sport to understand. The rules are few and fairly straightforward: two men enter a square ring standing toe to toe, with nowhere else to go but face each other, and with only their fists and their courage to determine the outcome. The basic strategy of boxing is twofold—either you hit your opponent enough times without being hit yourself so as to win on points, or you hit your opponent enough times until he can't continue. But to a purist, boxing is an art next to music itself.

The popularity of boxing in New Orleans dates to the early 1830s, when waves of Irish immigrants provided an enthusiastic audience. The Irish became masters of prize fighting in the 19th century as a way to augment their income and to gain social recognition. One of the earliest proponents of the art of manly self-defense was an Englishman named James Burke, also known as "Deaf Burke," who gave exhibitions at 84 Camp Street. On May 5, 1837, he met Irishman Sean O'Rourke at "the forks of the Bayou Road" just after high noon in a match that was heavily promoted by posting handbills in barrooms and on street corners. The fight itself was brief and unremarkable, but at some point after the third round O'Rourke's second apparently came too close to Burke and "received a severe blow from the *deaf 'un* himself." This apparently led to an all-out skirmish involving fists, sticks, and other weapons. Burke was followed by a group of Irishmen with "shelalahs [sic], dray-pins, whips, and what not" before someone handed Burke a Bowie knife and the reigns to a fast horse on which to make his escape.[47]

The mayhem continued when both sides returned to New Orleans and numerous altercations between the English and the Irish backers of both fighters took place in the general vicinity of the Union House at 68 Camp Street and Armstrong's, near Canal and Tchoupitoulas streets. Local police made more than a dozen arrests and the acting mayor, Paul Bertus, ordered out the Washington Guard to restore and maintain order.

Incidents like this, said to be instigated by "Irish hooligans," contributed in no small part to the general public's early disapproval of boxing and the prevailing attitude that boxing was no better than street brawling, pure and simple, appealing only to guttersnipes and hoodlums. It is no coincidence that the emergence of populist politics and boxing took a parallel course, with both camps courting the hordes of foreigners—the fight promoters for their dollars and the politicians for their votes. It is believed that the first organized system of "ruffianism for electioneering" in New Orleans was the work of an Irish prizefighter and promoter named Chris Lilly (Lillie), a former henchman for a notorious New York Tammany Hall crony named Isiah Rogers. Lilly was involved in a light heavyweight fight in September 1842 in New York against his bitter rival Thomas McCoy for 120 brutal rounds, Lilly anointing McCoy unmercifully—over 80 punches in the final round alone—until McCoy crumbled in a lifeless heap in the ring. Lilly quickly and wisely relocated to New Orleans to avoid prosecution. Tactics introduced by Lilly in New Orleans in 1848, and further refined during the elections in 1854, led to the ongoing corruption and poor administration that the city endured for countless decades.[48] That's an awful lot to lay on a single enterprising Irishman, as New Orleans politics had never been known on any level as a bastion of moral or political integrity.

In New Orleans, as well as most of America, prizefighting or boxing was a sport of questionable acceptance, often outlawed in most communities. Early bouts promoted and arranged by gamblers, brothel owners, and saloonists were often held in rural settings—in barns or in a makeshift clearing in the woods—anywhere that wooden posts and ropes could be hastily erected to define the ring and where paying crowds could be accommodated. Such settings were common "back of town," a short ride to the outskirts of New Orleans. Sometimes fights were held on barges anchored in the river to prevent police interference. Racetracks and ballparks located on the perimeter of the city were also popular venues. While paying lip service to the brutality of bare-knuckle fighting, New Orleans and indeed all of America was inwardly proud that their country could produce such men of strength, courage and stamina. Irish or Italian, it didn't matter where these fighters came from; almost everyone in New Orleans originally came from somewhere else. America in general, and New Orleans in particular, willingly absorbed immigrants into their vast melting pot, their gumbo, their free-form culture.

Bare-knuckle fighting was a mixture of boxing and wrestling, with a set of written rules compiled in 1743 by former champion Jack Broughton. These rules were designed to protect the fighters and put everyone on an even playing field, as it were. Under Broughton's Rules, if a man went down and could not continue after the referee finished a count of 30, the fight was over. However, it was also permissible for a fighter to take a knee at any time during the bout and thus ending the round and gaining a 30-second breather.[49] These rules were later modified by the Seconds of the Boxers in 1790.[50]

The next major evolution in boxing rules came in 1838 with the publication of

London Prize Ring Rules which required that fights be held in a 24-foot square ring surrounded by ropes and that tactics such as head-butting, biting, and hitting below the belt were declared fouls which would cost the fighter points that would influence the final outcome. However, matches under London Prize Ping Rules found that wrestling an opponent to the ground was permissible and would end the round. There was no set time for the length of a round, only for the interval between rounds. Rounds, as developed by the London Pugilistic Society in 1838 and revised in 1853 and 1866, would last as long as both fighters were standing. If a fighter went down, the round was over. Descriptions of fights that lasted for 70 rounds or more at first seem to be Herculean to the modern observer until one realizes that a round could last ten minutes or ten seconds. Combatants returned to their corner where their seconds or corner men would have 30 seconds to get their man ready to return to the bout.[51] A fighter's failure to return to the scratch line in the center of the ring within eight seconds resulted in his disqualification. This is widely held to be the origin of two popular idiomatic expressions—being "up to scratch" and the other to "toe the line," although some ascribe the latter's origin to the starting line in a foot race.

To protect themselves from low blows, it was customary for a fighter to wear a solid plaster belt around his mid-section beneath a colorful cloth or silk sash. And because fights were usually held outside, fighters wore leather boots with small spikes that could stabilize them on damp ground, but which could also be used to step on the feet of their opponent as yet another means of distraction.

In 1867, the Marquis of Queensbury Rules were published in England and it is with these 12 rules that we are most familiar.[52] For the first time the length of a round was set at three minutes with a one-minute break between rounds. The referee's 30-second count was reduced to ten seconds. Wrestling maneuvers were banned altogether, but perhaps the most significant development in the sport was the use of padded gloves. General opinion was that bare-knuckle fighting was nothing more than brawling that was as savage as a meat axe. With these new rules, boxing became more strategic, with more emphasis placed on defensive moves such as bobbing, jabbing, and counter-punching. Thus the "science" of boxing came into play.

In 1870, British heavyweight champion Jem Mace chose New Orleans as the site for his title bout against proclaimed American heavyweight champion Tom Allen for a $2,500 purse and the world championship. The two camps set out on May 10 for a location loosely described as "thirteen miles from New Orleans" which was, in fact, a small town known as Kennerville, easily reached on the Jackson Railroad. Mace defeated Allen in 10 rounds over 44 minutes before several thousand fans including General Phillip A. Sheridan and former American heavyweight champion John Heenan.[53] This match is thought to be the very first world championship prize fight in America and today a bronze statue in Kenner's Rivertown area commemorates the event.

New Orleans was the intended venue for the 1882 match between John L. Sullivan and Paddy Ryan which had to be relocated to Mississippi City (near Gulfport), as well as the famous 1889 fight between Sullivan and Jake Kilrain, which was moved to Richburg (south of Hattiesburg). The latter was the last bare-knuckle championship fight in America. Both fights were forced to relocate based on prevailing laws and political opposition from state and local authorities.[54] That is not to say that there was no boxing in New Orleans, just none with as high a profile as those fought for a national or world championship. Soon enough boxing promoters in New Orleans found a way around the 1882 state law which prohibited "personal combat with fists" by arranging bouts under the Marquis of Queensbury Rules which required, among other things, that fighters cover their fists with padded gloves.

One of the more popular boxers of the day was 20-year-old John Duffy, who was scheduled to meet J.L. Smith at Carver Park on Canal Street on June 15, 1884, in a triple bill that also featured two black boxers, Willis Kennedy from New Orleans against Steve Langster from Great Britain, and Fernand Chevalier against Jules Pujol, each bout for a $150 purse. Smith failed to show, but the other two matches entertained several hundred spectators. Two weeks later Duffy faced off against a fighter named the "Big Gas House Man" at the Southern Gymnastic Club Hall. In actuality, the "Big Gas House Man" was Ed Reynolds, a five-foot, seven-and-a-half-inch, 136-pound laborer who was not much competition for Duffy, who had three other fights during the remainder of 1884 alone.[55] Duffy would retire from boxing, choosing instead to become a boxing instructor at the Southern Athletic Club, earning the honorary title of "Professor." He also became one of the most popular boxing referees in the city.

Each of these pugilistic events was publicized well in advance and reported on in the newspapers and thus the police could have intervened, but chose not to. There were enough other things taking place in and around New Orleans that demanded the attention of a lax police force. The fighters held themselves out as amateurs and the purse was described as nothing more than a side wager between the fighters, thus not a "prize." At best, these bouts attracted a few hundred fans willing to pay the 25 cents for admission, and who were generally orderly and well behaved. In most cases the promoters didn't make any money on the event, so for the most part, the police were content to simply look the other way.

Between January and March of 1885 alone there were five notable boxing matches held at Sportsman's Park, the popular baseball facility located on the outskirts of the city at the end of Canal Street.[56] An unknown local laborer from the city's waterfront, Andy Bowen, made his debut in 1887 with a series of eight fights between January and September, mostly against marginal opponents. In 1889, the year of the Sullivan–Kilrain fight, Bowen is known to have participated in as many as four bouts.[57]

In January of 1890, New Orleans Mayor Joseph A. Shakspeare, a reform candidate elected with the backing of the Young Men's Democratic Association, refused to issue permits for any "glove contest." However, the New Orleans City Council revised City Ordinance 1194 to categorize prize fights sponsored by regularly chartered athletic clubs as permissible "exhibitions," thus outlawing all other types of fights.[58] There were also strict prohibitions against serving liquor and staging events on a Sunday. Fight sponsors had to post a $500 bond before each contest and tender a $50 charitable donation to City Hall that had to accompany any permit request. As a result, there were more than 15 significant fights held in New Orleans during 1890, starting with Andy Bowen and Louis Bezeneh in February at Sportsman's Park.

Boxing's popularity as a spectator sport was no longer limited to guttersnipes and hoodlums. Soon enough members of the socially prominent athletic clubs became an integral part of its growing appeal in New Orleans. This did not deter Louisiana Governor Francis T. Nicholls from pursuing anti-boxing statutes with state legislators who, in May of 1890, introduced Senate Bill No. 27, which was surreptitiously modified by the House of Representative to exempt exhibitions "which took place within the rooms of regularly chartered athletic clubs."[59] The Senate raised no objection to the House's modification and sent the bill to the governor for his signature. Nicholls was adamant in his refusal to sign the bill as amended, but the bill subsequently became law without his signature.[60] Nicholls would continue to rail against boxing for the remaining two years of his second term as governor, and later as Chief Justice of the Louisiana Supreme Court.

This clever bit of circumlocution in Senate Bill No. 27 provided a seemingly paradoxical distinction between "prizefighting" and "glove contests" would confound lawyers and legislators throughout much of the next decade. Yet out of this chaos the Young Men's Gymnastic Club was joined by dozens of newly chartered associations such as the Columbia Athletic Club, the Audubon Athletic Club, the West End Athletic Club, the New Orleans Athletic Club, and what would become the most famous of them all—the Olympic Club.

ONE

1883 to 1889

> "[W]e are a very excitable people—always craving a sensation of some sort—and partly to the equally palpable and still important fact that Muscle is King."
> —*New York Times*, March 9, 1860

Mayor William J. Behan and the city's civic and business leaders were gambling that 1883 would be a pivotal year for the city of New Orleans. The populace was still recovering from the massive flooding that swept through more than 260 crevasses along the levees from Memphis to New Orleans in 1882, washing away whole sections of rail lines and roads as well as a significant number of homes in New Orleans. Parts of the city were underwater for over 90 days.[1] At the same time the city was dealing with flood control they were also preparing to host the 1884 World Industrial and Cotton Centennial Exposition. The event was proposed by the National Cotton Planters Association the preceding year to celebrate the 100th anniversary of the nation's cotton industry first export to England in 1784. By 1884 over one-third of the cotton grown in the United States passed through the port of New Orleans. The port also handled the majority of the nation's sugar exports following the discovery by Norbert Rillieux, a Creole black man, of the process of boiling sugar cane to produce refined sugar. His 1843 breakthrough added to the overall tonnage of cargo passing through the port, which necessitated importing more and more slaves to harvest the labor-intensive sugar cane crop in Louisiana while exporting the refined sugar all over the world.

The site that Behan and the City Council selected for the exposition was upriver from the city, in the former town of Carrollton, where the cattle had been relocated from the bucolic lower City Park, the area closest to the river, and the swamp and weeds that covered upper City Park, the area closest to St. Charles Avenue, were filled in. Nearly every available inch of the 425-acre tract of the new exposition grounds was swarming with construction workers erecting everything from the massive three-story Main Building that, at 1,247,100 square feet, was one of the largest buildings in the world at the time, to the 500,000 square foot United States Pavilion, to the 117,000 square foot Horticultural Hall—the largest conservatory in the world—to the dozens of exhibition pavilions representing the numerous states and countries[2] that dotted the landscape now known as Audubon Park. Overcoming a financial shortfall that occurred when Louisiana State Treasurer Edward Burke absconded with nearly $1.8 million of the exposition's construction funds as he made his way to some foreign shore, as well

The 1884 World Industrial & Cotton Centennial Exposition saw the construction of several magnificent buildings, including the magnificent Horticultural Hall. At 117,000 square feet, it was the largest conservatory in the world at the time (Library of Congress).

as the typical corruption and scandals that always seem to accompany any public project in Louisiana, the exposition finally opened only two weeks behind schedule in December of 1884. By the time the celebration ended in May 1885 the city had hosted more than a million visitors, but the event ended deeply in debt.

In the period following the Civil War, the people of New Orleans spent the next 18 years applying their energies rebuilding their community and healing the wounds that had torn the country apart between 1861 and 1865. While most communities were trying to cope with recovering from the loss of whole swaths of young men wiped out by the Civil War, lost to the futile transience of political rhetoric, New Orleans, and to some extent Louisiana, were spared. Louisiana lost only 945 of the 620,000 killed, and of that only 214 were killed in battle; the remainder died of disease or as prisoners of war. However, Louisiana suffered disproportionately to other defeated Confederate states during Reconstruction due to the ongoing corruption from the back-to-back sham municipal administrations of Henry Clay Warmoth, P.B.S. Pinchback, and William Pitt Kellogg. Those making a legitimate effort to mend old wounds and rejoin the Union during this prolonged period of relative peace were weighed down by staggering debt in excess of $24 million[3]—approximately $542 million today—that left the city with scant resources for civic improvements and infrastructure maintenance. Even more so when combined with an overall slowdown in growth and immigration, and recurring outbreaks of yellow fever, cholera, and other diseases that continued to plague the city. In 1878 there were 4,046 deaths attributed to yellow fever alone. By 1883 the city recorded but a single death from yellow fever.[4]

The 1840 U.S. census shows that New Orleans was the third largest city in America, with the foremost and most active port in the country. By 1850 the city had dropped to the fifth largest. As 1883 dawned, New Orleans was still the tenth largest city in America,[5] but its place among the country's premiere urban centers had eroded such that they were never fully able to recover from the economic impact of the Civil War (1861–1865) and Reconstruction (1865–1877) which saw municipal corruption raised to the level of an art form, expanded first during the Federal occupation and then again during Reconstruction by Northern carpetbaggers who explored every conceivable form of graft known to man. The 1884 World Industrial and Cotton Centennial was an ambitious but ill-conceived attempt to tell America that New Orleans was ready to retake its place among the country's elite urban centers. While the exposition would be a critical success, it would unfortunately become a financial disaster. Cotton and sugar were still the port's principle exports, but could not fill the city's empty coffers fast enough.

Prior to the Civil War, being the second largest port in the country also meant that New Orleans was a major point of entry for immigrants. A wave of immigration between 1791 and 1809 brought new residents of all socio-economic strata to New Orleans, along with their diverse and colorful forms of culture and recreation. The 1830s provided another wave of immigration, primarily from Europe, and this fueled the city's rapid growth during the early part of the 19th century. These immigrants constituted a broad social under class, a diverse and disparate amalgam of ethnic, cultural, and racial groups whose activities were universally frowned upon by the enlightened and entrenched elite, the upper crust of society. These groups were defined not only by their economic circumstances, but also by what they did for a living and what they did during their free time. Their leisure activities would not only pucker many a blue-blooded brow, but were also, in many cases, downright illegal. Chief among this band of bodacious rogues were the Irish. Fleeing the economic depression that followed the Napoleonic wars (1803–1815), boatloads of Irishmen were shipped to New Orleans cheaply as "human ballast," replacing the boatloads of American cotton that had been shipped to Ireland and England.[6] To be Irish in New Orleans was to be just a cut above being a free person of color, and there was rampant anti–Irish prejudice in New Orleans as well as across the country.

While scores of immigrants worked as stevedores and dock workers along the New Orleans waterfront for as much as $4 a day, there were legions of Irish laborers toiling for as little as a dollar a day digging the New Basin Canal between 1831 and 1838. A massive undertaking, the 100-foot wide, 12-foot deep canal was designed to link Lake Pontchartrain with the American Sector of New Orleans, over a distance of just over three miles. An estimated 20,000 men died from cholera during its construction, providing inspiration for the limerick "Ten thousand Micks, they swung their picks, to dig the new canal. But the choleray was stronger'n they and twice it killed them all." Deceased workers were simply buried in the canal bottom or walls without ceremony or, in many cases, notice of any kind.[7] Those who escaped digging the canal became teamsters, longshoremen, rail workers, screwmen, soldiers and policemen. They settled all across the city and in the suburbs. The riverfront neighborhood located originally in the city of Lafayette along Magazine Street became known as the Irish Channel. Others, primarily fishermen, chose the eastern part of the city known as Irish Bayou. By 1850 nearly 20 percent of the city was Irish.[8] They gradually assimilated and were eventually accepted into the city's population.

Among the most beloved Irish immigrants to New Orleans was Margaret Gaffney Haughery, an illiterate widow who defied Union General Benjamin Butler to bring food to the city's poor and needy during the Civil War. When General Butler occupied New Orleans and imposed martial law in 1862, he set up barriers and posted curfews with standing orders to his soldiers to shoot anyone who attempted to ignore his directive. Margaret distributed food and milk to the needy outside those lines, and continued to do so despite several warnings from the sentries and pickets. Union soldiers finally arrested her and brought her before General Butler, where she promptly negotiated with the general for permission to cross the lines with aid and to get flour to her bakery. He informed her that she was to stay behind the lines or she would be shot or hung if she crossed them again. She queried the general if it was President Abraham Lincoln's expressed desire to starve the poor? General Butler replied, "You are not to go through the picket lines without my permission, is that clear?" "Quite clear," answered Margaret. To which Butler then responded, "You now have my permission."[9]

Major General Benjamin F. Butler was only in New Orleans from May 1, 1862, until December 16, 1862, during which he earned the nickname "the Beast of New Orleans" for hanging a man named William Mumford for pulling down an American flag from the New Orleans Mint building. Most notably, he also issued General Order Number 28 which stipulated that any female showing contempt for a Union soldier would be "regarded and held liable to be treated as a woman of the town plying her vocation." During Butler's brief seven-month tenure his brother Andrew succeeded in bilking the local gambling houses and brothels out of as much as $2 million while Butler succeeded in becoming the most hated man in the history of New Orleans and is still regarded as a scoundrel of the deepest dye. He was, however, no match for Margaret Haughery.

General Benjamin Franklin Butler led the Union occupation of New Orleans for a scant seven months in 1862, but earned the nickname "the Beast of New Orleans" for his treatment of its citizens during his tenure (Library of Congress).

Despite losing her entire family to cholera when she was only 23, Margaret worked her way up from being a wash woman in the laundry of the St. Charles Hotel and eventually built a successful baking business, Margaret's Steam and Mechanical Bakery. She generously distributed her profits to support the city's many orphanages and asylums. Following her death in 1882, citizens from all walks of life came together, donating their pennies and nickels to erect a statue in her honor. Margaret Haughery's monument is the first public statue erected to honor a woman in the United States.[10] It stands today in a small park at the intersection of Prytania and Calliope Streets in front of the former St. Theresa Asylum, one of the many beneficiaries of her generosity.

Between 1845 and 1851, a series of devastating potato famines fueled a mammoth wave of new Irish immigrants. Despite their humble beginnings and the systemic prejudice levied against them, the Irish somehow thrived in New Orleans and many moved beyond being common laborers to more refined occupations in the fields of medicine, engineering, and education. Until its sale to Capital One in 2005, the Hibernia National Bank, established in 1870, was the largest bank in the state.

Alongside the Irish were the Germans. Their history in New Orleans actually predates the Irish, going back to John Law and his ill-fated Mississippi Company scheme in 1720. The area they ultimately settled was upriver from New Orleans is generally known today as the river parishes—St. Charles, St. John, and St. James—and is often referred to as the German Coast. The village of Des Allemands was founded there in 1721 and still exists today. Des Allemands is French for "the Germans." All along the German Coast these hearty settlers quickly and easily assimilated into their adopted home. Those named Schneider became Schexnaydre, Wichner became Vicknair, Dubs became Toups, Wagensbach became Waguespack, and so on. Between 1718 and 1724 more than 10,000 Germans passed through New Orleans. To be German in New Orleans was a far better prospect than being Irish. Germans became well known for taming the Louisiana wilderness and were greatly appreciated. They became farmers, draymen and

This monument of Margaret Haughery is the first public statue erected to honor a woman in the United States (Library of Congress).

grocers; they operated hotels, breweries and bakeries, and thrived as merchants and bankers. During the 1840s the German community also settled downriver in the Faubourg Marigny and Faubourg Washington[11] attracted by relatively inexpensive land.

A "faubourg" was the French term for a suburb, usually delineated by a large land grant or plantation. The Faubourg Marigny, for instance, was the first neighborhood developed downriver from the city on land owned Bernard Xavier Phillippe de Marigny de Mandeville. One look at that name and you can bet that the land grant was because of his family's position back in France. Bernard Marigny, as he was most commonly known, was in fact the richest 18-year-old in the United States in 1800, having inherited vast land holdings in New Orleans and around Louisiana. He was educated in France and England, but was not a particularly industrious student. Rather, he was a fun loving, free spending rascal who did manage to learn a dice game called "hazards" in London, which he brought to New Orleans upon his return. Having learned only the rudimentary basics of hazards, Bernard improvised the rest and taught everyone he met how to play. Watching the Frenchmen squat and jump about during the game earned the players the derisive term "crapaud," or frogs, which Americans used to refer to Creoles in general. The name was eventually shortened to "craps" and became a sensation. And, as luck would have it, everyone that Bernard Marigny taught to play craps apparently played the game far better than he, resulting in large gambling debts. With his property already mortgaged to the Citizens Bank, his only recourse was to subdivide his property and sell it off piece by piece. His downriver estate became known as the Faubourg Marigny. Ironically, the street known today as Burgundy Street was originally called Rue de Craps. Marigny's land holdings on the north shore of Lake Pontchartrain became known as Mandeville, established three years before the city of Carrollton on the old Macarty Plantation.

Neighborhood development in New Orleans beyond the French Quarter spread upriver (to the west) into the Faubourg St. Marie and downriver (to the east) into the Faubourg Marigny and Faubourg Washington, a consolidation of six smaller faubourgs—Daunois, Montegut, DeClouet, Montreuil, Cariby, and deLesseps. These plantations too were surveyed and subdivided for residential and commercial development. Further upriver was the city of Lafayette (annexed in 1852), the city of Jefferson (annexed in 1870), and the city of Carrollton (annexed in 1874).

The Irish, Germans, and Italians who immigrated to New Orleans all had the same dream of a better life for their families, along with the hope that the next generation would be born in the United States, making them true Americans. To many it seemed as if it would take generations to wash away the field dirt from beneath their fingernails or the coal soot that covered their bodies like a cheap tattoo. Throughout their travails it was the promise of a brighter future that fueled their determination to become part of America's noble experiment in democracy.

With the annexation of the city of Lafayette in 1852 the city redefined its municipal districts. With the emergence of the American Sector as the city's preeminent business and residential district, the former Second District was now the First District, being the Faubourg Ste. Marie—from Canal Street upriver to Felicity Street. The former First District was now the Second District, consisting of the French Quarter from Canal Street downriver to Esplanade Street. The Third District was unchanged, being the

Faubourg Washington, from Esplanade Street downriver to the St. Bernard Parish line. The new Fourth District was the recently annexed city of Lafayette from Felicity Street upriver to Toledano Street, the border with the city of Jefferson. Eventually the city would establish seven municipal districts, often confusing in their delineation and composition, but no more so than many of the other geographical anomalies which thrive like nightshade in New Orleans.[12]

Not as prestigious as the First or Second Districts, the Third District is where many immigrant families would choose to settle. Land was inexpensive, but still close enough to the city and the business district that workers could easily commute by horse, carriage, or later street rail. Upwardly mobile, first generation Americans born of immigrant parents began their new lives in a place often referred to as the "poor Third" or the "dirty Third" for its hard scrabble roots. It was a pastoral, rural community that boasted the "best duck hunting" in the city.[13] Yet it was in the Third District that a group of 23 young men, eager to attain some measure of respectability unavailable to them in other closed circles, came together on May 3, 1883, to establish a new social and athletic club that they called the Olympic Club.[14] Being properly and legally chartered, they spent the first few months tending to the customary process of organization—electing officers and directors, safeguarding their meager finances, and finding a suitable clubhouse. They held semi-monthly meetings to review applications from potential new members and to discuss whatever club business was pressing at the moment. So, who were these intrepid young men?

John D. Carey was a 20-year-old cotton and sugar broker with the firm of Hyman, Hiller and Company who was unanimously elected the club's first President. William North was an employee of the Hart Piano Company who was elected First Vice-President. William Henry Wright was elected Recording Secretary. Benjamin G. Holscher, a 21-year-old insurance agent with L.H. Terry & Company, was elected the club's Financial Secretary, a position he would hold until 1891. Edward A. Koffskey was a 20-year-old cashier with the men's clothing firm of D. Mercier's Sons and was chosen to be the club's Treasurer. He would remain involved with the Olympic Club in various capacities through 1895.

The young men who comprised the Olympic Club were clerks and cashiers, musicians and merchants, bartenders and businessmen who the city's elite considered to be nothing more than a codfish aristocracy, and who the Creoles termed the "nouveau riche." But despite the disparagement of their neighbors across town, their membership ranks grew; they attracted men from other walks of life and other social classes who shared an abundance of energy and optimism, an enthusiasm for their native city and for their Third District neighborhood. In 1883 the Faubourg Washington was still very much a rural setting, with modest cottages and houses sprinkled between a wide variety of businesses.

On July 7, 1884, they opened their original clubhouse located in the former home of the late Dr. John Drysdale at 417 Royal Street between Elysian Fields and Marigny Street, near Washington Square.[15] Drysdale's widow had inherited several properties from her husband and leased the new organization this modest two story structure that offered a floor plan with sufficient space to convert its beautiful rooms into a central parlor, a meeting room, a library and reading room, baths and, of course, a gymnasium.

With membership now standing at 80, the new club appeared to be off to a solid start. The growing trend towards athletic development and exercise found many young men seeking just such a facility where they could engage in physical pursuits, but which also offered the additional advantage of a social club.

Despite its obvious and immediate attributes, the size of the facility at 417 Royal Street had been a point of contention among many of the members of the Olympic Club from the outset and the building soon proved insufficient to accommodate the growing membership. That the building was not centrally located in the Third District was another frequent objection and the Board soon identified and leased another building several blocks downriver at 636 Royal Street between Montegut and Clouet Streets,[16] on property once occupied by the Atlantic Press Yard No. 2 that operated a cotton press at that location. Also scattered throughout the neighborhood were breweries, stables, brickyards, coal yards, churches, schools, cotton storage sheds and seed oil mills, as well as dozens of residential cottages.[17] The location for the new clubhouse was selected because it was equidistant between Canal Street and the Jackson Barracks and was accessible at the time by two lines of street cars. Royal Street was cobble paved as far as Elmira Street (now Gallier Street) four blocks further downriver, but both Montegut and Clouet Streets were still uneven, rutted dirt roads.[18] This, however, was not at all unusual, for even as late as 1949 only 580 miles of the city's 1,148 miles of streets were paved.

The Olympic Club's new clubhouse would also be located just four blocks away from the newly formed Third District Building Association on Enghein Street (now Franklin Avenue) between Royal and Dauphine Streets. Chartered in April of 1887 and capitalized with 15,000 shares of capital stock at $200 per share, payable in installments of 25 cents per week,[19] the homestead provided investment capital for real estate development in the Third District. Three million dollars in 1887 would roughly be the equivalent of $73 million today, a considerable sum of money with which to finance and construct new residential and commercial buildings in the neighborhood. Among the initial 66 investors in the Third District Building Association were several Olympic Club directors, officers, and members including Louis P. Leonhard, Charles H. Genslinger, Joseph L. Sporl, Henry Thoele, Charles P. Drolla, Nathaniel H. Cloutman, Charles P. Leonhard, A.B. Cooper, M. Dardis, Victor and Henry Lambou, Charles Noel, Edward Koffskey, Benjamin G. Holscher, and Walter J. Wright.[20] The Olympic Club thus afforded members the perfect platform for young professionals to cultivate connections with fellow members socially, athletically, and economically, just as their more monied Creole and Anglo-American counterparts across town were doing. These brash upstarts had now established a business endeavor that would bring new development and jobs to the Third District and potentially bring new members to the Olympic Club. The Third District Building Association survived until well into the late 20th century.

The gentlemen of the Olympic Club rang in 1889 by announcing their plans to spend between $3,000 to $5,000 constructing a new state-of-the-art gymnasium.[21] There was also talk of adding a bowling alley and a shooting range, but the Olympic Rifle Club had already established a rifle range located on Poland Avenue, so perhaps what they intended was one designed for pistol shooting. In just a few short months, membership had advanced to 110, with another 15 applications in hand, and expectations were that the club would boast 200 members by April. To further that goal, they held a reception and dance on Tuesday, January 22, for the Lynwood Circle, a purely social club located on Esplanade and Gayoso Streets.[22] The Mardi Gras season had commenced on January 6—Twelfth Night—a strictly Catholic tradition celebrated 12 days after Christmas to mark the Feast of the Epiphany or the visitation of the three wise men. Final preparations for the various *ball masque* and parades occupied most of the month of February.

The Olympic Club spent the next few months completing the construction of the gymnasium, purchasing new equipment to outfit the facility, and continuing their ongoing membership drive. At the end of April, the Olympic Rifle Club went up against four other clubs at the Magnolia Garden (also known as Southern Park), scoring 1,084 points in the morning and 1,012 points in the afternoon to capture the second-place medal behind the Arnoult Rifle Club.[23]

By nine o'clock on Friday evening, May 4, 1889, the area surrounding the Olympic Club was blockaded with carriages. Membership was now approaching 200 and everything was in readiness to celebrate the club's sixth anniversary. The interior of the club was ablaze with electric lights illuminating immense, colorful Japanese umbrellas hanging from the ceiling. Strings of pagoda lanterns, multi-colored flag-draped palm trees, and gilt owls were strung waist high along the walls of each room. Music played continuously for the 500 attendees who danced the night away in the enormous new gymnasium on the first floor that had been converted into a ballroom for the evening. Outside, the long side yard had been floored and carpeted, tented and elaborately decorated with flags and lanterns, serving as a supper room throughout the evening.[24] Revelers enjoyed a diverse program of 30 dances until precisely ten o'clock when the Grand March, led by club president Charles Genslinger, wound its way through the rooms of the club.

Two weeks later Captain George Henry Mackenzie, the Scottish-American chess master from New York, visited New Orleans, causing quite a sensation. Although chess was popular and well known in New Orleans, it certainly would not rank at the top of the city's list of diversions and entertainments. But back in 1850, the city became involved in the competitive nature of the game after learning that a 12-year-old local prodigy named Paul Morphy defeated Hungarian chess master Johann Lowenthal in three straight games. By 1857, Morphy graduated from Tulane University's School of Law, but at the age of 19 was too young to practice law, so his father convinced him to participate in the First American Chess Congress tournament in New York city. There he dismantled his competition and was crowned the unofficial United States national chess champion. New Orleanians were captivated reading the reports of Morphy's travels through Europe the following year, devouring the details of each of his string of victories against most of Europe's established chess masters. The games were published move by move in the local newspapers. Morphy returned home in 1859 as the unofficial world chess champion, whereupon he promptly retired from playing chess to practice the law. He was often quoted as saying that he had learned how to play chess by watching his father and uncle play in their Royal Street home, better known today as the location of the world-famous Brennan's Restaurant. Thus the arrival of Captain Mackenzie in New Orleans was treated as a special event. During his visit he was the special guest of the Olympic Club, where on the evening of May 19, 1889, he systematically defeated 13 handpicked club members in 13 simultaneous, pre-arranged gambits before a large and enthusiastic crowd.[25] This exclusive exhibition was staged to draw interest to the club's upcoming chess tournament.

Several months later, as part of the formal opening ceremonies for the Olympic Club's new gymnasium, the club's newly hired boxing instructor, Professor John Duffy, put on a sparring exhibition with celebrated pugilist Mike Donovan in the gym's boxing ring. Donovan was a retired boxer who once fought John Shanssey in a bare-knuckle bout refereed by Wyatt Earp in 1869 in Cheyenne, Wyoming, and who was now a boxing instructor at the prestigious New York Athletic Club.[26] Duffy, the former Lightweight Champion of Louisiana, had met Donovan in 1884 when both appeared in John L. Sullivan's touring vaudeville show then appearing at the St. Charles Theatre.[27] Duffy was unabashedly promoting his forthcoming boxing match with Jimmy McHale from Philadelphia.[28] Also at the gymnasium's opening were William E. Harding, Sports Editor of the *Police Gazette* and former boxer Dennis Butler.

In 1859 New Orleans native Paul Morphy defeated the known chess masters in the United States and Europe to become the unofficial world chess champion (Library of Congress).

The Olympic Club was more than pleased to welcome such prominent guests, all of whom were on their way to the much-anticipated bare-knuckle heavyweight championship prizefight between John L. Sullivan and Jake Kilrain.[29] Newspapers across the country had been following the upcoming fight between heavyweight champion John L. Sullivan from Boston and challenger Jake Kilrain from Baltimore. Their every move was chronicled, their training regimens scrutinized and compared, their diets analyzed, and their travel schedules reported and tracked. Advertisements hawked the fighters favorite brand of nearly everything imaginable, from talcum powder to moustache wax. Whether or not the fighters knew of their "endorsements" is unknown, it is almost certain that neither man ever saw a penny for the use of their name.

News of the Sullivan–Kilrain match had many New Orleanians confused about

In 1882, Irish-American champion Paddy Ryan agreed to put his heavyweight title on the line by fighting the up and coming John L. Sullivan. There was also a $2,500 purse. The fight was originally scheduled to take place in New Orleans, but had to be relocated due to political opposition (Library of Congress).

the legality of such an event. If prize fighting was illegal, wouldn't the law simply say so in no uncertain terms? The Louisiana statutes on prizefighting, as in many other areas, were hazy on the matter. Known for its peculiar political history, Louisiana once had two duly elected governors. On January 8, 1877, Democrat Francis T. Nicholls and Republican Stephan B. Packard both claimed victory and both took the oath of office, albeit at different times. Packard would vacate his claim to the office a month later. So, something as simple as ambiguous or contradictory language in the law was not surprising. Yet there were many in New Orleans who questioned the legal footing being used by the fight's promoters, and New Orleans Assistant District Attorney John J. Finney conducted a brief review of the finer points of the governing law at a presentation to the Chess, Checkers and Whist Club, during which he informed his audience that in 1889 there was "no law directed especially against prizefighting."[30] The typical charge brought against those engaging in a boxing match was for a breach of the peace. Promoters who could afford to do so usually avoided this potential snare by paying for a police detail to maintain order.

In this instance, however, Governor Francis T. Nicholls had already stipulated that everyone involved in staging such an event in the state of Louisiana would be arrested for assault and battery, either as a principal or an accessory. This heavy-handed tactic had been sufficient in 1882 when employed by then Governor Samuel McEnery before the fight between John L. Sullivan and Paddy Ryan, forcing the relocation of the bout from the outskirts of the city at Fort Macomb on Chef Menteur Highway across state lines to Mississippi City (near Gulfport).

In the prior instance, both the Sullivan and Ryan camps were, from the outset, aware that the fight would take place somewhere in Mississippi along the Mobile Road within a hundred miles of New Orleans. The fighters had established their training facilities in Mississippi and were hard at work when word reached them that the Mississippi legislature was currently debating legislation that would outlaw prize fighting

On February 2, 1882, several thousand boxing fans traveled to Mississippi City (near Gulfport) to witness John L. Sullivan (*left*) deliver a first-class pasting to champion Paddy Ryan (*right*) beneath the live oaks at the Barnes Hotel (from an unknown 19th century publication).

with punishments including fines and imprisonment. Like two bands of gypsies, both camps beat a hasty retreat back to New Orleans, with Sullivan setting up at a rural resort in Carrollton and Ryan at the West End Hotel on Lake Pontchartrain. However, because of John L. Sullivan, the match attracted national attention, and it wasn't long before a congregation of churchmen called on Governor McEnery to persuade him to intercede and stop the fight, using the state law prohibiting prize fighting as their rallying cry. Representatives of the governor's office, accompanied by several well-known sporting men, were dispatched to both camps to inform the principals that any attempt to engage in prize fighting in Louisiana would be a serious violation of the law. After much hemming and hawing, and aided in no small part in learning that the proposed Mississippi law had failed to gain any traction and was, in fact, tabled for the foreseeable future, both camps swiftly decided to return to their original plan to hold the event in Mississippi.

On February 2, 1882, a special 14-car train left the Louisville & Nashville terminal in New Orleans at five o'clock in the morning with 1,500 fans including Frank and Jesse James and reporters from across the country.[31] The entourage arrived at Mississippi City, approximately equidistant from New Orleans and Mobile, at eight o'clock in the morning. At midday Sullivan and Ryan entered a makeshift ring erected under a grove of live oaks in front of the Barnes Hotel. Bare-knuckle fighting under London Prize Ring Rules was a mixture of wrestling and boxing, and Sullivan quickly proved to be the more adept at both phases of the sport. Throughout the first four rounds, both men exchanged short and quick punches and counter-punches, with the occasional right cross to the head or body, before clinching and wrestling each other to the grass to end the round. The total elapsed time of these 4 rounds was less than 1 minute and 20 seconds, typical of London Prize Ring Rules. After a bit sparring, Ryan caught Sullivan off-guard with an unexpected attack that felled Sullivan at the close of the 5th round. When time was called for the 6th round Sullivan popped up ready to go, but Ryan was slow to leave his corner to approach the scratch line. He had the look of an early Christian about to go up against a Roman lion. From that point forward Sullivan knew he had his man, delivering blow after blow through the 7th and 8th rounds. When Ryan's seconds would not allow him to answer the bell for the 9th round, the fight was awarded to Sullivan.[32] This was the beginning of the 25-year-old Sullivan's ten-year reign as the undisputed Heavyweight Champion of America,[33] and his two-fisted, ferocious style of fighting would earn him nicknames such as the "Boston Strong Boy" and "His Fistic Holiness." Sullivan's growing fame would make him an international celebrity and he would become the first athlete to earn over $1 million in his career.[34]

Despite infrequent local editorials against prizefighting,[35] New Orleans was quite content to allow prize fighters to train here and for boxing fans from across the country to crowd the local hotels and restaurants before boarding chartered trains to take them to the fight's ultimate destination. So, while prizefighting became more difficult, the contentious and confusing legal environment did nothing to stop promoters from arranging matches and actually contributed to a revival of interest in boxing in New Orleans.

When local fight promoters Bud Renaud and Patrick Duffy announced in early June of 1889 that heavyweight champion John L. Sullivan had agreed to return to New Orleans to defend his title against a young Irish-American from Baltimore named Jake Kilrain, the controversy over prizefighting was reignited. The portly Sullivan was whipped back into fighting shape by the well-known professional wrestler William "Iron Duke" Muldoon while Kilrain would be trained by Sullivan's chief rival, Charlie Mitchell. In 1883, Mitchell had been defeated by Sullivan in three rounds in New York and Mitchell now wanted another shot at Sullivan and his world heavyweight title.

As expected, details of the fight and its location were kept under wraps as politicians and policemen alike were trying to stop the fight before it began. Rumors of the fight's ultimate location were running rampant, with the fight said to be arranged in any number of possible venues from the middle of the Honey Island Swamp near the Louisiana–Mississippi border to the piney woods of Abita

Richard K. Fox was the owner and publisher of the *Police Gazette* and was an invaluable resource to New Orleans fight promoters Bud Renaud and Patrick Duffy in securing matches between promising fighters. He was known to be an ardent detractor of John L. Sullivan (from an unknown 19th century publication).

Springs north of Lake Pontchartrain and just about everywhere in between. Tickets at $10 for general admission and $15 for reserved seats were scooped up at a frantic pace, but the tickets didn't list a location. In today's dollars, these prices would be roughly $250 for general admission and $375 for reserved ringside seats. Patrons doled out their hard-earned greenbacks without any assurance that the fight would even occur. Were it not for the involvement of noted fight promoter Bud Renaud, the event may never have come off.

Born in 1853 into a prominent Mobile family, P.A. Renaud was nicknamed "Bud" by his uncle, John A. Soto, who later employed him at his New Orleans drugstore, Soto & Primo's. Renaud studied to become a prescription clerk, but was seduced by the pervasive gambling scene in the French Quarter, becoming proficient as a faro dealer. He would enjoy early success in a horse racing partnership with Barker Harrison, Alexander Brewster, and Charles Bush, which he parlayed into a wide variety of gambling ventures. Over the years, Renaud became quite well known throughout the Gulf Coast as a sporting man. For Renaud, organizing boxing events was little more than an amusing sideline, but it was one at which he excelled on a national scale. Having played a prominent part in arranging the Sullivan–Ryan bout in 1882, it was only natural that he get involved in the Sullivan–Kilrain match.

In predictable fashion, an executive order by Governor Francis T. Nicholls caused promoters to relocate the bout, and finally, on July 7, special trains from the Baltimore & Ohio and the Queen & Crescent railroads were chartered to accommodate the growing crowds for the trip. Fighters, their support teams, equipment, supplies and fans boarded the trains that would take them to the unknown fight venue. Hot on their heels was a massive contingent of the Louisiana State Militia, supplemented by local police, all engaged in a slow-speed land route chase, attempting to follow the two trains through a series of track changes and planned diversions, to no avail. The Mississippi State Militia joined in the chase, but spent a good deal of their time chasing shadows. The caravans came to a stop at around 8:30 in the evening approximately 105 miles northeast of New Orleans in a hamlet just south of Hattiesburg, Mississippi, known as Richburg.

The site was not much more than a rural lumber mill owned by former Colonel Charles W. Rich, but it was one which offered ample open area and a ready supply of lumber to construct the seating needed to accommodate several thousand fans from across the country. By agreement, the fight would be conducted under London Prize Ring Rules and the two sides settled on New Orleans politician and the future mayor of New Orleans, John Fitzpatrick, as referee. In Sullivan's corner were his seconds William Muldoon and Michael Cleary, bottleholder "Handsome" Dan Murphy, and timekeeper Thomas Costello. Kilrain was backed by seconds Charlie Mitchell and Mike Donovan, and bottleholder Johnny Murphy. His timekeeper was the legendary lawman Bat Masterson of Denver, Colorado.

At a little after ten o'clock in the morning on July 8, despite the best efforts of politicians and law enforcement officers in Louisiana and Mississippi, the two men entered the ring to square off under the sweltering Mississippi sun. Over the next 2 hours and 16 minutes, a crowd of mustachioed men in derbies and boaters watched Sullivan methodically destroy Kilrain in the 100-degree heat. The battle was fairly even in the early rounds, but Sullivan would eventually forge a devastating advantage. Both fighters reportedly consumed large amounts of whiskey and tea to remain hydrated and to sedate their throbbing bodies.

In the 44th round there was a surprised gasp from the crowd when Sullivan suddenly vomited profusely, usually an indication that a fighter was finished. Kilrain asked if he wanted to declare the fight a draw, only to be answered with a right hook that knocked him down. Despite Sullivan's weakened condition, Kilrain failed to capitalize on it and his fans were quickly disappointed as Sullivan rallied and continued his battering of Kilrain. Finally, and mercifully, at the conclusion of the 75th round, Kilrain's handlers threw in the sponge. Sullivan sported a slight cut under his right eye and a

On July 8, 1889, New Orleans photographer Thomas Pye captured this photograph of several thousand fight fans from across the country crowded around the makeshift ring in Richburg, Mississippi, to watch John L. Sullivan defend his heavyweight title against Jake Kilrain (Library of Congress).

small scratch on his left ear while Kilrain was badly bruised, bleeding from the nose, mouth, and ears. Thus ended what would be the last bare-knuckle championship fight in America.[36]

To the modern observer, the concept of fighting for 75 rounds seems overwhelming, but bear in mind that London Prize Ring Rules provided that a round would end if a man was knocked down or fell in the ring. Theoretically, a winded fighter could "slip" and fall to the ground and the round would be over, thus gaining him a 30-second reprieve between rounds before both fighters had to answer the bell for the next round.

It was said that Sullivan and Kilrain had "trouble finding a battle ground, and after the fight were hounded like horse thieves for finding it."[37] Immediately following the fight, both fighters and their supporters boarded their trains and took off, trying to remain one step ahead of the law for as long as they could. By order of Mississippi Governor Robert Lowry, both Sullivan and Kilrain were arrested in late July of 1889. Sullivan and his trainer, William Muldoon, were arrested in Nashville, and returned to Purvis, Mississippi, along with fight referee John Fitzpatrick for trial on August 15. Sullivan was sentenced to one year in the county jail, but was released on bond and he returned to New York on August 20. Muldoon and Fitzpatrick were fined $200 apiece which they readily paid.[38] Sullivan wound up paying out all of his winnings in fines and legal fees and swore he would never engage in another bare-knuckle fight. He was true to his word. Kilrain did not go to trial until December 14, having to wait for the trial judge, the district attorney and his defense team to return from the funeral of Jefferson Davis in New Orleans. An all-black jury found Kilrain guilty, sentencing him to two months in jail and a $200 fine.[39] Kilrain returned to New Orleans prior to serving his sentence and arranged matches with local fighter Felix Vacquelin at the West End Athletic Club on February 2, 1890, and with James J. Corbett on February 17, 1890, at the Southern Athletic Club. Both of these hastily arranged bouts were undertaken solely to help breathe some life into Kilrain's thread-bare pocketbook, drained from his loss to Sullivan, his fines, and his legal fees.

Ultimately, the acceptance and adoption of boxing by members of socially prominent athletic clubs such as the Young Men's Gymnastic Club and the Southern Athletic Club was an integral part of its growing appeal in New Orleans. Contests were originally arranged between club members, but in 1889 both clubs began to sponsor professional bouts. Boxing matches between non-members for public consumption, for a cash prize, was another thing altogether. For years, boxing promoters in New Orleans had been blatantly skirting the 1882 state law which prohibited "personal combat with fists" by arranging "glove contests" under the Marquis of Queensbury Rules, holding their events outside city limits where police were not likely to interfere. However, both the state legislature and the New Orleans city council were contemplating new legislation and ordinances to redefine and categorize prize fights sponsored under Queensbury Rules which would potentially change the old way of doing things dramatically.

Ever the opportunist, Olympic Club president Charles H. Genslinger had repeatedly read the comments and analysis delivered by Assistant District Attorney Finney on June 27 at the Chess, Checkers, and Whist Club regarding the persistent rumors of proposed legislation designed to regulate prizefighting and boxing exhibitions. Everyone knew that boxing or prize fighting, call it what you will, was taking place in and around

New Orleans on a fairly frequent basis. Between 1884 and 1888 there were several fights held at Sportsman's Park near the city limits, at the New Orleans Baseball Park on Canal Street, or outside the city limits in either Jefferson Parish upriver or St. Bernard Parish downriver,[40] but boxing or prize fighting was still technically against the law in Louisiana. This new legislation would either stamp out boxing once and for all or provide the springboard from which the Olympic Club could rise to new heights. Based on his discussions with the local legislative delegation, as well as many of the prominent members of the club who held positions of some political influence, Genslinger believed the latter scenario was not out of the question. His thought process did not have expanded membership as his primary focus. As President of the Southern League, Genslinger had seen the popularity of professional baseball grow into the national pastime and a thriving business concern. Genslinger had it in his mind that the Olympic Club could make money by sponsoring boxing matches on a grand scale. The profits from these boxing matches could then be used to fuel the expansion of the club and its facilities and amenities.

As Genslinger and the board pondered how to best position the Olympic Club to take advantage of the city's revived interest in boxing, the Olympic Rifle Club held its annual picnic and tournament at Boudro's Garden in Milneburg during which they announced plans for the opening of their new clubhouse on Poland Avenue between Royal and Chartres Streets in September.[41] The facility would serve as the rifle club's armory and clubhouse until 1897. While target shooting was still immensely popular and the event was well attended, providing spectators with the usual tests of skill and marksmanship, the conversation inevitably turned to boxing and how the Olympic Club might be able to profit from boxing.

To test the waters, the Olympic Club held a short program of boxing exhibitions billed as a benefit for the club's new boxing instructor, Professor John Duffy. Eleven boxers of all skill levels were enlisted for the event scheduled for Saturday, September 14, 1889.[42] Between 500 and 600 spectators, including delegations from other athletic clubs, filled a makeshift venue set up in an old cotton press yard in the vacant lot behind the clubhouse. Three preliminary bouts, a demonstration of club swinging, and a wrestling match all preceded the featured event between Peter Crawford and Louis Knoechel for a $1,000 purse. The referee was "a well-known resident of the Ninth Ward" who, while unnamed, was thought to be former mayor and current Olympic Club member J.V. Guillotte.[43]

The program began at ten o'clock, with the main event starting just after midnight. The police stepped in when the crowd's enthusiasm began to reach a point they considered to be too loud given the hour and the Crawford–Knoechel match ended in a draw after eight rounds. Having drawn fewer than a hundred people to the previous two exhibitions, Genslinger and the board were encouraged by the attendance and the absence of police intervention based on legal grounds, and made a persuasive argument to the Olympic Club's members to involve the club in prize fighting on a much larger scale.

It was an argument that Genslinger believed resounded with and was steadfastly shared by club members, so it came as a complete surprise when he and his ticket were emphatically turned away during the club's election of officers in November. Instead, the members overwhelmingly put their support behind Theodore Peterson, a 36-year-old former competitive billiard player who owned and operated Peterson & Janvry's, a saloon and billiard parlor at 205 Canal Street.[44] Conrad C. Julier and Walter J. Wright were retained as Recording Secretary and Treasurer, respectively. There were several changes to the Board of Directors as well, with two of the newly named directors being Charles Noel and Frank Zengel.

A spurned and insulted Genslinger, used to being the biggest toad in the puddle, immediately resigned from the Olympic Club, along with several other members, most prominently A.B. Cooper, William North, Nathanial H. Cloutman, Charles P. Leonhard, Benjamin Holscher, Charles Drolla, and Conrad Julier. On November 21, he and 26 other men met at the home of Herman Miester and quickly formed the Metropolitan Club[45] and what began as a routine change in leadership would gradually deteriorate into an all-out rivalry during the next two years.

Meanwhile, the newly elected Peterson lost no time in announcing the Olympic Club's third pool tournament scheduled for the coming year. Interested members, as well as some of the best competitive pool players in the country, had until year end to submit their names to the Competition Committee. The holiday season concluded with the club's customary final soiree on New Year's Eve and featured an assortment of festive food and refreshments, and dancing to music performed by the Nite Owls from eight o'clock until midnight when a fireworks display lit up the sky over the Third District.[46]

Two

1890

> "Officers of the law wonder why newspapers do not stop prize fights. It is too funny for anything when the very officials who could and ought to prevent such exhibitions of brutality are found occupying front seats at the fight."
>
> —*The Daily Picayune*, February 8, 1882

Joseph Ansoetegui Shakspeare was a businessman who operated a modestly successful ironworks foundry established by his father, Samuel, located at Girod Street and Dryades Street (now South Rampart Street). He entered politics with a single term in the state legislature before accepting the backing of a group of reform-minded New Orleanians seeking to overturn a political machine known as the Ring. Running for mayor on the Citizens' Democratic ticket in the election of 1880, Shakspeare defeated Ring candidate Jules Denis by more than 400 votes,[1] but could not assume office until the courts removed the incumbent mayor, Isaac W. Patton, who was also a member of the Ring.[2]

Shakspeare's first term from December 1880 through November 1882, was understandably difficult, being that he was the only reform candidate to be elected. However, Shakspeare did manage to restructure the city's remaining Civil War and Reconstruction debt and to enact a new city charter.[3] He returned to private life after his two-year term was over. A considerable amount of his private time was spent in the ongoing administration of the Shakspeare Almshouse, funded primarily with revenue derived from license fees imposed on gambling houses regulated under the Shakspeare Plan.[4]

Far from legal and yet typical of the type of political maneuvering which generations of New Orleans politicians raised to a fine art, the new mayor's plan was effective nonetheless. Following decades of periodic but futile efforts at reform and only token gestures made by corrupt city administrations that did little to halt the spread of vice in the city, the Shakspeare Plan involved limiting gambling houses to an area of central New Orleans loosely defined by Camp Street, Chartres Street, St. Louis Street, Bourbon Street, Carondelet Street, and Gravier Street, and requiring a monthly "donation" ranging from $100 to $150 depending on the size of the operation.[5] The city's gambling houses ran the gamut from elegant to tawdry, and this new legislation effectively reduced the number of gambling establishments from 83 to 16 and provided a steady revenue source for the almshouse.

In 1888 Shakspeare once again ran for mayor with the support of the business-backed reform faction known as the Young Men's Democratic Association.⁶ He easily defeated Ring candidate Judge Robert Davey by more than 7,600 votes during a contentious campaign and election.⁷ His second mayoral term, from April 1888 through April 1892, was a continuation of a series of civic projects—street repair and cobble paving dirt streets, installing electric street lights, replacing mule-drawn street cars with electric street cars, and constructing a new courthouse and jail complex on Basin and Saratoga Streets.⁸

So, it came as no surprise to anyone when the reform-minded Mayor Shakspeare announced a new ban on prizefighting on New Year's Day 1890.⁹ In his mind, athletic clubs were becoming more brazen in staging their "glove contests." In December alone there were two known fights, a particularly vicious battle between local heavyweight Felix Vacquelin against Lem McGregory, the "St. Joe Kid,"¹⁰ at the New Orleans Athletic Club and a bout between Andy Bowen and Jimmy McHale at the Southern Athletic Club.¹¹ The announcement of a series of boxing events to be held at the Young Men's Gymnastic Club put the city on notice that the Y.M.G.C. intended to test the legal climate.¹²

New Orleans Mayor Joseph Shakspeare, seated at his desk in City Hall, was a fervent reformer and outspoken anti-boxing advocate who did his best to transform the city during his term of office (The Historic New Orleans Collection).

Shakspeare ordered Police Chief David Hennessy to strictly enforce City Ordinance 1194 (1885) which prohibited "exhibitions, meetings, or assemblages for the purpose of prizefighting between human beings, whether engaged in with or without gloves, or under any device or design whatsoever, whether with or without prices of admission, are declared contrary to good order and police regulations of the city and are hereby prohibited."¹³ For all intents and purposes, the language in this ordinance would, to a reasonable person, appear to cover every possible contingency under which a boxing promoter might be tempted to stage a prizefight. However, the circumlocution and mysterious machinations of the New Orleans legal system would often afford attorneys sufficient latitude in the interpretation of the ordinance, dismissing the language as ambiguous and calling for further clarity, thus exonerating anyone being prosecuted for engaging in or promoting prizefighting. For instance, the participants in a bareknuckle bout might have been said to have been using gloves, albeit termed "skin gloves." Cash awards were not considered prizes, but side wagers between the participants that were only being held by the promoter. This sort of chicanery made the enforcement of the ordinance far less important to a police force stretched thin and dealing with more pressing issues throughout the city.

It was during a special meeting of the city's Committee on Police held on Thursday, January 9, 1890, that a group of representatives from several of the city's athletic clubs requested an amendment to the city ordinance be reviewed and considered. The fivemember committee voted four to one in favor of Councilman Hall's amendment to the ordinance to allow "exhibitions and glove contests between human beings for the development of muscular strength ... within the rooms of all regularly chartered athletic clubs in the city of New Orleans."[14] The usual restrictions against the sale of liquor and against allowing events to take place on Sundays were included, as was the condition of having a police presence available to inspect the gloves to be used and to maintain order throughout the event. Even a pragmatic group of politicians could see the wisdom in forging a compromise to please an estimated 10,000 or more registered voters who were athletic club members, representing just over 4 percent of the city's population.[15] The amended ordinance was recommended to be brought before the City Council and was formally approved and adopted there on January 28. With this piece of legislative largess in place, the city's various athletic clubs began scrambling to upgrade their facilities and arrange for boxing matches. New Orleans was now poised to join the ranks of New York and San Francisco, whose celebrated athletic clubs were already recognized nationally and internationally.[16]

The week following the Committee on Police meeting, the Olympic Club's 15-ball pool tournament got underway on January 15 in the club's gymnasium. Seating capacity was limited to 700 and the club promised to designate one night per week for ladies with special reserved seating. Over the next two weeks, club members and their guests were treated to some of the finest pool seen anywhere, with players vying to win 8 out of 15 games nightly in order to move on in the winner's bracket. David Moore finished in first place. A playoff between Isidore Busha and G.H. Miller was held on the evening of February 13 and resulted in Busha taking second place and Miller third.[17] Medals and monies were awarded before music and dancing entertained the contestants, members and their guests.

A little over two weeks after the City Council passed revised City Ordinance 1194, a largely unpublicized fight was arranged for January 26, 1890, between Joe Tanney of St. Louis and local fighter named Harry Lannon. Word of mouth was sufficient to attract approximately 200 people to travel from St. Louis Street in downtown New Orleans to the Shell Beach Station, then to Jackson Barracks and into St. Bernard Parish where the fight would be held "in the woods to the rear of Mr. R.E. Norton's plantation about a quarter mile below the slaughterhouse." Patrons slogged for nearly a mile from the rail depot to the site, crossing drainage ditches which were dutifully patrolled by swarms of flies feasting on the foul-smelling refuse from the slaughterhouse. After a delay of over an hour waiting for the fighters' seconds to arrive, it was learned that the stakeholder had absconded with the purse. Determined to stage a fight regardless, the boxers and their seconds agreed to fight for whatever gate receipts could be collected. Andy Bowen was selected as the referee and the bout was on. Tanney would knockout Lannon in the fourth round for what was originally a $100 purse, but Tanney now had to be content with receiving $18 in gate receipts for 14 minutes' work.[18] This incident was typical of the type of unsanctioned, word-of-mouth boxing events held out of the public eye that both the city and the state hoped to do away with. Upon reading the account of the fight in the newspapers, anti-boxing opponents appeared to have their first piece of ammunition to renew their fight against boxing statewide.

However, on January 31, 1890, the Southern Athletic Club, located on the northwest corner of Washington Avenue and Prytania Street, sponsored an evening of sparring exhibitions, the first being between Mike Cleary and Felix Vacquelin and the second between John Duffy and Joe Oliver. The main event of the evening was a 4-round match between lightweights Andy Bowen of New Orleans and Louis Bezeneh of Ohio. Originally scheduled to take place on December 1, 1889, at Sportsman's Park, the match between Bowen and Bezenah was quickly rescheduled for the Southern Athletic Club to take advantage of the newly revised city ordinance. Referee Jake Kilrain awarded the fight to Bowen on points. The evening finished with a lackluster sparring exhibition between Professor Mike Donovan and Mike Cleary.[19] While tame in comparison, the event was orderly and mildly entertaining.

Two days later Jake Kilrain stepped into the ring at West End where the local theatre had been converted into a boxing venue. Felix Vacquelin was scheduled to face Kilrain in a 6-round contest for a $2,000 purse. Despite newspaper editorials boasting about the demise of prize fighting in New Orleans, more than 1,500 people took the three o'clock train to the popular resort area north of the city on the shores of Lake Pontchartrain. Among those making the trip were "prominent educators, members of the exchanges and bon ton clubs, federal, state, and city officers, militia men and athletes, and race horse men." While perhaps not exclusively well heeled, the spectators were most definitely not the detritus of lower-class hoodlums and gamblers most often portrayed by the editorial press as being the only class of people who would deign to attend a prize fight. From the outset, it was obvious that Vacquelin was outmatched. A youthful but game Vacquelin attempted to go toe to toe with the far more experienced Kilrain, but in the end he was just no match and his side tossed in the sponge when the bell for the fourth round sounded.[20] Nonetheless he showed great pluck in trying to land a blow that might get the attention of the more experienced Kilrain. In a scant 15 minutes, Kilrain defeated Vacquelin, earning a hundred dollars per minute for his war chest.[21] The gate receipts were in excess of $4,500 so the event was considered to be both a financial and critical success.

Mayor Shakspeare invited a delegation of representatives from athletic clubs to City Hall on Thursday, February 6, to discuss the amended city ordinance passed by the council, but which still lay unsigned on his desk. The meeting quickly centered on the absence of the appropriate charitable donations from the Southern Athletic Club and the West End Athletic Club for their recent events. He threatened to veto the ordinance as written unless it was further amended to tighten up the charitable donation as part of the permit and license process.[22] These minor revisions were incorporated without much squabble or delay. From this point forward, the standard $50 charitable donation would accompany the permit application and fee.

Two weeks following his fight with Vacquelin, Kilrain met a rising young heavyweight fighter named James J. Corbett from San Francisco at the Southern Athletic Club. Kilrain's match against Corbett was by special invitation only, a fact which was poorly communicated to the club's military company who had been drilling on the streets of the Garden District along with several members of the Boston Club, all of whom tried to gain entrance without paying the $5 ticket price. Heated words were heard emanating from the gymnasium entrance and a disgruntled pile of members temporarily clogged access to the event. As a result, fewer than 500 people, including Mayor Shakspeare and two city councilmen, were inside the club to watch the exhibition, which began with a pair of 4-round preliminary matches. The first was between Louis Bezenah and Charley Johnson, followed by Mike Cleary and Mike Smith. After preliminary bouts, the crowd was treated to a display of "scientific" boxing provided by Corbett. Despite giving up at least 22 pounds in weight and at least two inches in reach, Corbett engaged in a strategy of hit and run, striking Kilrain rapidly in succession then moving quickly away to keep the bulky, brawny Kilrain off balance. Corbett never gave Kilrain an opening for anything more than an exploratory jab. At the end of the scheduled 6-round affair referee E.R. Violette declared Corbett the winner of the $2,500 purse. Although Kilrain groused that he had been told to fight would only go 5 rounds, he still took home $1,000 for his efforts.[23] Most accounts of the exhibition were surprisingly positive, as was the reaction of the mayor and city councilmen who assumed their evening would be marred by a brutal, bloody spectacle.

This was exactly what some boxing proponents had envisioned when they amended the city ordinance in favor of athletic clubs. A well-attended, well-behaved, appreciative and knowledgeable audience witnessing a relatively evenly matched group of boxers demonstrate the meaning of "scientific glove contest." Even staunch boxing opponent Mayor Shakspeare had to be able to take some comfort that they had not let the genie out of the bottle. Sensing a strategic advantage, J.H. Bruns and Louis E. Cormier of the Audubon Athletic Association contacted the officers and management of the city's other athletic clubs to arrange a meeting at their downtown clubhouse at 19 Exchange Place for the evening of Thursday, March 6, 1890. His plan was to propose an association of athletic clubs whose members would adopt a unified code of conduct for the events they staged and would also share information about "disreputable characters" in the boxing ranks.[24] While those in attendance all agreed in principle with the lofty goals proposed, such an association never materialized. Perhaps there was just too much to be done, too much competitive distrust, or too much fear of further city oversight and potential additional regulation.

By mid–March, the Olympic Club had completed the purchase of the property at 636 Royal Street, in no small part due to their close ties with the Third District Building Association. Another round of improvements was announced: enlarging the three first-floor parlors into a single room, adding a locker room next to the gymnasium, expanding the second-floor billiard room, widening the balconies, and the addition of bathrooms. New furniture and fixtures were also ordered and the exterior of the building was to be painted.[25] The club also announced the formation of a military company to be known as the Olympic Guards under the leadership of Civil War veteran Judge

Anthony Sambola, Captain John Coos, and Captain John Booth. Their first meeting was set for St. Patrick's Day, at which time 52 men signed up for service.[26] While there was no immediate threat of war on the horizon, it was common for military companies sponsored by a club or organization to become part of the state militia. Uniforms and arms were acquired and drill formations practiced on a regular basis. The Olympic Guards were mustered into service as D Company of the Third Infantry Battalion on Tuesday, April 8, 1890.[27] This added yet another dimension to membership in the Olympic Club.

The spring rainfall was heavier than usual throughout the Mississippi River valley and once again the city's attention turned toward their levee system. The river had already reached flood stage and numerous crevasses—deep fissures or breaches in the levee embankment—were showing up between Vicksburg and New Orleans. Although the state had spent more on levee construction and maintenance in the prior year than ever before, there was an immediate need for additional funds to bolster and shore up the levees. An unexpected windfall came when the Louisiana State Lottery Company offered Governor Nicholls $100,000 to use as he saw fit to address the problem.[28] This posed quite a conundrum for the reform-minded, anti-lottery governor who ultimately was forced to decline the lottery company's offer. His decision was fraught with political peril, especially if the river over-topped or broke through the levee at any one of the scores of crevasses already threatening the state from Ferriday to Belle Chasse.

Chartered by the Louisiana State Assembly in 1868, the Louisiana State Lottery Company sponsored daily and monthly drawings for prizes ranging from $100 to $300,000. There were also semi-annual drawings for a $600,000 grand prize which drew national and international players. Former Confederate generals P.G.T. Beauregard and Jubal Early presided over the monthly drawings and provided an air of respectability to the proceedings, in exchange for $30,000 per year in remuneration for less than two days' work per month.[29] In exchange for their exclusive right to conduct the lottery statewide, the privately-held company agreed to contribute a relatively minor annual sum of $40,000 per year through 1893 for the upkeep of Charity Hospital in New Orleans, with the lottery corporation keeping the remainder of their revenues. The company, owned by John Morris and Charles T. Howard, was suspected of paying substantial bribes to state legislators for the lucrative lottery franchise.[30] It is estimated that the Louisiana State Lottery Company returned 48 percent of its revenues to the company. In the spring of 1890 the end of their 25-year agreement was drawing near and a well-organized anti-lottery faction was gaining traction statewide. Even though it was "the most powerful gambling syndicate in the country"[31] at the time, it was in their best interest for the State Lottery Company to position itself as a philanthropic member of the community.[32]

Although Governor Nicholls declined the lottery's offer, Mayor Shakspeare could not afford to stand on principle and accepted a $50,000 donation from the lottery to be used for the levees around New Orleans.[33] This would put the reform-minded mayor squarely at odds with the growing number of social reform groups led by the Rev. Beverly Carradine of the Carondelet Street Methodist Church and the newly formed Anti-Lottery League of Louisiana led by Senators Murphy J. Foster from St. Mary Parish,

W.W. Heard from Union Parish, John C. Vance from Bossier Parish, and Joseph Henry, along with Representatives J.M. McCain, H.C. Newsom, Dr. D.W. Pipes from East Feliciana Parish, and G.L.P. Wren,[34] among others statewide.

Fortunately for all involved the city was able to shore up its levees to avoid a disaster. With the city successfully protected from this most recent round of devastating floods, at least for the present time, the populace could once again relax and enjoy life. The March 6 meeting of the city's various athletic clubs bore little fruit in terms of forming an association, but it did result in their organizing an amateur baseball league on April 6. The initial four clubs fielding teams were the Young Men's Gymnastic Club, the Southern Athletic Club, the Columbia Athletic Club, and the Olympic Club. Theodore Peterson of the Olympic Club was elected president of the Athletic Club League.[35]

The late spring and summer of 1890 were filled with a number of activities at the Olympic Club. On April 14, the rifle team participated in the Arnoult Rifle Club's annual picnic and shooting tournament along with five other clubs. Peter Tito of the Olympic Club took home a handsome silver goblet for top individual honors, scoring 296 out of a possible 325 points.[36] This was a warm-up for the state championship tournament which would begin in early May at the Metropolitan Club's range.

In May, the Olympic Club celebrated its seventh anniversary in their usual grand style. The gymnasium was once again transformed into a magnificent ballroom festooned with a tasteful array of evergreens. A large harp made entirely of flowers hung from the ceiling in one corner of the ballroom, and an assortment of other flowers and palmetto branches were strategically placed throughout the room to give it a tropical feel.[37] More than 50 young ladies, primarily the member's daughters, were promenaded through the ballroom to the delight of all present. The light and airy mood of the evening reflected the club's success in having exceeded the 300-member threshold, all of whom seemed to be dancing and enjoying the music of the Nite Owls and discussing the recent renovations to their brilliantly lit clubhouse, including the arrival and installation of their brand-new Emerson grand piano.

The members of the Olympic Club had every reason to be optimistic. With more than 300 current members, plus the addition of 10 to 20 new members every month, the club was bringing in several thousand dollars per year in dues, revenue that more than secured their day-to-day operating expenses. The clubhouse library boasted over a thousand volumes and received daily newspapers from major cities across the country. Belgian carpets and crystal chandeliers were prominent throughout the club rooms. The Olympic Rifle Club was in first place at the end of the first round of competition for the state championship, leading the Arnoult Rifle Club by a mere 17 points, but well ahead of the rest of the field.[38] And given the initial success of the boxing matches staged by the Southern Athletic Club, the Columbia Athletic Club, and the West End Athletic Club with no police interference or resulting city sanctions, even the most reluctant members of the Olympic Club acquiesced to the seeds planted by the relentless campaigning of Genslinger and his allies to hop on the band wagon and to expand into boxing. The argument gained traction among the club's leadership and it was announced in late June that the Olympic Club would throw their hat in the ring by inaugurating scientific glove contests.[39]

Tommy Ward versus Charles Wilson

On July 11, 1890, the Olympic Club's first official prize fight, although the club used the term "glove exhibition" so as not to run afoul of any alternative or opposing interpretation of the prevailing city ordinances, featured Tommy Ward from Zanesville, Ohio, against Charles "Kid" Wilson from England. There were some Olympic Club members who were ambivalent about jumping into the boxing business, counseling that a severe financial loss would be more than distasteful. Club President Theodore Peterson, a proponent of boxing, did not want to lose this opportunity to keep pace with the other athletic clubs in the city and offered to cover any financial losses realized by the Olympic Club out of his own pocket.[40] The club leased the vacant lot behind their clubhouse from the Atlantic Cotton Press and constructed a regulation ring—padded stakes were spaced eight-feet apart through which cloth covered ropes were strung around a ring of fine sawdust covered turf and packed river sand, all of which was covered by a canvas tarp. Four temporary carbon arc lights were placed over each corner of the ring. Canvas tarpaulins were on hand to cover the makeshift arena in case of rain. Elevated, terraced seating was also constructed to accommodate some 2,000 spectators, but the high wooden fence designed to encircle the yard could not be completed in time, allowing several hundred more interested non-paying onlookers to witness the event. Combined with the scores of freeloaders perched on the house tops and sheds adjoining the property, there were at least 3,000 on hand to witness the spectacle.

The two lightweights entered the ring a little after nine o'clock. Wilson was accompanied by Tommy Danforth, Felix Vacquelin, and Tom Casey, while Ward was seconded by James Sweeney, Horace Bourg, and Alphonse Lynch. They were joined by Professor John Duffy, who would serve as the referee, and timekeeper George Queen. After settling into their respective corners, the fighters met at the scratch line and were given their instructions by Duffy. At exactly 9:30, the bell sounded for the 1st round. The early rounds were marked by a vigorous give-and-take between Wilson and Ward, as punch and counter-punch were abundantly exchanged. In the 4th round Ward became the aggressor, but the 5th and 6th rounds were not much more than sparring. In the 8th round Wilson spotted an opening and landed a swift series of combinations followed by a strong right cross to the chin that knocked out Ward. An enthusiastic Wilson claimed the winner's share of the modest $400 purse.[41] At $2 per ticket, the club's first pugilistic event was a minor financial success, but a major critical success, even with the additional expense of constructing the ring and seating.

Two weeks later, a young New Zealander named Bob Fitzsimmons squared off against the New England Middleweight Champion Arthur Upham, from New London, Connecticut, in a much anticipated 5-round bout before the Audubon Athletic Club.[42] Both men were relative newcomers, Upham having defeated Jack Ashton to capture the New England Middleweight title in his first outing and Fitzsimmons with just two fights under his belt in California, both victories. Unbeknownst to Upham or the majority of the crowd, Fitzsimmons was actually a fairly experienced fighter, having engaged in 42 bouts in Australia before coming to America. His record in these fights was 20 wins against 6 losses, with 11 draws and 5 no decisions. Nevertheless, there were occasionally murmurs throughout the crowd about Fitzsimmons as a potential challenger to fight the great Jack Dempsey that most quickly brushed off as the whiskey and their wagers doing the talking. Eight hundred fans eagerly paid $3 per ticket and clamored into the Audubon Athletic Club at 19 Exchange Place in downtown New Orleans.

At nine o'clock, the lanky Fitzsimmons entered the ring followed by the shorter Upham. The New Zealander was seconded by Jimmy Carroll and Tommy Danforth, while the New Englander was backed by Professor John Duffy and Doc O'Connell. From the opening bell, it became apparent that Fitzsimmons was the better man, using his reach and height advantage to make short work of his opponent. The six-foot Fitzsimmons looked gangly and moved almost awkwardly around the ring in pursuit of Upham, flooring him in the 1st round, swelling Upham's mouth and nose in the 2nd round before sending him to the mat again. The 3rd round saw Fitzsimmons deliver one punishing blow after the other, first to Upham's body then to his head, then repeated blows to the body, with a volley of rights to the head and neck finally sending an exhausted Upham to the mat for the third time. The referee quite nearly called the fight before the start of the 4th round, but Upham and his corner persuaded him that their man could go on. By this point the crowd was convinced that Upham was done for and watched him slowly walk from his corner to the scratch line. Fitzsimmons immediately administered a sweeping right to the side of Upham's neck, dropping him yet again. As he staggered upright, Fitzsimmons threw another right cross with the same result. Upham had barely regained his footing before a left upper-cut sent him to the deck for the final time. Now the murmurs through the crowd about Fitzsimmons having a go at Jack Dempsey sounded more plausible.

The bout was another critical and financial success for the athletic club model and it seemed that all New Orleans was now caught up in the thick of boxing mania.

Utilizing the seating already constructed, the Olympic Club now made plans erect an arena to permanently enclose the ring and spectators. Great pains were taken in the design to prevent spectators from entering the ring by surrounding it with barbed wire gates.[43] Additional seating and reserved box seating were added. As construction crews worked furiously under the blazing summer sun, the Olympic Club and its members were enjoying their brief taste of success. They had recently received overtures from several London fighters regarding the possibility of coming to New Orleans.[44] European fighters were reaching out to every known fight promoter in America to grab their share of the spoils. Such thrilling accomplishments and accolades kept the Olympic Club from the realization that, for the moment, Louisiana was basically the only game in town as the bottom had temporarily fallen out of the fight game in New York, California, Illinois and several other states.[45] These states, like many others, had shored up their anti-boxing statutes, forcing boxing back into the shadows where an everyday bout might go overlooked, but where a fight involving a regional, national, or world title was out of the question. Had the Olympic Club comprehended the true nature of their success, perhaps the club's board would not have believed the press reports from around the country extolling the virtues of boxing in New Orleans and would have proceeded with measured caution. Then again, they too were swept up in boxing mania.

Andy Bowen versus Jimmy Carroll

The evening of September 16, 1890, saw the next fight sponsored by the Olympic Club and it was crackerjack. Local favorite Andy "The Louisiana Tornado" Bowen was going up against 38-year-old Jimmy Carroll from San Francisco in a bout promoted as being for the American and World Lightweight title. Bowen was something of an enigma. Described as being of Spanish descent, he was long thought to be part Negro, which Bowen consistently denied, often violently if someone belabored the question. To be even part-Negro would effectively prohibit Bowen from fighting for the big purses in any of the city's segregated athletic clubs. As a result, Bowen developed early on into quite a scrapper as a youth growing up near Annunciation Square, close to the rough and tumble New Orleans waterfront and its warehouses. On this night, a purse of $2,500 would be awarded to the winner, with the loser taking home $500. In current dollars, the winner's share would be worth $65,780 and the loser's share $13,150.

Crowd control was a problem from the outset. At least 5,000 people purchased tickets, but the Olympic Club had no way of easily sorting them out from those trying to sneak in. It was reported that there were at least a thousand ticketholders still outside who were unable to gain access when the bell sounded for the first round. Some of them may have been among those who tore down a portion of the wooden fence surrounding Alcee LeBlanc's home on Clouet Street to slip into the arena. Others used ladders to climb onto neighbor's rooftops, perched like so many blackbirds around the open-air venue. At this early point in his career Bowen was something of a favorite son and was presented with a large horseshoe wreath with "Good Luck" formed in flowers. Among the notables in the crowd was Billy Myer, who Bowen had defeated in May at the West End Athletic Club and who had announced he was prepared to challenge the winner of this bout. Master of Ceremonies Bruce Dixon introduced Professor John Duffy as the referee for the evening. Carroll entered the ring clad in pink and white striped tights and black shoes, looking in formidable condition for a 36-year-old. Bowen looked to be in peak physical condition and, at 23, drew the appreciation of the crowd. At precisely 9:30, referee Duffy brought the fighters to the center of the ring and dispensed his customary review of the rules. The

This rare photograph of lightweight boxer Andy Bowen dates from between 1890 and 1893. He made his professional debut on January 16, 1887 (from an unknown 19th century publication).

first set of gloves presented to New Orleans policeman Captain William Barrett were rejected as being too light, whereupon two pairs of five-ounce gloves were procured, weighed, approved, and laced up on the fighters.

Bowen had the advantage in the early rounds, but failed to press his opponent. Giving up at least two inches in reach to Carroll did not seem to be a problem. However, despite his age and inexperience—this was only Carroll's sixth professional fight—he knew he had to be patient. During the first seven rounds, each man sparred carefully while trying to size up their opponent. The occasional exchange of blows drew cheers from the crowd before settling back into the same comfortable routine. Most felt Bowen took the early rounds. In the 8th and 9th rounds Carroll became the aggressor, pressing Bowen non-stop until the very end of the ninth when Carroll received a strong left jab to the chin followed by a right hook to the side of his head. Bowen finally looked to have Carroll, working his ribs when the round ended. Both fighters had a little extra time between the 10th and 11th rounds to catch their breath as their gloves were examined for rosin by referee Duffy. Finding no evidence of tampering with the gloves the bout resumed, and for the next three rounds there was ample action on both sides with neither man gaining an advantage. Bowen was staggered by a hard left to the mouth followed by a strong right to his chest above the heart. Carroll pressed his attack only to have the bell sound to end the round.

From this point forward Bowen only grew weaker. He fought gamely and managed to roast Carroll's ribs in the 18th round, but he continued to fade. Carroll eventually won by a knockout in the 21st round.[46] Bowen did not take his first defeat lightly and his backers, Thomas Anderson and Albert Spitzfaden, immediately began lobbying the Olympic Club for a rematch. It would take Bowen nearly four years to arrange a rematch to avenge his first professional defeat. The fight was both a critical success and, even more importantly, a financial success, with 5,000 tickets sold at an average price of $3, the Olympic Club stood to gross at least $15,000 which, after the $3,000 in prize money and an estimated

Jimmy Carroll teamed up with Australian Bob Fitzsimmons and spent the better part of his career as a manager-trainer. He did compile a record of four wins, four losses, and three draws/no decision bouts between 1888 and 1896. Two of his victories were at the Olympic Club (collection of the author).

$3,000 in fight-related expenses and advertising, resulted in at least a $9,000 profit for the club, and perhaps even more. There were undoubtedly a fair number of reserved seats sold at $5 per ticket, but reports of the fight do not provide any clarity on the number of reserved seat tickets that may have been sold, thus we have used the more conservative ticket sales figures.

Even as the caliber of the fighters improved in direct proportion to the size of the purses being offered, there were still fledgling efforts by different groups across the New Orleans area to gain a foothold in the market. For instance, the newly formed Bench Athletic and Pleasure Club whose first and only exhibition on September 27, 1890, was between local fighters John Russell and Phil Cardenas for a $300 purse before 400 people.[47] There were many such organizations that folded after one or two events because they were poorly capitalized to begin with and could not afford to properly promote their event in order to draw a paying crowd of sufficient size to defray their expenses.

The Murder of David Hennessy

On Thursday morning, October 16, 1890, the city awoke to learn that Superintendent of Police David Hennessy had been attacked and shot multiple times by one or more unknown assassins on the corner of Basin and Girod streets just after 11 o'clock Wednesday night.

Following the weekly meeting of the Police Board dealing with two officers accused of taking bribes, and despite the rainy, chilly weather, Hennessy was walking home from the Central Station on Basin Street with William J. "Billy" O'Conner, his trusted friend and a captain with the Boylan Protective Police. Almost from the day he took office, Hennessy was on the receiving end of frequent death threats, and these threats only increased with his involvement in the very violent and very public feud between two Italian families, the Provenzanos and the Matrangas. It was believed that Hennessy was going to expose the Matranga family as head of the New Orleans' principal crime syndicate, with Joseph Machaca as their Underboss, as well as the involvement of New Orleans Police Detective Dominick O'Malley in trying to bribe and intimidate both potential witnesses and jurors in the employ of the Matranga family. With all the speculation about his pending testimony in the Provenzano–Matranga retrial scheduled for two days hence, it was the better part of prudence to have someone accompany Hennessy on the half-mile trek between the station and his home. That he employed a private bodyguard service might offer some commentary as to the lack of confidence Hennessy had in his own men.

That evening, as Hennessy and O'Conner walked up Rampart Street, they ducked into Dominic Virget's oyster saloon on the corner of Rampart and Poydras streets to escape the pouring rain and to enjoy a half-dozen oysters. Leaving Virget's, they parted company at Hennessy's insistence approximately two blocks from the modest residence at 275 Girod Street that he shared with his mother. The neighborhood was a rag-tag collection of cottages, rooming houses, and shops that were home to a wide variety of mostly working-class immigrants. Mrs. Hennessy had lived there for years and was unwilling to move, even after repeated offers from her son. Neither man paid any attention to the young boy who seemed to appear from nowhere, whistling an unfamiliar tune as he walked ahead of the chief.

The evening rain had stopped, but the night was filled with a damp mist that shrouded everything. Hennessy paused beneath the streetlamp in front of the secondhand store owned by Mrs. Ehrwald on the southeast or lower riverside corner of Girod and Basin Streets to search for his door key. Just steps away from where he had left Hennessy, O'Conner heard the unmistakable sound of gunfire, first that of one or more shotguns followed moments later by several pistol shots in rapid succession. As O'Conner rushed back up Girod Street through the eerie drizzle, he recognized the sound of men running. Scanning the area around Hennessy's home, he heard the chief call out and found the wounded Hennessy a half-block away from where they had parted, slumped on the front steps of the Gillis residence at 189 Basin Street between Girod and Lafayette streets. In a weak whisper, Hennessy informed O'Conner that it had been "Dagos" who had shot him.[48] Using the telephone at Feeney's Grocery Store just across the street, O'Conner first summoned an ambulance from Charity Hospital and then alerted the Central Station to send all available men to the crime scene, before returning to Hennessy's side.

Hennessy was carried to the residence of Auguste Gillis and her mother, where he was attended to in the front parlor. He was later removed by ambulance to Charity Hospital where he was treated by Assistant House Surgeon J.D. Bloom and several medical students who had the night shift. Their examination revealed that Hennessy had received several superficial wounds in the leg and forearm on both his left and right side that were not considered dangerous. There were, however, four "ugly, gaping wounds" on the left side of his chest, one of which was determined to be from a bullet that had penetrated the left lung pericardium and lodged under his eighth rib. This was the most dangerous wound and where the doctor directed his full attention. Following his initial treatment, Hennessy's wounds were dressed and he remained in the surgical amphitheater under heavy guard. Around one o'clock on Friday morning, a priest arrived to administer last rites and the chief's aged mother was allowed to see

New Orleans Police Superintendent David Hennessy was an integral part of Mayor Shakspeare's movement to clean up the crime and corruption that was rampant in the city (The Historic New Orleans Collection).

him. He reassured her and the others assembled that he would make a full recovery. As this was taking place, the police force, under orders from Mayor Shakspeare to "scour the neighborhood and arrest every Italian you come across," detained nearly 250 people, eventually making 45 arrests. Witnesses and suspects alike were detained at the Central Station.

Throughout the night, Hennessy was restless and his breathing was labored. Around two o'clock in the morning Dr. Bloom was joined by Dr. Samuel Logan who ordered the patient be given opiates to allow him to rest. This treatment was repeated at four o'clock by Dr. Harper who returned an hour later to find Hennessy's condition deteriorating rapidly. Hennessy was made as comfortable as possible, but succumbed to his wounds at just after nine o'clock in the morning, surrounded by his mother, friends, and colleagues.[49]

Hennessy's body lay in state at City Hall and received a hero's funeral. The crowd, which easily numbered in the tens of thousands, was said to surpass that which had assembled for Jefferson Davis' funeral several months earlier. A solemn mass at St. Joseph's Church on Common Street opposite Charity Hospital was followed by internment in Metairie Cemetery.

Despite the condemnation of the murder by the Italian community, personified by ex-Alderman Anthony Patorno, the headlines screamed "Assassination" and spoke of vendetta, pointing to the involvement "Italians of the Criminal Class." Every adult male Italian in New Orleans was now rolled up into one big criminal and was considered to be a member of the "Black Hand," and tensions were understandably and uncomfortably high. Statements were taken, witnesses were interviewed multiple times by multiple officers, and additional arrests were made as far away as Mobile, Alabama, but the progress of the investigation was slow. Eventually all but 19 of the 45 arrested would be released, and those who remained in jail were held without bail or legal representation. The investigation would grind along steadily and, given public sentiment, citizens were assured that the matter would be settled in due time. In the meantime, Mayor Shakspeare organized a Committee of Fifty to investigate the existence and activities of "secret societies," meaning the Black Hand and the newly identified "Mafia," and to determine how to eradicate them from New Orleans society.

Yet in spite of the city's shock and revulsion at the tragedy, daily life in New Orleans slowly found its way forward and gradually returned to its usual *laissez-faire* pace as citizens waited for the police investigation to conclude and for the trial of Hennessy's killers to begin. The fall social season concluded with a reception on October 21 for Olympic Club members and their guests that the club brought off despite inclement weather.[50] October also found the Olympic Rifle Club slipping into third place behind teams from the Southern and Arnoult clubs at Boudro's Gardens in Milneburg. Along with the usual brass band providing entertainment, refreshments were served in the garden pavilion. The day was highlighted by a ladies' shoot between Miss Moss and Miss Forester.[51]

The athletic prowess of the members of the Olympic Club was considerable in so many areas, but alas did not extend to the baseball diamond where their fledgling team, formed in April, went winless in the Athletic Club League's inaugural 15-game season.[52] The Southern Athletic Club eventually laid claim to the league pennant with a record of 12 wins against only 3 losses.

In November, the Olympic Club membership elected a 36-year-old board member and businessman named Charles Noel to succeed Theodore Peterson as president of the Olympic Club. Noel was a partner in the firm of Lambou & Noel, whose sawmill and lumberyard were located on the corner of Kentucky Street (now Alexander Street) and North Peters Street, downriver from the Olympic Club. He and the Lambou family, Victor and Henry, had been ardent supporters of the Olympic Rifle Club and on more than one occasion had allowed the rifle club to use their property as a shooting range. The men were also investors in the Third District Building Association, as indeed were many other Olympic Club members.[53] Other Olympic Club officers elected were William H. Wright (First Vice-President), E. Crassons (Second Vice-President), Walter T. Taylor (Recording Secretary), William D. Ross (Financial Secretary), and Walter Wright (Treasurer). Seven other members were elected to the club's board/governing committee.

The transition from Peterson to Noel was amicable and went smoothly, with the first and most pressing order of business being to finalize the club's next boxing event. First proposed in July of 1890, the bout between Jack Dempsey and Bob Fitzsimmons was agreed to in late September and the fight articles signed in mid–November.[54] This was the boldest and most audacious event proposed to date, with the Middleweight Championship of the World at stake, and the club now had just over 60 days to prepare for the bout, scheduled for mid–January of 1891. Noel persuaded the club to reach into the profits from previous prize fights in order to undertake yet another aggressive expansion of their wooden arena, increasing its seating capacity to accommodate another 2,000 patrons.[55] Construction crews worked furiously to complete the project in time for the big event. With an unheard of $12,000 purse on the line, plus the additional expense of expanding the arena, there was a lot at stake for Charles Noel and the Olympic Club.

Three

1891

> "It is very much better for the young, as well as the old, to possess the knowledge of the manly art of self-defense than it is to have them resort to knives and guns."
>
> —John L. Sullivan

Sadly, New Orleanians did not show much interest in the first fight card of the new year, the Audubon Athletic Club's match between two Boston welterweights, William "Doc" O'Connell and Eddie Conley, for a $1,000 purse which was set for Tuesday, January 12, 1891. Conley was handled by Howe Hodgkins and James Corbett, while O'Connell was handled by Bob Fitzsimmons and Jimmy Carroll. It was a disappointing crowd that watched O'Connell best Conley in the eighth round by a knockout. Nonetheless, the entire city was awash in boxing fever spawned by the national and international attention surrounding the upcoming bout at the Olympic Club. The biggest and most ambitious contest to be staged by the Olympic Club thus far took place on the evening of Wednesday, January 14, 1891, between the World Middleweight Champion, Jack Dempsey, and challenger Bob Fitzsimmons.

Jack Dempsey versus Bob Fitzsimmons

Dempsey was born John Edward Kelly in County Kildare, Ireland, on December 15, 1862, but emigrated to the United States as a child, growing up in Williamsburg just outside of Brooklyn, New York. During his teenage years, he found work as an apprentice cooper at Palmer's Cooperage in Brooklyn and it was there that he became friends with two other Irish lads—Jack McAuliffe and Jack Skelly. All three would eventually fight for world championship titles in New Orleans at the Olympic Club. He assumed the name Jack Dempsey for his first fight since even amateur fighting was illegal and kept the *nom de guerre* after he won the match. Undefeated in all but two of his first 64 professional fights, Dempsey soon earned the nickname "Nonpareil" meaning "unequaled."[1] In early 1885, Jere Dunn, a noted fight promoter from New York, set up shop in New Orleans and imported a number of prominent fighters. His most notable match brought Dempsey to New Orleans for the first time in 1885 to fight Charles Bixamos at Sportsman's Park on March 19, which Dempsey won by a knockout in the 5th round.[2] This was Dempsey's 24th professional fight.

Challenger Robert Fitzsimmons was born in Cornwall, England, but grew up in New Zealand where he apprenticed as a blacksmith in his older brother's forge. The day-to-day routine of pounding away at the anvil gave Fitzsimmons deceptively devastating power in his right arm.[3] At first blush Fitzsimmons, despite being nearly six feet tall, did not resemble the typical prize fighter. He displayed "magnificent shoulders and arms," but his lower body was so slim that he looked like "a case of arrested development."[4] His unusual physical appearance often caused his opponents to under-estimate him, plus he was an unknown commodity in America. Although this was to be Fitzsimmons' second fight in New Orleans, it was only his fourth fight in the United States. He had won two fights in May of 1890 at the California Athletic Club in San Francisco. He then took on Arthur Upham of Nova Scotia in New Orleans on July 28, 1890, at the Audubon Athletic Club for a $1,000 purse, Fitzsimmons pummeled Upham with a series of short, powerful strikes that traveled no more than a foot. With a 72-inch reach, these short punches from Fitzsimmons were both deceptive and devastating. As a result, Fitzsimmons won by a knockout in the 9th round.[5] Almost immediately following Fitzsimmons' win over Upham, the Olympic Club telegraphed Dempsey in Portland, Oregon, offering him a chance to defend his middleweight title against Fitzsimmons.

Jack Dempsey
WORLD'S CHAMPION

John Edward Kelly adopted the name Jack Dempsey for his first fight in 1885 and was the reigning Middleweight Champion of the World when he agreed to meet Bob Fitzsimmons at the Olympic Club (collection of the author).

At first, Dempsey insisted the fight take place before the Puritan Club in New York, but this was perceived by Fitzsimmons' backers as too much of an advantage for Dempsey. They preferred the neutral site offered by New Orleans. Following a brief but spirited bidding war with the Puritan Club, the Olympic Club hung out a $12,000 purse, the largest ever offered at the time. This, combined with a statement from Fitzsimmons that he wouldn't fight in New York for any price, convinced Dempsey to agree to fight in New Orleans. Dempsey had never seen Fitzsimmons, but he regarded his previous wins against McCarthy and Upham as "poor class," and had also heard the persistent stories about Fitzsimmons' loss to Jim Hall in Australia, so he felt highly confident in accepting the Olympic

Club's offer to return to Louisiana. And, of course, there was the promise of a huge payday.

The early money understandably made Dempsey the odds-on favorite. Fitzsimmons' principal financial backer was Major Frank McLaughlin, a director of the California Athletic Club, who placed the biggest single bet ever reported in New Orleans at that time—$50,000 on Fitzsimmons,[6] the equivalent of approximately $1.3 million today. New Orleanians were quick to follow the money and reluctantly embraced the lanky New Zealander as their favorite. Because of Dempsey, the fight attracted international attention and on January 14, 1891, the city was packed with strangers, but there were reports that only 140 tickets had been sold in early January. Nonetheless, the fight was a complete sellout by noon on the day of the fight. At a level price of $10 per ticket,[7] the potential gate could be in excess of $40,000 to the Olympic Club.

There was an overflow crowd outside of the Olympic Club by early afternoon. The brisk January

Bob Fitzsimmons
WORLD'S CHAMPION

Robert Fitzsimmons was a relatively unknown boxer from New Zealand who had only two fights in the United States before traveling to New Orleans. After defeating Arthur Upham at the Audubon Athletic Club in July of 1890 he was given a shot at the middleweight title against Jack Dempsey at the Olympic Club (collection of the author).

weather made them anxious to gain entrance to the fight, and the crowd pressed toward the doors around five o'clock and again around 6:30, but a large contingent of over a hundred policemen was on hand to hold them back until the doors opened at eight o'clock. The venue's 4,000 seats were quickly filled, joined by a standing room only crowd, estimated to be another 500, pressed together at the perimeter of the arena. The police presence was pronounced both inside and outside of the Olympic Club.

The club's arena had a retractable roof comprised of three-foot wide strips of waxed canvas strung on beams that could be adjusted by rope and pulley as desired, but the crisp January night kept the roof intact. In the center of the arena stood the 24-foot square ring comprised of turf and river sand that had been packed and rolled repeatedly to serve as the ring's sub-surface. On top of that was a single piece of raw canvas. The eight wooden stakes and ropes around the perimeter were padded and covered. Chairs for each fighter's seconds and corner crew were set up behind a barbed wire enclosure just four feet from the ring. The press was crammed into the next layer of seating around the ring. Every major newspaper in the country was represented at ringside, along with a few foreign correspondents. Although the arena had been wired for telegraph service, demand was such that use of the telegraph was prohibited that evening. Instead, messengers would have to carry all press copy directly to the Western Union telegraph office in the city at regular intervals throughout the bout. From there the news could be transmitted directly to each reporter's newsroom anywhere in the country. Among those anxiously awaiting the start of the fight were dozens of notables including Jake Kilrain, William Muldoon, James Corbett, Billy Myer, Andy Bowen and a host of titleholders both past, present and future.[8]

As part of the fight contract Dempsey had insisted that the official weigh-in take place immediately before the fight. He believed that no one of Fitzsimmons' height (five feet, 11 inches) could make the prescribed 154-pound weight and still have the strength to last through the fight. This was his first and most serious underestimation of Fitzsimmons. Both men and their entourage entered the arena just before 8:30 p.m. When Fitzsimmons shed his robe, it was reported that Dempsey rolled his eyes, demonstrating his amusement with the lanky Fitzsimmons, whose broad shoulders were supported on a lean mid-section and skinny legs. Earlier in the evening Fitzsimmons was one pound over the prescribed limit and was sent out to work his weight down with a brisk ten-mile run. Fitzsimmons was known as a diligent trainer whose daily workouts would include a 15-mile bicycle ride followed by a 15-mile walk, and then a 15- to 20-mile run between two hours of work in the gymnasium and ring. By the weigh-in both fighters were easily under the prescribed weight, with Fitzsimmons at 150 and a half pounds and Dempsey at 147 and a half pounds. This was the highest weight Dempsey ever carried as a middleweight. The referee for the night was Colonel Alexander Brewster, who had refereed the Sullivan–Ryan fight, and who would oversee the Marquis of Queensbury Rules during the scheduled 20 rounds.

As was now customary, the two fighters and their teams entered the ring area at nine o'clock. In Dempsey's corner were Mike Conley, Jack McAuliffe, Gus Tuthall, and his timekeeper Jimmy Colvine. Fitzsimmons was backed by Jimmy Carroll and Doc O'Connell, joined by his timekeeper W.J. Crittenden. Following a vulgar, but blessedly brief, attempt at entertainment by Irish comedian and singer Patsey Doody, the Master of Ceremonies for the evening, Olympic Club member and the former Mayor of New Orleans J.V. Guillotte, entered the ring at precisely 25 minutes after nine to introduce Brewster as the referee and Professor John Duffy as the club's official timekeeper. Dempsey and Fitzsimmons left their respective corners and shook hands as they met at the scratch line in the center of the ring. Dempsey was heard to offer Fitzsimmons a side bet of $1,000 which Fitzsimmons declined, saying he didn't have the money. It was then that Fitzsimmons' backer, Major McLaughlin, handed over $1,000 in cash to Jimmy Carroll, who was forced to return it by New Orleans police Captain W.J. Barrett, who had overheard the conversation as he stepped into the ring to deliver two pairs of five-ounce boxing gloves.

The two men now seated back in their respective corners could not have been any more different. In Dempsey's corner there were three bottles of beef tea, three bottles of rum, and four bottles of pale ale on ice. In Fitzsimmons' corner was a single bottle of water and a bucket. Dempsey appeared "graceful and symmetrical," while Fitzsimmons was "lank and lathy." Dempsey enjoyed the confidence of the crowd and was their sentimental favorite as the reigning champion. Fitzsimmons was a still a relative newcomer, a tall, awkward-looking fellow who was, however, impressive in his first appearance at the Olympic Club.

Time was called at approximately 9:30 and the battle was on. After a bit of sparring in the 1st round, Fitzsimmons cornered Dempsey and landed a right to the jaw. Dempsey attempted to counter with his left but fell short. The lanky New Zealander then began to bob and weave, using his long reach to deliver jab after jab to Dempsey's face. The round finished with Dempsey repeatedly clinching Fitzsimmons, then stepping back each time to deliver rapid combination blows with some effect. Fitzsimmons again took the lead in the 2nd round, with Dempsey taking more of a defensive tact. In a lightning quick move though, the challenger tagged the champion with a right to the nose that staggered Dempsey and had him retreating as he then took a left to the neck. He returned a blow to Fitzsimmons' ear, but was then countered quickly to the head. Judging by the look on the champion's face as he sat in his corner, he knew he had a fight on his hands.

In the 3rd round Dempsey was rushed by Fitzsimmons and was pinned to the ropes where he received a barrage of head and body punches. Every attempted counter was in vain as Fitzsimmons proved to be the quicker man. The two traded punches in the clinch with Fitzsimmons getting the better of these exchanges as well. Fitzsimmons led off the 4th round with three damaging shots to Dempsey's stomach. The champ countered once before receiving another four solid rights that nearly floored him towards the end of the round. Both men appeared fresh at the start of the 5th round. They traded jabs and moved cautiously for several seconds before Fitzsimmons unleashed a right to the body, countered by a left to the face. Fitzsimmons delivered another right to the chin and quickly ducked under Dempsey's counter. Dempsey was seen smiling following the exchange, but was quickly back to business when Fitzsimmons landed a left to the nose, followed by two blows to the chest and two more to the face. Dempsey had no other tactic but to clinch until the round ended.

Dempsey landed a right to the chest to begin the 6th round, but was immediately pounded in the ribs and once again resorted to the clinch. After one break Dempsey caught a clout to the nose and was forced into his corner, where Fitzsimmons landed several staggering jabs that went unanswered. Fitzsimmons sensed that he had hurt Dempsey at the end of the 6th round and pounced on him straight away in the 7th round, landing an uppercut that floored Dempsey and drew blood from the nose and mouth. The remainder of the round saw Fitzsimmons pursuing Dempsey around the ring delivering blow after blow. The champ had little time to recover between rounds and was battered at will for much of the 8th round, during which Fitzsimmons was untouched.

The 9th round was a repeat of the 8th, with Fitzsimmons easily landing punches and Dempsey trying to fight back. However, with his eyes nearly swollen shut, Dempsey could only land a few ineffective punches to Fitzsimmons' neck and upper body, receiving far worse than he gave.

With the fight all but a foregone conclusion, an astonished crowd watched Dempsey begin the 10th round fighting for pride alone. He was dropped by body shots, rising only to be floored again. Fitzsimmons continued to wallop Dempsey, putting him down three more times before the end of the round. As Dempsey lay on the mat at the end of the 10th round, it was reported that Fitzsimmons stood over Dempsey and whispered to him that he should just stay down. At this point Dempsey's childhood friend Jack McAuliffe entered the ring brandishing a pocket knife, thinking Fitzsimmons was trying to hit Dempsey when he was down, and threatened to stab him if he didn't walk away immediately.

Staggering to answer the bell for the 11th round, Dempsey continued to absorb punches at a murderous rate and was floored a total of seven times. Dempsey displayed the heart of a champion, however, even going so far as to pick up the towel his corner had thrown in, saying "a champion never quits." The 12th round began with two determined fighters trading punches, Fitzsimmons with several combinations to the head, Dempsey with an uppercut. After a right to the stomach Dempsey went down again. He rose groggy, but game nonetheless. Fitzsimmons, however, did not let up sensing the outcome was certain. Dempsey was once again battered and beaten in the 13th round. He was on the receiving end of a steady stream of punches that seemed to detonate on impact and was repeatedly knocked down until finally his seconds entered the ring to stop the fight. It was at that point that Fitzsimmons picked up Dempsey and carried him back to his corner.

Forty-nine minutes after the opening bell sounded, 28-year-old Bob "Ruby Robert" Fitzsimmons was declared the winner of the match and the new World Middleweight champion. The winner's share of the purse for this fight was $11,000 (worth approximately $290,000 today), with the loser receiving $1,000. The capacity crowd of 4,500 cheered both fighters.[9] With gate receipts of at least $30,000, the Olympic Club netted $15,000 for the evening after deducting the $12,000 purse and approximately $3,000 in expenses.[10]

In the wake of his victory Fitzsimmons agreed to take part in an exhibition two weeks later at the Olympic Club.[11] Two dates were advertised—Friday, February 6, and Monday, February 9, to be headlined by Fitzsimmons along with Jimmy Carroll, Andy Bowen, Felix Vacquelin and several others. The first event was somewhat subdued following the announcement of a split between Fitzsimmons and his manager/trainer Jimmy Carroll. The 460 fans who attended saw Englishman Joe Fielden go three rounds with John Cash of New York, followed by an excellent sparring exhibition between Fitzsimmons and Vacquelin. Featherweights Patsey Doodey and Kid Wilson were followed by lightweights Andy Bowen and Billy McMillan, after which Mike Smith and Tom Casey went their three rounds. The evening ended with Fitzsimmons and Fielden going four rounds. By agreement, Fitzsimmons would receive 60 percent of the gate receipts and the Olympic Club would retain the rest.[12]

Whether it was Fitzsimmons' disappointment with the paltry gate receipts—somewhere in the vicinity of $150—or a misunderstanding as he later claimed, Fitzsimmons, was a no-show for the Monday night event. He maintained that his participation had been arranged by Jimmy Carroll, but that he was only aware of the Friday night commitment. He went on to explain that on Monday night he was watching Mike Conley defeat Billy Woods at the Audubon Athletic Club[13] and the miscommunication was as a result of his recent split with Carroll. Irrespective of Fitzsimmons' explanation, the management of the Olympic Club was understandably upset at being stood up, misunderstanding or not, and publicly expressed their displeasure in the newspapers. Before leaving for Chicago, Fitzsimmons paid a visit to the Olympic Club to scold management for publicly implying that he was in any way responsible for the Monday night debacle, referring to the story which had been reported in the newspapers and which was now working its way across the country. Still embarrassed by the entire incident and now stinging from Fitzsimmons' verbal abuse, the Olympic Club held a special meeting on Friday, February 27, during which they banned both Fitzsimmons and Carroll from future consideration and revoked their honorary membership.[14] It was customary to grant all fighters and their seconds an honorary, non-dues paying membership in the club as part of their overall strategy to remain in compliance with the law. Should the police suddenly decide to stop the fight, the club could maintain that it was simply an exhibition between some of their members, which couldn't possibly be against the law.

"Who Killa Da Chief"

Beginning in mid–February and throughout March, the citizens of New Orleans were preoccupied with the trial of the alleged assailants of murdered Superintendent of Police David Hennessy. With a frenzy of headlines such as "Who Killa Da Chief," the trial began on February 11th with the difficult task of selecting an impartial jury, a process which occupied several days, examining and interviewing more than 1,300 potential jurors.

During the course of the trial, more than 140 witnesses provided contradictory and confusing testimony that described how Chief Hennessy had taken sides in a bitter feud between the Provenzano and Matranga families for control of the lucrative dockworker contracts for the waterfront along the port of New Orleans. Between 1888 and 1889, several murders involving both families caused Hennessy to attempt to broker a truce during a meeting at the Red Light Club on Customhouse Street (now Iberville Street) between Bourbon and Dauphine Streets.[15] Despite Hennessy's efforts, and a handshake agreement to stand down, the fragile truce would not hold. Within weeks, in the early morning hours of May 6, 1890, Antonio Matranga and five others were attacked as they rode in a wagon at the corner of Claiborne Avenue and Esplanade Street. Hennessy had arrested six members of the Provenzano family who were believed to be directly involved, however, it was well known that Hennessy was planning to testify at their trial, validating new evidence that would exonerate the Provenzano family, thus pointing the finger back at the Matranga family.[16]

There had been plenty of distraction during the Hennessy trial. In one such instance, heavyweight champion John L. Sullivan, in town to appear in a legitimate stage performance of *Honest Hearts and Willing Hands* at the Grand Opera House, was escorted into the courtroom in the middle of a witnesses' testimony, causing quite a stir and eliciting a mild rebuke from the judge. Sullivan was seated next to the jury box and for the balance of the day conversed freely with the jurors during the trial. By Wednesday, March 11, closing arguments had not been concluded[17] by Lionel Adams for the defense and by District Attorney Charles Luzenberg for the state, when, at six o'clock in the evening, Judge Joshua G. Baker adjourned the proceedings until ten o'clock the next day. On Thursday morning, the courtroom was packed to hear the closing arguments from both sides. Impassioned rhetoric and a mind-numbing series of alternative versions of just how the defendants came to be identified, arrested, held without bond, and charged were offered. Alibis that had been established were now reviewed in excruciating detail. The motives, memories, and statements of each of the individual witnesses for both sides were called into question. Finally, at just before 6:30 in the evening, the case was turned over to the jury for deliberation.

On Friday, March 13, at 2:30 in the afternoon, the jury entered the courtroom in St. Patrick's Hall. Access to the courtroom was restricted, but the chamber was still packed to overflowing when Judge Baker was handed the verdict from the jury foreman. After staring at the written verdict for what seemed an eternity, he declared a mistrial in the case of three of the defendants—Emmanuele Polizzi, Antonio Scaffedi, and Pietro Monasterio. Murmurs throughout the courtroom were vigorously gaveled down by Judge Baker, who then moved on to the jury's acquittal of the remaining six defendants. After a moment of stunned silence, the courtroom erupted with such furor that it could wake snakes. The accused were quickly escorted back to their prison cells at the Central Station where they were to continue to be held as they were still the subject of other indictments pending against them. The jurors, when interviewed, stated that they believed the state had presented a poor case and that they had reasonable doubts.[18] Almost immediately rumors began circulating that the jury had been tampered with, the accusations becoming focused on one individual in particular, jury foreman Jacob M. Seligman. Allegations of bribery dogged Seligman for weeks following the trial and he was later dismissed from his position with the stock exchange and expelled from the Young Men's Gymnastic Club. He eventually relocated to Cincinnati to escape the indignation of the citizens of New Orleans. Dominick O'Malley, a former New Orleans police detective and an investigator on Lionel Adams' defense team, was later charged with bribing the jury and was tried and convicted along with six accomplices. No charges were ever brought against Seligman.

The city was a simmering powder keg when several prominent citizens, remnants of Mayor Shakspeare's Committee of Fifty, called for a meeting at the Clay statue on Canal Street and Royal Street "to remedy the failure of justice in the Hennessy case." Approximately 1,500 people gathered to hear the exhortations of William S. Parkerson, an attorney and president of the Southern Athletic Club, as he circled the towering monument three times demanding the crowd "set aside the verdict of that infamous jury."[19] By ten o'clock there were between 6,000 and 8,000 angry citizens assembled. Brief, forceful speeches from two other attorneys, Walter Denegre and John C. Wickliffe, worked the crowd up into a frenzied, fevered pitch. The men had established a makeshift arsenal in a large ground floor room at the home of Franklin B. Hayne one block away on the corner of Bienville and Royal streets, stocked with over 150 shotguns, Winchester rifles, numerous pistols and, of course, plenty of ammunition. As the crowd eagerly filed through the room, weapons and cartridges were passed out until the room was empty. The rowdy procession flowed with the force and fury of the Mississippi River, making their way toward the Orleans Parish Prison located near Congo Square, where they were joined by hundreds more, ready to participate in whatever was going to happen.

A packed courtroom listened to the verdict of mistrial for three of the defendants and not guilty for the remaining six defendants. Allegations of jury tampering and bribery immediately hit the headlines, but could not prevent what happened next (*New Orleans Daily Picayune*).

At the prison, they met several thousand additional onlookers who had already assembled. A single patrol wagon summoned from the Central Station, jammed with a dozen or so city policemen that tried to intercede, but they were pelted with mud and rocks by the mob. In the waning hours of Friday evening a determined crowd of vigilantes stormed the prison, breaking through the North Liberty (Treme) Street door. They stalked the prison corridors, confronting panicked deputies and demanding the know the whereabouts of the Italian prisoners, who apparently had been released from their cells by Warden Lemuel Davis and were now scattered throughout the facility. Within a matter of two hours, two men were lynched outside the prison and nine men were beaten and fatally shot at various locations within the prison.

Three men were killed on the prison's third floor gallery walkway that led to the Fourth Precinct Station: Joseph P. Macheca, a shipping magnate and suspected Mafia leader who was accused of organizing the assassination. He was the person who rented

Incensed over the not guilty verdict in the Hennessy trial, it was an armed and dangerous crowd of six to eight thousand angry citizens that forced their way into the Orleans Parish Prison to execute eleven Italian prisoners accused of being involved in the murder of David Hennessy (from an unknown 19th century publication).

the shanty room on Girod and Basin Streets, in Pietro Monasterio's name, from which the assassins launched their attack. He died of a gunshot wound to the face. Antonio Marchesi, Sr., a fruit peddler who lived across the street from Hennessy, survived the prison attack, but died the following morning from a massive gash above his right eye caused by the iron gate on the third floor when it was broken down by the mob. The force of the blow caused the iron gate to penetrate his skull. His thumb, forefinger, and middle finger had been blown off when he grabbed a pistol aimed at his chest. His adolescent son, Asperi Marchesi, who was accused of having whistled to the shooters to signal Hennessy's arrival, survived the attack unharmed. The last victim was Antonio Scaffidi, a fruit peddler who had survived an earlier attack in prison in October 1890 from a newspaper vendor named Thomas Duffy. He was accused of being one of the principal shooters.

Several men were cornered and attacked in the courtyard of the adjoining women's prison: Pietro Monasterio, a shoemaker whose shop on the corner of Poydras and Basin Street Hennessy passed most evenings as he walked home, was accused of pointing out Hennessy to the assassins. He was shot numerous times. James Caruso, a stevedore, was cornered with Monasterio and the two received 42 wounds to the head and body from at least six different weapons. Charles Traina, a laborer at the Sarpy rice plantation upriver from New Orleans, was one of the men thought to have fired at Hennessy. Loretto Comitz, a tinsmith, died alongside Traina. Both men were beaten and shot to death. Rocco Geraci, also a stevedore, was discovered in the prison courtyard and shot twice in the head. Frank Romero, a ward-level politician known as "Nine Fingered Frank," was kneeling in the courtyard begging for his life when he was shot. Antonio Bagnetto was also accused of being one of the principal shooters. He was only slightly wounded when he was discovered hiding among the dead. He was dragged outside of the prison and lynched from a tree directly opposite the prison's North Liberty (Treme) Street entrance. He was shot several times as his body swung from the tree limb.

The crazed mob found their final victim hiding beneath a stairwell. Emmanuele Polizzi, a street vendor who often played the part of a madman during the trial. Polizzi was wounded before he was dragged from the prison and lynched from a lamppost at the corner of St. Ann and North Liberty (Treme) Streets. He too was accused of being one of the principal shooters. Traina, Caruso, Geraci, Romero, and Comitz had not yet gone to trial, but were hunted down and killed nonetheless. The bullet riddled bodies of Polizzi and Bagnetto were allowed to remain hanging outside the prison for several hours while inside the prison throngs of people filed through the corridors to view the massacred prisoners.

Inexplicitly, two of the most visible prisoners, Charles Matranga and Bastiano Incardona, both of whom had been found not guilty by the directed verdict from Judge Baker[20] and who were widely considered to be the chief lieutenants to ringleader Macheca, were never found by the mob and thus avoided the attack. There were persistent rumors that the mob had been instructed by Parkerson not to harm Matranga or the Marchesi boy. Deputies repositioned the bed in Matranga's cell and concealed him beneath the mattress. Six others escaped by hiding elsewhere within the prison.[21] The acquittal of Matranga and Incardona, followed by their survival inside the prison, gave rise to a whole new and disturbing set of questions regarding the true motives behind the mob violence. There was a sizeable contingent of citizens of the opinion that the mob's actions were instigated behind the scenes and financed under the table by the Matranga family, the original target of Chief Hennessy's investigation and who stood to benefit the most from his demise. The conspiracy theories swirled and circulated, but nothing further ever came of them.

Across the country, however, newspapers described how eleven innocent Italians had been lynched by a blood-thirsty, vigilante-style New Orleans mob. Cities with large Italian communities such as New York, Chicago, and San Francisco called for Federal intervention and reparations. Mayor Shakspeare was quoted as saying that "the Italians had taken the law into their own hands and we had to do the same."[22] President Benjamin Harrison eventually agreed to pay a $25,000 indemnity[23] to the families of the deceased prisoners and the incident placed such strain on American-Italian relations that both countries recalled their ambassadors. The episode, framed as the "retribution of the righteous," introduced Americans to the term "Mafia" and thereafter Italian men, irrespective of class or social standing, were suspected of being Mafioso, a stereotype that lingered well into the late 20th century. While largely consigned to the footnotes of

American history, the lynching—so described even though only two of the eleven victims were lynched—is better remembered in Italian history. Calls for retaliation from both sides lost momentum and threats were generally ignored as the outrage and indignation from both local and national sources would eventually subside, returning the city to a tense but typical day-to-day routine. Louisiana had one of the largest concentrations of Italian immigrants in America at the time, the majority primarily from Sicily having arrived by ship on the Palermo to New Orleans route.[24] Naturally they were reticent to return to their jobs for fear of further reprisal. The city's waterfront and warehouses, the fruit and vegetable markets, grocery stores and other businesses that were Italian-owned were mostly empty until an uneasy calm could be restored.

Back to Normal

For their part, the Olympic Rifle Club continued to participate in ongoing league competition as well as other tournaments, placing a close second to the Expectation Rifle Club by a mere eight points, followed by a stellar performance the following week by Joseph McMahon in individual competition with a score of 302 out of a possible 400 at the Southern Rifle Club picnic.[25]

The Olympic Club celebrated their eighth anniversary in the usual grand manner with yet another elaborate reception at their clubhouse for members and their guests. Nearly all of the 518 members were in attendance and danced to the music of renowned cornetist Armand Veazey's celebrated orchestra. As expected, the clubhouse was all abuzz with latest news in the wake of the murders at the Orleans Parish Prison, but before long their attention returned to boxing. Not only had the Dempsey–Fitzsimmons fight been a financial success for the club, but the recent decision to change the club's charter to that of a stock company would provide additional funds to finance future enhancements to their clubhouse facilities and the arena. The club issued 2,000 shares of voting stock at $25 per share, payable in installments.[26] The additional capital, combined with the profits from the Dempsey—Fitzsimmons fight, would give the Olympic Club a sizeable war chest to accomplish their ambitious plans. On the drawing board was the purchase of the properties directly behind their clubhouse and next to their arena, where they would erect a new building to house a larger natatorium, bowling alley, shooting range, and gymnasium. The country was emerging from yet another recession that had lasted nearly 12 months during which business activity had declined more than 20 percent.[27] The Olympic Club, however, seemed to be immune to the dismal economic fortunes experienced elsewhere and was enjoying their time on the national and international stage. Their foray into boxing had born fruit in an abundant harvest.

The Metropolitan Rifle Club staged their second rifle tournament of the season on Sunday, May 3, 1891, between eight local clubs. Competition was from 150 yards with three rounds of shooting—morning, noon, and evening. The Arnoult Rifle Club was in first place after the first day of competition with a score of 5,271 out of a possible 5,400 points, with the Olympic team right on their heels at 5,223 points.[28] The tournament lasted throughout the month of May, concluding on May 30, 1891. Charles

Ahrens of the Arnoults took top individual honors and the Arnoults won the team competition. Among the Olympic Rifle Club's top shooters were Harry Bouck (Bonck), Captain H.P. McNeely, Lem McNeely, and John Hammel.[29]

Andy Bowen versus Billy Myer

After a four-month hiatus, the Olympic Club launched their next boxing match, which turned out to be one of the ugliest events to take place at the Olympic Club. On the evening of Tuesday, May 19, 1891, was a bout between lightweights Andy Bowen and Billy Myer, a rematch from a year earlier at West End Athletic Club won by Bowen. Both camps trained furiously for the match, with Myer setting up once again in Carrollton Gardens while Bowen teamed up with Bob Farrell, a lightweight who had once been in John L. Sullivan's training camp, training in Abita Springs, a resort town located 60 miles north of New Orleans. Myer was considered to be an experienced fighter, yet if Myer was a fighter, Bowen was an assault engine, known for his tenacity and power.

Although beaten and bloodied in the early rounds, Myer was the aggressor throughout the fight. Bowen appeared uncharacteristically cautious, almost afraid to lead, but still managing to send Myer to the grass three times. Throughout the middle rounds, Myer repeatedly taunted Bowen to lead, dropping his guard or turning his back on Bowen. The one time that Bowen was induced to lead he was met with a right hook that felled him like an ox. Despite the blood flowing freely from Myer's nose and mouth, despite his black and puffy eye, Bowen could never finish off Myer. From the 18th round on the fighting was particularly ugly and most present felt the "Streator Cyclone" (Myer) had the advantage over the "Louisiana Tornado" (Bowen). The hideous affair saw Myer cautioned by referee Alexander Brewster for multiple fouls in rounds 20 through 24. After another series of fouls by Myer in the 24th round, referee Brewster abruptly ended the fight, much to the delight of the 3,000 fans present. Newspapers across the country initially reported that the fight had been awarded to Bowen on fouls,[30] but Brewster later declared the match to be a draw and the $3,000 purse was to be divided evenly.[31] This of course meant that all bets were off, much to the displeasure of all who had placed what they believed to be a winning wager on Bowen.

Alexander Brewster, the referee, was known from one end of the city to the other. He was a former director of the Metropolitan Police Board, and was currently serving as the Registrar of Voters in Orleans Parish, but he was also a nationally respected boxing referee, having worked such high-profile fights as the Sullivan–Ryan fight in 1882 and the Dempsey—Fitzsimmons fight in 1891. He repeatedly turned down the Sullivan–Kilrain fight in 1889. As a sporting man he was involved as a director of the Crescent City Jockey Club and served as Commodore of the Southern Yacht Club. It was once rumored that Brewster would be named as Chief of Police to replace the murdered David Hennessy.[32] However, since Brewster also owned one of the few legally sanctioned gambling houses in New Orleans, his decision came under greater than average scrutiny. This was the first incident to blemish the Olympic Club's sterling reputation for fair dealing, and it would be the last event Brewster officiated at the Olympic Club. While the club more than covered the purse and fight-related expenses, the fight itself and Brewster's decision made the event a critical disaster, one that sent the Olympic Club's management back to the drawing board.

As expected, the Olympic Club's proposed charter change became official at the club's annual meeting, raising an additional $50,000 in capital for the Olympic Club coffers. With virtually no indebtedness, the club was financially secure and began soliciting bids for the new building as well as for improvements to the existing clubhouse. They would need the additional space. The Oriental Club, a social club established in 1876, had recently relocated their clubhouse from Dauphine Street and Elysian Fields Avenue to the Olympic Club's old clubhouse in the former Drysdale residence at 417 Royal Street. However, lingering financial strain, brought about in no small part by the flagging business circumstances of the majority of their members during the most recent recessions in 1887–1888 and 1890–1891, forced the liquidation of the Oriental Club's assets in early 1891[33] and their remaining 115 members were now welcomed into the Olympic Club,[34] swelling their membership rolls to nearly 700.[35]

Concurrent with the club's charter change and their absorption of the Oriental Club's members, Olympic Club representatives and agents were busy trying to arrange future pugilistic events. The Competition Committee was all smiles when they were informed on July 7, 1891, that their proposal for a match between John L. Sullivan and Frank "Paddy" Slavin had been successful. They beat out the only other bidders, the California Athletic Club and the Granite Athletic Club in Hoboken, New Jersey.[36] The Olympic Club knew, however, that the fight itself was not yet a given. Agreements were almost always contingent on a set of very specific performance hurdles being achieved by both parties, but anyone with a say in the matter agreed that if the match was to occur, it would be in New Orleans at the Olympic Club.

Later that month, several representatives from the Olympic Club—Reuben M. Frank, Joseph Sporl, Frank Zengel, W.H. Douglas, Frank Williams, Charles Dickson, and Charles Noel, along with another 65 New Orleanians—boarded a train bound for Minneapolis to watch the much ballyhooed fight between Bob Fitzsimmons and Jim Hall.[37] The Olympic Club was among the dozen or so clubs across the country that had bid aggressively for the contest over the past 12 months, all of which had ultimately lost out to the Twin City Athletic Club of Minneapolis, who scheduled the event for Wednesday, July 22, 1891. Back in New Orleans, the Olympic Club issued 4,000 invitations for members and locals to come to their arena where they would "broadcast" the results of each round received by telegraphic updates directly from ringside in Minneapolis.[38] Officers and directors would take turns reading aloud the operator's transcription of events. And since the event was not considered to be a boxing event under the city ordinance, the club was prepared to sell alcoholic spirits and everyone expected the night to be a boisterous, but grand time.

However, as promised by Minnesota Governor William Rush Merriam, and chronicled almost daily in the news, the state militia was called upon to assist the local sheriff in enforcing the state law against prize fighting. With no last-minute reprieve forthcoming, the Twin Cities Athletic Club had no choice but to cancel the fight, to refund ticket sales, and to graciously accept their huge financial loss, with both fighters pocketing the forfeit money plus expenses.[39] It was not as if there had never been a boxing event in Minnesota before. Indeed, there had been at least 28 fights conducted in Minneapolis and St. Paul alone during 1891, six of those at the Twin Cities Athletic Club. And it was not just the national attention drawn to a prominent fight. In February of 1891, there were two title fights—Tommy Ryan versus Danny Needham for the World Welterweight Championship, and Harris Martin versus Denny Kelliher for the Northwest Middleweight Championship. In April of 1891, there was a third title bout pitting Charles Kemmick against Jim Scully for the American Welterweight Championship.[40] All 28 of these prize fights were advertised well in advance and held in public spaces. In addition to the Twin Cities Athletic Club, events took place at the Olympic Athletic Club, the Newmarket Theatre, the Comique Theatre, the Washington Rink, the Pence Opera House, the St. Paul Armory, and several other venues between the two cities. This was becoming an all too familiar scenario in cities across America as fight promoters are caught off guard when the state and local government suddenly takes exception to a high-profile event and sends in the troops to ensure the event is cancelled. No matter that the event had the potential to inject thousands of dollars into their economy. And while politicians might be tempted to look the other way from time to time, inevitably the hue and cry of reform-minded citizens promising to make trouble come election time would drown out the hope of any sort of compromise. On this time around it was Minnesota's turn just as it had been Louisiana's turn in 1882 for Sullivan–Ryan and again in 1889 for Sullivan–Kilrain.

As a result of the fight's cancellation, it was a reinvigorated group of Olympic Club officials who caucused during the train trip back to New Orleans from Minneapolis, discussing how their now revived chance to bid for the Fitzsimmons–Hall match might fare. Reuben M. Frank remained in Minneapolis to negotiate with both camps. In typical fashion, both sides now felt they had the upper hand—the fighters holding out for a $12,000 purse and Frank holding fast to his last $9,000 offer. The fighters wanted to meet immediately, but the Olympic Club wanted the fight to take place in December. A rival bid of $10,000 from the Pokegama Athletic and Sportsman's Association in Grand Rapids, Michigan appeared to queer the deal for the Olympic Club.[41] While he was in the middle of these negotiations, however, Frank was successful in signing Jimmy Carroll and Billy Myer to meet in New Orleans in December.[42] Negotiations with Fitzsimmons also broached the possibility of matching him against Ted Pritchard, the English middleweight champion, during Mardi Gras. These back-and-forth negotiations were nothing new to the Olympic Club. In less than two years into the fight game, they had seen dozens of proposed matches dissolve after weeks or months of such negotiations, only to be renewed at a later date.

Harry McEnery, a sportswriter for the *Daily Picayune* better known by his byline moniker "Bantam" for his bi-weekly column "Bantam's Budget," informed Olympic Club officials and his readers that, while in Minneapolis for the Fitzsimmons–Hall fight, he had spoken with James J. Corbett, who indicated that he was eager to meet John L. Sullivan. If for some reason the Sullivan–Slavin match did not come off, perhaps a Sullivan–Corbett match might be possible.[43] Corbett was gaining a reputation in New Orleans following his victory over Jake Kilrain. In May of 1891 Corbett fought Peter Jackson for 61 rounds before the California Athletic Club before referee Hiram Cook declared the bout to be no contest.[44] When he fought the up and coming Corbett, Jackson was an experienced and feared heavyweight fighter with 93 bouts under his belt since his debut in 1882.

With the return of the club's management from Minneapolis on Thursday night, September 17, 1891, the Olympic Club entertained members of the press corps during one of their typical informal social gatherings featuring songs, speeches, and both humorous and dramatic recitations accompanied by champagne and cigars. There was also a brief address from William A. Brady, the dramatic and business manager for James Corbett, who spoke of his client's willingness to meet Charles Mitchell, Paddy Slavin, or John L. Sullivan, in no particular order, although most believed that Corbett's prime target was Sullivan. This was the second time in as many weeks that the idea of a Sullivan–Corbett match had been mentioned, and there were those at the Olympic Club who began to explore the possibility.

Much later in the evening Acting-President Joseph Sporl returned from a prolonged interview with the Orleans Parish Grand Jury, informing members that he felt quite positive about the club's status in the face of a new legal challenge.[45] Sporl obviously underestimated the determination of the grand jury who later found the Olympic Club to be in violation of Act 25 of 1890—once again trying to reconcile the blurred lines between "prizefights" and "glove contests."[46] As a result, in a preemptive strike by the city, both Cal McCarthy and Tommy Warren were indicted by the grand jury for training and preparing to engage in a prizefight, scheduled to take place as advertised at the Olympic Club in just four days. It was their interpretation that, under Section One of Act 25 of 1890 that stipulated it would be illegal "to go into training preparatory to such fight, or act as trainer for any such [fight]" and since both McCarthy and Warren were openly training for an advertised prizefight, also prohibited under Section One, the indictment should be issued. The fly in the ointment was, of course, the language in the act which stated, "Provided, this act shall not apply to exhibitions and glove contests between human beings, which may take place within the rooms of regularly chartered athletic clubs." However, this interpretation of Act 25 of 1890 speaks volumes as to the activist inclination of the grand jury. Rather than dismay, the club's officers and directors were actually eager to meet the legal challenge head on at trial. And, in typical Olympic Club bravado, they announced yet another round of improvements to their facility.[47]

Better known as "Bantam" for his bi-weekly sports column "Bantam's Budget," McEnery was one of the very first dedicated sportswriters in New Orleans. He covered a wide variety of sports and recreation in the city, but his first love was boxing (*New Orleans Daily Picayune*).

Cal McCarthy versus Tommy Warren

Released from police custody on bail, both fighters being primed and ready, McCarthy and Warren faced off on the evening of Tuesday, September 22, 1891, before a sparse crowd of only 1,500 at the Olympic Club arena, including "those who represented the best elements" and who were all very orderly. The neighbors would probably not have known there was an event at the arena save for the usual crowd outside attempting to satisfy their curiosity about the fight without having to pay the piper. From the moment both fighters entered the ring, the crowd immediately remarked at the physical conditioning of the two featherweights, but gave the nod to the slightly taller and heavier McCarthy. At a quarter after nine o'clock the bell sounded and the fight was underway. The first three rounds were marked by brief bits of sparring followed by alternating attacks from each man, blows exchanged and a return to sparring in order to absorb the lessons learned about their opponent. Thus far it was all very scientific, but ultimately unproductive. There was plenty of give and take during the next several rounds, each man scoring with their jab. McCarthy gradually gained the upper hand as Warren began to tire, working the body repeatedly to further weaken the young Californian. In the 19th round, coming out of a clinch, Warren's eye caught an inadvertent elbow which drew blood. McCarthy continued to land stinging blows to Warren's swollen lamp for the next two rounds, which only caused Warren to overcompensate in order to protect the eye. In the 20th round McCarthy threw a wild roundhouse that Warren tried to avoid, catching the point of McCarthy's elbow again, this time in the jaw. In the 21st round McCarthy delivered a left jab to Warren's mouth, quickly followed by a right upper-cut to his jaw that staggered Warren, who tried to clinch but only succeeded in dragging both men to the mat as he fell. Both men remained on the deck for an eight-count. Upon regaining their footing, McCarthy was the first to land a punch, another right upper-cut to the jaw that sent Warren down to his hands and knees. Trying to rise after the second eight-count, Warren's legs gave out and he collapsed for the final time. McCarthy's victory allowed him to claim the winner's share of the $2,000 purse. The uncharacteristically poor attendance was attributed to the fact that the required city permit was only obtained at the 11th hour due to the grand jury's legal complications, and there was

Although seeking to challenge the legal system, the Olympic Club was still cautious in advertising the McCarthy–Warren event. They specifically state that the bout was not a "prizefight," but rather a "Grand Glove Contest" (*New Orleans Times-Democrat*).

simply not enough time for the club to properly advertise the fight in advance[48] to assure patrons that the match would actually come off. Resigned to a financial loss, the Olympic Club's management now had to hope that the upcoming jury trial would vindicate them and provide them with an opportunity to quickly recover their modest loss in the very near future.

On September 29, 1891, in Section A of New Orleans Criminal Court presided over by Judge Robert H. Marr, that McCarthy and Warren appeared to face the grand jury's indictment, represented by vaunted legal team of W.L. Evans and Arthur Dunn. The city would be represented by District Attorney Charles H. Luzenberg. Testimony for the defense was solicited from several witnesses referred to as "the best class of citizens" such as prominent attorney and politician Charles P. Drolla, New Orleans coroner Dr. Charles L. Seeman, as well as other lawyers, business owners, and even William H. Williams, Sporting Editor of the *Times-Democrat*. Drolla testified that he knew the difference between a prize fight and a glove contest, having been present at the Sullivan–Kilrain prize fight which he stated was "an exhibition of brutality." He further stated that "there was nothing repulsive in the mill at the Olympic Club. It was no prize fight, but a scientific glove contest, under the supervision of the police." J.H. Kennard, an attorney who was present at the Sullivan–Kilrain fight and at the McCarthy–Warren contest, testified that the chief difference between a prize fight such as Sullivan–Kilrain and a scientific glove contest such as the McCarthy–Warren fight was the structure, with the former being under London Prize Ring Rules and the latter being under Marquis de Queensbury Rules. The lack of consistently timed rounds, the crudeness of the ring, and the element of bare knuckles made the Sullivan–Kilrain match a prize fight, while the structure of timed rounds, timed intermission between rounds, and the use of padded gloves made the McCarthy–Warren match a scientific glove contest. Additional testimony was provided by witnesses other than the Olympic Club's officers and members, including police Captain William J. Barrett and State Representative B.C. Shields. Each of these fine gentlemen, to a man, testified that they did not believe the exhibition glove contests presented by the Olympic Club constituted a prizefight. W.L. Evans' closing argument touched on Article Two of the Olympic Club's Articles of Incorporation which mentioned "exhibitions of athletic sports." He also highlighted City Ordinance 4336 (amending Ordinance 1994) legalizing glove contests taking place under police supervision, and Ordinance 4522 (amending Ordinance 4336) which required a permit be issued by the city upon payment of a charitable donation not to exceed $500, all of which were judiciously complied with by the Olympic Club in each of their exhibitions.

District Attorney Luzenberg attempted to persuade the jury that a right hook to the jaw, whether gloved or not, still had the potential to draw blood, to crack teeth, to break the jawbone, or to cause unconsciousness. He argued that repeated blows to the eyes from either bare knuckles or gloved fists could cause blindness, that a single jab to the nose from either bare knuckles or gloved fists could still break the recipient's nose. He further explained, that each form of fighting was as brutal as the other, irrespective of bare knuckles or gloved fists; irrespective of a three-second round or a three-minute round; irrespective of a turf ring or a padded canvas ring. And, in the end, the fighters, whether using bare knuckles or gloved fists, both received a monetary reward—

a prize. Thus, he concluded, both forms of boxing were, in fact, prizefights. Although logical, Luzenberg's argument and lack of corroborating witnesses made no impression whatsoever on the jury. Judge Marr's charge to the jury was essentially that while there was a state law against prizefighting, there was no legal definition of what constituted a prizefight. It would be up to the jury to decide for themselves based on the testimony given whether or not they believed a prizefight had taken place. Without ever leaving their seats in the jury box, it took the 12-man jury a mere five minutes to return a unanimous verdict of Not Guilty.[49]

Having cleared this legal hurdle, the Olympic Club vigorously returned to arranging future events and pressed forward with their pending bouts, beginning with a series of six sparring exhibitions on October 6 to benefit Tommy Warren.[50] The grand jury had a number of vocal anti-boxing proponents in their ranks who were determined to force the city and the state to abolish the sport by legislative fiat. Therefore, not being entirely satisfied with the most recent jury verdict in Judge Marr's court, these activist grand jury members prepared a special report which they delivered to the city, commenting upon the defect in the law that was the source of such confusion, and urging the city and their state representatives to address this in the upcoming legislative session.[51]

Meanwhile, having spent the better part of 18 months since his resignation from the Olympic Club trying to increase the membership, footprint, and public profile of the Metropolitan Club, Charles Genslinger was now ready to take on the Olympic Club head to head. He had announced plans for the club's magnificent new clubhouse across the street from the Olympic Club and had raised additional funds to begin construction on an arena intended to rival that of the Olympic Club in both design and amenities. However, the completion date was still some six weeks away. Nonetheless, Genslinger was anxious to arrange for a prizefight. Scheduled in advance of the Olympic Club trial, the Metropolitan Club matched Charlie Porter from Texas against local Joe Fernandez on Monday, October 19, 1891. In an abundance of caution, the club only allowed members and a few invited guests to attend so as not to draw any attention from the authorities. As a result, there were only approximately a hundred spectators on hand, seated around the temporary ring erected in the club's main gymnasium for the event. Herbert Rathery of Denver was chosen as the referee and he accompanied Porter and Fernandez into the ring following the conclusion of a three-round exhibition between Ed McCune and Charles Fox. For eight rounds, the sparse crowd watched two uninspired and clearly under-trained fighters go at each other in a way that did not involve much science. Fernandez was one dimensional and continually refused to heed the advice of his trainer and corner crew during the fight. Porter, on the other hand, adapted to the advice given him between rounds, and that proved to be the difference in the end.[52] It was an eventful evening, marking the club's first fight, but the true test would have to wait until a proper prizefight could be staged in their new arena.

The Metropolitan Club's new arena was hastily completed ahead of schedule and preparations were underway for their first big event. For weeks, the club had been negotiating a match between two unbeaten featherweights, George Siddons from Chicago and Charles Fox from Galveston. On November 7, 1891, the fight card opened with a typical 4-round exhibition between "Freckles" and "Joe," two of Professor John Duffy's teenage students, whose enthusiastic performance whet the appetite of what was described only as "a large crowd." Just before 9:30 in the evening, Siddons and Fox entered the ring. The crowd instantly noted a marked contrast in the physical appearance between the tall, slender Siddons and the shorter, stocky Fox. Local fighter Andy Bowen was selected as the referee and before long the set-to was underway. Frequent cries of foul from both sides marked the action, with Siddons clearly having the better time of it. Fox gamely managed to last 15 rounds, but the fight went to Siddons.[53] With the success of their first foray into the fight game, the Metropolitan Club immediately began trying to arrange a bout between Siddons and Tommy Warren.

John Griffin versus Jimmy Larkin

Two weeks later, across the street, the Olympic Club proceeded with bringing off their own featherweight match between John Griffin of Brooklyn and Jimmy Larkin of Jersey City for the American Featherweight Championship. Between 2,800 and 3,000 were in the Olympic Club arena on November 19, 1891, to watch the two featherweights do battle. Professor George Soule and J.M. Coos provided the customary pre-fight announcements to the crowd, pointing out the numerous policemen stationed throughout the facility. Just after 9:15 the two bantams met at the scratch line and the bout was on. In the 3rd round, an unsteady Larkin was knocked clean out of the ring and returned to the battleground with a pronounced limp. To no one's surprise, in the 4th round Griffin took the fight directly to Larkin with a relentless attack to the head and body. He floored Larkin with a left jab-right cross combination, followed by a devastating right hook to the jaw, taking less than 60 seconds to knock out the fading Larkin to claim the victory and the title.[54] This was the third title fight held at the Olympic Club and clearly demonstrated the club's growing stature in the national boxing pantheon.

Meanwhile, the Metropolitan Club, having announced plans in late June for their new arena, celebrated their second anniversary with a gala reception which included a special ceremonial groundbreaking for the Metropolitan's new clubhouse.[55] Members of the Olympic Club had watched all winter as the impressive three-story building designed by the firm of Duval and Favrot took shape across the street. The club also continued to aggressively purchase property adjoining their clubhouse and now owned nearly half of the block. Genslinger and the Metropolitan Club were demonstrating their determination to surpass the Olympic Club.

When it became known that longtime boxing instructor and referee at the Olympic Club, Professor John Duffy, was in failing health, his friends and supporters at the club decided to hold a benefit to help with his medical expenses. With the Griffin–Larkin bout already scheduled, the club decided to hold the benefit a month later on Monday, December 21, 1891, at their arena. More than 2,000 patrons saw seven mediocre sparring matches and one Greco–Roman wrestling match before the night was capped off with a lively exhibition between Bob Fitzsimmons and local fighter Felix Vacquelin.[56] Nonetheless, Duffy received nearly $1,000 from the affair.

Jimmy Carroll versus Billy Myer

On the heels of the Duffy benefit, the Olympic Club had one final match proposed for 1891 between Jimmy Carroll and Billy Myer, scheduled for Thursday, December 22, 1891. At some point between their February expulsion and the Duffy benefit, Fitzsimmons and Carroll reunited to resolve their differences and resumed their partnership, also smoothing over their brief dispute with the Olympic Club. By now Jimmy Carroll was a familiar face to New Orleans boxing fans, having first been introduced to him the previous year when he successfully defended his American Lightweight title by beating Andy Bowen in 21 rounds.[57] He was also Bob Fitzsimmons' de facto trainer and manager when Fitzsimmons defeated Dempsey earlier in 1891 and was a frequent member of the corner crew of seconds for numerous fighters appearing in New Orleans. At 38, the aging titleholder was still an impressive fighter, and his conditioning was unquestioned.

Thirty-three-year-old Billy Myer from Streator, Illinois, was also familiar to New Orleans, having faced off against Andy Bowen twice in the last two years. The first meeting resulted in a loss at the West End Athletic Club and the second was referee Alexander Brewster's recent controversial draw at the Olympic Club.[58] Myer came into his ninth professional fight with a record of four wins, one loss, two draws, and one no decision, but boxing fans who took the time to examine Myer's record knew that he too was an impressive fighter. On February 13, 1889, he battled World Lightweight Champion Jack McAuliffe for 34 rounds at Burche's Opera House in North Judson, Indiana, approximately 60 miles southeast of Gary, Indiana. Myer drew first blood in the 29th round and knocked McAuliffe down in the 43rd round, but referee Mike McDonald declared the bout to be a draw after 4 hours and 27 minutes.[59]

In the longest fight thus far at the Olympic Club, Myer needed 43 hard-fought rounds to tame the plucky Carroll before 3,000 fans. The two had traded punches evenly throughout the night, and it seemed like a toss of the coin could easily determine the winner, depending of course on who you talked to and who they had bet on. Both Myer and Carroll's

Having defeated Andy Bowen at the Olympic Club in September of 1890, Carroll travelled to Amsterdam to face Jimmy Dime, losing by a knockout. He returned to the friendly confines of the Olympic Club to meet Billy Myer from Streeter, Illinois, in December of 1891 (from an unknown 19th century publication).

eyes glazed with competitive cruelty and all during the fight Myer was at his best in close, consistently crowding his opponent who fared better at long range. By the 13th round most of the crowd still had the fight a draw. But following a cursory left jab from Myer, Carroll turned his head a bit more than usual to avoid the blow and Myer threw a quick right. Carroll hit the mat like a felled tree. There was no need for referee John Duffy to even begin the ten-count, Carroll was out cold and remained down for several minutes until his seconds carried him out of the ring. As fate would have it, in a bout where each man gave as good as he got, it was a single opportunistic blow to Carroll's jaw that sent him to the canvas.[60] Myer had earned himself another shot at Jack McAuliffe and the world lightweight title. This was the Olympic Club's fourth title fight of the seven regulation, non-exhibition or benefit, events in 18 months. Having sold 3,000 tickets at $4, the club realized a profit of $6,000 after deducting the $5,000 purse and approximately $1,000 in expenses. Olympic Club officers and members, guests and patrons, everyone but Jimmy Carroll was elated with the outcome. Even those members who had been vocally critical of the club's involvement had reason to be pleased.

Spirits were generally high during the holiday season as Olympic Club officers and members eagerly awaited the new year. One could argue that they had every reason to feel that way. The club had successfully defended their right to hold "scientific glove contests" in the courts, they were secure in the financial condition of their club. and they were feeling less threatened by Genslinger and the Metropolitan Club. A few Olympic Club members even treated themselves to a Christmas present, purchasing $5 reserved seat tickets to watch Andy Bowen take on Austin Gibbons at the Metropolitan Club's newly completed arena on the evening of Tuesday, December 29, 1891. Those who attended the fight witnessed a terrific lightweight battle during which Bowen had the upper hand throughout most of the first 44 rounds. When Gibbons drew blood in the 45th round, he went from hunted to hunter, pounding Bowen with a whirlwind of blows to the head. Bowen fought back gamely, but Gibbons aggressively took the fight to Bowen, fiercely working combinations to Bowen's ribs like a pile driver, moving Bowen back against the ropes. Gibbons had his right cocked and ready to deliver when referee John Duffy interceded, awarding the match to Gibbons. Had Duffy allowed Gibbons to follow through with his punch it would have caused Bowen's head to bash against the wooden corner post with devastating effect. As it was, the slumping Bowen had to be carried back to his corner.[61]

Charles Genslinger had thrown down the gauntlet with a successful series of fights at the Metropolitan Club. Several thousand people filled his costly new arena, nearly a mirror image of the Olympic Club arena in terms of design and amenities. Gate receipts were more than sufficient to cover the purses offered and related fight expenses, but there was not much leftover to make a dent in the cost of building the massive arena and their beautiful new clubhouse. All in all, it was a respectable first effort, but Genslinger put himself at a disadvantage by attempting to do everything at once. The Olympic Club had grown gradually, expanding both their clubhouse and arena progressively over time, taking on very little debt, and putting less of a strain on their club's finances. They were also very fortunate that some of their bold moves paid off.

During 1891 the Olympic Club promoted five "scientific glove contests." Their efforts were highly successful, as shown below.

Date	Match	Gross Receipts	Purse and Expenses	NET to Olympic Club
January 14	Dempsey–Fitzsimmons	$30,000	$12,000 + $3,000	$15,000
May 19	Bowen–Myer	$9,000	$3,000 + $1,000	$5,000
September 22	McCarthy–Warren	$4,500	$1,500 + $500	$2,500
November 18	Griffin–Larkin	$6,400	$2,500 + $1,000	$2,900
December 22	Carroll–Myer	$12,000	$5,000 + $1,000	$6,000
		$61,900	**$30,500**	**$31,400**

All figures estimated.

With these five events, the Olympic Club grossed approximately $1,628,900 in today's dollars and netted approximately $852,600 for the year. They also hosted four benefit exhibitions during 1891—a member's only event and a benefit for Bob Fitzsimmons in February, a benefit for Tommy Warren in October, and a benefit for Professor John Duffy in December. Even with the additional expenses related to settling their legal affairs, completing their charter change and stock offering, plus further property acquisition and construction projects, the club still was an extremely profitable venture and continued to attract new members. Although the stakes had been raised, Genslinger wasn't done yet.

Four

1892

"The bigger they are, the harder they fall."—Bob Fitzsimmons

Even as Olympic Club director Frank Williams scoured the athletic clubs and gymnasiums of New York trying to arrange matches for Mardi Gras, the rivalry between the Olympic and Metropolitan clubs began to heat up. The first boxing match of 1892 took place at the Metropolitan Club on January 21 between featherweights George Siddons and Tommy Warren for the Featherweight Championship of America. Although the club offered tickets at rather modest prices—$2 for general admission, $3 for a reserved seat—there were less than 2,000 fans strolling through a building designed to hold 10,000 or more. The "tough element" was noticeably absent given the affordable ticket price and the "sport and the swell mingled good naturedly in the excitement-seeking brotherhood of Fistiana." It turned out to be an easy victory for Siddons, who knocked out Warren in the waning moments of the 9th round to claim the winner's share of the $1,500 purse.[1] It was only a modest financial success for Charles Genslinger and the Metropolitan Club, but a success nonetheless. Assuming they sold 2,000 tickets at $2 each, the club stood to gross $4,000 and net approximately $2,000 after expenses.

Tommy Callaghan versus Cal McCarthy

The Olympic Club kicked off their 1892 season with a bantamweight bout between Irish champion Tommy Callaghan from Newcastle, England and Cal McCarthy from New Jersey on Wednesday, January 27, 1892. McCarthy had beaten Tommy Warren at the Olympic Club just four months prior and was the fan favorite to defeat the unknown Englishman making only his second appearance in the United States. Callaghan's backers hoped that a victory against McCarthy would put their man in line to face World Bantamweight Champion George Dixon. Ornate banners depicting the national colors of both Ireland and England were commissioned and draped over the ring for the fight, and which the Olympic Club announced they would award to two lucky ticket holders through a special drawing on the night of the fight.[2]

From the opening bell, McCarthy set a furious pace in an effort to overcome Callaghan's height and reach advantage. Throughout the early rounds he proved his cleverness by coming inside and engaging Callaghan at close range, most effectively with a swift right upper-cut that he landed in the clinches. He was also well aware of Callaghan's powerful right and moved quickly to confuse the ungainly Callaghan. During the middle rounds McCarthy fought with an air of confidence not seen since his victory over Warren, taking an aggressive tact to the tiring Irish lad. Late in the 14th round McCarthy saw an unexpected opening and felled Callaghan with a combination uppercut to the stomach and a vicious right cross to the jaw that dropped the Englishman for the count.[3] With just over 2,000 tickets sold, the fight was considered only a modest financial success for the Olympic Club.

And so, what had been a simmering feud between the Olympic Club and the Metropolitan Club was beginning to come to a full boil. Having resigned in a pique after losing his reelection bid in 1889, Genslinger left to establish the Metropolitan Club, setting up right across the street from the Olympic Club at 625 Royal Street. They had gone toe to toe with the Olympic Club during 1891, staging a match between featherweights George Siddons and Charlie Fox on November 7 to compete with the Olympic's Griffin–Larkin match on November 19 and another between lightweights Andy Bowen and Austin Gibbons on December 29 to compete with the Olympic's Carroll–Myer match.[4] While each of the Metropolitan's three fights was modestly profitable, they did not result in the waves of additional new members that Genslinger had envisioned and thus the club was having trouble overcoming the tremendous financial burden placed on them by Genslinger's ambitious, and some might say vindictive, plans to drive the Olympic Club out of the fight game. Genslinger's haste to beat the Dutch out of the Olympic Club required him to finance, construct, and appropriately furnish, in a little over one year, facilities that would outshine those that the Olympic Club had built and paid for gradually over the past ten years. Construction of a magnificent four-story clubhouse on Royal Street, designed to rival the Olympic Club in amenities and furnishings, as well as building the club's gymnasium and 10,000-seat arena, was all proving too much for Genslinger and his fledgling Metropolitan Club.[5]

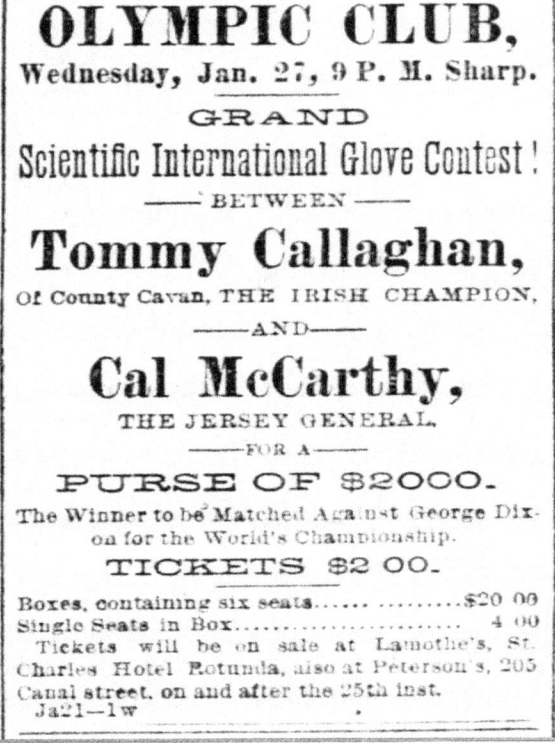

Advertised as a "Scientific International Glove Contest" in order to placate the authorities, the winner of this bout was next in line to face bantamweight champion George Dixon for a title shot (*New Orleans Daily Picayune*).

Despite the acceptance of infrequent glove contests at other athletic clubs in New Orleans, to this point these events had generally only been open to members and their invited guests. The city still had a voracious appetite for boxing that was met with unsanctioned fights that continued to be sporadically staged illegally outside the city limits. One such match occurred in the wee hours of Sunday, February 21, 1892. Rumors ran wild all Saturday night through the city's saloons, groggeries, and sporting houses: there was to be a bare-knuckle fight on Sunday morning at an undisclosed location downriver in St. Bernard Parish. To those who delighted in flaunting the law, this fight would tick all the boxes. A bare-knuckle brawl on a Sunday was just too good to pass up. The word quickly spread and nearly 500 people gathered at the landmark Clay Statue on Canal Street just after dawn and traveled in groups of 40 to 50 by street rail downriver to St. Bernard Parish to see a finish fight with "skin gloves" somewhere in the woods near the slaughterhouse. Upon their arrival, they found an additional 200 men waiting to get in. Freeloaders who had unsuccessfully swarmed the gate were perched on the outhouse rooves and cisterns surrounding a large, isolated brick building. There, in the interior courtyard of Patton's Tallow Factory, a sleepy and shivering crowd was primed by a steady stream of bottles of free whiskey and other potentially combustible potables passed among the pugnacious patrons, each man doing his level best to keep the rest of the crowd from getting drunk by drinking as much as he could as fast as he could before the bottle was wrested away from him. A crude boxing ring was pitched, a pair of yellow wooden stools appeared for the fighters, and at seven o'clock in the morning, Charley Johnson and Alphonse Garcia made their way to the ring. Before long the fight was on, with Ed Williams serving as the referee.

Both Johnson and Garcia were relatively well-known club fighters, albeit just a cut above being suitable to act as sparring partners for more talented fighters. For a quarter of an hour, the sleepy and shivering crowd watched Johnson brutally pound Garcia for 4 rounds, hitting him everywhere from the blinkers to the bellows seemingly at will. Frequent altercations between pockets of inebriated spectators, now numbering around 600 in total, delayed the match between rounds, as the arguments often spilled over into the ring itself. Mercifully, before the 5th round, Garcia's seconds threw up the sponge.[6] A drunken and thoroughly disgusted crowd slowly made their way back to the city, some to attend church, some to find breakfast, but most to sleep it off.

This was precisely the type of unseemly, unauthorized, and illegal event that everyone, politicians and athletic clubs alike, wanted to eliminate. Johnson and Garcia were known to boxing fans around New Orleans, so what, other than the promise of a lucrative payday, would have drawn them to participate in such an event? On Monday morning, St. Bernard Parish District Attorney James Wilkinson issued orders for the arrest of the fighters and their seconds—Arthur Upham, Charles Porter, Ed McCune, Frank "Dutch" Neil and Joseph Suarez Garcia.[7] The following week ministers across the city could point to this horrid, violent spectacle, with who knows how many men losing who knows how much of their hard-earned wages to the ever-present gambling sharps while under the influence of an abundance of cheap liquor, all in violation of the Sabbath. Anti-boxing proponents and reformers had yet another bit of evidence for their cause.

On the other end of the spectrum, the Olympic Club's long-term plan was to once again improve and expand their facilities. To that end, with great fanfare and flourish, and perhaps a slight snub of the nose to Genslinger, the club laid the cornerstone for their own new clubhouse on Sunday, February 28, 1892.[8] At four o'clock in the afternoon, the assembled membership, invited guests, and newspaper reporters listened to speeches about a "new era of progress" symbolized by the construction of the club's new headquarters—a four-story edifice designed by local architect Dietrich Einseidel. The new building was planned to be three stories high in the French Renaissance style of architecture, with an angled tower and Mansard roof, surrounded by galleries, forming a fourth story. The building would have 80 feet fronting on Royal Street, with annexes surrounding approximately 140 feet deep. Upon passing through the clubhouse's ten-foot-wide front entrance, a visitor would enter an area approximately 26 feet by 40 feet housing several parlors which would be used as informal meeting rooms. At the rear of the first floor were parlors for reading and literary rooms. Six billiard and pool tables occupied much of the second floor, with several smaller rooms at the rear of the second floor which were divided into smoking rooms. Along one wall in the center of the second floor was a bar that would rival any found in the city.

The third floor was divided into four large rooms, each 16 feet by 18 feet, which were able to serve a variety of purposes, along with a secretary's office approximately 13 feet square. In the rear of the main building was a "glazed" building, the upper walls and roof comprised of an architectural glass specially coated with a transparent film which allowed the building to be open to the light, but also to be structurally strong. This building would have the footprint of a 30 foot by 50 foot structure covered by a 29-foot-high arched roof.

The natatorium was on the Montegut Street side of the property and was 35 feet by 75 feet. There was also a 150-foot-long shooting range and a bowling alley on the Montegut Street side of the gymnasium. The gymnasium was housed in a two-story building behind the clubhouse, and was approximately 74 feet by 180 feet with locker rooms on each floor. Above the gymnasium was a rubber-surfaced running track approximately 220 feet around (24 laps to the mile). The main entrance to the gymnasium was on the Chartres Street side of the property. The rear door of the gymnasium opened almost directly into the large wooden arena.

The now-famous arena was located on the Chartres Street side behind the main building in a large part of the property purchased from the Atlantic Cotton Press. Its exterior consisted of overlapping corrugated sheet metal panels nailed to a wooden super structure, all of which was protected by barbed wire and canvas tarpaulins. The frame of the building was 130 long by 177 feet wide, with 30-foot-high walls, and an expanded seating capacity of nearly 10,000 plus standing room for another 500 to 600 fans. It was one of the largest amphitheaters in the United States and featured a retractable roof consisting of a series of three-foot-wide waxed canvas tarpaulins that could be adjusted to various lengths like a window shade by means of ropes and pulleys. Clusters of incandescent electric lights and four large carbon arc lights over each of the ring's corners provided more than ample illumination. Carbon arc lighting was the first practical electric lighting system, invented by Humphrey Davy in the early 1800s. Although commonly used for street lights and lighthouses, it produced a high intensity beam that was perfect for illuminating the ring. Of course, in a city known for excess, having one world-class arena would not do. Not 300 feet away the Metropolitan Club completed construction of their own arena, equal in size and amenities to the Olympic Club.

Even with all the excitement and activity surrounding the construction of two new clubhouses being built by the Metropolitan and Olympic Clubs, everyone, including the Olympic Club and the Metropolitan Club, was focused on trying to arrange a revival of the Fitzsimmons–Hall fight cancelled in Minnesota back in July of the previous year. The Olympic Club also made an offer to match Fitzsimmons with Charlie Mitchell for $12,000 in February. So when the Olympic Club announced their proposal to match Bob Fitzsimmons and Irish champion Peter Maher for a $10,000 purse, the Metropolitan Club jumped in with an unheard of $25,000 bid and there was speculation that the bidding war would reach $50,000 or higher.[9] Fight promoters and athletic clubs across the country shook their heads in disbelief at what was going on in New Orleans. A $25,000 purse to see the great John L. Sullivan defend his World Heavyweight title was one thing, but the Fitzsimmons–Maher match was to be a middleweight bout, and more than double any purse Fitzsimmons had been offered in the past.

Frank Williams was still in New York working diligently to arrange bouts for the Olympic Club to coincide with their pending Sullivan–Slavin fight, which at this point was still very much in the works.[10] Over a period of several days he was able to convince both the Fitzsimmons and Maher camps to accept the Olympic Club's smaller $10,000 purse by casting serious doubt on the Metropolitan Club's financial capacity given their brief and uninspiring history thus far, and citing their ambitious capital outlays, dismissing any thought of a bidding war. Articles were signed and the fight was scheduled for March.[11] Williams was also successful in signing Jack McAuliffe and Billy Myer to meet in conjunction with the Fitzsimmons–Maher event,[12] but this match would later be postponed by mutual consent until a future date that year.

Bob Fitzsimmons versus Peter Maher

Following the success of the Dempsey–Fitzsimmons fight on January 14, 1891, the Olympic Club was eager to arrange another match featuring Fitzsimmons. The brief dust-up following the botched exhibition that caused the club to ban Fitzsimmons and Carroll was because of previous commitments to Fitzsimmons' touring theatrical schedule, and as a result the first open date was in early 1892. There were some who were quick to dismiss Fitzsimmons' theatrical pursuits. After all, he was in no danger of eclipsing Edwin Booth on stage. In general, his performances almost always included him working on a punching bag as well as providing an exhibition of blacksmithing, with Ruby Robert banging away bare-chested on an anvil. He often credited his apprenticeship in his brother's blacksmith shop as the source of his tremendous upper-body strength. For this trifle Fitzsimmons could earn as much as $1,000 per week for a few hours work without having to dish out or take a physical beating.[13] Considering that an annual income of $4,000 in 1892 would make one rich, Fitzsimmons was smart to honor his theatrical tour commitments.

As was popular during the time, successful boxers toured the country and often held exhibition matches of four rounds or less, followed by an open challenge to the audience for $50 to anyone who might last four rounds against the celebrated pugilist. There always seemed to be some ploughboy who fancied he could take a punch and deliver better than he got. Fitzsimmons had arranged two such exhibition matches following the Dempsey fight, the first on April 27, 1891, against Abe Coughle at the Battery in Chicago which he won by a knockout in the second round, and the second match on May 1, 1891, against Harris "The Black Pearl" Martin at the Washington Rink in Minneapolis. Martin lasted the requisite four rounds, but no decision was given.[14] In the meantime, discussions had been concluded which called for Fitzsimmons to meet Peter Maher, the Irish Heavyweight Champion, at the Olympic Club in New Orleans for a $10,000 purse to be split 90 percent to the winner, 10 percent to the loser.

Born in Gunnode, Tuam, Galway, Ireland, on March 16, 1869, Peter Maher made his professional debut two days after celebrating his 18th birthday, knocking out his opponent in the first round. He captured the Irish Middleweight Championship several months later in only his seventh fight with a 5th-round knockout of John Seenan at the Rotunda Concert Hall in Dublin. Two years later he would defeat Harvey deCross on points to become the Irish Heavyweight Champion. With a record of 44 wins against only 2 losses and 2 no decisions, this would be Maher's 49th professional fight, but only his 10th fight in the United States. His American fights were split primarily between Philadelphia and New York, so the Irish champion was virtually unknown in New Orleans. Local fight fans learned that Maher had a reputation for delivering powerful punches, but without the refined boxing skills necessary to protect what many perceived to be a glass jaw.[15] The fight articles were signed on January 20, 1892, and the date was set for March 2, 1892, which was Ash Wednesday, the day after Mardi Gras.[16]

The Metropolitan Club tried to counter with a match between Welterweight Champion Tommy Ryan from Chicago and Danny Needham from San Francisco for a $13,000 purse, but had to postpone the bout due to the sudden illness of Tommy Ryan. Genslinger was still scrambling to salvage the event when Ryan's trainer, Jack Burke, offered to fight instead of Tommy Ryan. This match was set for March 3, the day after the Fitzsimmons–Maher contest.[17] With a bona fide fight on the card, Genslinger now tried to have Mayor Joseph Shakspeare intervene because of conflicting dates between the clubs' events, a problem caused by Genslinger himself. Genslinger requested that the mayor rescind the mandatory city permit for the Fitzsimmons–Maher fight at the Olympic Club.[18] The mayor quickly surmised that Genslinger was trying to get the bulge on the Olympic Club because of his club's scheduling problem. Not wishing to appear to be taking sides, Mayor Shakspeare listened respectfully to Genslinger's argument, then tele-

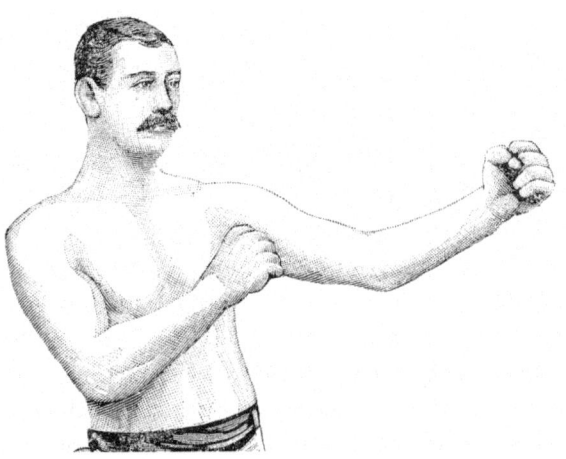

Irish Middleweight Champion Peter Maher was an experienced boxer, having engaged in 48 bouts, winning 44 of them before stepping into the ring at the Olympic Club to face World Middleweight Champion Bob Fitzsimmons (from an unknown 19th century publication).

phoned Olympic Club president Charles Noel to arrange a meeting. In the end the mayor, who was openly opposed to prizefighting, wisely decided not to step in between the two clubs, sagely recommending that they work out their differences,[19] and secretly hoping that their rivalry would destroy each other, solving his boxing problem in the process.

The city would almost certainly be overflowing with tourists during Mardi Gras and, anticipating another financial windfall, the Olympic Club once again expanded their arena to accommodate 10,000 fans[20] and heavily promoted the Fitzsimmons–Maher fight. Men throughout the city spoke of little else but the upcoming fight. Hotels, saloons, factories, workshops, and stores were all pulsating in anticipation of the event. Those who had witnessed Fitzsimmons dismantle Jack Dempsey two years earlier made him the odds on favorite locally. It is estimated that over $150,000 was bet on Fitzsimmons in New Orleans alone, with an equivalent amount being wagered in San Francisco and New York. The event was sold out well in advance, providing at least a guaranteed $45,000 gate to the Olympic Club. After deducting the $10,000 prize money and another $15,000 for construction, marketing, and other expenses, the club stood to make a $20,000 net profit.

On the evening of March 2, 1892, a sea of electric lights sizzled and the eight carbon arc lights occasionally sparked around the Olympic Club arena, threatening to ignite the flags of England and Ireland strung over the ring to honor both fighters. Flags from France, Germany, Switzerland, Italy and several other countries were also displayed in honor of the visiting dignitaries from other countries who had reigned over the city's Mardi Gras festivities earlier in the week. The night's entertainment was scheduled to open with a series of round-robin matches between Paddy Slavin, Charlie Mitchell, Felix Vacquelin, and Arthur Upham. Mitchell beat Upham on points in 4 rounds, followed by Slavin and Vacquelin fighting 3 rounds with no decision. Slavin then fought 3 rounds against Mitchell, again with no decision. The capacity crowd was done with the appetizers and was ready for the main course.

From the opening bell, Fitzsimmons appeared eager to

Champion Bob Fitzsimmons possessed a powerful upper-body atop a slender lower body that caused many of his opponents to underestimate him (Library of Congress).

take the fight to Maher, but after Maher received a left to the ear he rushed Fitzsimmons like a bull, connecting with a solid combination to the body. Fitzsimmons sported a large red welt on the right side of his body for the duration of the bout. A sharp left opened a nasty cut on Maher's lip that was to be the subject of a hail of blows throughout the fight. However, for the remainder of the first round Maher stunned the crowd by pounding Fitzsimmons steadily and only the end of the round saved this from being an unanticipated short match. Fitzsimmons' corner crew revived him in time to answer the bell for the second round, most of which he spent dancing and avoiding any close quarter battle with Maher. Fitzsimmons did manage to use his reach to continually jab at Maher's cut lip. Both fighters spent the 3rd round sparring and trying to regain their strength, cautiously circling and exchanging a series of light blows.

During the 4th round Maher continued to expend energy without inflicting serious injury on Fitzsimmons. Maher would lead, but Fitzsimmons would duck or dance out of reach, landing a punch or two to Maher's mid-section as he moved away. Fitzsimmons diligently worked Maher's seeping saucebox with his jab, further infuriating Maher, whose wild roundhouse swings resembled saloon salvos more than the attack of a trained prizefighter. Maher would try to corner Fitzsimmons, but the New Zealander was too quick for him.

Both fighters began the 5th round looking weary. They exchanged blows to the head, and Fitzsimmons jabbed Maher's lip even harder, so much so that Maher's face looked like a "beefsteak." Maher continued his bull rushes, but Fitzsimmons avoided him, landing counter-punches to Maher's head and neck in the process. The sixth round began with Maher landing a strong left to Fitzsimmons' jaw and both fighters engaged

After a first round scare, Fitzsimmons had the upper hand for much of the remainder of the fight, winning in 12 rounds (*New Orleans Times-Democrat*).

in heavy in-fighting during their frequent clinches, but without inflicting any serious damage except to their stamina. It was during the 7th round that Fitzsimmons delivered a pivot blow and dealt Maher a particularly brutal right to the neck. A pivot blow is a back-handed punch delivered as the boxer turns completely around on his heel, the acceleration of the pivot adding to the power of the punch.[21] As there had been no agreement against using the pivot blow, referee John Duffy paid no heed to cries of foul, but did warn each corner that the move was not to be tried by either side from that point forward. The 8th round saw more cautious sparring between the two embattled warriors. They exchanged blows to the head and neck with Fitzsimmons gaining the upper hand as he punished Maher's bleeding lip. A pale and woozy Maher continued to lose momentum due to the continuous loss of blood.

Neither fighter landed a punch of any significance in the 9th round, but Maher continued to fade. Both fighters began the 10th round on the defensive, with Maher decidedly more so than Fitzsimmons. They traded glancing blows to the upper body, but their attempts at heavier, more effective punches were lackluster, most missing wildly. As the bell sounded to begin the 11th round, both men began cautiously, and it appeared that Fitzsimmons was content to work Maher's bloody mouth with his jab, a strategy which Maher seemed determined not to defend, as if he hoped Fitzsimmons would somehow eventually tire from battering him. His constant ineffective sparring, combined with the loss of blood from his cut lip, was taking the steam from Maher's stride. Fitzsimmons could sense the advantage was his and became more aggressive in the 12th round while Maher became even wilder and weaker. As the round was nearly at its end, Fitzsimmons landed a bunch of fives to Maher's already bleeding mouth and it was reported that Maher told Fitzsimmons in the ensuing clinch that he was finished. Fitzsimmons then let up on Maher for the remainder of the 12th round. As the bell signaled the end of the round, Maher's side received their battered fighter and, upon examination, signaled their defeat by throwing in the sponge and Fitzsimmons was declared the winner. Fitzsimmons walked across the ring to shake Maher's hand and offered him a flask which both men drained in short order.[22] Fight patrons were treated to a roaring title defense and their faith in Fitzsimmons had been rewarded, although Maher was by no means a walkover.

As Genslinger had feared, with the lack of a title fight to offer, the following night fewer than 700 paid spectators went to the Metropolitan Club to see the Needham–Burke fight, resulting in a loss in excess of $5,000 for the club.[23] The proximity of the two events favored the Olympic Club, just as Genslinger feared, but his ego would not allow him to postpone the Needham–Burke fight. For their part, the Olympic Club not only covered the purse and expenses, but was able to recoup the cost of expanding their arena as well.

With this challenge behind him, Fitzsimmons next set his sights on a rematch with his old nemesis Jim Hall, who had beaten Fitzsimmons under rather questionable circumstances in Australia before either man sailed for the United States. Fortunately for him, Fitzsimmons arrived in America first and, with the financial backing of Major Frank McLaughlin of San Francisco, his career began in earnest. Hall was always a bit resentful of this and he often dogged Fitzsimmons across the country, acting as both official and unofficial second to Fitzsimmons' opponents, giving belligerent and provocative interviews in the press, and generally calling out Fitzsimmons on every possible occasion, especially following Fitzsimmons' surprise defeat of Jack Dempsey. Their match in Minneapolis had been summarily cancelled at the 11th hour by the Minnesota governor in 1891 and the roles were now reversed—it was Fitzsimmons who was now pushing to arrange a match with Hall to settle the contentious argument once and for all. And every boxing promoter across the country wanted a shot at putting the two rivals together in the ring.

As a back-drop to the Fitzsimmons–Hall feud, discussions between the Sullivan and Slavin camps had once again broken down, and now James J. Corbett had come out and publicly challenged Sullivan. When informed by the Olympic Club that Charlie Mitchell had the right of first refusal to meet Sullivan, Corbett publicly dismissed Mitchell's ability to attract backers. According to those involved with the negotiations, Sullivan had agreed to meet either Slavin, Mitchell, or Corbett, in that order, for $25,000 and it was now up to the Olympic Club to arrange things with a suitable opponent.[24] With Slavin out of the picture and with Mitchell's apparent lack of financial support, Corbett repeatedly declared in the press that he was the most logical choice to face the champion. Corbett's disparaging assessment of Mitchell's lack of financial backers proved to be correct and within a matter of weeks an agreement was reached to pit John L. Sullivan against James J. Corbett in New Orleans at the Olympic Club in September of 1892. The purse varied between $20,000 and $25,000 depending on the club's ability to set the date of the match. Sullivan wanted to fight in August ($20,000) while the club wanted the event to take place in September ($25,000).[25] An agreement was eventually reached in mid–March and the fight articles were sent to each man for signature the following day.[26] The fight would take place in early September.

Having nearly defeated John L. Sullivan in 1888, Mitchell felt he was first in line for a rematch against the champion. His title shot would not materialize as the Olympic Club believed that the up and coming James Corbett made a better match (from an unknown 19th century publication).

Charlie Mitchell was now the man left out. Englishman Mitchell was well known in boxing circles. He had been the instructor at the International Athletic Club in London since 1880 and had fought extensively across Europe. Mitchell had developed a penchant for using the London Prize Ring Rules to his advantage against opponents who outweighed him by 30 or more pounds. He toured North America with Paddy Slavin and Jake Kilrain and was in Kilrain's corner in July of 1889 for his fight against Sullivan. Mitchell had previously faced Sullivan twice, losing in 1883 in New York and battling for over two hours to a draw in the driving rain in 1888 in Chantilly, France at Baron Rothschild's chateau. As the leading heavyweight contender, he now lobbied in the press for his right to meet Sullivan again, accusing Corbett of meddling in the negotiations. An obviously frustrated and irate Mitchell even confronted Corbett at Miner's Bowery Theatre in New York where Corbett was giving a vaudeville boxing exhibition, cursing and goading him, insulting him, and offering to fight him on the spot, but Gentleman Jim simply ignored Mitchell and walked away from the frustrated fighter.[27] Mitchell would eventually get his chance against Corbett in 1894, losing by a knockout in the 3rd round.

The whirlwind of activity only intensified as the Olympic Club began proposing matches at an unprecedented rate, even for them. Over the next several months the club spent considerable time and resources arranging yet another title bout. To date the club had successfully put on 12 regulation fights between July 11, 1890, and March 2, 1892, leading up to what would become the crowning moment in New Orleans boxing history. What the Olympic Club had planned next would change the boxing world— three world championship fights to be held during a single week—a Fistic Carnival.[28] From early March when the reigning World Heavyweight Champion John L. Sullivan agreed to meet a young upstart banker from San Francisco named James Corbett, the next six months were filled with tumultuous goings-on as Olympic Club officials scrambled to put together the remaining match. Frank Williams had signed Billy Myer and Jack McAuliffe to fight in March as the undercard to the Fitzsimmons–Maher fight, but they agreed to move the fight to September. With two of the three title bouts in hand the Olympic Club now needed the third title fight to complete the Fistic Carnival.

As the Olympic Club was riding this most recent wave of good news, the Metropolitan Club offered their next match between featherweights George Siddons from Hartford, Connecticut and Johnny Van Heest, from Cincinnati, Ohio. It was a very lonely crowd of less than 800 patrons that roamed the club's brand-new arena, and Genslinger had yet another disappointing turnout on his hands. The city's favorite referee, Professor John Duffy, brought the two bantams to the scratch line for their instructions and just after 9:30 the bell sounded to start the match. Siddons and Van Heest traded punches for the better part of 7 rounds with the advantage tilted to Siddons' side of the ledger when the underdog Van Heest overcame his opponent's advantage in height and reach with a surprise combination left to the nose and right to the point of the chin that crumpled Siddons, who hit the floor as limp as a cloth bag.[29] Siddons struggled to his feet by climbing up the ropes, knowing that Van Heest would soon to step in for the finish. He tried to avoid Van Heest and, when he could no longer count on his weak legs, sought to clinch, only to be greeted with the final blow. Siddons was on his knees, propped up on one unsteady hand when Duffy finished his ten count.

Gate receipts were insufficient to cover the purse and expenses and it seemed a foregone conclusion that the Metropolitan Club was not only out of the fight game, but would probably have no alternative other than to merge with the Olympic Club. It was an oft-repeated joke that "the Olympic and Metropolitan Clubs of New Orleans are going to consolidate. If they do it will most likely be in the way a live man consolidates with a raw oyster. The Olympic Club would not be the oyster."[30]

For the most part, the relationship between the members of both clubs was cordial enough, to the extent that each club fielded a baseball team for a road trip to play at St. Stanislaus College in Bay St. Louis, Mississippi, on Thursday, May 12, 1892. It was an exciting game marked by "several extra-base hits, excellent fielding, costly errors, and multiple lead changes." Ultimately the game was called after nine innings at a 15–15 deadlock. The two teams returned to Bay St. Louis the following weekend with the Olympics losing to the Metropolitans 15–6.[31] Genslinger, as an officer and shareholder with the New Orleans Pelicans and the Southern League, was a baseball man at heart, but could take little comfort from this victory.

Even as New Orleans was basking in the national limelight of the sporting world, rumors coming from Baton Rouge hinted at yet another attempt to craft legislation aimed at doing away with both public and private boxing events, whether it be called a prizefight or a glove contest. Olympic Club president Charles Noel did not appear overly concerned, at least publicly. He was also aware of the organized public opposition to the Louisiana State Lottery Company that had been steadily gaining traction in their efforts to block the renewal of the lottery's franchise slated for 1893. There were several reform movements that were part of a national trend to reverse the *laissez-faire* policies of a series of weak presidential administrations beginning with Chester Allen Arthur (1881–1885), followed by Grover Cleveland (1885–1889), and now Benjamin Harrison (1889–1893). On the local level, reform groups were faced with a surfeit of corrupt state and local politicians and their political machines spawned during Reconstruction and the years that followed. The national economy was still recovering from back-to-back recessions, and as a result the cumulative frustration of a large segment of the populace threw their energies behind one or more of the social and political reform movements such as the temperance movement, the women's suffrage movement, and a host of other populist movements designed to change the status quo and overcome the rampant vice and crime which many of boxing's most out-spoken detractors believed went fist in glove.[32]

Noel, however, insisted that the Olympic Club move ahead with the Fistic Carnival in addition to their other usual activities. To that end, the Olympic Rifle Club engaged in a series of competitions throughout the summer[33] and the club held its annual meeting to elect officers and directors, but there was still an awful lot of work left to do. The Olympic Club's Fistic Carnival had its main attraction in the Sullivan–Corbett match. The McAuliffe–Myer bout, originally scheduled to occur on the undercard during the Fitzsimmons–Maher event in March, was postponed by mutual agreement until September. That gave the club two title matches, but they still lacked the third and final piece of the puzzle. Like a sideshow juggler trying to keep a dozen colored balls moving without collapse, the Olympic Club had their hands full with multiple possible combinations of fighters that had been proposed and with whom negotiations continued at a frenetic pace until late July. Among the matches that Olympic Club officials were trying to finalize were Jimmy Carroll and Joe Choynski, Bob Fitzsimmons and Jim Hall, Jim Hall and Joe Choynski, and Bob Fitzsimmons and Ted Pritchard.

Fitzsimmons was the obvious first choice. He was very well known in New Orleans, an extremely popular fighter and, as the current Middleweight Champion of the World, considered an extremely bankable draw. Along with every other fight promoter in the country, the Olympic Club tried repeatedly to have Fitzsimmons agree to fight his Australian nemesis Jim Hall, but to no avail. They then tried to match him with English Middleweight Champion Ted Pritchard, but that fell through as well. No sooner had a suitable opponent been found than Fitzsimmons held out for more money, a tactic that was his signature strategy, supported by Jimmy Carroll, Fitzsimmons' friend and manager/trainer. By continually squabbling over money Fitzsimmons would ultimately miss out on being part of the greatest prizefighting event the world had ever seen.

As negotiations continued apace, renovations and improvements continued frenetically at the Olympic Club. In addition to expanding the seating capacity in their arena to 10,000 and replacing the original sawdust and packed river sand ring with a raised wooden platform with a thick, felt-padded canvas covered floor, the club added other amenities such as new, thicker waxed canvas tarpaulin panels for the retractable roof, additional electric lights and additional telegraph connections for the press.[34]

On the main floor of the arena, in the area closest to the ring were the 300 reserved box seats. Olympic Club members and their guests could enter through the club's main entrance on Royal Street, going through the clubhouse and the gymnasium and finally into the arena. General admission ticket holders entered around the corner through one of the two entrances on the Chartres Street side of the arena. Once inside, one could walk along a wide aisle which separated the general admission seats from the reserved box seats, and could select their preferred vantage point in one of the 13 sections of amphitheater-style, terraced wooden bench-style seating. This section on the main floor of the arena could accommodate 6,000 people. Above the main floor was a second-floor gallery surrounding the perimeter of the arena that could accommodate 4,000 people, bringing the total seating capacity to 10,000 people. The arena's plenums could accommodate an additional 500 to 600 standing room only customers.

The press area downstairs was the most interior seating in the building, surrounding the central boxing ring in trenches along two sides of the ring, with seating behind smooth board planks joined to form a narrow tabletop they could use for taking notes during the event. The press area was slightly lower than the ring to allow patrons in the reserved box seats directly behind the media to have an unobstructed view of the action in the ring.

Spaced evenly above the four corners of the ring at the center of the arena were four electric arc lights with four additional electric arc lights placed higher around the second tier of seats, all supplemented with numerous incandescent fixtures throughout the arena. There was a reserve of oil lamps for emergency use should the arena suffer an electric outage during an event. During the most recent renovations in early 1892 the arena was wired for additional telegraphic service so that members of the press could communicate the details and results of the fight to their readers almost instantaneously. That service was expanded to accommodate the anticipated influx of national and international newspapermen.

The space directly above the ring was an opening approximately 15 feet to 20 feet wide, covered by a series of overlapping retractable waxed canvas tarpaulin panels as their roof, similar in many respects to the system used in the Roman Coliseum. The prize ring itself was a regulation 24-foot square with three padded wooden posts on each side through which padded ropes were strung to define the ring. There was an exterior extension to the ring approximately seven feet wide which would allow the fighters' seconds access to their corner between rounds and provide the referee, who was not usually in the ring with the fighters during the bout, the ability to circumnavigate the ring to supervise the action. In the event of a knockdown, a foul, or a clinch that seemed to linger, the referee would enter the ring to take the appropriate action. Furthermore, the referee's walk was cordoned off with barbed wire to prevent rowdy spectators from entering the ring either during or after the bout. In its time and place, the Olympic Club arena was a modern marvel.

Back on the other side of Royal Street, the Metropolitan Club inexplicably decided to stage another fight despite lackluster crowds for almost half their previous fights. To the surprise of many, it was to be a rematch between George Siddons and Johnny Van Heest who had battled just four weeks earlier. That fight failed to draw more than 800 spectators, and unfortunately for Genslinger and the Metropolitan, non-title featherweight matches were not much of a fan favorite, as opposed to the heavier weight classes. The event on the evening of Saturday, May 28, 1892, would fare even worse than their first meeting. Following a disappointing undercard of amateur fighters engaged in unenthusiastic sparring, a sparse crowd of 400 watched the two featherweights go at one another for 46 rounds before referee John Duffy was forced to stop the fight a few minutes before the clock struck midnight to prevent the club from being in violation of Sunday laws.[35] Once again the Metropolitan Club failed to see gate receipts exceed the purse and expenses. Those who previously believed that the Metropolitan Club was finished were now certain that Genslinger's folly would finally go toes-up before the end of the summer.

Throughout June and July, the Olympic Club continued to attend to the myriad details of the upcoming triple event, including putting together the third title fight in the Fistic Carnival. The public was so wrapped up in the preparations for the event and its ever-changing participants that no one paid much attention to the arrest of Homer Adolph Plessy for refusing to ride in the Negro car of the East Louisiana Railroad in violation of the Separate Car Act of 1890. Plessy was a native New Orleanian generally described as being a French-speaking Creole and a free man of color. He was often disparagingly termed an "octoroon," meaning he was classified as being one-eighth black. In an action designed to test the existing law, on June 7, 1892, with the knowledge and backing of the Citizens' Committee of New Orleans, Plessy purchased a first-class ticket from New Orleans to Covington and deliberately sat in the whites-only car. He was arrested not long after the train left the station. The Committee then arranged for Plessy's legal representation, hoping to strike a well-timed blow against Louisiana's segregation laws.

Losing the case first in Orleans Parish Criminal Court and again on appeal in the Louisiana State Supreme Court, the case was appealed to the United States Supreme Court in 1896. Plessy's case would be argued by former Solicitor General Phillips and the prominent legal scholar and author Judge Albion W. Tourgee. The case, inscribed as *Plessy v. Ferguson*, made history by actually affirming the "separate but equal" Jim Crow doctrine outlined in Act 111 of 1890 of the statutes of Louisiana which would only be abolished 68 years later by the Civil Rights Act of 1964, making it one of the most cited cases currently studied in law schools across the country. The *Ferguson*

The streets around the Olympic Club were packed with thousands of boxing fans eager to witness the Fistic Carnival. The club's massive wooden arena can barely be seen at the right-center of this image (private collection).

named in the case was J.H. Ferguson, the presiding judge in Orleans Parish Criminal District Court who ruled against Plessy in June 1892. Homer Plessy was a resident of the Third District and purchased his ticket for his brief but historic train ride at the train station located on the corner of Press Street and Royal Street, often referred to as the northwest depot, just three blocks upriver from the Olympic Club complex.

As part of their preparations for the Fistic Carnival, Olympic Club member Reuben M. Frank, who had been central in the negotiations that brought the Fitzsimmons–Maher fight to New Orleans, successfully struck agreements with every railroad operating in the New Orleans market to offer attractive package deals for the Fistic Carnival. These packages included reserved seating for all three fights with reduced round trip train fares for those traveling to the event.[36] Finally, in early August, the club reached an agreement between "Handsome" Jack Skelly from Brooklyn and George "Little Chocolate" Dixon, a Canadian now based in Boston.[37] What raised more than a few eyebrows was the club's decision to include Dixon, a black man, on the card. Although Dixon was the reigning World Bantamweight and World Featherweight Champion, and was widely acknowledged to be a formidable fighter, he was still a black man. Heretofore no black man had ever fought at the Olympic Club. In the end, Frank Williams successfully persuaded Noel and the rest of the Olympic Club board to sign Dixon.

Yielding to pressure from a variety of sources, the club agreed to consolidate the Fistic Carnival into three successive days rather than spreading them out over a week.[38] In the first days following the announced completion of the three matches in early August ticket sales were brisk, but not overwhelming. However, a week before the event was to take place, the Olympic Club announced that ticket sales had reached $160,000 for all three events[39] and just a few days later informed the public that there were no reserved seats remaining.[40] Fight fans across the country combed through every edition of their local newspaper daily for information about the event and newspapers everywhere were glad to provide even the most innocuous information to their readers. Every nuance of the fighters' training routine and support personnel, their daily diet, their sparring partners, their living quarters, and even their personal hygiene was grist for the mill. For weeks before the fight, newspapers nationwide reported on the odds for each fight and described the betting activity in great detail.[41] Nationally, the odds on the Sullivan–Dixon–McAuliffe trifecta was three to one, while Corbett–Dixon–McAuliffe was six to one. Local betting shared the country's sentimental bias in favor of Sullivan, but could not bring themselves to bet against Dixon once they learned of his record and the lack of any significant fight record for his opponent.

Jack McAuliffe versus Billy Myer

Irish-American Jack McAuliffe was born in County Cork, Ireland in 1866 and emigrated to America with his parents in 1871. He had his first amateur fight in 1883 and turned professional soon thereafter, his first bout taking place in Jersey City on July 25, 1885, against Joe Milletechia. McAuliffe won by technical knockout in the 2nd round. He won the American Lightweight title, at the time set at under 135 pounds, from Harry

Gilmore on January 14, 1887, in a fight that lasted nearly two hours and which was held off the beaten path in a barn in Lawrence, Massachusetts.

A strong fighter with cat-like reflexes and surprising power from either hand, McAuliffe knew the Olympic Club well, having accompanied his friend Jack Dempsey there in 1891 to face Bob Fitzsimmons. McAuliffe claimed the vacated World Lightweight title in 1884 when Jack Dempsey moved up to middleweight, and he jumped at the chance to face Billy Myer, who he had fought previously in 1889 at Burche's Opera House in North Judson, Indiana. During that match Myer had drawn first blood and twice floored McAuliffe, who was fighting with his right arm broken for 56 rounds, during a 64-round draw that lasted nearly four and a half hours. The undefeated champion wanted vindication and readily accepted the Olympic Club's offer.

Thirty-three-year-old Billy Myer was a native of Streator, Illinois, just southwest of Chicago, who had his first professional fight in 1883 and who now had ten professional fights under his belt, including the previous match against McAuliffe. He too was well known in New Orleans, having fought Andy Bowen at the West End Athletic Club in 1890 and again at the Olympic Club in 1891. He also fought Jimmy Carroll at the Olympic Club in December of 1891. Former Wild West lawman and noted boxing aficionado Bat Masterson described Myer as "the quickest man on his feet and the hardest man to get at" that he ever saw.[42] He too was eager to meet McAuliffe for another title shot and the "Streator Cyclone" was considered a very bankable attraction for the Olympic Club.

Another prominent boxer in the Irish-American aggregation, Jack McAuliffe was the defending World Lightweight Champion when he met Billy Myer at the Olympic Club on September 5, 1892 (collection of the author).

On Monday, September 5, 1892, New Orleans had a carnival-like atmosphere. It began raining around four o'clock in the afternoon just as the early birds were beginning to make their way to the Olympic Club. The inclement weather continued throughout the night, keeping the club's roof closed, but the waxed canvas sections could not stop the rain from seeping in and eventually soaking the crowd. It was estimated that the fight drew as many as 5,000 visitors to the city, and despite the inclement weather it seemed that all of them were determined to attend the fight. Police were stationed several blocks away from the Olympic Club to direct the considerable carriage and tally ho traffic coming down Royal Street. Members with valid tickets were allowed to proceed down Royal Street where they could enter the arena through the main clubhouse entrance. Non-members with valid tickets were directed along a different route to the Chartres Street entrance. Pedestrian traffic coming from the two street rail lines that served the area clogged the neighborhood, attracting the usual pickpockets and ruffians. By nine o'clock that night there were 6,500 patrons primed and ready to watch Jack McAuliffe and Billy Myer battle for the Lightweight Championship of the World.

Just before nine o'clock, former Mayor J.V. Guillotte entered the ring as Master of Ceremonies and gave the usual admonishments to the audience, reminding them that police Captain William Barrett and his team of over a hundred uniformed officers would not tolerate behavior unbecoming gentlemen. Professor John Duffy then entered the ring and was introduced as the referee for the event. He was followed by the two pugilists for the official weigh-in at the edge of the ring, with Myer coming in at 137 and a half pounds, McAuliffe at 137 and a quarter pounds. Captain Barrett then inspected and weighed the gloves to be used and declared them to be within specifications at five ounces. As the boxers entered the ring itself, a loud cheer arose as they met in the center of the ring to hear Duffy's instructions regarding the proper application of Queensbury rules and warning against the use of either a pivot blow or sternum punch. After a cursory handshake, they returned to their respective corners to await the signal for the fight to commence.

At the bell both men anxiously raced to the center of the ring. A somewhat pale McAuliffe slipped on a lead to Myer's mid-section, but quickly rebounded, only to receive a left from Myer. From that point forward, McAuliffe became the more aggressive of the two, stalking Myer around the ring, but with little impact.

The 2nd round had both men trading heavy blows and engaging in frequent clinches. Upon breaking one such clinch Myer landed a solid left to McAuliffe's nose, to which McAuliffe responded with a right to the head that felled Myer. McAuliffe continued to strike Myer at a furious pace for the remainder of the 2nd round and relentlessly throughout the 3rd round. The 4th round saw both men drop the other with strong right hooks to the head. The crowd cheered wildly with each staggering shot delivered. McAuliffe and Myer continued to trade punches to the head and body, but neither could put the other away. Rounds 5 and 6 were a flurry of body blows and clinches, as both men were beginning to tire, but gaining strength from the exhortations of the crowd. The middle rounds continued to be a grind, with each man occasionally landing an upper-cut that would momentarily stun his opponent, only to be countered when they tried to follow through. Fatigue began to take its toll during the 9th round, allowing McAuliffe to floor Myer once again with a right cross at the conclusion of the round.

Courtesy of a sweeping right from McAuliffe, Myer came to grief for good, hitting the canvas for the last time in the 15th round. Referee Duffy completed the standard ten-count as Myer lay helplessly tangled on the ropes. A great many locals in the crowd were disappointed, having seen Myer fight previously in New Orleans, but a resounding cheer greeted McAuliffe as his seconds hoisted him on their shoulders and carried him around the ring. The intermittent lightning flashes and thunder that had occurred all night were nearly drowned out by the roar of the crowd's adulation. A bottle of champagne was opened in McAuliffe's corner and a glass offered to Myer as the two exhausted warriors toasted McAuliffe's victory that allowed him to retain his World Lightweight title, and take home the $9,000 purse.[43] If this is what New Orleans had to look forward to in the next two fights, then the success of the Olympic Club's Fistic Carnival was assured.

George Dixon versus Jack Skelly

Twenty-two-year-old George Dixon was born in Halifax, Nova Scotia, and, at five feet, three inches, the slender young man at a strapping 87 pounds looked like he might be more comfortable in jockey silks than as a prizefighter. Nonetheless, the diminutive Dixon made his professional debut as a boxer in 1886, winning his first six fights, three of those by knockout. Fighting mainly in the Boston area, he defeated Cal McCarthy in 22 rounds on March 31, 1891, to take the World Featherweight title (below 126 pounds), becoming the first black boxer to claim a world title in any weight class. He followed that up by taking the World Bantamweight title (below 118 pounds), beating Abe Willis on July 28, 1891, at the California Athletic Club in San Francisco. Dixon is widely credited with having developed shadow boxing, a training exercise used at the beginning of a fighter's workout to prepare his muscles for actual sparring or bag work and to hone his rhythm and technique.

George Dixon was the defending World Featherweight Champion when he met the unknown Jack Skelly on September 6, 1892. Dixon was the first and only black boxer to appear at the Olympic Club (collection of the author).

Dixon had just beaten Fred Johnson at the Coney Island Athletic Club in Brooklyn on June 27, 1892, by knockout, a fight probably witnessed by Frank Williams of the Olympic Club, who then approached Dixon about defending his title in New Orleans as part of the Fistic Carnival. Dixon was understandably skeptical at first, primarily concerned about the reception a black man might receive in the Deep South. After receiving assurances from sports writers who had been to events at the Olympic Club and other boxers who had fought in New Orleans about the reputation of the Olympic Club for fair dealing, Dixon was persuaded to accept.

Jack Skelly, on the other hand, was a relatively unknown featherweight from Brooklyn who might even be better described as an amateur, having only just made his debut on December 24, 1891, in a 4-round loss to another newcomer, Johnny Gorman from Queens. With no reliable boxing history to his credit, Skelly was inexplicably given a shot at the title against Dixon. Even the loser's share of the $7,500 purse and a shot at the title before the vaunted Olympic Club in New Orleans was too good of an offer to pass up even for an afternoon farmer like Skelly. For this bout he trained in earnest and was even photographed following one of his workouts by the soon-to-be famous New Orleans photographer Ernest J. Bellocq from the New Orleans Camera Club.[44]

On Tuesday night, September 6, the featured match between champion George "Little Chocolate" Dixon and the unknown Jack Skelly became the second championship fight to take place in as many days. Even more significantly, this marked the first time a black man was allowed to fight at the Olympic Club and the first time that blacks were admitted as patrons to the Olympic Club, albeit in a segregated section upstairs in the north gallery.[45] Additional police were detailed to the gallery to oversee the "cloud of coloreds," numbering approximately 350 or more, including several prominent black politicians.[46] In retrospect this was a very respectable turn out considering that tickets for the event were $5 apiece and the average black resident of New Orleans was not generally overburdened with so much surplus cash to be able to spend 1 percent or more of their annual disposable income on a single sporting event that might only last an hour or so.

Betting was light, as most Southerners wanted to back the unknown, white Skelly, but thought better of it the more they read and learned about Dixon. The Sullivan–Dixon combination had fallen to 2-to-1, while Corbett–Dixon was also now two to one. Individually, Dixon was 10-to-3 and Skelly was 3-to-1. No one thought it would be an easy fight, but informed, albeit reluctant, sentiment favored the "dusky champion."[47]

The storm front that had intermittently soaked the city the day before had passed for the moment, allowing the Olympic Club to retract their canvas roof, providing a very welcome light breeze in the stifling heat of an Indian summer. Although the management of the Olympic Club had resigned themselves that this would be the least attractive of the three bouts, there were still approximately 4,500 spectators on hand to view the weigh-in, with Skelly tipping the scales at 116 and a half pounds to Dixon's 118 pounds. There was scant applause when Dixon entered the ring, but a rousing reception for Skelly a few moments later. Skelly was accompanied by Jack McAuliffe, Joe Choynski, and Jimmy Carroll, all of whom were training together at the facility owned and operated by Bob Fitzsimmons, Robinson's Cottage in Bay St. Louis, during preparation for the fight.

Luck of the draw, settled by a coin toss, gave Skelly what had come to be known as the "loser's corner," that being the side where Jack Dempsey, Peter Maher, and Billy Myer had when they all met their defeat. The gloves being weighed and approved, the combatants were laced up, referee John Duffy provided his usual thorough instructions to the anxious boxers and the stirring crowd, and the men returned to their respective corners to await the opening bell. No sooner had that bell sounded than Skelly charged Dixon, throwing a wild left hook for Dixon's head that Dixon easily dodged, countering with a left jab that found Skelly's forehead. Some intermittent sparring during the remainder of the first round signaled to the crowd that the seemingly outmatched Skelly might actually have a chance against Dixon. They were to be disappointed in the 2nd round as Dixon worked Skelly's body with successive lefts before landing a right to the nose that drew blood.

The 4th and 5th rounds found Dixon landing punches to Skelly's face and body almost at will. A groggy Skelly tried to clinch to save himself the beating, but Dixon would answer with his left to Skelly's already broken and bloody nose. The 6th round was a breather for both men, especially Skelly. The 7th round saw Dixon batter Skelly with a series of back-to-back combinations that made his midsection look like a boiled lobster until a left hook caught Skelly squarely on the jaw, knocking him cock-eyed and sending him to the mat. A wobbly Skelly survived the count and slumped in his corner between rounds.

The bell for the 8th round was a telltale moment. The crowd watched Dixon spring to the center of the ring while an obviously dazed Skelly, looking quite fishy about the gills, slowly approached his opponent, but it was like trying to stop a charging rhino by pelting him with balls of cotton. Many in the crowd began to leave, sensing that the fight was a foregone conclusion. Dixon pummeled Skelly and dropped him twice, the second time for the full ten-count, ending any hope Skelly had of taking the featherweight title by a knockout in the 8th round.[48]

So brutal was the beating applied by Dixon that the New Orleans *Times-Democrat* opined that it was "a mistake to match a Negro and a white man, a mistake to bring the races together on any terms of equality, even in the prize ring." Dixon, a Canadian who now lived in Boston, had faced nearly 30 white fighters prior to meeting Skelly, but all of these bouts were primarily in the Northeast, either in New York, California, Massachusetts, or Connecticut. This would be the first and last fight Dixon would participate in in the South, save for a brief four-round victory over Charles Slusher in Louisville, Kentucky, in 1896.[49] Olympic Club officials had every reason to ignore the harsh reaction to the fight being expressed primarily in Southern newspapers. The reaction outside of the South was that Skelly was courageous and plucky, but seriously over-matched against Dixon.[50] In the main, the Olympic Club was justifiably proud of having achieved two massively successful championship fights back to back, racist sentiment be damned. Gate receipts were estimated at $70,000 for the first two fights[51] and both events had come off without so much as a hitch. Everything was ready for the main event between Sullivan and Corbett.

John L. Sullivan versus James J. Corbett

John L. Sullivan was probably the wealthiest and best-known athlete of his time. Born in the Boston suburb of Roxbury in 1858, into a desperately poor Irish family, young John showed a penchant for serious scrapping early on. Soon enough he graduated from bar brawls to the underground world of bare-knuckle boxing. He had his first professional fight on April 6, 1880, in a three-round exhibition against Joe Goss. In his first 33 fights Sullivan was undefeated, with 10 of those victories coming via knockout. However, the ravages of the ring combined with a life well lived, perhaps to excess at times, was slowing the "Boston Strong Boy" down. After compiling a remarkable record of 36 consecutive wins over the previous six years, in the following 15 months between November 1886 and January 1888, Sullivan had only three fights, earning two wins and a draw during a paltry 12 rounds of work.[52]

Sullivan relished his 1889 victory over Jake Kilrain and soon afterwards he was challenged in succession by Frank "Paddy" Slavin, Peter Jackson, and Peter Maher. Instead of stepping back into the ring, he returned to the vaudeville stage and embarked on a tour of Australia, greeted by the cheers of strangers and leaving with their money jangling in his pockets. After a two-year hiatus, he was now considering a return to the ring. The Olympic Club thought they had the match between Sullivan and Slavin all tied up in late 1891,[53] and Sullivan genuinely wanted to give the Australian a shot at the heavyweight title, but, as so often happens, negotiations fell apart. Slavin was subsequently matched against Charlie Mitchell and they met five months after the Fistic Carnival at the Olympic Club[54] in March of 1892 as part of the undercard for the Fitzsimmons–Maher bout. Sullivan informed his backers that he still wanted to fight in New Orleans and eventually the fight with Corbett was arranged. The cornerstone for the Fistic Carnival was in place.

One of the thousands of Irish immigrants that landed in New Orleans in 1854 was Patrick J. Corbett, late of Ballycusheen, Balinrobe in County Mayo, Ireland. Experiencing the typical difficulties of an Irishman trying to gain a secure financial foothold in New Orleans, he was finally seduced by the stories of the unlimited opportunities still coming from post–1849 Gold Rush California, and Corbett set off for San Francisco to make his fortune. There he married and started a family, with James J. Corbett being the third of nine children.

Born in 1866, and pugnacious even as a schoolboy at Sacred Heart College and St. Ignatius College, young James Corbett had eight exhibition bouts before his first two professional fights in 1886 against Billy Welch, los-

This 1887 print depicts John L. Sullivan at the height of his career. The pastoral background is not that unusual as many early fights took place in rural settings (Library of Congress).

ing the first, but winning the second by a knockout. While working as a bank clerk during the day, he scuffled with fellow Bay Area fighter Joe Choynski three times during 1889, the first being stopped by the police, but with Corbett winning the next two.[55] While this gave him something of a local reputation, Corbett had yet to travel further than Portland, Oregon to fight. The match in New Orleans with Jake Kilrain at the Southern Athletic Club in 1890 gave Corbett the national reputation he needed, resulting in more visible fights against Mike Donovan and Peter Jackson that placed him among the top contenders for the heavyweight title. Seasoned observers of the sport drew comparisons with the boxing style of the great British champion Jem Mace. With this momentum, Corbett challenged Sullivan in February of 1892 and it was left to the Olympic Club, who offered a staggering $25,000 purse, to settle the details. Corbett was confident that his 13th professional fight would be his lucky charm.

There was not a single professional fight of any significance scheduled anywhere in America on the night of September 7, 1892. The sporting world was completely focused on New Orleans and the showcase match between champion John L. Sullivan and challenger James J. Corbett for the Heavyweight Championship of the World. This attention would place both the Olympic Club and the city of New Orleans center stage in the national and international spotlight. Press coverage of the fight even overshadowed coverage of the lackluster presidential race between Benjamin Harrison and Grover Cleveland and begrudgingly shared front-page column space with the gruesome reports of a horrific cholera outbreak that was ravaging the midwest and northeast.

Following his match with Sullivan, the dashingly handsome Corbett embarked upon a lucrative theatrical tour. This cabinet card is an advertisement for his appearance at the Haymarket Theatre in Chicago (Library of Congress).

Newspapers, theatres, and athletic clubs across the country arranged to receive fight updates via telegraph to rebroadcast in their city. Theatres announced that they would provide fight updates between acts to assuage an audience full of fidgety husbands. Newspapers in Boston, New York, and Philadelphia advertised an elaborate system of colored lights that would be projected in the night sky above their office buildings to inform citizens of what was happening in New Orleans.[56] The *Boston Post* advertised an intricate

It was standing room only at the Olympic Club arena on the night of September 7, 1892, to watch champion John L. Sullivan face off against challenger James J. Corbett. Not a single professional fight was scheduled anywhere in America as the entire sporting world looked to New Orleans for the outcome of the "Second Battle of New Orleans" (*Chicago Daily Tribune*).

series of flashing lights to inform viewers of the progress and results, the corresponding signal code requiring two full front-page columns to explain to their readers. In New York, the dome of the Pulitzer Building in Manhattan would illuminate the result of the fight, red for Sullivan, white for Corbett, and both in the event of a draw. The *Police Gazette* optimistically declared that "the whole civilized world" was anxiously waiting for news of the fight.

Betting was 4-to-1 on Sullivan, 3-to-1 against Corbett. Marsh Redon and the majority of the most popular New Orleans pool operators—a person that we would today term a bookmaker or bookie—saw a significant flow of money from out-of-town visitors. Trains from every major city in America were chartered to bring an estimated 12,000 spectators to New Orleans. The champion departed Boston on the "Sullivan Special" which made its way through the midwest, before turning south to New Orleans where the champion set up camp at the St. Charles Hotel, and training at the New Orleans Athletic Club. Corbett's route from New York, where he had been training with Mike Donovan, was down the Atlantic seaboard through North and South Carolina, Alabama, and Mississippi to New Orleans where he also settled in at the St. Charles Hotel and finished off his training at the Southern Athletic Club. Both men faced daunting challenges en route as zealous lawmen, spurred on by ambitious politicians, attempted to detain and arrest the fighters for training in their jurisdiction. Louisiana was not alone in having statutes and ordinances prohibiting training as well as fighting in their state.

During the seven long months since Sullivan had agreed to fight Corbett, it seemed that all of America had been waiting for the event that was about to take place.[57] The intermittent rain of the last two days had subsided and the sky was clear, but on the evening of Thursday, September 8, 1892, it was hot and humid nonetheless. Businesses closed early to allow people to have their dinner before heading to the Olympic Club. Near sunset, a steady stream of carriages, cabs, and tally hos began funneling down Canal Street through the French Quarter into the Third District. Customers who had not arranged for transportation in advance groused about the sudden increase in the price for hire, but their complaints fell upon deaf ears. To onlookers it seemed that every possible form of transportation had been pressed into service, from old coaches filled chock a block with all manner of mustachioed men, to beer wagons overflowing with jovial riders, to packed hacks not seen since the Civil War, all jostling down the cobble-paved streets, occasionally jolting and jerking their passengers in the process.

The New Orleans police were used to handling large crowds during Mardi Gras and for previous events at the Olympic Club, but even this was a strain for the experienced men in blue. As they had for the two previous nights, the police had checkpoints positioned at the intersections of Enghein Street (now Franklin Avenue) and Dauphine Street, Royal Street, and Chartres Street. By seven o'clock the traffic was nearly double what they had previously seen. As usual, vehicles were routed according to the passengers' ticket, with club members going down Royal Street, and non-members being funneled down Chartres Street. Pedestrians coming from the street rail were encouraged to follow the same route, but the surge of foot traffic overwhelmed street traffic and congestion and confusion took hold. Those without tickets were permitted to congregate in front of the Olympic Club on Royal Street. Each and every carriage was met upon its arrival with a hearty cheer as its passengers decamped. Upon the appearance of Sullivan's entourage, the police cleared the sidewalk in front of the club to allow the Sullivan party to enter the clubhouse without incident. Fifteen minutes later Corbett's group arrived and were quickly escorted into the clubhouse. Charles Noel presided over the coin toss to determine the combatant's corners, which Corbett won, selecting the "lucky" corner that both McAuliffe and Dixon had used. Both men looked hale and hearty and neither man exhibited any outward sign of nervousness. They repaired to separate

This card allowed a member of the Olympic Club to enter the clubhouse through the club's main Royal Street entrance, then traverse the building to the arena and ultimately access Reserved Box Number 49, ringside at the arena (The Historic New Orleans Collection).

rooms on the second floor of the clubhouse to change their clothes and to prepare for the coming clash.

At five minutes before nine o'clock, New Orleans police Captain William Barrett entered the ring and the excited murmur of the crowd began to escalate. He was followed by former Mayor J.V. Guillotte who, as Master of Ceremonies for the evening, cautioned the crowd about proper deportment during and after the event. By this time, fans who were not otherwise fortified by the libations procured from flasks hidden in their coat pockets could quench their thirst with bottles of either ginger ale or sarsaparilla being hawked by an armada of vendors working throughout the arena.

Sullivan was the first to enter the ring, dressed in green trunks with black shoes and socks. He was joined by Charley Johnson, Phil Casey, Joe Lannon, and Jack McAuliffe, as well as timekeeper Frank Morgan. When Corbett joined him in the ring a moment later, accompanied by his corner crew consisting of Bill Delaney, Jim Daly, John Donaldson and Mike Donovan, with Bat Masterson as his timekeeper, the crowd was struck by Corbett's pale appearance next to the bulky Sullivan. To many, Sullivan was larger than life, but in the ring he was only feet, ten and a half inches and better than 215 pounds. At six feet, one inch, Corbett was taller than Sullivan, but at least 25 pounds lighter. At the same time, the spectators also noticed an undeniable air of confidence in Corbett and his seconds as they prepared for the battle. Corbett had been trained by one of the most respected instructors in the country, Mike Donovan, to avoid Sullivan's trifecta of terror. First, avoid the left chop designed to beat down his opponent's guard to provide an opening for the inevitable right to follow; second, avoid his formidable right jab that could rattle your teeth if it landed; and third, avoid his right cross that typically caught his opponents on the side of the head.

In pre-fight ceremonies on behalf of the club, police Captain Barrett presented referee John Duffy with a silver ice bucket and ladle engraved to commemorate the event before turning his attention to weighing and approving the gloves to be used. Once ready, the two gladiators moved to the center of the ring to receive their gloves and Duffy's typical instructions. The champion stood, arms folded, glaring at Corbett who had his eyes fixed on Duffy, not because he was intimidated by Sullivan, but as if ignoring the champion, letting him know that he wasn't even thinking about him. If Corbett's apparent nonchalance was intended to infuriate Sullivan he was successful.

At ten minutes after nine o'clock, the assembled thousands rose to their feet as the bell sounded the beginning of the first round. Both men smiled at each other before Sullivan swiftly succumbed to his pent-up anger and moved in on Corbett, missing with a left jab. The crowd and Sullivan got their first glimpse of Corbett's boxing style as he deftly parried Sullivan lead, then moved away quickly. To the crowd this seemed more like sparring and what started with a few hisses soon began to sound like an open steam valve. Corbett would not fall prey to Sullivan's bull rushes and would not allow himself to be trapped in a corner. Not a single blow was landed by either man in the 1st round, not for lack of effort by Sullivan.

The first two minutes of the 2nd round resembled the first round until Sullivan finally pinned Corbett against the ropes, landing two strong jabs followed by a right upper-cut. Donovan yelled out instructions to Corbett who continued to prance around the ring "like a hunted deer," throwing just a single punch to Sullivan's mid-section. It was evident to all watching that Corbett's strategy was to wear down the portly Sullivan, making him expend his energy chasing Corbett around the ring. No one doubted that Sullivan could still lay Corbett down neatly with either his left or his right, but as clumsily as their man was floundering around the ring, they were beginning to think that he now lacked the legs to deliver such a blow. Just when everyone had figured out Corbett's strategy, he changed tactics. In the 3rd round, as Sullivan landed a glancing blow to Corbett's side, Corbett stopped and delivered a "rib roaster" to Sullivan's chest, followed by two strong lefts to Sullivan's jaw. Once again Sullivan's counter punches had no effect on the younger man. Another series of combinations to Sullivan's body and head drew blood, the last breaking the champion's nose. The rumors about Corbett's speed were true enough, but that the few blows Sullivan managed to land had no discernable impact on Corbett caused the champion to grow progressively angrier, even as his fans grew more and more worried about the sums they had wagered. The smoke from thousands of cigars could not be disbursed by the arena's small fans, but the haze did not seem to bother either fighter. The 4th and 5th rounds were a continuation of the waiting game, with Corbett drawing more than a few snide jeers from the gallery gods and from Donovan as well who felt that Corbett's hit-and-run strategy was allowing Sullivan to recover too quickly. He pressed Corbett between rounds to work Sullivan's body and end the bout quickly. Those who had bet on Sullivan were now resigned to the fact that their champion was not the man they thought him to be—the champion of old was, at the age of 34, old.

In the 6th round Corbett took the fight to Sullivan, but was greeted with a right to the ribs which brought about a return to the hit-and-run style that continued to infuriate Sullivan. Corbett struck Sullivan's broken nose twice in rapid succession at the bell. Casey and Lannon had a time getting Sullivan ready to answer the bell for the next round, but answer it he did, quickly striding to the scratch line. Corbett pelted the big man with a sequence of nasty left jabs to the head followed by a right cross to the jaw, much to the delight of the crowd. To appease Donovan, Corbett also went to work on the champion's fleshy mid-section, sinking multiple blows that finally doubled Sullivan up in obvious pain as the bell sounded to end the 7th round.

The 8th round saw a pale and panting Sullivan attempt to take back control of the fight, but Corbett continued his barrage of speedy left jabs followed by a terrific right hook to the body, landing this combination three times back to back to a now exhausted Sullivan. His staunchest supporters blindly believed that it was Sullivan who was waiting for Corbett to tire of dancing around the ring before their man would finish him, but sadly there was no real correlation between their eyesight and their wagers. The combination of continued blood flow from his broken nose, his frustration in not being able to hit Corbett with any real consistency or force, and the cumulative effect of Corbett's surprisingly powerful punches was taking its toll on the fading Sullivan.

The 9th and 10th rounds were more sparring than anything else, both men trading several ineffective jabs. Towards the end of the 10th round Sullivan did manage to deliver a solid left hook to Corbett's ear, then followed with a strong jab to his eye, but Corbett clinched and delivered three lefts to the champion's head as the round ended. Donovan renewed his plea to Corbett to just get it over with, not out of fear of Sullivan who Donovan now told Corbett "couldn't dent a pound of butter." Rather, it was clear to Donovan, and becoming more so to the crowd, that the once feared champion was done. It was actually out of respect for Sullivan that Donovan wanted his man to end the fight. A champion like Sullivan deserved a better end than to flail around helplessly in the ring.

By the time the bell sounded to begin the 11th round, it seemed that everyone in the Olympic Club arena was familiar with Corbett's fight plan except Sullivan: begin with some casual sparring, step in to deliver a volley to the head or body, then dance away before the big man had a chance to react. When an exhausted Sullivan dropped his guard, almost as if inviting a knockout blow, Corbett would pounce, dispensing a flurry of damaging blows to the jaw. This strategy played out through the 13th round, and Sullivan was clearly feeling the impact. The 14th round exploded with some sharp "hot work," with Sullivan smashing Corbett with a left uppercut, countered by two right hand punches from Corbett that caused the blood to reappear from Sullivan's smeller. Sullivan was losing steam with each exchange. Each man seemed content to trade a few jabs during the 15th round, but little else.

Sullivan tried one last rush at the start of the 16th round, only to be met with a left to the mouth that forced him to gasp for air. Corbett quickly repeated the combination of body and head blows, sliding off before Sullivan could return fire. Both men were content to take the 17th round off, with nothing of note occurring. Although he answered the bell for the 18th round, it was clear that Sullivan was gassed. His breathing was labored, audible 20 feet away over the non-stop "tap-tap-tap" of the ringside telegraph operators and the intermittent exhortations of the crowd. He landed the occasional jab, but received two, three, or four blows for every one delivered. Corbett's rights to the head were having more and more effect on the sluggish champion. Corbett was obtaining an appreciative audience, with the crowd admiring and acknowledging his speed and subtle power. Truly this is what everyone meant when they talked about the "science" of boxing. Corbett had the advantage of height and reach and was clearly the better conditioned of the two, but Sullivan was still an imposing physical specimen and still quite capable of delivering a savage knockout blow with either his left or right. The problem was that, try as he might, at this point Sullivan was not even a caricature of his former self and couldn't catch Corbett in order to deliver the blow.

During the 19th round Corbett struck Sullivan at least four times for every feeble attempt from Sullivan, who simply refused to go down. In the 20th round Corbett took the fight squarely to Sullivan, punishing him on the ropes, his repeated blows to the chest robbing Sullivan of his wind, causing him to once again drop his guard, resulting in a slew of jabs to the head. But Sullivan would not go down. Corbett clearly had the advantage and the majority of the crowd was now solidly in his corner. A dazed Sullivan was nearly blind as a post hole with his eyes bloated and swollen, but he would not go down.

Sullivan was still breathing heavily when he stood for the 21st round and Corbett knew he had to end the fight in this round. He landed blow after blow to the jaw of the man who was a living legend, pummeling the man whose name struck terror in the heart of any who was fool enough to challenge him. Sullivan backed away trying to save himself, but let down his guard again and provided Corbett with the opening he had waited for. As the fighters stood in the center of the ring, a solid right cross to the jaw drew more blood from the champion's nose and eyes before one final right hook felled Sullivan. He struggled to rise, taking a few steps before Corbett's inevitable combination to the jaw caused Sullivan's knees to buckle, dropping the champion like a sack of Irish potatoes, collapsing and remaining down as referee John Duffy slowly approached the fallen champion. A gradual hush fell over the crowd so that the only clear sound was Duffy's voice marking each number in the slow ten count. For the briefest of moments, the entire arena was so quiet that you might have heard the watch ticking in the pocket of the man standing next to you as everyone in the arena processed what they had just witnessed. Then the outbursts of applause and cheers from more than 10,000 throats erupted to celebrate the victory of the new champion and to honor the fallen Sullivan. Before long the bell ringing of churches throughout the Third District spread the news across the city. Telegraph lines erupted with the details of the fight, a battle so epic it would have a place among the chapters of Tolstoy or Dickens. The night skies over Philadelphia, Boston, and New York were illuminated to indicate Corbett's great victory. The news spread like wildfire.

The torch had been passed to the former bank clerk from San Francisco who won over the crowd with his agility, his speed, his footwork, and his clever fight management. He backed up his quiet air of confidence with skillful and tenacious fighting. It was a fight that would never be forgotten. Billed as "The Second Battle of New Orleans," a capacity crowd witnessed Corbett out-maneuver, out-fight, and out-last the champion from the outset.[58] The post-fight coverage was as extensive as the pre-fight hype, being chronicled in newspapers from San Francisco to New York. A London newspaper quipped that "the overbearing insolence of 'the Boston Bully' has been checked in the only way it could be checked, by his getting a sound drubbing from a fisticuffs man."[59]

This fight marked the beginning of the modern era in boxing—from London Prize Ring Rules to Marquis of Queensbury Rules, from quasi-legal bare-knuckle bouts held at all hours in barns, fields or the back room of some squalid saloon or barrelhouse, hopefully out of the sight of the local police, to matches using approved and inspected padded gloves held indoors on a cushioned ring in the electrically illuminated Olympic Club arena where scores of policemen were on hand to ensure order.

The betting had been fast and furious on the fight. Jack McAuliffe, victorious on Monday night against Billy Myer, had given his friend Dick Roche a check for the entire $18,250 balance in his account at the National Bank of Commerce in New Orleans to wager on Sullivan. Luckily for McAuliffe, Roche did not place the bet. The biggest loser that could be identified was former baseball umpire "Smiling" Jack Kelly of New York who wagered $21,000 on Sullivan. Charles Johnson, Sullivan's backer, lost $17,000 that night. The celebrated ex-lawman Bat Masterson was rumored to have won $4,000 on Corbett and to have convinced many of his friends from Denver to back Corbett as well.[60] "Yank" Sullivan of Syracuse, NY laid $650 on Sullivan at six to one and $250 on Corbett at four to one, while Emmett Driscoll of Boston wagered $4,000 on Sullivan at four to one.[61] New Orleanians bet heavily on Sullivan—among them being L.H. Klein ($7,300), Larry Killion ($5,000), James Doherty ($2,500), George Moolie ($2,300), and John Kennedy ($2,300). One local who fared well was popular lightweight boxer Andy Bowen, who won $1,150 on Corbett.[62] However, the majority of the winners and losers went unidentified, having placed their wagers through betting syndicates or pools. It was estimated that over $300,000 was bet in pool rooms in New Orleans alone.

Press coverage of the fight's aftermath was no less intense as it had been in the months leading up to the battle. There were stories of Corbett collecting his winnings at the Olympic Club the afternoon following the fight, on Sullivan's declaration that he had seen the elephant and was now done with prizefighting, and on what the future might hold for boxing. Following a benefit for Sullivan in New York, Corbett immediately embarked upon a cross-country theatrical tour that reportedly brought him as much as $150,000 in gross receipts. Contenders lost no time challenging Corbett, anxious to line up a lucrative payday for themselves and perhaps a title to boot. In New Orleans, observers of the fight game and the Olympic Club raced to tally the actual three-day take. There was little doubt that the event was both a critical and financial success for the Olympic Club. Ten days after the event, President Charles Noel and Contest Committee Chairman Joseph Sporl were honored at an impromptu celebration at the club during which they were presented with gifts and toasted with testimonials. Chief of Police Charles Drolla presented Noel with a gold watch and chain and Sporl with a diamond tie stud.[63] Refreshments were served and the testimonials continued informally amid handshakes and backslapping. There seemed to be enough glory and glad-handing to go around.

The first indication that something might be problematic came when a number of Olympic Club members learned that the 11-member board had voted eight to three to pay themselves $5,250 for "services rendered."[64] Club President Charles Noel was to receive $1,500 and the five members of the contest committee were allotted $750 apiece. An impromptu meeting of the club's shareholders was called for Monday, September 26, at the Olympic Club. There was a growing furor over the board's action, especially since the membership at-large still had no idea of the actual official financial results of the recent three-day event. Estimates of the three-day attendance and aggregate gate had been reported elsewhere,[65] and these estimates varied significantly. Thus far the club had yet to release this information to its members. After all, some of the more vocal members argued, the board had already failed to publish the club's customary annual report in June, and now they appeared to be dodging a true accounting of the Fistic Carnival. So, if they could vote themselves this extraordinary "bonus" without scrutiny, what else might they have done behind closed doors? Following an evening of sometimes spirited and frequently argumentative discussions, it was finally resolved to appoint a special 15-member ad-hoc committee to immediately investigate the club's finances.

The board cooperated fully with the ad-hoc committee, although one of the directors, William D. Ross, filed suit against one particularly outspoken member, Jules Janvry, for slander, seeking $10,000 in damages. Ross had been employed by the Olympic Club as its financial secretary for many years. Janvry was the co-owner of a successful saloon and billiard parlor, Peterson & Janvry's at 205 Canal Street. His partner in the venture, Theodore Peterson, was a former president of the Olympic Club. It had been rumored for some time that Janvry wanted Ross' position with the club, and over the past several months Janvry had repeatedly accused Ross of falsifying the club's books to anyone who would listen. The current situation emboldened Janvry to become even more vocal during the September 26 meeting and it was then assumed that other board members were contemplating similar action against the most outspoken club members.[66]

Tensions were still elevated when the ad-hoc committee convened the membership to present their report on the night of Thursday, October 6. After a thorough review of all expenditures and receipts related to the Fistic Carnival, read aloud by club secretary William D. Ross, the club's balance sheet indicated that the club was indeed in sound financial condition. The astonished club members learned that the total gate from the Fistic Carnival was $101,557 for the three nights. Less prize money of $41,000 and $5,000 in expenses, the club was left with a net profit in excess of $55,000 for the event.[67] That would equate to roughly $1.45 million today. The "bonus" payments turned out to be nothing more than reimbursement for legitimate out-of-pocket expenses related to putting together the Fistic Carnival, despite accusations to the contrary. This explanation did not sit well with the most vocal members. If it was simply a reimbursement then why was a board vote required to distribute the funds? Committee chair W.L. Hughes calmed the crowd and informed the assembled members that the club's audit committee would publish a more detailed report on the event within a month.

All of the previous grumbling and general discontent notwithstanding, there was now a motion to commend the club's officers and directors for their hard work. Surprisingly, the motion passed by nearly unanimous acclamation.[68] On the surface it appeared that harmony had been restored and the Olympic Club could now move forward, retaining its position as the premiere boxing venue in the country. But distasteful accusations had been leveled, fingers had been pointed, derogatory slurs had been shouted, the insults and invectives had been delivered and, unfortunately, the wounds inflicted went deeper than anyone could have imagined at the time. Had this occurred a generation earlier and there would have been at least a dozen duels fought as a matter of honor. Only later would the general membership realize the damage that had been done.

The Crescent City Athletic Club

In late October, three weeks after receiving the unanimous acclamation of the Olympic Club membership, Charles Noel and Joseph Sporl unexpectedly resigned from the Olympic Club and organized the Crescent City Athletic Club.

Charles Noel was personally offended by the reaction of the membership of the Olympic Club who questioned the lack of transparency in accounting for the money from the Fistic Carnival (*Louisville Courier Journal*).

Stung by their friends' accusations of impropriety, they were now determined to take their new club to the prominence of the Olympic Club.[69] The news broke while Noel was in New York, ostensibly on Olympic Club business. Even as the local newspapers were reporting on Noel's possible future matches for the Olympic Club, the major out-of-town papers were reporting that Noel had resigned.[70] By mid–November Noel's resignation and the formation of the Crescent City Athletic Club was news across the country.[71]

As upsetting as this unexpected turn of events was, this was not the first such challenge to the Olympic Club. After being defeated in 1889 for reelection as President of the Olympic Club, Charles H. Genslinger resigned and organized the Metropolitan Athletic Club. He was a prominent businessman who was also President of the New Orleans Pelicans, the city's professional baseball team, and the Southern League, as well as a member of several other prominent social,

The Mascot was an irreverent, sometimes controversial weekly New Orleans newspaper that flourished from 1882 until 1892. It was at one time the largest illustrated weekly journal in the South. This cover page deals with the departure of Charles Noel and others from the Olympic Club (Louisiana Division/City Archives, New Orleans Public Library).

fraternal, and benevolent organizations. Genslinger deliberately located the Metropolitan Club's new clubhouse at 625 Royal Street in the former residence of Cassius Meyer, which was almost directly across the street from the Olympic Club at 636 Royal Street. Try as he might, however, Genslinger could never overtake the Olympic Club, but he did avoid being absorbed by his nemesis. The Metropolitan Club would eventually be forced to merge with the Crescent City Athletic Club in March 1893.[72] Genslinger subsequently left New Orleans, continuing his involvement with a succession of successful athletic clubs in Ohio, New York, and Illinois.

The newly chartered Crescent City Athletic Club leased a clubhouse on the edge of the city's business district at 18 North Rampart Street just off Canal Street. Noel and company set about renovating the building to match the caliber of furnishings and fixtures found at the Olympic Club. At the same time, they also began clearing and preparing a site on the northeast corner of Canal Street and Carrollton Avenue, with plans for the construction on a massive, barn-like arena. Noel and Frank Williams now engaged in an aggressive bidding war for boxing matches on behalf of the new club, hoping to draw crowds large enough to justify the larger purses they offered. The Olympic Club's new president, Charles Dickson, was the first to blink, stating that his club "would not pay such extraordinary big prizes, but will give a reasonable amount."[73] Wasting no time, the new management of the Olympic Club announced the details of their next triple event to be held March 1–3, 1893. The festivities would begin with a featherweight championship bout, followed the next night by a wrestling match, and concluding the following evening with a heavyweight fight. There was no thought of trying to replicate the out-sized success of the Fistic Carnival. What may have sounded good at first blush was, to many, not of the same caliber as the Fistic Carnival. And how could it be? Having set the bar so high, they were in many respects a victim of their own success. To make matters worse, officials from the city's various carnival organizations immediately voiced their opposition to having prizefights during Mardi Gras, not wanting to taint the carnival atmosphere with a "considerable proportion of the rougher element."[74] Despite the national and international accolades garnered by the Olympic Club in the wake of their highly successful Fistic Carnival, the city's old money social organizations paid no heed. Boxing was still the domain of ruffians and rascals.

There were complex boundaries drawn between the public and private lives of the city's social elite who would condemn boxing in public, but enjoyed a certain anonymity when they attended an event at the Olympic Club with their social peers. Such a social paradox was not unusual in New Orleans where gentlemen often split their time between their storybook families at home and their quadroon mistresses in the modest one-story cottages back of town provided for them by their "protectors." Bachelors and married men alike attended one or more of the Quadroon Balls, lavish affairs held at the Orleans Theatre, just a few paces from the St. Louis Cathedral. The families of these mixed race young ladies dressed them to the nines, showcased them in ornate tableaus, and negotiated a suitable arrangement with an interested gentleman who became her protector. Such unmentionable arrangements were, in fact, quite well known and were responsible, in great part, for the city's escalating problem with dueling. "There were hundreds of duels growing from these [quadroon] balls, and many a young Creole, whose marble slab in the old St. Louis Cemetery testifies that he 'fell in a duel,' lies there because of his attentions to a quadroon girl."[75]

Representatives from several carnival organizations and social clubs repeatedly approached the mayor to insist that he refuse to issue any athletic club the required permits not only during Mardi Gras, but also the weeks immediately before and after the carnival celebration. It was their contention that "the prize fights which take place in this city are not attended by the class who come to our carnival," and they feared that respectable people would not travel to New Orleans at the same time with such disreputable scoundrels and strangers. The next few months would indeed prove challenging for everyone concerned, white shoe and hoi polloi alike.

Looking back on the events of 1892, the Olympic Club experienced its most successful year of operation in its brief history—five major fight events drawing unprecedented crowds to their arena, estimated to be between 35,000 and 38,000, garnering critical acclaim for their facilities and arrangements from both national and international observers, and in the process ensuring the financial security of their club. And as an ancillary benefit, all but crushing the potential threat posed by Charles Genslinger and the Metropolitan Club.

1892: The Olympic Club

Date	Match	Gross Receipts	Purse and Expenses	NET to Olympic Club
January 27	McCarthy–Callaghan	$8,000	$2,000 + $1,000	$5,000
March 2	Mitchell–Upham			
	Slavin–Vacquelin		$2,500 + $500	($3,000)
	Slavin–Mitchell			
	Fitzsimmons–Maher	$49,750	$10,000 + $1,500	$38,250
September 5	McAuliffe–Myer	$101,557	$9,000 + $1,000	$55,057
September 6	Dixon–Skelly		$7,500 + $1,000	
September 7	Corbett–Sullivan		$25,000 + $3,000	
		$159,307	**$64,000**	**$95,307**

All figures estimated.

Although the recent unfounded accusations of financial impropriety had resulted in the creation of yet another competitor with the formation of the Crescent City Athletic Club, the Olympic Club could comfortably boast a bank account flush with cash and ongoing international recognition as one of the world's premiere sporting clubs. In short, the Olympic Club believed they had nothing to fear from either the struggling Metropolitan Club or the upstart Crescent City Athletic Club.

1892: The Metropolitan Club

Date	Match	Gross Receipts	Purse and Expenses	NET to Olympic Club
January 22	Siddons–Warren	$4,200	$1,500 + $1,000	$1,700
March 3	Burke–Needham	$3,700	$13,000 + $1,000	($10,300)
April 27	Van Heest–Siddons	$1,700	$1,000 + $800	($100)
May 28	Van Heest–Siddons	$800	$1,200 + $500	($900)
		$10,400	**$20,000**	**($9,600)**

All figures estimated.

The overall quality of the events offered by the Metropolitan Club simply could not compare to those provided by the Olympic Club and this was manifest in the Metropolitan's poor attendance and gate receipts. Equally troubling to the membership of the Metropolitan Club was the tremendous initial capital outlay solicited by Genslinger for purchasing the real estate and constructing their new arena, designed from the outset to be even larger than the Olympic Club's arena, and for building and furnishing their new clubhouse. With only 350 members at this point there would need to be a dramatic turnaround in their boxing program in order for the club to survive. The frustration of failure lingered in Genslinger's psyche like a brooding and demanding house guest who could not be appeased. His plan was too ambitious, trying to pull together in 12 months what the Olympic Club had achieved gradually over ten years. Metropolitan Club shareholders might be willing to reach a bit further into their wallets to help tide the club over until it became profitable, but there would have to be immediate tangible evidence of a significant change in direction to attract new members and to retain existing members.

FIVE

1893

"You become a champion by fighting one more round. When things are tough, you fight one more round."
—James J. Corbett

Although only 28 years old in 1892, Charles Noel was not only President of the prestigious Olympic Club, but was a well-established partner in two highly successful businesses—the Jackson Saw Mill and the Lambou & Noel Lumberyard, both located a short distance downriver from the Olympic Club. He was one of the initial investors in the Third District Building Association and had been instrumental in organizing one of the first paid fire departments in the city. Noel was also an emerging political figure who had recently been elected to the New Orleans City Council to represent the Ninth Ward in the Third District. It was rumored that he had aspirations of running for mayor. He was a former fire commissioner who, despite being of diminutive stature, was a man who was used to having his opinions heard and, even more importantly to him, was also used to getting his way. In short, he was as fond of personal criticism as the Devil was of holy water.

Noel and his management team at the Olympic Club believed they had been blindsided by the unwarranted accusations of financial impropriety in their handling of payments to members of the Olympic Club board and Contest Committee. From his vantage point, he was a respected businessman, a valued member of the community who had just been elected to serve on the New Orleans City Council, and the chief architect of the Fistic Carnival that filled the coffers of the Olympic Club to overflowing. As the club's ad-hoc committee would discover, and which the club's financial audit later proved, these purported "payments" were merely reimbursements for the out-of-pocket expenses incurred by the accused individuals during the course of arranging the Fistic Carnival. There was nothing untoward in the actions of Noel and his fellow Olympic Club officers who had successfully pulled together the unprecedented Fistic Carnival.

Although less divisive among the membership, Noel and his supporters gave short shrift to the persistent hue and cry from those members they believed to be uninformed, but who nonetheless comprised an extremely vocal faction within the Olympic Club that wanted to avoid what they perceived as a tremendous financial risk posed by promoting boxing on the scale that Noel had just produced and had repeatedly stated that he wanted to expand upon. While it was true that none of the city's other athletic clubs had achieved the notoriety, acclaim, and reputation of the Olympic Club, neither were the other athletic clubs in the city offering the extremely generous, some might say outlandish, purses that the Olympic Club dangled in front of these fighters. Indeed, few if any of the athletic clubs in America offered such out-sized purses, at least none that could be taken seriously. The $12,000 purse paid by the Olympic Club for the 1891 Dempsey–Fitzsimmons bout was the largest purse in either Dempsey's or Fitzsimmons' careers to that point, and an unprecedented, historic prize for a middleweight championship fight anywhere for that matter. While other athletic clubs throughout the country might impetuously throw out a huge offer in the heat of the moment, such as during the ongoing bidding war that took place off and on during 1891 and 1892 for the match between Bob Fitzsimmons and Jim Hall, none of these fights were ever brought to fruition. The following year the Olympic Club then hung out a $25,000 purse for the great John L. Sullivan, which was the largest purse the great champion ever fought for. Likewise, James Corbett was never offered or fought for a larger purse during the remainder of his career. In the span of 32 years, the purse offered for a world heavyweight title fight went from $1,000 in 1860 for the Heenan–Sayers fight in England, to $2,500 for the Mace–Allen championship bout in 1870 in Kennerville, Louisiana, to the $25,000 purse for the Sullivan–Corbett fight at the Fistic Carnival. To some this was a scene straight out of a 1636 Dutch tulip auction. Surely this bubble would also burst in time.

In Noel's eyes, these other athletic clubs were all gum and no substance. Across the board, he believed they simply lacked the nerve to act. Noel, on the other hand, had backed his play to the tune of more than $41,500[1] and had come up aces. Now feeling angry, unappreciated, and that he and the others had been treated like a bunch of malicious mountebanks, Noel and his supporters broke off from the Olympic Club to set up a new venture. Enticed by the lure of even bigger profits, Noel wanted his new Crescent City Athletic Club to stage even bigger events, with even larger purses. To do so he would have to attract both new members and additional working capital needed to erect a clubhouse and arena that would compete with the Olympic Club, the Metropolitan Club, and the handful of other smaller venues scattered throughout the city. In addition, Noel would also have to contend with sporadic, but increased competition coming from other athletic clubs in New York, Illinois, California, and Florida who had witnessed firsthand what the Olympic Club had done in New Orleans and wanted to replicate that success back home.

Noel commissioned architect Dietrich Einseidel to draw up the plans for a massive new arena.[2] At the same time, the new club leased a suitable property for their clubhouse at 18 North Rampart Street and renovations were initiated. The new clubhouse was located on the edge of the city's business and residential corridor, and there simply was no room available for the new arena to be constructed contiguous to the clubhouse. After an exhaustive search, Noel decided that the new arena would be constructed on a large tract of land available on Canal Street bounded by Carrollton Avenue, Customhouse (Iberville) Street, and North Pierce Avenue. It was an unusual decision to have the clubhouse and the arena located more than a mile apart, and his decision had many observers scratching their heads. Nevertheless, the property was acquired and construction commenced in January on the club's arena.[3]

Given their remarkable record of success, Noel and his supporters had deservedly gained a certain level of credibility and respectability in the boxing world from their prior activities, allowing them to quickly sign Andy Bowen to fight Joe Fielden from Great Britain on January 5, 1893. However, on such short notice the club had to hustle to erect even a temporary facility on the vacant lot on Canal Street and Carrollton Avenue. In the shadow of the new arena's wooden framework now under construction, a large canvas tent was raised to provide some measure of insulation from the blustery New Orleans winter. Wooden bleachers were hastily slapped together, although sufficient to comfortably accommodate the 3,000 fans who hoped to see their local man regain some of his lost luster against the man from Britain. When Fielden sparred with Bob Fitzsimmons back in February of 1891 at the Fitzsimmons benefit at the Olympic Club, he tattooed the lanky New Zealander, leaving a nasty black eye to remember him by. Not long after, fight promoters began trying to match Fielden against Bowen. Once the fight articles were negotiated and signed, Bowen set up training camp in Mississippi City (near Gulfport), and Fielden did his training at an undisclosed location in New Orleans.

Among the crowd were politicians, businessmen, and professional men who greeted Joseph Sporl, vice-president of the Crescent City Athletic Club, as he escorted Fielden into the ring at ten minutes past nine o'clock. While Fielden was getting settled into his corner, Charles Noel climbed into the ring to address the crowd, welcoming them to the new club and promising them a steady succession of "exhibitions by the greatest athletes of all branches," or weight classes. He then stated that the usual rule of law and order would be observed at all times, a caution to the small number of "the tougher element" that peppered the crowd. The ever-present and immensely popular Professor John Duffy was then introduced as the referee for the evening, but his greeting was overshadowed when Bowen and his entourage entered the ring.

At 9:30 the bell sounded to start the 1st round. Patrons immediately contrasted the swarthy Bowen with the pasty Fielden, who cautiously sized each other up with exploratory jabs and the occasional combination. During one movement by Fielden, Bowen landed a combination right to the heart and a left to the mouth that sent the Englishman to the mat, as much from being off balance as from the force of the blows. Fielden recovered quickly and the two fighters exchanged punches for the balance of the round, which was scored in Bowen's favor. The next two rounds went to Bowen with the 4th and 5th rounds going to Fielden. The battle raged on, but Bowen was wearing Fielden down, knocking him down several times in the 21st round before finally sending him down for the count in the 22nd round.

Bowen claimed the $1,500 winner's purse and Fielden went home with the $500 loser's share. At an average of $2 per general admission ticket, the Crescent City Athletic Club grossed $6,000 that night, perhaps more given the probable sale of several $3 reserved seats and $25 boxes. A modest but auspicious beginning for the fledgling promoter.[4] While those involved may have noticed the similarity to the Metropolitan Club's initial events, with the net proceeds from their first event being wholly insufficient to replace the cash the club was burning through to complete their clubhouse and arena, Noel and his supporters were as convinced of the ultimate success of their new venture even as they were blinded by the prospect of future glory.

In spite of the seemingly unflagging popularity of boxing in New Orleans, there was still a large contingent of vocal citizens and clergymen opposed to the brutality and viciousness related to the sport and the dope fiends and drunkards they were certain it attracted. Editorials against prizefighting, though infrequent, kept the hope alive that one day the city would be able to rid itself of this scourge. The reformers were not so much against the celebrity and notoriety of championship-caliber bouts such as the Fistic Carnival, but against those unseemly fights that still took place largely out of sight. Events such as the Tanney–Landon fight under the trees of Norton's plantation in St. Bernard Parish in January of 1890 or the early morning parade to see Alphonse Garcia and Charles Johnson in an interior courtyard of Patton's Tallow Factory near the slaughterhouse in February of 1892 were still all too commonplace. To most observers there was nothing "scientific" or sporting about 600 people, liberally fortified with free whiskey at seven o'clock in the morning, watching one man make a chopping block out of another for 3 rounds until his seconds mercifully threw up the sponge signaling defeat. Even though both fighters and their seconds were later arrested and prosecuted for violating Act 25 of 1890,[5] the public's distaste for this side of boxing was wearing thin. And yet these types of fights occurred frequently in and around the New Orleans area. For every one of these fights that they knew about there must have been dozens that went unchronicled. Nearly a year after the Johnson–Garcia fight, however, a legal exhibition, albeit on the very fringes of the law, would reignite community sentiment against boxing.

On St. Charles Avenue, in the first block off Canal Street, there was an arena that was little more than the squalid back room of a guzzle shop that had been expanded to accommodate a boxing ring. Dark, dirty and foul smelling, it operated with a modicum of legitimacy only because it was owned by Professor John Duffy, the celebrated boxing referee and instructor whose infectious good humor could make a stuffed bird sing. It was here that Duffy had arranged a routine amateur glove contest to take place in the wee hours of Friday, February 3, 1893, and it was here that two black men squared off just after midnight in front of a mixed audience of 200 black and white patrons seated on opposite sides of the ring.

George Goodrich was a steamboat hand known to frequent the dives and rum holes along Franklin Avenue in the Third District. His opponent was Joe Green, a local bricklayer who was a protégé of Duffy's. What made the bout legal was that the men did not fight for money. They were to fight a 3-round match with the winner receiving a medal from Duffy. The fighters and their friends made money through side bets with the saloon's patrons. Although witnesses provided several different, often conflicting, versions of what transpired, the unfortunate result occurred after Green leveled Goodrich in the 2nd round. When Goodrich attempted to rise he slipped, some said he slipped on water, others said it was his own blood. Either way, in trying to regain his balance, Goodrich fell out of the ring, hitting his head on the brick floor, breaking his neck. No one yet realized that he was dead, though the rumors circulating through the barroom that he might be caused many patrons to quit the premises. A group of men were pressed into service to carry the limp and lifeless Goodrich to what passed for a dressing room, laying him down on a pile of filthy rags heaped on one side of the room.

Duffy was summoned, and he thought Goodrich was fine and said so to those gathered around to gawp at the lifeless fighter, adding that he had seen this before and that Goodrich would come around. "A crowd of bewildered and half frightened negroes and white men and boys crowded about the body of the fighter, and simply gazed at the prostrate man." After several minutes, they made some effort to revive him until an ambulance arrived. The attendants held a candle over Goodrich's body, declaring the boxer dead, having seen no response from him while hot wax dripped onto his face. "The grim reaper had played the part of time keeper and had counted the pugilist out," the *Times-Democrat* stated rather melodramatically. Several arrests were made, but no one was ever prosecuted in Goodrich's death.[6]

The city's attention would be diverted in the complete opposite direction later that very same day when the Crescent City Athletic Club threw open the doors of their stunning new clubhouse with tremendous fanfare and publicity.[7] Several hundred people, including Mayor John Fitzpatrick, strolled through the old Letchford mansion on North Rampart Street that had been magnificently transformed into the opulent phenomenon Charles Noel envisioned. In what could only be described as putting butter on bacon, the clubhouse was complete with French lace curtains and a Steinway grand piano in the main parlor, lavish drawing rooms, an impressively stocked library and reading rooms, meeting rooms, cardrooms, billiard rooms, and a bar.

Noel and his supporters were still basking in the glowing newspaper accounts of the club's grand opening when yet another new athletic club quietly came onto the scene on February 28 with their first bout between local fighters Jack Everhardt and Joe Oliver, a finish fight for the Lightweight Championship of Louisiana. The Boulevard Club was located uptown near the old Exposition Grounds (Audubon Park) on Exposition Boulevard near St. Charles Avenue. Perhaps having learned from watching the Metropolitan Club struggle by throwing out large purses, the new club offered a very modest $500 purse and priced tickets for $1.50 for general admission.

In the 1st round Everhardt floored Oliver at least a half-dozen times, Oliver lingering as far as a six-count, before the end of the round mercifully provided him a chance to recover. At the call for the 2nd round, a still groggy Oliver endeared himself to the crowd for his pluck, but was soon on the receiving end of a fusillade of gloved fists from Everhardt. Referee John Duffy had his hands full keeping Everhardt away from Oliver when he went down for the second time, but there was no need when moments later Everhardt landed a jolt to Oliver's jaw that put him on the canvas for good.[8] Press reports relay that a large crowd tested the new club's seating capacity, but there was no actual attendance mentioned. Like so many small venues, this was their first and last foray into prize fighting. On any scale, boxing was a tough business to gain a secure foothold in and most clubs that tried once quickly decided their members could enjoy watching events at one of the other more established clubs.

All of this activity on the periphery had momentarily sidetracked boxing fans from the next triple event quietly being organized by the new leadership at the Olympic Club. However, by mid–February ticket sales from across the country indicated that the event would be a financial success.[9] The card was to feature welterweights Australian George Dawson against Tommy Ryan from Redwood, New York on Wednesday, March 1, followed the next night by a match between William McMillen from Washington, D.C., and Billy Hinds from Providence, Rhode Island. Also slated for Thursday night was a wrestling match between Ernest Roeber from New York and Evan "Strangler" Lewis from Wisconsin. Friday, March 3, would be the feature event with a heavyweight contest between Australian champion Joe Goddard and American Ed Smith.

General admission tickets for the event on Wednesday night, March 1, were $3, dropping to $2 for both events on Thursday night. Tickets for the Friday night heavyweight bout were $5 for general admission and $7 for reserved seats.[10] In a cruel twist of fate reminiscent of the recent Metropolitan Club event, the Ryan–Dawson fight had to be cancelled. As he had with the Metropolitan Club a year earlier, Ryan claimed illness, but offered to fight at a later date. There was no time to arrange a suitable replacement, so Dawson was paid the forfeit money and tickets were refunded. For the first time in their brief history, the Olympic Club was out of pocket for the training and other fight-related expenses. Although Ryan was believed to be a talented fighter who would participate in 86 more fights during his career, now twice burned, New Orleans boxing promoters would never again sign the untrustworthy Irishman. Ryan would finally meet Dawson on April 8, 1893, in Chicago, winning on points in six rounds, and would go on to win the World Welterweight title on July 26, 1894, from Mysterious Billy Smith at the Twin Cities Athletic Club in Minneapolis.

William McMillen versus Billy Hinds

Everything was ready and everywhere throughout the arena the telltale signs of the Olympic Club were evident. The bright lights chased away the shadows cast by the Ryan–Dawson debacle. Yet it was a disappointing crowd of no more than 2,000 fans on hand Thursday, March 2, to witness the boxing match between McMillan and Hinds, to be followed by the wrestling match between Roper and Lewis. Although billed as a "finish" fight, that being until one man knocked out the other, the club allotted an hour for the boxing match, which perhaps gave some indication that the match was destined to be one sided. At precisely eight o'clock Judge Anthony Sambola, a distinguished Civil War veteran and prominent jurist, welcomed the sparse crowd and introduced Professor John Duffy as the referee. The two welterweights lost no time answering the bell.

Hinds appeared to be the better conditioned and stronger of the two, but as experienced boxing fans learned from the Sullivan–Corbett fight, appearances could be deceiving. McMillan did nothing to make the crowd think he was a force to be reckoned with, as his hunched over, stooped fighting stance made him look smaller and more frail than Hinds. During the 1st round it became evident which way the fight was destined to go as McMillan proved to be quick on his feet and quick with a right that found Hinds' jaw frequently, sending Hinds to the mat towards the end of the round. He recovered and was on his feet before Duffy could count to five. Hinds managed to elude McMillan for the remainder of the first round.

McMillan continued to land his left jab with visible effect during the 2nd round. Hinds attempted to clinch to avoid further punishment and to try to figure out how to press his attack. McMillan was not a mixer, so Hinds relied on cornering McMillan on the ropes, delivering a series of ineffective punches that only served to stimulate McMillan, who countered with a flurry to Hinds' head and body. Hinds' eye puffed up and became McMillan's target as the bell sounded to begin the 3rd round. Hinds sought the safety of long range, trying to escape by circling constantly, but McMillan cleverly drew him in and when Hinds took the bait he repeatedly received a cocked right hand from McMillan that drew blood from Hinds' mouth and nose. From that point on in the round McMillan let up his attack, answering only when rushed by a fading Hinds.

McMillan was quick to answer the bell for the 4th round, his relentless barrage of jabs reopening Hinds' cuts, covering his face, neck, and chest with blood. Hinds tried to stand his ground, but was rewarded with jab after jab until Hinds could move in to clinch. In breaking from one clinch McMillan danced away to his right and Hinds' pursuit led him to collide with one of the ring posts. Hinds resolutely brought the fight to McMillan, scoring occasionally on a combination, but it was too little too late. When the bell rang for the 5th round Hinds approached McMillan with the haggard look of one who knows he will finish the fight on the mat. McMillan feinted with his right, then drove a left hook to Hinds' mouth, followed by a right cross to the jaw that sent Hinds reeling back into his corner. As Hinds turned back into the ring McMillan crossed him with a savage right that sent Hinds down for the count.

Evan "Strangler" Lewis versus Ernest Roeber

While the boxing match was of little consequence outside of the ring, the wrestling match was actually of more interest to the sparse crowd. Those familiar with wrestling were well aware of exactly what was on the line—that a win by Lewis would unify the World Catch-as-Catch-Can and American Greco–Roman titles. Catch-as-catch-can is an open style of wrestling in which nearly all tactics and holds are permitted, and is an amalgam of many different styles of wrestling, but mainly British and Irish wrestling. It became immensely popular in the United States as a carnival stunt during which the touring show would offer a cash prize if a local man could defeat the carnival's strongman wrestler. Greco–Roman wrestling, on the other hand, was a more traditional style of wrestling familiar throughout the world.

At nine o'clock the two wrestlers entered the ring, which was now covered with a mat, which in turn was covered with a thin layer of fine sawdust. Cheers greeted the two combatants. While most felt Lewis to be the favorite, there was some concern that his wife's recent death had interrupted his training and his concentration. Physically the two were evenly matched, both standing five feet, seven and a half inches and weighing approximately 180 pounds. In Lewis' corner were two of Bob Fitzsimmons' trainers, Martin Julian and Frank Bosworth. Roeber was attended by Duncan McMillan and the celebrated pugilist from California, Joe Choynski.

The first bout was catch-as-catch-can, which Lewis won in a little over seven minutes. After ten minutes' rest the two men locked arms for the Greco–Roman bout which Lewis eventually won after a prolonged 28-minute struggle to drop the big German Roeber. The third and final bout was another catch-as-catch-can affair, this time easily won by Lewis in less than a minute.[11] The success of the wrestling match proved to those present that, in many respects, wrestling was more physically demanding than boxing. The Hinds camp would disagree and their man announced before he left the Olympic Club that he intended to retire from boxing.

Denver Ed Smith versus Joe Goddard

The boxing event scheduled for Friday night did not fare much better, with only 3,000 on hand to watch Denver Ed Smith face Australian champion Joe Goddard. The Australian Goddard received a significant amount of pre-fight hype, garnering the "tag of terror" handle, and described as a "strange anomaly of a boxer without science, who was invincible." Once again, Judge Anthony Sambolla introduced Professor John Duffy, who in turn introduced the undercard for the evening between George Dawson and Eddie Greeney. The two welterweights provided the crowd with a three-round sparring exhibition that included imitation knock-downs and vigorous, if sometimes comic combinations, and concluded with a double knockout. The overall mood in the arena was so light that not even this delay could dampen the crowd's spirits.

Englishman Edward Corcoran adopted the *nom de guerre* Denver Ed Smith when he emigrated to America in 1884. He battled many of the best heavyweights of his day (from an unknown 19th century publication).

When Goddard entered the ring, there was a murmur of surprise. The six-foot Australian looked thin at his announced weight of 180 pounds, with especially slender legs supporting a well-muscled upper body. As Goddard settled into the "unlucky" corner, Smith entered the ring fully clothed, stripping down to his fighting togs in front of the crowd in theatrical fashion. At 165 pounds, he was much lighter than Goddard. When the men met at the scratch line, Smith objected to the other man's gloves, claiming that Goddard's gloves were too short and that his wrists were encased in a sticky plaster bandage. After yet another delay during which Smith's objections were dismissed, the fight finally got underway at ten o'clock.

Both men spent the better part of the 1st round sizing each other up, each offering an exploratory salvo to determine his opponent's counter-strategy. After an aggressive lead by Goddard that forced Smith into the corner of the ring, he followed up in lively fashion and sent Smith to his knees for an eight-count. As the two were set to resume, the bell clanged to end the round. Smith was up first and waiting for Goddard at the start of the 2nd round. The men exchanged blows and chased each other around the ring, occasionally landing a telling blow to the head of their opponent. Smith began attacking Goddard's body, trying to rob him of his wind, with some effect, a strategy that he continued through the next several rounds. Goddard continued to fade, but bravely rose to answer the start of each round, far from fresh, but not willing to give in. Finally, in the 16th round, Goddard landed an unexpected uppercut to Smith's jaw that sent him down for an eight-count. This only served to anger Smith who renewed his attack on Goddard with a series of hard combinations that drew blood from the Australian's nose. The 17th round began slowly, each man still trying to recover from the cumulative pounding given and received, and was marked by frequent clinches. All of a sudden Smith went on the offensive, perhaps sensing that Goddard had nothing left. A volley of jabs to the mouth, followed by uppercuts to the chin, caused the groggy Goddard to clinch. Duffy had more than usual difficulty in separating the two, Goddard hanging on to Smith shoulders and neck helplessly as the round ended. The 18th round saw the two men stagger to the scratch line and unleash punches with whatever reserve of strength they could muster. However, before the round could end Smith saw an opportunity and threw a right hook that caught Goddard squarely on the jaw, sending him to his knees. Steadying himself with one hand on the ground, Goddard appeared to be listening to Duffy, waiting for the eight-count to rise, but when he did not his corner jumped through the ropes to retrieve their man before Duffy got to ten. Smith laid claim to the winner's share of the $10,000 purse as well as a new pair of shoes from "Pokorny, the artist shoemaker."[12] For the past two years Michael Pokorny had custom made fighting shoes for Andy Bowen, Jack McAuliffe, and dozens of other fighters across the country from his St. Charles Avenue store and workshop. The business, established in 1860, later known as M. Pokorny & Sons, a retail shoe store that existed on St. Charles Avenue for more than 140 years.

With the cancellation of the Ryan–Dawson match on Wednesday night and the poor showing for both Thursday and Friday nights, the Olympic Club experienced their first real financial setback. With gate receipts estimated to be $3,000 on Thursday and $15,000 on Friday, the club nearly broke even. It was generally thought that the poor attendance meant that fight fans were saving their money for the upcoming Fitzsimmons–Hall fight at the Crescent City Athletic Club. All Dickson and the Olympic Club could do now was to wait to see what would happen across town with the most recent challenge from Charles Noel. Observers of the boxing scene in New Orleans could easily imagine that somewhere in the rooms of the Crescent City Athletic Club Charles Noel was smiling, having outmaneuvered his former club by securing the fight that everyone in the country wanted to see and that he wagered everyone would pay dearly to see. Noel had arranged two bouts—a preliminary match for March 7 and the main event for March 8.

Charles Noel had pushed and cajoled his contractors to erect the club's new arena in record time, rising from the ground like the legendary beanstalk. He succeeded in opening a superbly appointed facility, on par or exceeding that of his nemesis, the Olympic Club. Since the Bowen–Fielden fight, the skeleton had been fleshed out, seats constructed, an upper gallery added, and the roof completed. The ring stood on a raised platform covered with pine boards which were padded with thick felt covered with white duck canvas. The new Fistic Carnival provided by Charles Noel, especially the upcoming fight between Fitzsimmons and Hall, was the topic of conversation in saloons and salons, in clubs and companies, and among almost everyone on the streets of New Orleans.

On Tuesday night, there were only between 1,200 and 1,500 fans scattered throughout row after row of empty seats in the Crescent City Athletic Club's massive new arena to watch the first match of the evening that pitted Austin Gibbons from New Jersey against Mike Daly from Maine for a $3,500 purse. In the days leading up to the fight, the odds favored Gibbons at 10 to 7, which held for the latecomers who placed their wagers at ringside. There was a smattering of sporting men from all parts of the country including Bat Masterson, Charlie Mitchell, and Joe Choynski. Unfortunately for the Crescent City Athletic Club, there was a crowd estimated to be twice that size mingling outside of the arena, unwilling or unable to pay the $3 ticket price, but anxiously awaiting news of the fight. They would have to linger for nearly two hours, through 31 rather lopsided rounds dominated by Gibbons before Daley retired.

With an optimistic estimate of 500 reserved seats at $4 per ticket and the remaining 1,100 general admission seats at $3 each, the club received approximately $5,300 in gate receipts on the night. Less the $3,500 purse and approximately $500 in expenses, they stood to make $1,300 on the fight. This was before trying to recoup the mounting, ever-present, and ongoing cost of building their beautiful new arena, renovating and furnishing their new clubhouse. Without a doubt, Noel and his backers had rolled the dice, and all eyes were on the Crescent City Athletic Club's main event.

Immediately upon resigning from the Olympic Club, Frank Williams and Charles Noel joined the scores of athletic clubs nationwide trying to arrange a match between Bob Fitzsimmons and Jim Hall. This was a fight that Hall had been pushing for ever since he landed in America, and, after his victory over Peter Maher, one that Fitzsimmons now wanted to settle once and for all. Between 1887 and 1890, Fitzsimmons and Hall had fought each other five times—three different four-round bouts with no decision, one bout won by Fitzsimmons (January 19, 1889), and one bout won by Hall (February 11, 1890). All five of these fights took place at Foley's Hall in Sydney, Australia. In 1890, San Francisco promoter Major Frank McLaughlin had offered to bring Australian Jim Hall to America to try his hand there. Hall had just defeated Fitzsimmons in a controversial bout on February 11, 1890, for the Australian Middleweight Championship with a 4th-round knockout that still stirs debate even today. However, an injury to Hall's hand prevented him from making the trip and so McLaughlin offered the trip to Fitzsimmons instead.

Now, with the World Middleweight Championship to his credit, Fitzsimmons was looking forward, not backward. His interest lay in challenging for the world heavyweight title.[13] Despite his success, Fitzsimmons was hounded incessantly by Hall and the time had come to put an end to the accusations and vitriol from Hall. Their ill-fated rematch in Minneapolis had been cancelled in July of 1891 and athletic clubs across the country had been scrambling in a wild bidding war to bring the two together ever since. However, by December of 1892 Charles Noel and Frank Williams from the newly formed Crescent City Athletic Club in New Orleans and Judge Newton from the Coney Island Athletic Club in New York were the last men standing in a bidding war for the right to stage the match. It appeared that, at long last, both Fitzsimmons and Hall were agreeable. It also appeared that the New York group would prevail when they offered a $45,000 purse, $5,000 higher than the highest bid from the Crescent City group.

The same sporting men and pundits throughout the country who questioned the initial $10,000 purse offered for the Fitzsimmons–Maher fight were totally at a loss for words to understand the logic of the Crescent City Athletic Club in offering a $40,000 purse to these two men. Charles Noel and Frank Williams had both earned a credible reputation in the boxing community in a very short time and were well respected, but this was beyond the pale in the eyes of many of their critics. Many believed that Noel was off his chump at $40,000 and Newton was even crazier at $45,000 for a middleweight fight, world championship or not. There was some doubt regarding the sincerity of Judge Newton's bid on behalf of the Coney Island Athletic Club, but unlike many of the shill organizations that only bid in order to raise the purse to benefit their favorite fighters, the New York club was a relatively new, but reputable venue. They had staged their first event on Monday, August 8, 1892, and 10,000 people were on hand to watch the card that included three matches, two featherweight matches featuring Eddie Pierce against George Siddons followed by Jerry Barnett against Billy Plimmer, and a middleweight bout between Charley Kammer and Jim Sullivan.[14] Then, on Halloween night 1892, the club staged a twin bill that offered a 10-round bantamweight bout between local products Kid Hogan and Adolph "Dolly" Lyons that was followed by a 15-round heavyweight battle between Joe Choynski and George Godfrey. The crowd was estimated to be more than 8,000 fans.[15]

Judge Newton and the Coney Island Athletic Club posed a legitimate threat to Charles Noel and the Crescent City Athletic Club in this bidding war. In a surprise move, the historically and notoriously greedy Fitzsimmons camp now insisted on fighting in New Orleans and the Crescent City Athletic Club's lower offer was accepted. You could have knocked Judge Newton into a cocked hat, and indeed most of the country was flabbergasted and more than a little dumbfounded. But at the end of the day the astonishing decision was made to stage to the fight in New Orleans for a $40,000 purse. Boxing enthusiasts, writers, and promoters across the country would watch with great interest to see if Noel could once again back his bluster. Noel, on the other hand, had carefully calculated that he could cover the purse and expenses if he could fill his new 13,000-seat arena at an average of $3.50 per ticket.

It was generally believed that Fitzsimmons wanted to return to New Orleans because it was the scene of his first major victory, plus he owned and operated a well-regarded training camp complex, Robinson's Cottage, in nearby Bay St. Louis. However, it was later revealed that Charles Noel had appealed to Fitzsimmons' only known vice—his notorious greed. He offered Fitzsimmons a $2,500 "bonus" if the fight were held at his new club in New Orleans.[16] In so doing he was also appealing to Fitzsimmons' outsized ego, lowering the loser's share of the purse from $5,000 to $2,500, thus adding to Fitzsimmons' potential payday if and when he defeated Hall. Fight articles were drawn up and signed, with the date being set for Thursday, March 9, 1893.

Bob Fitzsimmons versus Jim Hall

The Crescent City Athletic Club completed construction on their brand new wooden arena on Canal Street in January and enlarged it in February, adding an upper gallery in anticipation of drawing a record crowd for the Fitzsimmons–Hall event. This was the largest purse ever offered in the United States to date and the World Middleweight title was on the line. Noel was gambling heavily that fight patrons were ready for another epic battle to rival the spectacle he had provided a scant eight months ago when Corbett defeated Sullivan. Unfortunately for Noel, in the minds of most pugilistic patrons, the fight between Fitzsimmons and Hall had none of the trappings of another David versus Goliath.

There was ample room for cabs and carriages to traverse Canal Street to the arena and the street rail line had extra cars at the ready to accommodate the crush of the anticipated crowd Noel had told them to expect. There would be none of the typical congestion and confusion fans experienced in getting through the French Quarter into the Third District to the Olympic Club. Unfortunately for Noel, these preparations would not be necessary. Despite all of the pre-fight publicity, less than half of the arena was filled by the time the doors opened at eight o'clock. Attendance was estimated at between 6,000 and 5,000 in a facility constructed to easily accommodate 13,000 or more.[17] In yet another questionable decision, unquestionably fueled by sheer greed and hubris, Noel and the club priced their general admission tickets at $10 and $15 for reserved seating, not the original $3.50 and $5, respectively, first contemplated. Advance sales were understandably weak with beleaguered boxing patrons staying away in droves, deterred by the high ticket prices.[18] Noel was still outwardly confident, and inwardly hopeful, that there would be a last minute rush to the box office to see the fight.

To some extent ticket sales were also jeop-

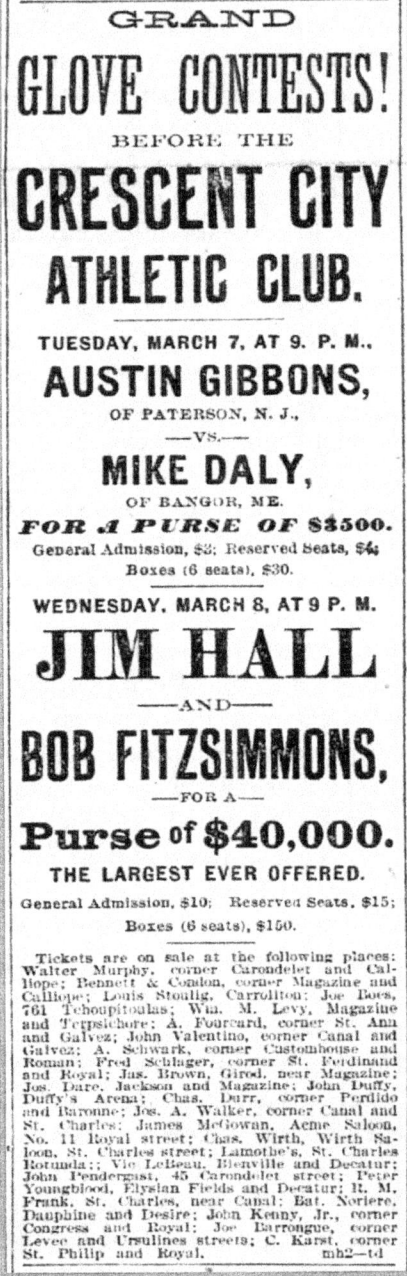

The Crescent City Athletic Club heavily advertised the mill between Fitzsimmons and Hall, including the unheard of $40,000 purse. Despite a large number of ticket sellers, listed at the bottom of the advertisement, the club did not sell many tickets (*New Orleans Daily Picayune*).

ardized by a minor dispute raised at the eleventh hour by some of the city's other athletic clubs as to whether or not the fight was legal because it was not being staged under the club's own roof. The operative language of the ordinance was "within the rooms of all regularly chartered athletic clubs in the city of New Orleans." It was well publicized that the Crescent City Athletic Club was headquartered on North Rampart Street while the new venue was prominently located approximately one mile away on Canal Street, obviously not adjacent to that building and, therefore, technically not part of the "rooms of ... the club." Many opined that the two fights would never come off, but after some last minute legal wrangling, the matter was eventually resolved in Crescent's favor, the requisite city permit was issued, and the two fights were allowed to go forward. While this may have caused some to hold off buying their tickets, for most it was the huge increase in ticket prices, well over 200 percent, that ultimately deterred them.

At precisely nine o'clock on the evening of March 8, 1893, Hall entered the arena with Charlie Mitchell, Squire Abingdon, Jack McAuliffe, and his trainer named Klein. Famed Western lawman and boxing enthusiast Bat Masterson was tapped to serve as Hall's timekeeper. Two minutes later Fitzsimmons entered the arena accompanied by his older brother Bill, his manager Martin Julian, and trainer Frank Bosworth. New Orleans native Dominick O'Malley was to serve as Fitzsimmons' timekeeper. Fitzsimmons carried a small American flag as earlier that day he had visited the New Orleans Criminal Court complex to become an American citizen.

Although the weights were not announced at ringside before the fight, Hall looked to weigh in at 170 pounds and Fitzsimmons declared his avoirdupois to be at 162 pounds. Any disparity between the two men was not apparent to the crowd. Both men entered the ring and stared at each other in the center of the ring, halfheartedly listening as referee Professor John Duffy delivered the standard admonitions against deplorable conduct unbecoming gentlemen and cautioned the crowd that unruly behavior would not be tolerated by him or the cadre of New Orleans' finest on hand throughout the arena. Captain Barrett of the New Orleans police department then stepped into the ring to deliver the approved gloves, which were promptly laced up on each fighter. At a quarter after nine o'clock the two men shook hands and returned to their respective corners to await the bell. The small but appreciative crowd comprised of "prominent lawyers, doctors, merchants, bankers, journalists, and educators" also included boxing champions from all weight classes and sporting men, as well as "lesser lights" scattered throughout the building.

Although Hall had been established as the favorite nationally, based almost solely on his own widely circulated stories of his prior defeat of Fitzsimmons in Australia, those in New Orleans who had seen Fitzsimmons systematically dismantle Dempsey in 1891 and Maher in 1892 laid their money of the New Zealander. The money from the East Coast went against Fitzsimmons, as much as from Hall's bragging as from their displeasure in Fitzsimmons' defeat of Dempsey. From the start of the fight, there was a sense throughout the arena that Fitzsimmons had the upper hand. After a brief bit of sparring in the 1st round, Fitzsimmons took the fight to Hall, who hovered in his corner for most the round. The two traded punches, but only Fitzsimmons landed anything of notice, and won the round.

In the 2nd round Fitzsimmons recommenced hostilities, going to body blows straight away and forcing Hall to clinch. Hall looked to be the better fighter on open ground, avoiding going toe to toe with the dangerous Fitzsimmons, who continued to press his attack. Hall landed a left to Fitzsimmons' head and Fitzsimmons countered with a right hook. There were several sharp exchanges and Hall had Fitzsimmons on the ropes briefly, but failed to take advantage, allowing Fitzsimmons to escape. Although most believed Hall to have carried the round, the official scorer's tally showed the round was scored even. The 3rd round was telling, the crowd now believing that either man could come out on top. As expected, Fitzsimmons forced the fighting, even when Hall outmaneuvered him in the clinches. Fitzsimmons landing several punches to Hall's face and body, but without any visible effect. Hall's wild swings were easily dodged and countered. Fitzsimmons now seemed fresh while Hall seemed to be clumsy. Some vicious in-fighting in the clinches took place, with Fitzsimmons landing several short but powerful shots that caught Hall's attention without drawing blood.

Both men seemed rejuvenated as the bell sounded for the 4th round. Hall sported a sarcastic smile that displayed a remarkably cool air of confidence. The newly minted American Fitzsimmons was also calm and collected and immediately launched his attack with a strong left that grazed Hall's mouth. This was followed with a bit of cautious sparring and circling, both men looking puzzled as they glared at each other. Suddenly, Fitzsimmons launched a right hook with crushing force to the jaw of a thoroughly unprepared Hall, who must have been musing about how he was planning to spend the winner's share. Hall was already unconscious when he hit the canvas covered cork floor, striking his head with a resounding thud. Referee Duffy engaged in a slow count, but the crowd issued a resounding roar before he made it to four, knowing instinctively that Hall was out. The fallen Hall remained motionless as Duffy eventually and inevitably reached ten. Mitchell and McAuliffe scrambled into the ring to attend to their man, who lapsed in and out of consciousness and had to be carried back to his corner.

The fight lasted 13 minutes. Fitzsimmons danced around the ring waving an American flag over his head. During the next 20 minutes Hall sat slumped in his corner, unresponsive to the efforts to revive him. A physician in the crowd briefly examined him and pronounced him unconscious, but uninjured. Hall eventually came to in his dressing room some 45 minutes after the conclusion of the fight.[19]

The out-of-town money was on Hall and they lost heavily. Charlie Mitchell and James Corbett had wagered $2,800 and $200, respectively, on Hall. The size of Corbett's bet should have alerted Hall's camp that the current World Heavyweight Champion wasn't totally confident in Hall or, conversely, that he feared Fitzsimmons. New Orleanians, however, had backed Fitzsimmons and they were well rewarded for their faith in him. In addition to Mitchell and Corbett, noted backers of Jim Hall who lost were Jack McAuliffe ($1,500) and Bat Masterson ($2,000). Local fight promoter Bud Renaud and Pat Duffy were among the Fitzsimmons camp that went home flush, winning $12,500 and $20,000, respectively.[20]

But the biggest losers on the night were Charles Noel and the Crescent City Athletic Club. The fortunes of the Crescent City Athletic Club were not at all what they had expected. They had promised Fitzsimmons a $2,500 "bonus" for insisting on New Orleans as the fight venue, but only paid him $1,000 prior to the fight. Already heavily

After months of speculation and false starts, it took champion Bob Fitzsimmons, shown raising an American flag, just 13 minutes to knock out his nemesis, challenger Jim Hall. Although this image depicts the Crescent City Athletic Club arena as being packed, there were fewer than 5,000 in attendance (*New Orleans Times-Democrat*).

in debt, and with a gate estimated to be at or below $25,000, they had no way to cover the $37,500 winner's share of the purse. Charles Noel had no idea what to expect early the next morning as both fighters showed up at the Crescent City Athletic Club to collect their share of the purse. The antagonists were greeted separately by Noel and other club officials, and each was led to a different room on the main floor of the clubhouse. To all assembled there seemed to be nothing out of the ordinary—sealed envelopes containing checks for the fighter's winnings were presented along with several rounds of champagne and the requisite toasts. Reporters peppered the men with questions with the usual questions regarding their views on the previous night's affair and their plans for the future. Hall put out feelers for another match while Fitzsimmons announced that he would be heading to Chicago for an exhibition after a brief visit to his training camp in Bay St. Louis.

Fitzsimmons delayed his travel plans after opening the Crescent City Athletic Club's envelope. The enclosed check was for substantially less than the $37,500 he expected to find. His manager, Martin Julian, contacted Noel who contritely explained the club's financial predicament. The parties agreed to meet on Monday, March 13, to resolve the matter. Fitzsimmons and Julian were accompanied by Judge Henry L. Lazarus as legal counsel. The Crescent City Athletic Club was represented by Noel, Frank Williams, Rueben Frank, Louis Grevenig and several other members, most assuredly being attorneys. After several hours of arguing, handwringing, and negotiating behind closed doors a compromise was reached. Although Noel steadfastly refused to disclose the terms of the settlement, obviously wishing to avoid the humiliation and scandal that would accompany such a story, it was learned that Fitzsimmons was given $5,000 in cash and notes secured by the club's property for the $31,500 balance. Charles Noel's huge gamble had gone toes up on him. This was just the sort of outsized financial risk the dissenting Olympic Club faction had warned of several months prior.

Fitzsimmons later sued the Crescent City Athletic Club on multiple occasions and eventually recovered an additional $13,000 from which his attorneys took $3,000 for legal expenses.[21] From a contract under which he should have received 90 percent of the purse or $37,500 he received only $19,000 and would only net $16,000 after his legal expenses. While still larger than any purse he had ever received, it was far less that the $40,000 that was fixated in the nation's memory and plastered across the nation's headlines.

The Crescent City Athletic Club had made a significant capital outlay in advance of this fight renovating and furnishing their new clubhouse, purchasing the real estate and for the design and construction of their opulent arena on Canal Street, accruing organizational, marketing, and travel expenses related to the fight, and, of course, the looming liability for the prize money. The failure of the Crescent City Athletic Club was more than a black eye for Charles Noel and the club; it caused fight promoters to question New Orleans as a viable fight venue in the future. The periodic anti-boxing sentiment in Louisiana,[22] as elsewhere across the United States, began to gain traction as word of the failure of the Crescent City Athletic Club became known. Promoters were being lured by other cities, particularly from Texas, California, and Nevada, and from this point on the popularity of boxing in New Orleans began a gradual downward spiral as the national spotlight began a slow fade.

If one needed further evidence of the precarious position athletic clubs engaged in the principal business of promoting boxing placed themselves in, just four days before the Fitzsimmons–Hall event, the floundering and failing Metropolitan Club adopted a resolution that consolidated it with the Crescent City Athletic Club.[23] Noel, Williams, and Frank had not learned from any of the missteps made by Charles Genslinger in allowing his wounded ego to accept questionable risks in trying to vindictively overtake the Olympic Club. Now their own bristling egos, combined with a healthy dose of pure greed, brought them to the same position. For those members of the Metropolitan Club who had just joined the Crescent City Athletic Club, the future was all cold coffee.

To pile on the agony, on March 10, 1893, Edwin H. McCaleb, attorney for the state of Louisiana in the collection of delinquent state licenses, filed suit in Civil District Court against the Olympic Club and the Crescent City Athletic Club for $18,000 and $10,000, respectively, under the Revenue Act of 1892.[24] The suit stipulated that the Olympic Club owed the state $2,000 per year for the period from 1888 through 1891 and $5,000 per year for 1892 and 1893. The Crescent City Athletic Club too owed the state $5,000 per year for 1892 and 1893. While the suit posed no credible threat to the Olympic Club, this unexpected turn of events appeared to be the death knell for Charles Noel and company, and a pivotal factor in the future disposition of the Crescent City Athletic Club.

The officers and directors of the Olympic Club felt vindicated—they had successfully overcome recent legal challenges, they had sufficient cash reserves to satisfy the state's claim for back license fees, and they had defended their position as a preeminent boxing venue from threats posed by the Metropolitan Club and the Crescent City Athletic Club. But they had not done so without some collateral damage. The Olympic Club tried to repair the damage by arranging a contest between local favorite Andy Bowen and "Texas" Jack Burke for the vacant Lightweight Championship of the South and a $2,500 prize.

Andy Bowen versus Jack Burke

A former day laborer who grew up as poor as Job's turkey, New Orleans native Andy Bowen was a hard-nosed scrapper who would come at you like an alley cat on his ninth life. Bowen made his professional debut in 1887 and his first eight professional fights resulted in seven wins and a single draw.[25] He garnered local attention with his 3rd-round knockout of New Jersey's Tom Ryan on August 4, 1889,[26] and the spotlight became even brighter following a 2nd-round knockout of Jimmy McHale at the Southern Athletic Club on December 22, 1889.[27] Before long Bowen was attracting large local crowds and on September 16, 1890, he made his debut at the Olympic Club. Unfortunately for Bowen, Jimmy Carroll from San Francisco would knock him out in the 21st round.[28]

New Orleans native Andy Bowen was the Lightweight Champion of the South appearing for the third time at the Olympic Club on April 6, 1893. His opponent was Texas Jack Burke. No one realized that history was about to be made that night (*New Orleans Times-Democrat*).

Bowen's opponent, Jack Burke, was born in Chicago, but grew up in Galveston. He made his professional debut on September 19, 1889, in a 9-round draw against George LaBlanche in Seattle. Following mixed success in four local fights, Burke was in New Orleans for a match between Danny Needham and Tommy Ryan, who Burke had been training. When Ryan fell ill, Burke stepped in against Needham, but was not truly in fighting shape and was easily knocked out in the 10th round.[29]

On the night of April 6, 1893, a crowd estimated to be between 8,000 and 8,500 was on hand for the fight, the largest since the Sullivan–Corbett title bout eight months earlier at the Fistic Carnival. At approximately nine o'clock the two fighters and their seconds entered the ring. Bowen was accompanied by his trainer Charles Kennedy, backers Thomas C. Anderson and Albert Spitzfaden, and timekeeper Frank Carambat. Burke was joined by his trainer George

LaBlanche, John A. Sullivan, and timekeeper Joe Davis. Local businessman and New Orleans City Councilman Charles Dickson, who succeeded Charles Noel as president of the Olympic Club, introduced Professor John Duffy as the referee for the match, who in turn delivered the customary admonitory address to the spectators. In his trademark loquacious manner, Duffy specifically drew their attention to Captain W.J. Barrett and Captain E.J. Donnelly of the New Orleans Police Department, assuring the crowd that there was sufficient force capable of handling any unseemly and uncalled for breach of order or decorum.

After a few moments of cautious sparring, Bowen took an aggressive approach, rushing Burke from the moment Duffy called "time." His first approach was so hurried that he lost his balance and fell, drawing jeers from the crowd. Quickly on his feet, Bowen engaged Burke in short-range fighting during the 1st round. A few solid punches were landed in the 2nd round, but most were without effect. However, in the 3rd round Bowen landed a solid right to Burke's head followed by a few body punches. The balance of the round was a cycle of in-fighting and clinching, most of which were scored in favor of Bowen. The 4th round was nearly through before Burke delivered a severe uppercut which caught Bowen solidly, saving the round for Burke. From the 5th round through the 28th, the fight was fairly, but fiercely fought. Burke's tactic was to try to land another surprise uppercut while Bowen worked fiercely on Burke's ribs and body. At some point during the 14th round Burke broke a bone in one of his hands and thereafter began to fight a very different style. Bowen was still the aggressor, but now had to try to corner Burke to exchange blows. When they did mix it up, Burke favored his remaining good hand.

Those who had seen Bowen fight before were surprised when he failed to follow up on those instances when he had a clear opportunity to put the fight away such as in the 28th round when Bowen scored a clear knockdown. While Burke was still determined to battle, his corner advised him to stay down to recover as the referee counted. When Duffy reached five in the count the bell sounded to end the round and Burke was saved by the bell. For the next several rounds there were a few spirited exchanges, but nothing of any consequence.

At the end of the 34th round, the crowd began to grow weary after nearly two and a half hours. Some spectators left, but those who

Chicago native Jack Burke grew up in Galveston and was a rising lightweight when he stepped into the ring to meet local favorite Andy Bowen at the Olympic Club on April 6, 1893 (from an unknown 19th century publication).

remained began whistling and humming the popular folk tune "Home Sweet Home." With a badly injured hand, Burke clearly had no disposition to fight and would break and run whenever Bowen approached. At the end of the 41st round Burke's people approached Duffy about declaring a draw, but Bowen's side protested. Duffy announced that this being a finish fight, there would be a conclusion to the fight. The exchange drew calls from the crowd for Burke to stand and fight. In the 48th round both men were understandably showing visible signs of fatigue. The drawn and drained fighters staggered around the ring, stalking each other in slow motion, their labored breathing as if they were sniffing the air trying to catch the scent of their prey. At one point during the round Burke was knocked down and completely dazed, but Bowen appeared too groggy to finish him off. From this point on Bowen had the best of each round, landing numerous punches, but none of them with enough force to put Burke away.

Around 3:30 in the morning, at the start of the 94th round, Olympic Club president Charles Dickson took Duffy's place as referee, allowing Duffy a few minutes respite after more than six hours in the ring. He returned a few rounds later. In the 105th round Bowen mustered up enough strength to take a vicious swipe at Burke, but wound up stumbling over Burke and to the floor, turning a complete somersault. The crowd by this time was now howling for a draw. Duffy consulted with Captain Barrett and Dickson to gauge their thoughts on declaring the match no contest. He would not stop the fight as most athletic clubs prohibited a fight ending in a draw. In that event, they would be forced to refund the gate to fight patrons as well as provide them with tickets to a rematch. More than 2,500 were in attendance that night, mostly laborers who had come to support Bowen. As the fight dragged on into the night, many could not believe what they were witnessing. By the waning hours of the fight many of those still in their seats were either asleep or thinking about breakfast.

After 108 rounds, referee John Duffy announced to the crowd that he would allow two more rounds before ending the fight. He visited each man's corner to repeat his announcement. Exhausted, battered, and broken, neither fighter had much of anything left in the tank. Staggering around the ring, not a single blow was delivered in either of the two final rounds, the boxers so fatigued that their halfhearted swinging was like soap bubbles bouncing off each other. Just before five o'clock in the morning, Duffy entered the ring and threw up his hands, saying, "Gentlemen, this fight is off. I declare it to be no contest." While in hindsight many would agree with his decision, there were still many who did not agree, including Olympic Club president Dickson. The decision was later changed to be a draw.

A decision of "no contest" occurs when the referee determines that the fight should be concluded for reasons beyond the control of the fighters. In a "no contest" bout, the purse is split between the fighters. This is different from a "draw," which occurs when the referee stops the fight because one of the fighters is unable to continue from an accidental injury or from a fall. In a "draw," the club would have to refund the gate and all bets are nullified.

After 7 hours and 19 minutes, this was the first draw fought before any regularly organized athletic club in New Orleans. Duffy would later state that his decision of "no contest" was not in the typical sense given the circumstances. The fight between

Bowen and Burke would become part of boxing history as the longest prize fight in United States history,[30] a record that stands to this day.

Desperate to generate positive cash flow in the wake of the Fitzsimmons–Hall debacle, the Crescent City Athletic Club reduced their ticket prices to $1 for general admission and $1.50 for reserved seats for their next event which pitted Burke's trainer, George "The Marine" LaBlanche against Australian Billy McCarthy on Thursday, May 18, for a $2,000 purse. The public may have lost its taste for high priced boxing, but they were more than willing to shell out a buck to see an old-fashioned slugfest. There were more than 4,000 in the big arena to watch the two middleweights have to, however it was evident by the 2nd round that LaBlanche was not in shape for the fight. Nevertheless, he lasted until the 16th round when McCarthy landed back-to-back right uppercuts to send LaBlanche to the deck. He gamely struggled on the ropes, but could not get to his feet by the completion of the ten-count.[31] Noel publicly expressed his satisfaction with the gate, but with the majority of ticket sales being $1 general admission and with less than a hundred reserved seat tickets sold at $1.50, the club once again would clear a little over $1,500 on the event after the purse and fight-related expenses were deducted. The ship was slowly sinking and was still taking on water. Noel could not bail fast enough and was coming to the realization that, try as he might, he could not right the ship.

Andy Bowen versus Jack Everhardt

Following the celebration of their tenth anniversary, the Olympic Club decided to bring Andy Bowen back in June to face another local, Jack Everhardt. The evening of May 31, 1893, saw four street-rail lines—Rampart, Dauphine, Levee, and Barracks—carrying capacity loads into the Third District beginning two hours before the fight. In scenes reminiscent of the good old days, the surrounding streets were filled with cabs and tally hos shuttling patrons to the Olympic Club arena. A near-capacity crowd of more than 9,000 spectators cheered when both fighters entered the ring, although it was evident that the Everhardt faction, representing the Sixth District uptown, clearly outnumbered the Bowen group.

At precisely nine o'clock, referee Lloyd Gearhardt brought both fighters to the scratch line and, after the usual cautions against ungentlemanly behavior, the fight began. No one on hand expected the bout to drag on for six hours. At just after three in the morning, at the call for the 85th round, Everhardt, beaten into jelly, could not rise from his stool, even with the help of his seconds. He had to be carried back to his quarters. The fight was awarded to Bowen, who in truth had done most of the fighting throughout the match.[32]

With estimated gate receipts of $9,500 less the $2,500 purse and $1,000 in expenses, the Olympic Club stood to make approximately $6,000 on the event.

To everyone's surprise, the Crescent City Athletic Club defied liquidation and announced a match between featherweights Jack Daly from Delaware and local Owen Harney. Noel and his club offered a $1,000 purse and were praying that continued low ticket prices would attract a crowd, especially to see a hometown boy. It was not in the cards for either Harney or the Crescent that night. A gathering of less than 2,500 sat through 10 rounds during which Daly's superior height, reach, and skills won the decision from referee George Scott.[33] With an estimated $2,750 in gate receipts, less the $1,000 purse and $500 in expenses, the club once again netted approximately $1,250 on the night. Such meager results wouldn't even satisfy the club's outstanding legal bills, much less stave off liquidation.

The end seemed evident to everyone except the Crescent City Athletic Club. Facing lawsuits from Fitzsimmons as well as from the club's contractors who had yet to be paid for work on the arena, their landlord for unpaid rent on their clubhouse, and legal fees from their lawyers, the Crescent City Athletic Club finally threw in the towel. In the past few weeks the majority of their members had resigned and joined the Elks, who also agreed to take over their clubhouse.[34] By mid–August there was a judicial notice of liquidation for the club's furnishings and fixtures, the proceeds of which were garnished by Bob Fitzsimmons[35] who wanted to force the Crescent City Athletic Club to merge with the Olympic Club.[36]

The state of Louisiana eventually stepped in, having successfully argued that their position as creditor gave them seniority and thus preference over the club's other creditors..[37] The club still owed the state $10,000 for two years of unpaid licenses. The last remaining asset of the club, their arena and the land on which it stood, was auctioned for $10,100 on December 20 to a buyer identified as the Southern Improvement Company, Limited.[38] Despite receiving a judicial judgment, even Charles Noel's lumber company had to swallow over $5,850 in losses[39] for unpaid building materials.

New Leadership

During the Olympic Club's mid-year meeting, a new slate of officers and directors was elected. Businessman Charles Dickson had been quickly elected President following the abrupt resignation of Charles Noel in November of 1892, but the membership was ambivalent about the decline of the club's status under Dickson's leadership. As a result, 38-year-old businessman William A. Scholl was elected the tenth president of the Olympic Club.[40] Also elected as part of the Scholl ticket were P.R. Coyle, Andrew P. Marmouget, Edward Koffskey, Joseph Kantz, John Belou, Walter J. Wright, N.D. Hughes, E. Ruty, Conrad C. Julier, and F. Dufreche. In addition to Dickson, his ticket included such well-known names as John Carey, Herman Eicke, Henry Peters, Frank Zengel, and Victor Lambou. There was clearly a desire among the members to shake things up, given all of the controversy and legal wrangling they had experienced in recent months. They were looking for a change.

The members spent the remainder of the month of June watching their rifle club acquit themselves favorably in tournaments sponsored by the Louisiana State Rifle League at Boudro's Garden in Milneburg. At mid-year, the Olympics were in second place behind the Arnoult Rifle Club by a mere 52 points.[41]

By the middle of July, the Olympic Club was preparing to report on its financial condition to the membership. Secretary William D. Ross informed its assembled membership that the club had assets of $87,146.28 and liabilities described only as "less than a third of that amount."[42] Membership rolls now stood at 1,150, of whom 408 had joined during the past year, and this was net of 70 resignations, 6 deaths, and 193 members who had been dropped from the rolls during that time.

In mid–August, members were shocked to learn of the death of 30-year-old physician Charles Seemann, a former Olympic Club director who was currently serving as the Coroner for Orleans Parish.[43] Seemann typified the caliber of the young men who comprised the Olympic Club: a successful business or professional man who dedicated himself to his family and his community. Membership standards were high and integrity and decorum were cornerstones of the Olympic Club tradition, so what transpired next shook the club to its very foundation.

The evening of Wednesday, August 30, 1893, began as usual for the recently elected president of the Olympic Club, William Scholl. Nearly every evening after dinner, weather permitting, Scholl would walk the seven blocks from his home at 407 Royal Street to the Olympic Club to attend to any club business before relaxing with other members. On this particular evening, Scholl arrived at the clubhouse at approximately seven o'clock to find 50 or more members on hand—some engaged in conversations and smoking, some quietly reading, others playing billiards or pool. Following a brief visit with John Booth and Conrad Julier in the third-floor business office, Scholl stopped on the second floor and approached fellow member Leon Frank to play a game of billiards. They selected an empty room on the eastern side of the building near the front window.

Around the same time, members gathered outside enjoying the evening breeze on the second-floor gallery porch noticed two medium-sized men exit their carriage in front of the club while, at nearly the same time, a second carriage dropped off another man who appeared to be smaller than the others. The trio entered the club and made their way to the second-floor bar. Members recognized two of the men as Bernard Klotz, Sr., and his son, Bernard "Buddy" Klotz, Jr., but they did not recognize the third man with them. A round of drinks was ordered and several toasts were offered, each becoming louder and nastier than the previous one. To those within earshot, it was uncomfortably clear that the Klotz's maliciousness was directed toward the club's officers, particularly William Scholl, who was playing billiards just a few feet away in another room.

When informed of the Klotz party's language, Scholl thought nothing more of it and continued his billiard game with Leon Frank.

On June 11, 1893, William A. Scholl was elected President of the Olympic Club. The popular businessman had been on the Competition Committee for the club's highly successful Fistic Carnival (*New Orleans Daily Picayune*).

He may have had a passing thought that possibly the elder Klotz still harbored some degree of animosity towards him—Scholl had been unexpectedly and summarily dismissed from Bernard Klotz & Company three weeks earlier, having been accused by the elder Klotz of secretly conspiring against him in a pending business opportunity. As far as Scholl was concerned that was all water under the bridge.

Before long, both Klotz, Sr., and his son appeared at one of the other pool rooms at the rear of the second floor and engaged two young men there, asking to be shown the proper way to shoot the ball. Klotz, Jr., then walked to the front of the building to the room where Scholl and Frank were playing. Frank immediately recognized the younger Klotz, who asked him who he was playing with. Upon hearing that it was club president William Scholl, the younger Klotz eyed Scholl, who was chalking his cue. He then calmly walked up to Scholl and was reported to have said, "You son of a bitch, you are a thief." Klotz then quite unexpectedly slapped Scholl across the face. Bernard Klotz, Sr., overheard his son's remarks and added, "You are right, my boy, he is a thief." A moment of confusion and concern followed as Frank and several others began to slowly withdraw from the immediate vicinity. The younger Klotz suddenly moved towards Scholl as if to strike him again, but suddenly drew a pistol from his coat pocket. The elder Klotz then rose from his seat, drawing his own pistol, and walked through the bar towards his son and Scholl. He was heard by multiple witnesses to say, "Give it to him, Buddy!" as he continued to move toward the front of the building.

As Scholl struggled to protect himself, Bernard Klotz, Jr., pressed his pistol into Scholl's stomach and fired. A panic ensued and another shot rang out, believed to be fired by the elder Klotz, which wounded Scholl in the chest and arm. Injured and bleeding, Scholl awkwardly retreated, stumbling through the bar and down the rear stairway as a third shot was fired by the younger Klotz. When he reached the first floor, Scholl encountered James C. Peyton, the club's Collector, who inquired about the commotion upstairs. Scholl informed Peyton, "They are shooting at me," before continuing his escape through the rear of the building. Ed Donnegan, John Cullen and several other club members who had left after the first gunshots now returned to the club, noticing the Klotz group quickly move past them to board a waiting carriage, which then departed quickly up Royal Street. Various witnesses reported hearing Klotz, Sr., instruct the carriage driver to "cut him off before he escapes," obviously referring to Scholl. In all of the ensuing excitement no one could locate the wounded Scholl. A search of the adjacent property found Scholl lying in the loft of an adjoining building. He was carried back into the club's first floor reading room and attended to, assured that proper medical care was on the way. Scholl was later taken by ambulance to Charity Hospital. Within 30 minutes of the shooting, three policemen from the Second Precinct station arrived at the Olympic Club, interviewed and took statements from several eyewitnesses, and then left to apprehend the Klotz party.

Corporal Daly, Officer Bitterwolf, and Officer Whalen had already arrived at the residence of Bernard Klotz, Sr., at 157 Annunciation Street, between Melpomene and Robin streets near Annunciation Square, and had been there for some time when a carriage pulled up to the home. The officers approached the carriage and found that the only passengers were Klotz and his son. There was no sign of a third man in the carriage. The pair was immediately placed under arrest and transported to the Second Precinct station. In addition to Klotz and his son, the police also arrested James Hickory, the cab driver. Another contingent of police were dispatched to Klotz's business later that evening where they arrested John Ryan, a deliveryman who worked for Klotz and Clarence Routh, the night watchman at the Klotz factory on South Peters Street. Routh was later identified as the third man with Klotz and his son at the Olympic Club. However, at this point everyone was considered a possible accessory to the crime and all five men were booked at the Second Precinct station.

Within minutes of Klotz's booking, two prominent New Orleans attorneys, W.L. Evans and Arthur Dunn, presented themselves at the Second Precinct, stating that they had been retained to represent Klotz and to investigate the incident on his behalf. This may explain how the police arrived at Klotz's home so much sooner than he did, for they could only assume that, after a fruitless search for the wounded Scholl in the vicinity of the Olympic Club, Klotz stopped by his factory to drop off Routh and to telephone Evans and Dunn. The two attorneys arrived at approximately nine o'clock to speak with their clients and found the prisoners unfazed by their arrest and present circumstances. Evans and Dunn then left the police station and attempted to visit Scholl at the hospital, but were informed by Dr. Albert B. Myles, Chief Surgeon at Charity Hospital, that Scholl was stable and resting, but unable to receive visitors.

While Evans and Dunn were at Charity Hospital, Police Detective Littleton interviewed both Klotz and his son at length. Klotz. Sr., informed the detective that Scholl was a former trusted employee who had been dismissed by Klotz on August 11, 1893, on grounds that Scholl had conspired with the American Biscuit Company against Klotz in the sale of the company, a statement that Scholl had repeatedly denied in the past. Scholl, in fact, held a 10 percent stake in the business, but had no capital of his own invested.[44] But what made the shooting of William Scholl so shocking to the New Orleans community was not so much the assault itself, but the people involved in the incident.

Born in New Orleans on December 23, 1855, William Scholl began his education in the city's public school system, but left at the age of ten to work for the auction house of Vincent & Company. He was 32 years old when he joined Klotz in 1887 and he rose rapidly within the company, earning a 10 percent interest in the business. As a minority partner, he had been granted 10 per-

On the night of August 30, 1893, Bernard Klotz, Sr., and his son, Buddy, attacked and shot William Scholl in the second floor billiard room of the Olympic Club in front of several witnesses. Klotz had fired Scholl only three weeks earlier (*New Orleans Daily Picayune*).

cent of whatever profits Bernard Klotz declared and distributed. Scholl joined the Olympic Club in 1889, probably upon the recommendation of Bernard Klotz, and was elected as a Director in 1892, becoming involved with the club's highly successful Fistic Carnival in September of 1892. In the September 4, 1892, edition of the *Daily Picayune*, Scholl was described as being "connected with the Klotz Manufacturing Company where he holds a responsible position and is highly respected." On June 8, 1893, William Scholl was elected President of the prestigious Olympic Club and, following his dismissal from Bernard Klotz & Company,[45] had easily and quickly secured a position with the E.T. Brakenridge Lumber Company[46] located on the New Basin Canal. He was considered an aspiring 38-year-old with tremendous potential.

His attacker, Bernard Klotz, Sr., was considered by many in New Orleans to be the adopted son of Margaret Haughery, who gained her reputation as a humanitarian during the Civil War by confronting the Union pickets when crossing posted barriers to bring food to the poor and needy, defying the martial law curfew imposed by Union General Benjamin Butler.[47] As early as 1859, Margaret Haughery owned and operated Margaret's Steam and Mechanical Bakery at 74–78 New Levee Street (later South Peters Street), producing assorted cakes, crackers, and breads. Following his service in the Confederate Army during the Civil War, Bernard Klotz was employed by Margaret as her chief baker and in 1878 was admitted as a partner in the business. The business prospered until Margaret's death on February 9, 1882. For some inexplicable reason, Klotz waited for more than six months before seeking to be appointed liquidator of the business.[48] His delay in so doing would prove crucial in understanding later developments. In mid–February, Klotz promptly filed to dissolve the partnership known as Margaret Haughery & Company and announced the formation of a new partnership with P.A. Joyce, the company's bookkeeper, under the name of Bernard Klotz & Company. It was not until August 16, 1882, that Klotz filed a petition in New Orleans Civil District Court to be appointed liquidator of Margaret Haughery & Company,[49] more than six months after Margaret's death.

Margaret's personal attorneys and the executors of the Haughery estate, Charles Macready and Nicholas Burke, formally objected to Klotz's actions, principally because the six-month time period specified under the partnership agreement for Klotz to liquidate the affairs of the partnership had expired and that Klotz had failed and neglected to do so as provided in Haughery's will.[50] They stipulated that Klotz was well aware of the terms of both the partnership agreement and Margaret's will. Additionally, and more significantly, Macready and Burke believed that if Klotz were to become the court-appointed liquidator of the business, he would deliberately underestimate the value of the business so that he could purchase it himself under much better terms. Klotz protested that he had been too busy running the business, assuring the bakery's customers that there would be no interruption in either products or services. In his eyes, it was a simple oversight for the courts to sort out. The case was tried before Judge Aristice Louis (A.L.) Tissot on August 23 and 30, 1883. Charges and counter-charges of financial impropriety and self dealing were made by attorneys for both sides who provided witnesses to support their claims. Macready and Burke's attorney, Thomas Gilmore, attempted to portray Margaret Haughery as little more than an illiterate and doddering old widow more concerned with giving her money away to charity than in running her business and was, therefore, surreptitiously being taken advantage of by Klotz.

In turn, Klotz attorney A.J. Murphy attempted to prove that both Macready and Burke had bilked the estate out of tens of thousands of dollars in legal fees and that it was they who were enriching themselves in this protracted process. Nonetheless, Judge Tissot ruled in favor of Bernard Klotz on September 4, 1882, and Klotz became the court-appointed liquidator. A week later Klotz filed the business inventory with the court.[51] The appraisal firm of Gast & Llambias calculated the total assets of Margaret Haughery & Company to be just over $36,100 which was significantly lower than the appraisal of $49,258 conducted nine months previously on behalf of the executors in February of 1882 following Margaret's death. The ongoing objections of the executors notwithstanding, the court approved Klotz as liquidator and accepted the appraisal. On October 5, 1882, the inventory and assets of the business were auctioned by Hoey & O'Conner for a paltry $7,000.[52] As Macready and Burke had repeatedly warned the court, Klotz had low balled his appraisal and then manipulated the auction process in his favor. To no one's surprise, Macready and Burke filed an appeal before the Louisiana State Supreme Court, which decided in favor of the estate on April 25, 1883. However, by this time Klotz had already liquidated the business and was operating his own bakery at the same location. An advertisement in the *Daily Picayune* on May 26, 1883, stated that Bernard Klotz & Company were the "successors to Margaret Haughery & Company, operating Margaret's Steam and Mechanical Bakery."[53] All the parties could do now was to argue over the meager proceeds of the liquidation.

A hearing was requested by Macready and Burke, which was granted and heard before the Louisiana State Supreme Court on March 23, 1887. The argument was presented that Klotz had once again unfaithfully discharged his duties as liquidator of Margaret Haughery & Company for his own enrichment and to the detriment of the estate. Among the more salient facts brought out by Thomas Gilmore, attorney for Macready and Burke were

- that Margaret Haughery herself believed her 50 percent interest in the business and real estate to be worth at least $30,000 when she revised her will in October of 1881;
- that Bernard Klotz had offered Margaret Haughery's estate $32,000 for her interest in May of 1882, while he was supposedly too busy running the business to file as liquidator of the partnership, and that he later withdrew his offer when a counter-offer of $35,000 was proposed;
- that in July of 1882, Klotz had submitted a second offer to the estate for $30,000 which was ultimately rejected as it was in the form of a series of unsecured personal notes; and,
- that Klotz now expected the executors of the estate to accept a mere $3,500 as being their half of the proceeds of the liquidation performed by Klotz on October 5, 1882.

They further pointed out that Klotz had systematically withdrawn $46,000 against his original capital of $10,000 without informing either Margaret or her executors and had operated the business for the past five years without compensating the estate a single penny of the profits from running the business or, at the very least, even a modest rent on the property. Finally, and perhaps most damaging to Klotz, Macready and Burke outlined how the October 5, 1882, liquidation performed by Klotz had been an orchestrated ruse, with Klotz himself acquiring the inventory and assets of the business at substantially below-market prices through a series of "straw-men."

It was shown that bakery's machinery, entered as being worth $8,000 on the books, was sold to J.B. Camors for $1,417 and that the same machinery was still in Klotz's possession at his bakery five years after its sale to Camors. Jaeger & Depass, a general mercantile store located between South Peters and Tchoupitoulas Streets, purchased all of the "odds and ends" of the business which they promptly turned around and sold to Bernard Klotz on the same day for the same price they paid. The flawed appraisal also listed 775 barrels of flour, the majority of which were purchased by either Charles H. Schenck or J.J. Reiss, two of the three individuals who posted surety for Klotz's bond as liquidator of the business. Once again, their purchases were resold to Klotz on the same day for the same price. In light of this overwhelming evidence, the court ruled against Klotz,[54] who naturally applied for a rehearing on April 16, 1887. But after all of the evidence and testimony in the case was once again reviewed by the court Klotz's appeal was denied on May 28, 1887.[55]

Legal entanglements dogged Klotz through much of 1888 when he was sued first by the city of New Orleans over the agreed upon price per pound in a contract to provide bread to the city's prison[56] and then again by Macready and Burke over the surety provided by Charles H. Schenck and J. J. Reiss for Klotz's bond as liquidator of Margaret Haughery & Company.[57] After several months of negotiations the suit with the city was ultimately settled, but Klotz lost the case related to his surety.[58] Klotz uncharacteristically decided not to appeal the lower court's ruling, but his legal troubles were far from over.

On May 27, 1888, Klotz announced that he was moving the business to a new larger factory on South Peters and Fulton Streets, basically right across the street from the former bakery.[59] The three-story building had its offices, shipping and receiving, and sales offices on the ground floor. The bakery operation on the second floor could process more than 400 barrels of flour daily, capable of producing over 3,000 barrels of crackers per day and over 200 distinctive styles of crackers, cakes, and bread. It also processed a wide selection of pasta and noodles. The third floor was home to an extensive candy plant capable of turning out 10,000 pounds of stick candy per day as well as other tempting confections, glazed fruit, and other candies. From this facility, the company served not only New Orleans and the local region, but also Central and South America through its steamboat and maritime division.[60] Klotz financed this new facility by seeking out and affiliating with what was commonly known as "The Cracker Trust," a combination of 35 similar manufacturers across the country under single ownership. In becoming part of the Trust, Klotz would have to sell the business, property, equipment and the associated goodwill to the American Biscuit Company, the forerunner of Nabisco. This he agreed to do in writing, for which he received $300,000 of the company's stock at par.[61]

Two years later, on June 2, 1890, Klotz entered into a lease agreement with the American Biscuit Company for the old factory at 74–78 New Levee Street. By signing the lease agreement with American Biscuit Company, Klotz was clearly acknowledging that the company was the rightful owner of the property, for who would agree to pay rent to someone who did not own the property. For reasons known only to Klotz, he then refused to pay the rent stipulated in the lease for six months. Jacob Loose, president of the American Biscuit Company, dispatched one of his managers, a gentleman by the name of Summers, to New Orleans to assume control of Bernard Klotz & Company. When Klotz refused to provide access to the books and records of the business and further refused to recognize the authority of either Summers or the American Biscuit Company, Loose himself traveled to New Orleans to meet with Klotz. Receiving the same reply in person from Klotz, the company was forced to take legal action. For all intents and purposes, Klotz was now attempting to repudiate the entire transaction.

On November 21, 1890, the American Biscuit Company sought to enjoin Klotz,[62] maintaining that they had purchased the inventory and assets, including the real estate, of both Bernard Klotz & Company and Margaret Haughery & Company and that Klotz was now an employee of the American Biscuit Company. Klotz, on the other hand, sought to prove that the American Biscuit Company was an illegal monopolistic trust and that he had been induced to join the trust unwittingly. He filed to have the entire transaction annulled. As part of the filing Klotz tendered the shares of American Biscuit Company he had received. With the growing anti-trust fever sweeping the country at the time courtesy of the recently enacted Sherman Anti-Trust Act, it was not surprising that on January 8, 1891, the United States Circuit Court held for Klotz.[63]

It seems likely that Bernard Klotz believed he had dodged another bullet and had finally acquired undisputed ownership of the old Margaret's Steam and Mechanical Bakery as well as his new facility across the street. But what Bernard Klotz imagined was the beginning of a new era in 1891 for Bernard Klotz & Company would once again run afoul of his questionable business decisions, resulting in a brand new legal challenge. His old nemesis, Charles Macready, now filed suit to force the sale of the original bakery building and property at 74–78 South Peters Street in order to disgorge the 50 percent ownership interest in the property to the estate of Margaret Haughery. Incredibly, although Klotz had continued to operate the business on the premises following the sham of a liquidation sale back in October of 1882, he still had not paid the Haughery estate a single penny in rent during the past eight years. Macready's argument was successful and the two properties were seized by the Orleans Parish Civil Sheriff. An order was entered for the auction of the property on May 2, 1891.[64] Klotz petitioned for a jury trial on April 17, 1891.[65]

While he was dealing with Macready's new lawsuit, Klotz was also receiving disturbing reports from his salesmen and customers that the American Biscuit Trust was intentionally dumping crackers and bread in the New Orleans market in an effort to drive Klotz out of business. Considering the entirety of his ongoing six-year legal battle with Macready and Burke, his several lawsuits with the city over the prison bread contracts, and the recent lawsuit with the American Biscuit Company, Klotz's legal bills were no doubt rapidly mounting. Now faced with a serious new threat to his business, without question Klotz was feeling the financial strain.

Following the Civil War, the United States economy was in nearly constant recession, with the period between 1873 and 1896 being coined as the Long Recession, with back-to-back periods of moderate to severe economic slowdown, each lasting anywhere from ten months to five years. Both Margaret's Steam & Mechanical Bakery and Bernard Klotz & Company struggled to maintain their market share and, on the surface, the business appeared to be thriving. However, a series of departures of minority partners and key employees beginning in 1884 and continuing until 1893 would indicate that Bernard Klotz was not the astute businessman people generally believed him to be and that his company was not as profitable as it would appear on the surface. The partnership Klotz formed with P.A. Joyce in August of 1882 was expanded in August of 1884 to include George E. Courtain, who was dismissed a year later; David Hughes and Charles W. Dodd both resigned in 1884 to join other bakeries; Mike McGraw was hired in November of 1884 to spearhead the company steamboat sales and resigned within 18 months to return to the river; Hugh Fitzpatrick was admitted as a partner in March of 1886, bringing his expertise in candy making, and left the company in 1890 following the sale to American Biscuit; P.A. Joyce retired in August of 1889; and, of course, William Scholl was admitted as a partner on March of 1891 and was dismissed on August 1, 1893.

These personnel losses, on top of Klotz's aggressive expansion and sometimes questionable business decisions with their attendant ethical shortcomings, quite possibly had Klotz backed into a corner, hanging onto the ropes. As a further complication to his already perilous financial condition, Klotz was reported to have lost a considerable sum betting on the prizefight between John L. Sullivan and James J. Corbett held at the Olympic Club on September 8, 1892. Rumors swirled that Klotz had lost more than $10,000 on this fight alone[66] (approximately $260,000 today) which, when combined with his legal bills and the possibly of other significant gambling losses, put Klotz in a difficult financial position. On June 13, 1893, Klotz was twice accosted by men near his factory at the corner of Poydras and South Peters streets, once in the morning and then later in the afternoon.[67] Word on the street was that these supposedly random altercations were nothing more than an indiscrete attempt to force Klotz to make good on his gambling debts. By some strange machination in the depths of Bernard Klotz's twisted logic, William Scholl had become the focal point for all of Klotz's gambling debts as well as his other legal and monetary problems. Although he summarily dismissed Scholl from the company in mid–August, on the night of August 30, 1893, Klotz set out to fix the flint with his antagonist, the man he somehow believed was at the heart of his troubles. He and his son confronted an unsuspecting and unarmed Scholl at the Olympic Club, assaulted him, and shot him twice in front of several witnesses.

Upon hearing of the shooting all New Orleans was stupefied. After even a cursory reading of the events as published in the daily newspapers, how on earth did Klotz think he and his son could get away with such a brazen and deliberate act of violence in front of so many reliable witnesses? Wasting no time, the Board of Directors of the Olympic Club met on September 6, 1893, and unanimously voted to expel Bernard Klotz and his son.[68] This was certainly nothing more than a symbolic act, but it was also one which sent a resounding message to the New Orleans community at large, and the potential jury pool, as to who they believed the guilty parties to be.

As Klotz and his son sat in jail, he was also being sued by J&M Schwabacher for nearly $10,000 in past due bills, and on September 7, 1893, his factory was once again seized by the Civil Sheriff.[69] To many this appeared to be extreme for a business valued at more than $100,000 to be used to secure a $10,000 debt, so perhaps it is reasonable to assume that Klotz's precarious financial condition was, in fact, well known in the New Orleans business community after all, at least to the city's banking concerns. Given Klotz's prior history of vigorous legal defense, his refusal to fight the Schwabacher suit puzzled most observers. Across New Orleans, it seemed that everyone in town had a viable theory as to what Klotz was doing. Many assumed that he would simply mortgage the property to pay Schwabacher, while others posited that he deliberately wanted his business to fall into the hands of his old friends to hold and operate as caretakers until both the criminal and civil suits in the Scholl case were behind him. That way he could claim to have no assets and a meager net worth should a judgment for damages be levied against him. In the meantime, he responded to the inventory dumping by American Biscuit Trust by opening an office in St. Louis, home of the American Biscuit Trust, on September 16, 1891. Over the course of the next several weeks, Klotz's agents and salesmen aggressively canvased the St. Louis market offering merchants in that area low-priced goods with growing success, so much so that American Biscuit eventually ceased its dumping in New Orleans. Although a small victory for Klotz, this tactical maneuver cut deeply into his bottom line even further.

As more and more New Orleanians were learning more about Bernard Klotz's questionable business acumen, William Scholl was recovering from his wounds and was released from Charity Hospital. He was able to return to work at the lumber company and to resume his duties as president of the Olympic Club. Throughout the summer, boxing fans in New Orleans were at the end of a nearly four-month drought with the demise of the Metropolitan Club and the Crescent City Athletic Club, the Olympic Club was basically the only game in town. However, their forced abstinence was almost over. Agreed to and signed before the Scholl shooting, the Olympic Club planned to stage a battle between two featherweights, Wisconsin native Johnny Van Heest and Australian Hugh Napier in September, but many wondered if the Scholl shooting would postpone the event. As fate would have it, Scholl had made a nearly complete recovery[70] and fight patrons were eager for another contest, so management decided to press ahead with the Van Heest–Napier bout.

Johnny Van Heest versus Hugh Napier

A featherweight match typically did not draw a capacity crowd, and on September 20, 1893, there was a modest crowd on hand to watch the two bantams battle. Napier was rumored to be a miniature version of Bob Fitzsimmons, with an advantage of both height and reach over Van Heest. In that light, much of the early money was bet on the secretive Australian who refused to allow just about everyone from either the press or the Olympic Club to watch him train at Wyman's Gardens in Carrollton. The air of mystery surrounding Napier only made him a more attractive prospect to defeat Van Heest, who the local crowd was well familiar with from his two earlier matches against George Siddons at the Metropolitan Club in April and May of 1892. Van Heest did his training north of New Orleans in Abita Springs with Andy Bowen. In the days leading up to the fight a rumor began circulating that the winner of this fight was a shoo-in for a title shot against featherweight champion George Dixon at the Coney Island Athletic Club for a $10,000 purse. Had the current champion been anyone but George Dixon the Olympic Club might have had an opportunity to stage that title match in New Orleans under its own arena, but there was little doubt that Dixon would never stand for it given the city's reaction to his defeat of Jack Skelly less than a year earlier.

When the two men entered the ring at 8:45 the crowd was abuzz with their usual appraisal and commentary on the size and conditioning of the two men. Napier appeared to be the more genial and confident, Van Heest the more serious and businesslike. They were joined by Professor John Duffy and, with the weigh-in having been conducted earlier in the day at the Olympic Club, the fighters' gloves were approved and laced up by police Captain William Barrett. Duffy delivered his standard pre-fight speech, and the bout began a few minutes after nine o'clock.

The two featherweights were about as evenly matched as could be. Napier was a relative newcomer, making only his fourth professional appearance and sporting a record of one win and two losses. At nearly 23 years of age, Van Heest was already a wily veteran, having made his professional debut on October 1, 1887, and was entering his 54th fight with a record of 41 wins, 3 losses, and 9 draws/no decisions. The two featherweights, each touching just over five feet, six inches in height, traded punches for 28 evenly matched rounds. Napier had the advantage on several occasions, but failed to finish Van Heest, who landed a terrific combination of a right to the head followed by a left to the jaw that staggered the Australian. Sensing victory, Van Heest continued stalking the plucky Napier, ducking and sidestepping his wild roundhouse swings until an opening presented itself and Napier went down as a result of a terrific collision between his jaw and Van Heest's right hook. Referee John Duffy was still in his long count when Napier's seconds entered the ring and carried their man away. Van Heest was awarded the winner's share of the $2,000 purse.[71] Estimating 4,000 general admission sold at $1, plus a handful of reserved seats at $1.50 each, the gross gate was in the neighborhood of $4,300 and the net proceeds somewhere between $1,800 and $1,900 on the evening. Although not the windfall they were hoping for, it was nonetheless another modest financial success for the Olympic Club.

The same could not be said for the Crescent City Athletic Club. Still trying desperately to remain afloat, the club experienced a torrent of member's resignations, and was the subject of constant legal pressure from Bob Fitzsimmons. In an interview in New York, Fitzsimmons floated the idea of organizing all of the Crescent City Athletic Club's creditors, of which he still believed himself to be the largest, to assume control of the club and join the bidding war for the long-awaited match pending between champion James Corbett and challenger Charlie Mitchell. His overly simplified "back of the envelope" sketch of the potential financial solution intrigued many, but was ultimately rejected as being unworkable.[72]

During the first week of October, New Orleans was frequented by "Jupiter Pluvius" nearly every day non-stop, inundating the city and battering both buildings and citizens with stiff tropical winds. Despite such weather being commonplace during the height of hurricane season, to many this was nothing to fear as it was thought to be far too late in the season for a storm. Nonetheless, the city's drainage system was taxed to the limit handling the constant rainfall. Experienced residents of New Orleans knew instinctively that somewhere out in the Gulf of Mexico there was a storm and the city braced itself just in case the storm was headed their way. On Thursday morning, October 5, New Orleanians read with horror about the disaster this most recent storm had caused just south of the city. The unnamed storm[73] struck the barrier islands and settlements along the Gulf Coast with frightful ferocity. The greatest loss of life came in the small community of Cheniere Caminada, a stretch of scrubby oak groves (*cheniere* in French) cultivated during the period of Spanish rule by a sugar planter named Francisco Caminada. It was here that the shrieking winds pushed the storm surge ashore, sweeping away over 1,100 of the town's 1,200 residents, destroying every structure in the town and washing away most of the surrounding landmass. Another 850 lives were lost in Grand Isle, the Chandeleur Islands, and neighboring communities.[74] A rag-tag fleet of fishing luggers and other rescue boats carried those who survived back through the labyrinth of waterways up through Barataria Bay into Lake Salvador. As the story goes, these distraught souls believed that they were headed west to safety and kept repeating to themselves "west we go," when they were actually headed north. In any event, they named their point of embarkation on the Salaville Canal "Westwego," which still exists today.

Among the many people whose travel plans were interrupted by the savage storm was Bob Fitzsimmons. While in New Orleans discussing legal matters related to his pending divorce from his first wife Louisa, Fitzsimmons candidly admitted that he had no longer held out any real hope of collecting any of the remaining money owed to him by the Crescent City Athletic Club. Little did he know how accurate that statement was, as later in the day Louisiana Attorney General M.J. Cunningham filed a petition to have the State of Louisiana appointed as receiver for the Crescent City Athletic Club based on the $10,000 in past due license fees due to the state.[75] When this action hit the headlines it reopened old wounds and caused another wave of anti-boxing sentiment that many felt would be resolved at long last with joint action from local and state lawmakers and the courts.[76] Central to the issue was the ongoing lack of any reasonable and defensible legal definition of prizefighting that would put "scientific glove contests" and prizefights on the same level.[77] Although this long standing legal conundrum was more than a huckleberry above a persimmon to most New Orleanians, there was mounting pressure from several different sources to address the matter once and for all.

As if in denial of the swirl of events going on around them, the Olympic Club scheduled two fights for the evening of October 17, 1893. The first match, which had also been planned prior to the Scholl shooting, was between local lightweights Jack Everhardt and George Pierce in a ten-round bout for a $600 purse. This was the 22-year-old Everhardt's eighth fight and his third bout at the Olympic Club, coming in with a record of six wins against one loss and one draw/no decision. He entered the ring with an air of confidence, and was actually conversing before the fight about a rematch with Andy Bowen right after he dispatched Pierce. The newcomer Pierce, on the other hand, had trained hard for three weeks at Parmentalo's gym on the corner of Desire and Dauphine streets in the Third District, but had no such lofty expectations. He was prepared to do his best in his professional debut, but was just hoping to earn his laurels before the prestigious Olympic Club.

Everhardt easily sized up the inexperienced Pierce, and, after a handful of ineffective exchanges drew blood from a solid early punch to Pierce's sneezer, which he continued to punish with non-stop combinations to the face throughout the 1st round. Everhardt maintained his attack with a series of salvos to Pierce's head and neck until midway through the 2nd round when Everhardt had turned his opponent's nose into something resembling a seeping pomegranate. He finally sent the drained and outmatched Pierce to the canvas with a savage right cross. Referee John Duffy wisely and mercifully counted him out quickly to end the match. Everhardt would take home $550 and Pierce received $50 for his trouble. Losing to Everhardt in his debut, Pierce quickly decided he did not like groveling in the dust of defeat and never boxed again.

The second match of the night had also been in the works before the Scholl shooting and would feature a bantamweight bout between Jack Levy of New York and Johnnie Gorman of New Jersey for a $1,000 purse. It took the "Lilliputian lord" Gorman 8 rounds to knock out the affable Levy before a meager 2,500 fans.[78] It was yet another barely profitable event for the Olympic Club. Although the lower weight classes often provided truly professional caliber boxing, it was the higher weight classes, middleweight and heavyweight, that consistently attracted the largest interest and crowds.

With these two minor events off the calendar, the Olympic Club now turned its full energies to entering the bidding fracas surrounding the negotiations for the Corbett–Mitchell fight that for the past year had nearly become a full-time occupation for athletic clubs and fight promoters across the country. In behavior reminiscent of a gambling addiction, the Olympic Club pursued the Corbett–Mitchell fight with dogged determination. What is amazing is that none of the officers and directors at the Olympic Club appeared to be aware of the rapid decline in out-of-town interest in boxing in New Orleans as a viable boxing venue. Surely they had listened to and learned from their recent conversations with fight promoters, managers, and others in the boxing game around the country that the failure of both the Metropolitan Club and the Crescent City Athletic Club had tarnished the city's reputation as a trustworthy fight venue while the renewed state and local legal assault on boxing had placed boxing in New Orleans on extremely unstable footing in their eyes. The sporting community had seen this same anti-boxing sentiment take root in other cities and most were fairly certain that New Orleans was headed toward the same inevitable fate. The Corbett–Mitchell mill eventually came off on January 25, 1894, before the Duvall Athletic Club in Jacksonville, Florida, with Corbett successfully defending his heavyweight title for the first time against the aging Mitchell by knocking him out in the 3rd round. Newspaper accounts of the affair commented unfavorably regarding the unfinished arena and the club's general "lack of enterprise in the arrangements."[79] It was Mitchell's penultimate battle in the ring after nearly 17 years in the ring.

As if on cue, the state of Louisiana sought an injunction against the Olympic Club once again seeking a legal remedy to its stipulation that the "scientific glove contests" allowed under current state and local statutes were nothing more than prizefights.[80] Caught wholly unaware at this most recent action, the Olympic Club argued that the courts had already ruled on the matter two years ago before Judge Robert Marr in the McCarthy–Warren case. But what concerned the Olympic Club this time around was that the state not only wanted to prevent any future boxing events, but further sought to revoke the club's charter as a punitive measure. This sent a chillingly clear message to the other athletic clubs in the state who had been content to allow the Olympic Club to be their vanguard and fight their legal battles for them.

On Tuesday, December 12, 1893, the parties met in Division D of Civil District Court before Judge Nicholas Henry Rightor. The state was represented by Attorney General M.J. Cunningham, Edwin H. McCaleb, Jr., and B.R. Forman, while the Olympic Club would be represented by Henry P. Dart, Frank Zengel, and Charles H. Luzenberg. Dart had represented the Olympic Club in the past, but the inclusion of Zengel and Luzenberg was an interesting decision. Luzenberg was an obvious choice, being the former New Orleans District Attorney who had unsuccessfully prosecuted the Olympic Club in the McCarthy–Warren case two years prior. He was there, no doubt, to provide insight into the government's case as a former prosecutor. Zengel, however, had been one of the renegade Olympic Club members who had sided with Charles Noel and was a founding member of both the Crescent City Athletic Club and its successor, the recently chartered Auditorium Athletic Club. While he was a young but respected attorney, it was a quixotic decision to include the 28-year-old Zengel on the defense team.

After three days of testimony, the jury took less than 30 minutes to return a nearly unanimous verdict in favor of Olympic Club.[81] Opinion throughout the city was sharply divided and the press dusted off their series of past editorials[82] bemoaning the deficiencies of the legal system to resolve what to many seemed a simple proposition. A contemporary reading of the testimony finds witnesses splitting hairs so fine as to be laughable. In their view, a "prizefight" was a bare-knuckle brawl outdoors under London Prize Ring Rules while a "glove contest" was indoors with the contestants wearing gloves under Marquis de Queensbury Rules; a contestant in a glove contest was not offered a prize, but a cash purse instead.[83] Herman J. Seiferth, city editor of the *Daily Picayune*, described his viewing of the Sullivan–Corbett match as "a scientific triumph over a magnificent physical wreck," while the Fitzsimmons–Maher match was described as "a contest between science and brute force." Prominent local jeweler A.M. Hill testified that he had attended many of the Olympic Club's contests, that he had never witnessed any brutality, and that no one was ever seriously hurt.[84] Dr. W.R. Mandeville testified that all of the contests he witnessed at the Olympic Club were "characterized by no brutality whatsoever and were simply exhibitions of great skill."[85]

Everyone in the courtroom was anxious to hear the testimony of New Orleans police Captain William Barrett, a veritable fixture at events at the Olympic Club and elsewhere. He explained the differences between London Prize Ring Rules and Marquis of Queensbury Rules. He then went on to explain the difference between the matches for "points" at the Southern Athletic Club and the contests before the Olympic Club, to which the impartial lawman responded by saying that the pugilists performing at the Olympic Club were attempting to knock each other out while the participants at the Southern Athletic Club were merely trying to score points by striking their opponents. Defense attorney Henry Dart inquired what would happen if a boxer at the Southern Athletic Club would strike his opponent enough times with enough force, to which Barrett replied that the man would probably be knocked out. Following Captain Barrett was J.C. Campbell, president of the Southern Athletic Club, who spent considerable time on the stand testifying along the same lines as Barrett.

The prosecution called Colonel Boylan of the Boylan Detective Agency and former Chief of the New Orleans police force. He spoke quite eloquently about the crowds of "tough characters" who attended events at the Olympic Club. He further stated that the same element was present at the prizefights in Mississippi as well as during Mardi Gras. However, he could offer no direct testimony as to the difference between glove contests and prize fights, nor could he quantify the number of petty crimes assumed to have been committed by the "tougher element" as they allegedly preyed upon the unsuspecting fight patrons.

Lamar C. Quintero took the stand next, describing the two prize fights he had attended. The first was the Sullivan–Kilrain fight in Richburg, Mississippi, and the second being the Fitzsimmons–Maher fight at the Olympic Club. He offered that, in his opinion, the Fitzsimmons–Maher fight was the more "disgusting and brutal" of the two because Maher was "covered in blood throughout the fight." On cross examination Mr. Dart inquired why Mr. Quintero's version of brutality differed so starkly from the majority of the previous witnesses, to which the witness apologetically stated that perhaps his "moral and humane nature was more developed than that of the other witnesses who had testified."

As incredulous as the testimony and decision in the case might seem to many impartial observers, in the end the Olympic Club had successfully avoided yet another legal attack on their organization. However, any hope of reentering the bidding war for the Corbett–Mitchell fight was now out of the question as the contestants had agreed on Jacksonville, Florida, as their preferred venue. However, the fight itself was on hold while the matter worked its way through the Florida court system. Skeptics who only considered Jacksonville's lack of boxing history (table below) to be against them when competing against more experienced clubs in larger cities also eager to land the most sought after title bout in two years also failed to understand the determination and resources at work.

Number of Boxing Events

City	1891	1892	1893	1894
New Orleans	10	11	15	12
Chicago	22	27	25	30
New York	16	37	35	31
Brooklyn	9	20	39	6
Philadelphia	10	37	43	52
Boston	5	4	23	21
San Francisco	29	38	13	5
Minneapolis/St. Paul	27	10	19	13
Jacksonville	0	0	0	1
TOTAL	**128**	**184**	**202**	**171**

One of Jacksonville's most prominent citizens, 36-year-old James Edward Theodore "J.E.T" Bowden, scrambled to organize the Duvall Athletic Club after reviewing the Florida statutes and finding no specific prohibition against boxing. The determined dry goods merchant attracted additional financial backing and travelled to meet the boxers and their representatives in New York. After some discussion and negotiation, Bowden agreed to match the $40,000 bid from the Coney Island Athletic Club that Judge Newton had nervously offered before the actions of the New York legislature provided Newton with a veritable pugilistic shroud. Upon his return to Jacksonville, Bowden was greeted with a torrent of telegrams protesting the proposed event. Florida Governor Henry L. Mitchell was also on the receiving end of the anti-boxing campaign and Mitchell, a former Florida Supreme Court associate justice, took Bowden to court. When it became apparent that Bowden would prevail, the state dropped its case and the fight was allowed to proceed. Bowden then informed the fighters that the fight articles had to be amended as the purse had to be reduced from $40,000 to $20,000 because of legal expenses. Both men had been in training in anticipation of the fight and Mitchell went as far as saying that he would forgo the purse and fight Corbett privately if need be.[86] Many of the 3,000 spectators had not even reached their seats before the bout was over, even though the fight began 35 minutes late. After months of legal wrangling, the fight lasted 6 minutes and 35 seconds. The event was a disaster both critically and financially, and was the first and last fight sponsored by the Duvall Athletic Club.

Back in New Orleans, rather than contemplate the sure-fire probability that Attorney General Cunningham would appeal the lower court's verdict to the state Supreme Court, the officers and members of the Olympic Club no doubt took a deep cleansing breath and gratefully concentrated their energies on enjoying the approaching holiday season.

Six

1894

As the new year opened, nearly the full gamut of legal proceedings would be front page news. First, the anti-lottery faction was successful in their lawsuit to block the renewal of the Louisiana State Lottery Company's charter.[1] This did not deter John Morris from moving the entire operation to Honduras, from which he illegally sold lottery tickets back in America. Next, newspapers across the country were monitoring with great interest the legal challenge in Florida to the Corbett–Mitchell fight.[2] Then, as anticipated, the state of Louisiana filed their appeal in the Olympic Club case with the state Supreme Court, and finally, the New Orleans grand jury formally indicted Bernard Klotz, Sr., Bernard Klotz, Jr., and Clarence Routh for the attempted murder of William Scholl.[3]

Later in the month the Klotz family was once again indicted for "assault with a dangerous weapon" by Olympic Club member Henry P. Labatut, whose accusation included a detailed description of the attack upon William Scholl during which it was alleged that one of the Klotzes pointed their gun at Labatut and threatened to shoot him if he interfered.[4]

The crack legal team of Henry Dart, Frank Zengel, and Charles H. Luzenberg was reassembled to mount what had become the three-legged stool of the Olympic Club's standard defense against the state,[5] being that

- Louisiana Statute No. 25 of 1890 does not define the crime of prizefighting.
- Reference to any other system of laws to obtain such a definition is prohibited by both the 1879 Louisiana Constitution and by relevant case law; and
- the proviso of Louisiana Statute No. 25 of 1890 exempting "glove contests and exhibitions between human beings in the rooms of regularly chartered athletic clubs" prevails so long as these exhibitions are not accompanied by disorder or unlawful assembly and are held under strict police surveillance.

This strategy had prevailed in every prior court challenge and there was every reason to believe that the Olympic Club would once again be successful. There was nothing in the law that adequately defined a prizefight; no term of art that said a boxing match deemed to be disgusting or brutal was, in fact, a prizefight; no characterization of its patrons being from the wrong side of the tracks would transform a scientific glove contest into a prizefight. Despite renewed editorial opposition from the city's newspapers, chiefly from *The Times-Democrat*,[6] the Olympic Club felt confident that they would once again be exonerated.

In the interim, Olympic Club members spent the better part of February and March discussing and debating the ongoing delays and maneuvering in the Klotz trial. Those claiming to have been present grew in number almost in direct proportion to the details provided in their individual accounts of the mayhem and the amount of alcohol they consumed. Through it all, the club's officers and directors, in a show of extreme confidence in the club's legal position, were busy putting together a match between Jack Burke and Jack Everhardt scheduled to take place in May.

On April 23, 1894, the Louisiana Supreme Court announced its decision. Speaking for the majority, Justice Lynn B. Watkins provided an elaborate opinion which emphatically shifted the responsibility for the current legal stalemate from the courts to the legislature, indicating that the legislature alone had the ability to remedy the situation. Chief Justice Francis T. Nicholls provided the dissenting opinion, cautioning legislators about converting the present prohibitive statute into a more permissive one, a position not wholly unexpected from the staunch anti-boxing former Louisiana governor. Justice Joseph A. Breaux sided with Justice Watkins and thus the court affirmed the verdict of the New Orleans jury, essentially exonerating the Olympic Club.[7] Knowing that the state still had ten days to request for a rehearing by the court, William Scholl and the other officers of the Olympic Club were reluctant to express their exuberance publicly. Instead they answered all inquiries by saying that they were wrapped up in planning the club's spectacular eleventh anniversary celebration and preparing for their upcoming glove contests. A damper was firmly placed on their frail hopes when, as expected, the state filed for a rehearing on Monday, April 30, and everyone now held their breath awaiting the court's decision.[8] When the court refused the rehearing on May 14 there was an initial sigh of relief until, upon a more detailed reading of the court's decision, it was discovered that the court had remanded the case to the lower court for a new trial due to certain perceived irregularities in the presentation of evidence.[9] A minor technicality, perhaps, but certainly enough to cause concern.

As they awaited their next round in court, William Scholl and the Olympic Club were still trying to arrange a match between Bob Fitzsimmons and Joe Choynski, raising the club's bid to $7,000 which was quickly rejected by Fitzsimmons who predictably countered with a $15,000 demand.[10] The Olympic Club raised their offer to $8,000, but was outbid by a group from Boston that acceded to the fighters' demand for a $15,000 purse.

The news of the Olympic Club's new trial was barely out when many New Orleanians learned, to their surprise, that a new boxing entity, the Auditorium Athletic Club, had been formed by Frank Williams and Frank Zengel out of the remnants of the failed Crescent City Athletic Club. Williams and Zengel were both members of the Olympic Club and founding members of the Crescent City Athletic Club. With the anti-boxing sentiment from both the public and private sectors steadily growing, pundits predicted another pugilistic funeral. The new club first made its presence known by advertising an exhibition featuring the enormously popular World Heavyweight Champion James J. Corbett on Friday, March 2, with general admission tickets going for 50 cents and reserved seats for a dollar.

On the evening of the event, a lackluster crowd of 3,000 roamed freely throughout the largely vacant wooden arena on Carrollton Avenue and Canal Street, many of them women eager to catch a glimpse of "Gentleman Jim" to see for themselves if he was as handsome in person as the stories and engravings of him in the newspapers seemed to indicate. Shortly after eight o'clock in the evening, Professor John Duffy kicked off the festivities by introducing the first of several preliminary exhibition bouts, a three-rounder between Owen Harney and Jack Everhardt. This was followed by a demonstration of French-style boxing known as "savate" featuring Professor Duson and his pupil Baquie, whose athletic antics had them leaping, gyrating, and kicking with great exertion, providing an interesting and entertaining diversion, for which they were cheered and applauded for their efforts by an appreciative crowd. Next on the card was a spat of uneventful sparring between Johnnie Eckhardt and Lucas Siefcar, both relatively unknown to New Orleans, but who amused the crowd nonetheless. This was followed by an unusual three-round exhibition match between welterweight George Pierce, who towered over lightweight Andy Bowen. A sedate set-to between Louis Knoechel (Knuckles) and Joseph Cornu was followed by an entertaining exhibition between John Duffy and Pat Allen, much appreciated by the crowd. There may have been a few in the crowd who remembered Duffy from his earlier fighting days or who took lessons from the affable Irish "Professor" before he became a nationally recognized boxing referee.

Finally, Corbett arrived and was greeted with cheers and thunderous applause, crawling through the ropes and stepping to the center of the ring to address the audience. After thanking them for their warm welcome, he treated them to a master class in scientific boxing against Professor John Donaldson, stopping from time to time to explain his technique and method of boxing.[11] While disappointing financially, the uncontroversial event was successful in drawing the public's attention to the new venture, without attracting the ire of either the clergy or the reform-minded citizenry.

Just seven days after the state Supreme Court handed down their decision in the Olympic Club case, the new Auditorium Athletic Club was first out of the gate, announcing a match between Andy Bowen and Stanton Abbott, the lightweight champion of England. The fight would take place at the old Crescent arena on Carrollton Avenue and Canal Street, now called the Auditorium Club, on Monday, May 7, for a purse of $2,500 in a fight to the finish. This term "finish fight," or a fight to the finish, was a central element in the brutality thesis put forth by the anti-boxing faction, arguing that the longer two men beat on each other without result, the bloodier and potentially more dangerous the fight became, pandering to the bloodlust of a lower class of citizen. When contacted by state Attorney General Cunningham in this regard, Frank Zengel was quick to agree and the club modified the fight articles for the bout to go no more than 10 rounds so as not to run afoul of a still as yet "uninterpreted" law in exchange for the state's agreement not to interfere with the event.[12]

Despite having 5,000 patrons on hand, the immense arena designed to hold 13,000 looked nearly empty. Many felt that Bowen had seen better times and was no longer the threat he was when he fought Billy Myer in 1891. Too many punches over the course of too many rounds had taken their toll on Bowen. No one would dare insinuate that Bowen was a pushover or a pug, but rather that he now faced a younger, stronger Englishman who looked formidable, at least from the newspaper's published descriptions of his training workouts. The sparse crowd watched as Bowen and Abbott fought to a draw after ten mediocre rounds in which "both science and brutality were absent."[13]

Still, at $1.50 per general admission ticket, the new club covered the purse and expenses with room to spare. After an eight-month involuntary hiatus, the renewed interest in boxing among "that class of people" seemed to be gaining momentum. One can only assume that the newspaper's writer was referring to the many laborers in the crowd supporting Bowen, but which also included bankers, professional men, and merchants. All of these fans would have to wait another three weeks before the next event.

Jack Burke versus Jack Everhardt

Originally scheduled by the Olympic Club for Monday, May 21, 1894, the match between Jack Burke and Jack Everhardt had to be postponed due to a training injury experienced by Everhardt that delayed the event until Saturday, May 26. The club extended free general admission for its members and reserved seating for only $0.50 while the general public would pay $1 for general admission and $1.50 for reserved seating,[14] hoping that a packed arena would demonstrate to observers, including politicians and potential jurors, the public's great love of boxing in general and the Olympic Club in particular. Not even their cut-rate prices could overcome an unexceptional matchup. Everhardt, while a strapping physical specimen, was totally lacking when it came to the rudiments of boxing. He was a "miserable judge of distance" and those who had seen him before the Olympic Club were unimpressed with his deficit of boxing acumen. Burke was chiefly remembered for his marathon match with Bowen that lasted 110 rounds just a year earlier. But even before his broken hands prevented him from engaging Bowen, the punches he managed to land had little or no power behind them.

The bout was scheduled to go 15 rounds, a decision specifically designed to deflect the state attorney general's previously expressed legal objections to "finish fights," being a match that would last until one man could no longer fight. Scattered among the meager crowd was a number of state legislators who wanted to see what a "scientific glove contest" looked like firsthand. Unfortunately, what they witnessed was a ludicrously out-of-shape Burke continually attempting to avoid a knockout blow from a trim but clumsy, overly aggressive Everhardt, who was ultimately awarded the decision from referee Lloyd Gearhardt at the conclusion of the 15th round. Although the country was once again in the midst of yet another recession, with unemployment reaching anywhere from 12 percent to over 18 percent, in the end it was not the cost of the ticket, but the caliber of the card that determined the attendance.[15] To many, the once lustrous Olympic Club, while not tarnished, had lost some of its sheen.

James Barry versus James Gorman

The following month, on Saturday, June 2, the Olympic Club featured a 25-round match between bantamweights James Barry and James Gorman for a $7,000 purse. In a hard fought and evenly matched bout, it would be Barry's conditioning that allowed him to outlast Gorman for ten rounds, eventually winning by a knockout in the 11th.[16] The winner of this match was to take on the winner of the upcoming Levy–

Connors match. That contest took place less than two weeks later, on Thursday, June 14, when the Olympic Club brought back English champion Jack Levy to face off against Johnny Connors from Springfield, Illinois, in a 25-round bout for a $1,000 purse. During the 1st round Connors concentrated on head blows with the effect of closing Levy's left eye and reducing his face to "a mass of crimson jelly" by the 3rd round. Referee Lloyd Gearhardt repeated his warnings to Connors about dirty fighting—specifically sliding the heel of his laced glove across Levy's face when coming out of clinches—behavior so obvious that it drew boos from the sparse crowd. A drained and battered Levy was barely able to answer the bell for the fifth round and succumbed to back-to-back right hooks to the jaw.[17] Anyone present who believed that what they had just witnessed was "scientific," had only to watch Levy's seconds carry their bloodied fighter back to his corner to try to revive him. Despite the times, this was a tough way for a man to earn $300 to be sure.

Between the two June events, the Olympic Club membership reelected the full Scholl-led ticket, which faced only token opposition. Scholl campaigned on a populist-style platform which promised to improve the club's facilities and amenities.[18] Following the election, the final event to take place in June was the telegraphic rebroadcast of the Fitzsimmons–Choynski fight which had been successfully blocked in the Florida courts and was now set to take place in Boston.[19] The match was held in mid–June, and was declared a draw when police intervened in the 5th round to stop the fight, much to the dismay of Fitzsimmons, who had Choynski on the ropes both figuratively and literally.[20] Recording Secretary James C. Peyton called out the news received by the Olympic Club's telegraph to several hundred members scattered throughout the clubhouse. Between telegraph messages the crowd engaged in a spirited discussion on the two boxers and wagered on the outcome, both activities enhanced by generous libations flowing freely from the bar.

July began with the much anticipated benefit for longtime club secretary William Davidson Ross. There were a dozen three-round sparring exhibitions and personal appearances by several prominent names in the sporting world, including Jack Dempsey.[21] Later in the month the club returned to its familiar game plan, announcing a new Fistic Carnival to be held in September. Current pending offers to several fighters—among them James Corbett, Bob Fitzsimmons, Peter Maher, Joe Choynski, and Jack McAuliffe—were going to be consolidated in an effort to recapture the old magic.[22] William Scholl and other club representatives were candid about the club's willingness and ability to provide the liberal purses they had in the past, especially as they had already announced plans for improvements to the club's facilities.

Scholl had campaigned on a promise to actually build the long-awaited natatorium facility and on Tuesday, July 24, he informed the press that plans from the architectural firm of DePass & Behan were now finalized. The Olympic Club would construct a new two-story brick building behind the existing clubhouse on Chartres Street that would house the natatorium and a new gymnasium on the bottom floor and over 1,500 lockers on the upper floor. The first floor would also feature 24 white marble Turkish baths with hot and cold running water.[23] Scholl wanted to placate the anti-boxing sentiment that existed within the Olympic Club by demonstrating to them, and anyone else watching, that the club was more than just a de facto boxing enterprise.

Across town, the Auditorium Athletic Club returned to the spotlight with a bout in August between Andy Bowen and Jimmy Carroll, both well known to the New Orleans boxing public. Their offering was a long-awaited rematch of their 1890 fight at the Olympic Club which Carroll won. Despite what many felt would be an attractive match, the event was far from a sell out. The Auditorium Club could only attract another modest crowd of 5,000 on Wednesday, August 8. During 25 rounds neither man gained the advantage over the other and neither man drew blood. Bowen out-punched Carroll two to one, but retreated into what had become his customary aggressive-passive cycle—after pummeling his opponent, he squandered the opportunity to put away Carroll by failing to follow through. In the end, in an occurrence becoming all too common in boxing circles, referee John Duffy declared the match a draw.[24] The lackluster crowd appreciated the effort of the two fighters, but was disgruntled with Duffy's decision as that meant all bets were off. This was the second consecutive draw fought at the Auditorium Club and as the fans filed out the doors many of the departing cranks let management know that they expected more.

For a change of pace, the Olympic Club announced a continuous pool tournament for the Louisiana state championship, set to take place in the second-floor parlor of their clubhouse over three weeks in August. Medals and cash prizes were offered and the event secured the participation of serious stickmen Dave Moore, Henry Miller, Marc Tarleton, Pete Miller, Theodore Peterson, and Ed Tarleton. All of these contestants were either touring professionals or owned pool parlors in the city. This was another plank in Scholl's platform of providing other-than-boxing entertainment and activities for his membership.

Even as planning for the pool tournament was underway, Scholl traveled to New York where he was able to obtain an agreement, with the help of Richard K. Fox of the *Police Gazette*, between Bob Fitzsimmons and Dan Creedon to meet in September for a $5,000 purse.[25] He also offered $25,000 for a match between James Corbett and Peter Jackson and $3,000 for a match between Peter Maher and Frank Slavin. As he waited for a response to these offers, a new wrinkle was added to the mix: The Edison Kinetoscope Exhibition Company offered to pay $15,000 to film the Corbett–Jackson fight.

The first known boxing film was the Jack Cushing–Mike Leonard fight filmed June 14, 1894. The 6-round bout was filmed in Edison's Black Maria Studio in West Orange, New Jersey, prolonged between rounds by the film crew constantly adjusting lights and restocking film. Each round was filmed individually. Leonard eventually knocked out Cushing in the 6th round.[26] The new Edison offer was an interesting development, but not much more than a publicity gimmick as the filmmakers asked for the ring size to be reduced to a minuscule ten feet by ten feet to accommodate the limitations of the camera. The Edison group also required that the event be private, as the positioning of the camera and the crew around the smaller ring would effectively block the view of an audience. There had been numerous interruptions during the filming of the Cushing–Leonard fight when fans leaned over the ropes for a better view, blocking the camera. While this was an intriguing new wrinkle on the promotion of boxing to the masses, Corbett's manager William Brady reminded the Edison people that they already had an offer of $25,000 from the Olympic Club on the table and politely declined the opportunity.

Back in New Orleans, the Olympic Rifle Club participated in the first of three shoots to occur in August and September as part of the Louisiana State Rifle League's state championship competition. Five 12-man teams were scheduled to participate: the Olympic Rifle Club, the Volunteer Rifle Club, the Broadway Rifle Club, the Imperial Rifle Club, and the Jackson Rifle Club. Scholl was making good on his promise to involve the club in more non-boxing activities while awaiting word from Richard Fox in New York on his proposed boxing matches.

Desperate for a winner, the Auditorium Club reached back for a nostalgic favorite in Jack Dempsey, pitting the Nonpareil against Australian Billy McCarthy on September 5 for a $2,000 purse. Counting on Dempsey to be a sure-fire draw, ticket prices were raised to $2 for general admission and $3 for reserved seats. The crowd started building outside of the Auditorium Club arena around seven o'clock the night of the fight, lingering long after the scheduled start with the hope that ticket prices would be lowered. They would be sorely disappointed. Bob Fitzsimmons made something of a grand entrance just before nine o'clock and paid a visit to Dempsey's dressing room before being seated in Mayor John Fitzpatrick's ringside box. Not long after he was seated the two fighters and their seconds entered the ring, received their instructions from referee John Duffy, and the fight commenced.

Dempsey had the better of the fight throughout the scheduled 20 rounds, but when Duffy declared the bout a draw there was a protest from Dempsey, who believed he should have been awarded the decision on points. He was reminded that the fight articles stated that the fight was automatically a draw if both men were still standing after 20 rounds. The crowd agreed with Dempsey, but to no avail. No one knew it at the time, but this would be Dempsey's penultimate battle. Although the attendance provided more than enough to cover the purse, the third consecutive draw had fight fans up in arms. Many accused the club of kowtowing to the anti-boxing gang by watering down the fight articles and limiting the number of rounds.[27]

Unbeknownst to the sparse crowd inside the arena, at approximately quarter to ten o'clock, with the fight already well underway, nearly a hundred men made their way up a wooden exterior stairway thinking they might be lucky enough to catch a glimpse of the fight through the cracks in the wooden planks. They were turned away by police stationed on the stairway's top landing, but they had nowhere to retreat to as the swell of men from the street continued. Suddenly, a section of the stairway collapsed, sending 40 or more men to the street some 15 feet below. Police quickly restored order and ambulances carted off 20 young men with minor injuries.[28]

The Triple Event

In early August, Bob Fitzsimmons agreed to defend his World Middleweight title against Dan Creedon before the Olympic Club for a $5,000 purse. The fight articles were executed in New York at the offices of *The Police Gazette*, signed by William Scholl on behalf of the Olympic Club and by Bob Fitzsimmons. The contract was promptly dispatched to St. Louis for Creedon's signature. With the Fitzsimmons–Creedon fight in hand, the Olympic Club set about arranging for two other matches to fill out their new triple event. As in the 1892 original, the club hoped to arrange all three bouts to be for world championships. There was considerable talk of having James Corbett face Peter Jackson, but this was a match that everyone in the country was trying to land with the same fervor that they had gone after the Fitzsimmons–Hall and the Corbett–Mitchell matches. No one counted on having a reluctant champion in Corbett, who declared both publicly and privately on many instances that he preferred the stage to the ring. Fitzsimmons was now pursuing Corbett as vehemently as Jim Hall had once pursued the New Zealander. Fitzsimmons was eager to add the heavyweight title to his resume, but Corbett would have none of it. In the interim Fitzsimmons was content to accept a very modest purse for what in his mind was only an appetizer in Creedon until he could get to Corbett for the main course and a much larger payday.

Jack Everhardt versus Stanton Abbott

Only days after the Fitzsimmons–Creedon fight was announced, the club signed the English Lightweight Champion, Stanton Abbott, to fight Jack Everhardt on Tuesday, August 21, 1894, for a $1,500 purse. As this was not a world championship title fight the club considered it to be merely a warm up for the Triple Event, a match that would shake off the dust at their arena and get their service personnel back in fighting shape so to speak. On the night of the event an extended thunderstorm made everything "bustle and confusion." Hacks and carriages clogged Royal Street, carrying a sizeable portion of the 7,000 hearty souls who braved the inclement weather to nearly fill the arena. Just before nine o'clock the combatants entered the arena with their seconds for the weigh-in at ringside, Abbott tipping the scales at 132 pounds and Everhardt just a half pound heavier. The arena's retractable roof was closed against the rainstorm, but there were intermittent rivulets of runoff that floated down onto the crowd. Abbott drew the 'loser's corner," many of whose past occupants had gone down in defeat. The fighters met at the scratch line and were given their instructions by referee Lloyd Gearhardt. At 9:20 the bell tolled to begin the melee.

At one time or another, scrappy New Orleans native Jack Everhardt was the Middleweight, Welterweight, and Lightweight Champion of the South who often fought men much larger than him. The bout on August 21, 1894, against Stanton Abbott would be his fourth appearance at the Olympic Club (from an unknown 19th century publication).

The opening rounds were

uninspired, with each man preferring to clinch rather than to counter the other's attack, a tactic which opened up by the middle of the 3rd round. By the 4th round both men engaged in infrequent waves of equal give and take, each drawing blood from well-placed right hooks. Four more rounds of alternating concentration on body blows followed by close in-fighting, moving to sustained jabs to the head and neck followed by more in-fighting. The next 3 rounds saw plenty of cautious sparring, devoted to what appeared to be an ongoing "studying modes of attack," which those present would have called coasting, but which allowed both Everhardt and Abbott to regain their strength. Few punches of any consequence made an impact, although towards the end of the 11th round there was a protest from Abbott's corner that the New Orleanian had engaged in unfair tactics, but their argument was in vain. Everhardt was content to grind down Abbott, sending the English champion to the mat several times. In the 25th round Everhardt floored Abbott almost immediately for an eight-count. Upon rising Everhardt began pushing Abbott onto the ropes, at one point almost sending him through the ropes, and drawing more cries of foul. In trying to steady himself Abbott left himself wide open to Everhardt's onslaught. He dropped to a knee, awaiting the eight-count from referee Gearhardt. Regaining his footing, Abbott was greeted a hard left that drove the Englishman to clinch, in so doing Everhardt swung him to the side, bashing his head into one of the ring's padded wooden stakes. The roar of the crowd intensified as Everhardt continued his attack, pushing Abbott to the floor, then pounding him with a strong combination. Everhardt landed a hard right to Abbott's jaw that put him down for Gearhardt's ten-count. Both corners emptied, words were exchanged, but Everhardt was declared the winner.[29] Gearhardt, who throughout the latter rounds was on the receiving end of a relentless barrage of boos for his dismal handling of the fight, primarily for failing to warn Everhardt for his thug-like style of boxing, was the last to leave the ring. While financially successful, the evening was a continuation of subpar boxing that Scholl and the Olympic Club had hoped desperately to avoid. Boxing fans could go just about anywhere to see two palookas dust each other off, but they expected more from the Olympic Club.

Following the Abbott–Everhardt mill in late August, an agreement was reached between the world bantamweight champion Billy Plimmer from England and Johnnie Murphy from Boston for a $4,000 purse. With time running out and the third match of the triple event missing, the Olympic Club was running out of viable options. There would be no last-minute windfall, so Scholl and company resigned themselves to arranging a rematch between Everhardt and Abbott to fill the bill. It was clearly not the match they hoped for, but their last match had drawn 7,000 fans, so the return bout had promise.

Billy Plimmer versus Johnnie Murphy

First up on Monday night, September 24, would be Billy Plimmer against Johnnie Murphy for the World Bantamweight Championship. At that time, the recognized weight limit was 110 pounds or less, so when both men weighed in over the limit—Murphy at 113 and a half pounds and Plimmer at 113 pounds even—the prospect of a title match was off the table, which seemed of little concern to the 4,000 eager fans assembled. When Professor John Duffy introduced John Eckhardt, the famed New York referee who would oversee the match, he was greeted with a resounding complimentary cheer from the crowd. So intense was the pugilistic community's dislike for Lloyd Gearhardt over the Everhardt–Abbott fight that he would never referee an event at the Olympic Club again.

Plimmer was the taller of the two and had the better of the fight for the majority of the 25 scheduled rounds which saw a game but fading Murphy hang on to avoid defeat starting in the 5th round. Each man scored a clean knock down and the match slowly unfolded without incident, without either man seizing the advantage, and without a clear victor. In what had become the new normal in the New Orleans boxing world, with both men standing at the end of the fight, the match was automatically declared a draw.[30]

Jack Everhardt versus Stanton Abbott

On Tuesday night, the 25th, there were only 5,000 fans gathered to watch lightweights Jack Everhardt and Stanton Abbott in a rematch of their August 21 fight at the Olympic Club that drew 7,000. To diffuse any lingering animosity for those who had witnessed the prior fight, the Olympic Club offered an undercard to begin the evening. A 6-round exhibition between two lightweights—Young Griffo (Albert Griffiths), one of a growing number of young Australian fighters who found steady work in America, and his trainer Micky Dunn, who towered over his charge by nearly ten inches. The lighthearted match showcased the talented 25-year-old Young Griffo, nicknamed the "Australian Will o' the Wisp," who already had 173 professional matches under his belt by the time he stepped into the ring. Young Griffo ducked and dodged the salvos of his taller, heavier, and deliberately slower opponent, entertaining the crowd with dazzling feints and skillful footwork. Although classed as a lightweight, that would be from the waist up only, his lower body resembling that of a heavyweight. The crowd demonstrated their appreciation with an extended ovation at the conclusion of the 6 rounds. Little did anyone know at the time, but this lighthearted exhibition was to be the highlight of the evening.

Upon the entrance of Bob Fitzsimmons, Jake Kilrain, Jack Dempsey, and Johnnie Murphy, the crowd burst into a series of sustained ovations as each man found their seats in their respective reserved boxes at ringside. A booming cheer filled the air when Professor John Duffy was introduced as the referee for the main event. A few minutes before nine o'clock, Abbott and Everhardt entered the ring, Abbott first followed by Everhardt only seconds later. There was prolonged parley during the weigh-in about deciding the fight on points, with the eventual agreement that the fight would be declared a draw if both men were still standing at the conclusion of the scheduled 25 rounds. This news was greeted with a chorus of boos and curiously a few cheers from the impatient crowd, perhaps a glimmer of things to come. At a quarter after the hour the fight was finally ready to commence.

From the opening bell through the conclusion of the 25th round, the fight was marked by a general lack of enthusiasm on the part of the antagonists. Punches were exchanged, energies expended, occasionally a combination made someone in the crowd stand up and take notice. But for 25 tedious rounds, the two men pawed at each other, clinched, poked, sparred, and danced. Compared to the opening exhibition with Young Griffo, the Everhardt–Abbott match was "tame and disappointing" by comparison, resulting in yet another 25-round draw.[31] Most in attendance agreed that both Abbott and Everhardt had missed their true calling, whatever that might be other than pugilism. Postfight Abbott was an outspoken critic of the "bloomin' pillows" used for gloves, asking the press how a man was supposed to do any damage with five-ounce padded gloves.

Bob Fitzsimmons versus Dan Creedon

Shrugging off their disappointment in the first two matches of the triple event, a crowd of nearly 7,000 turned out on Wednesday night the 26th to witness the feature match between Bob Fitzsimmons and Dan Creedon for the World Middleweight Championship, defined in the fight articles, at Creedon's insistence, as being below 150 pounds. Somewhat surprisingly, Fitzsimmons was only a two and a half to one favorite in the betting parlors throughout the city despite being the crowd favorite. With a training camp established in Bay St. Louis on property he purchased after the Dempsey fight, the lanky champion was a frequent fixture at fights at the Olympic Club and other venues in New Orleans when not touring the country with his theatrical shows. To many in the crowd, the cherry on top of tonight's fight was the prospective future match between Fitzsimmons and the current heavyweight champion James Corbett that the Olympic Club was still trying to piece together. If and when Fitzsimmons defeated Creedon, his constant challenges to Corbett could no longer be ignored by the reluctant champion.

Bob Fitzsimmons would defend his World Middleweight title for the last time against Dan Creedon at the Olympic Club. He wanted to move up to the heavyweight class and would eventually capture that title in 1896 against Peter Maher. He would become the first boxer to win three world championships in three different weight classes when he won the Light Heavyweight title in 1903 (from an unknown 19th century publication).

Patrons had hardly settled in their seats when the bell for the 1st round sounded. Creedon tried to set the pace, but Fitzsimmons was content to study his opponent, dodging and dancing around him without any serious attack until just before the end of the round when Fitzsimmons unleashed a strong left jab, right hook combination followed by three powerful jabs to the head that clearly stunned Creedon. Answering the bell for the 2nd round, Fitzsimmons calmly walked up to Creedon and landed a jolting left that caused the challenger to try to cover up before the inevitable right from Fitzsimmons could catch up to him. Fitzsimmons was now the aggressor, stalking Creedon, scoring with a torrent of different punches that came so fast that Creedon simply had no defense. He couldn't clinch as Fitzsimmons would dance away for just the briefest moment before stepping back in to wail away at the beleaguered Creedon. A jolting left upper-cut sent Creedon to the mat "in a heap," but he managed to rise before Duffy finished the ten-count. Fitzsimmons moved in for the kill, landing a succession of lefts to the head before throwing a terrific right hook that broke Creedon's nose and knocking him backwards several steps before he collapsed, at this point thoroughly thrashed and utterly defenseless. The fight was over in 4 minutes and 40 seconds.[32]

The Olympic Club's triple event ended on a high note. For Scholl and the club, the three-day carnival drew approximately 16,000 fans and resulted in gate receipts approaching $32,500 against combined purses of $9,000 and estimated expenses of $3,500 for an anticipated net to the club of $20,000 or more. Although the event did not result in the same degree of success as the Fistic Carnival, President William Scholl had every reason to be pleased with the preliminary results. When the final accounting was completed in the coming days, not only should the club have the necessary funds to follow through on his promised building program and renovations, but the club's reputation as the premiere boxing venue in the city would still be beyond doubt. Even with the uneven caliber of boxing and the fans' sometimes dissatisfied reaction to the Everhardt–Abbott fight, Scholl reasoned that he and the club had little to fear from the upstart Auditorium Athletic Club. His only concern now was getting through the upcoming trial of Bernard Klotz and his son for their shooting attack on him back in August of 1893.

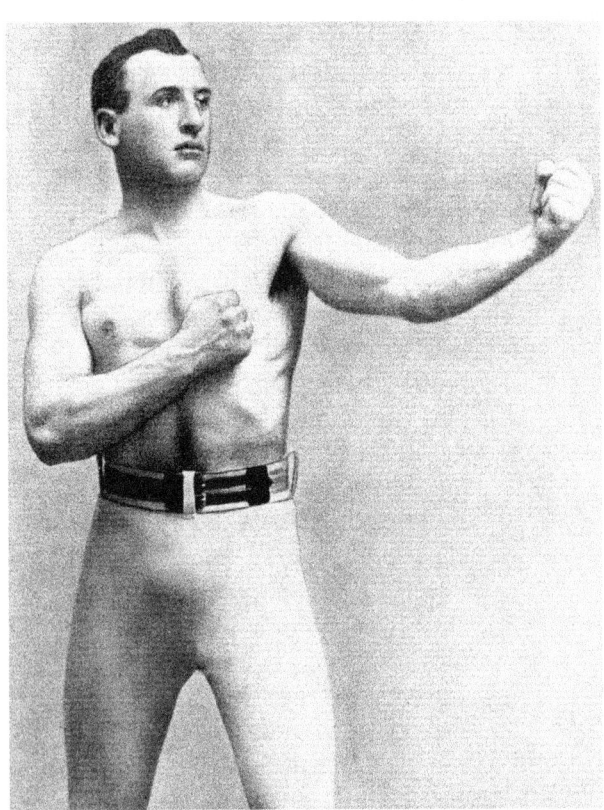

New Zealander Dan Creedon was undefeated in 29 fights and was the reigning Australian Middleweight Champion making his first attempt to win the World Middleweight Championship title against Bob Fitzsimmons (from an unknown 19th century publication).

The Trial of Bernard Klotz

More than a year had elapsed between the arrest of Bernard Klotz, Sr., Bernard Klotz, Jr., and Clarence Routh and the start of their trial. Exactly 413 days, in fact, as tallied and prominently printed daily on the newspaper's front page by the *Times-Democrat*. It was a lengthy period of wearisome legal wrangling over potential jurors and alleged "irregularities" in juror selection, complete with charges of jury tampering, during which Klotz and his son were both found to be in contempt of court.

Finally, on October 17, 1894, Judge James C. Moise convened Division B of Criminal District Court in the case of the City of New Orleans versus Bernard Klotz, Sr., Bernard Klotz, Jr., and Clarence Routh for the attempted murder of William A. Scholl on August 30, 1893. The Klotz group was represented by former Assistant District Attorney Lionel Adams, who from the outset of the proceedings attempted to set up a self-defense plea, stating that his clients had a pre-arranged meeting with Scholl at the Olympic Club by Scholl's request, during which meeting Scholl attempted to strike Buddy Klotz with his pool cue. Klotz and his father were simply trying to defend themselves. As improbable as this line of defense would appear, during five days of testimony, Adams paraded a string of 24 character witnesses, from Chief of Police D.M. Gasser to the *Daily Picayune*'s sportswriter Harry "Bantam" McEnery, and highlighted by what felt like an entire convent full of nuns from both the Sisters of Charity and the Mount Carmel Asylum, all of whom extolled the positively saint-like character, integrity, and virtue of Bernard Klotz, Sr. At first blush these witnesses provided a glimmer of hope for the Klotz faction. That was until Assistant District Attorney John J. Finney established during his cross examination of these witnesses that none of them had actually been present at the Olympic Club on the night that Klotz and his son shot an unarmed William Scholl.

Then Adams called defense witness Mike Shea to the stand. Shea operated a barroom where the defense alleged that Buddy Klotz and William Scholl met on the afternoon of August 30, 1893, during which Shea claims to have overheard a heated argument between the two men. Shea testified that he threw both men out of the bar, but that as he was so doing he heard them agree to meet later that night when Klotz's father could be present. Finney, who succeeded Lionel Adams as Assistant District Attorney, so thoroughly discredited the contrived testimony of Mike Shea on cross examination, that reporters covering the trial felt that Shea may well be charged with perjury.[33]

In an effort to shore up Shea's poor performance, Adams then called Bernard Klotz, Jr., to the stand. Klotz testified that, on the afternoon of August 30, he had quite unexpectedly encountered William Scholl on the street and invited him for a drink. It was then that the younger Klotz supposedly informed Scholl that the elder Klotz magnanimously wished to heal the breach caused by Scholl's inexcusable disloyalty in the American Biscuit Company matter and to see if they might not salvage the relationship. This preposterous and highly questionable statement drew snickers from the observers in the courtroom. Klotz continued unfazed by the reaction in the courtroom, saying that he had told Scholl that, being the gentlemen that they were, the Klotz's were offering Scholl an olive branch. Another round of snickering earned a prolonged gavel pounding from Judge Moise. Klotz then characterized Scholl's reaction as argumentative and unappreciative of his charitable overtures, resulting in their being thrown out of Shea's bar. Both Shea and Klotz stipulated that this occurred between three and five o'clock on the afternoon of August 30, 1893, but neither could be more specific regarding the time.

Klotz then dutifully recited his version of the events of the night of the shooting at the Olympic Club. In an attempt to shore up Adams' self-defense theory, he stipulated that he and his father just happened to be carrying pistols as was their habit, and that it was Scholl who was the aggressor. For the first time, the younger Klotz admitted that it was he who had fired all three shots, trying to refute prior testimony from several prosecution witnesses that his father had fired the second shot that wounded Scholl in the chest and arm. Clearly young Klotz was willing to admit to being the sole shooter and, in so doing, clear his father of the attempted murder charge.

Adams then called George E. Courtain, a bill of lading clerk and former partner at Bernard Klotz & Company, who testified that around five o'clock on the afternoon of August 30 he answered a telephone call in the second-floor bakery shop of the Klotz plant from William Scholl, who asked to speak with Buddy Klotz. He later recanted this testimony, stating that what he actually heard was Klotz telling his father that they were going to meet Scholl at the Olympic Club that night.

Klotz attorney Lionel Adams provided the closing argument for the defense. He reiterated his client's assertion that Scholl was a disloyal and ungrateful employee who had betrayed his employer and that it was the Klotz family who had attempted to extend a peace offering to Scholl that was abruptly and abusively rejected; that it was Scholl who had assaulted Bernard Klotz, Jr., at the Olympic Club and that Klotz had only fired in self-defense; that it was Bernard Klotz, Jr., and only he who had fired all three shots at Scholl in self-defense; and that Scholl was trying to implicate Bernard Klotz, Sr., in the shooting out of his ongoing malicious hatred for his former employer.

Assistant District Attorney John Finney then provided the closing argument for the prosecution. He systematically laid out the undisputed facts provided by direct testimony from dozens of sworn prosecution witnesses, renewed his disbelief in the incredulous testimony provided by Mike Shea, and guided the jury through the events that occurred the night of August 30, 1893, that had resulted in the attempted murder of William A. Scholl. The parade of character witnesses was a canard; none was present when father and son attacked William Scholl, but the jury had heard the testimony of dozens of witnesses who were present and saw Klotz and his father insult, assault, and shoot William Scholl. Finally, he dismantled Adams' assertion of self-defense by pointing out that the third shot fired was from 15 feet away at a wounded man fleeing his attackers, and who were heard instructing the waiting carriage driver to "cut him [Scholl] off before he gets away."

After eight grueling days—three days for jury selection and five days of testimony and cross examinations—both sides were more than ready to rest their case. The trial had been marked by months of multiple postponements and continuances, accusations of jury tampering and other irregularities in the jury selection process, the near depletion of the available jury pool surprisingly enough by reason of sympathy for the Klotz family, and multiple contempt citations for the failure the Klotzes to appear at trial,[34] the matter was finally in the hands of the jury. At two o'clock Judge Moise read the jury their charge and ordered them to begin their deliberations. Approximately five hours later, at seven o'clock that evening, the jury had reached their verdict. Given that Bernard Klotz, Jr., had sworn that he fired all three shots, the jury was willing to accept his version of events and allowed him to bear the full weight of the verdict: guilty on the count of felonious assault with intent to slay and kill. Incredulously, Bernard Klotz, Sr., and Clarence Routh were declared to be not guilty and were immediately discharged.[35] Bernard Klotz, Jr., was led away to the sheriff's office to begin serving his sentence.

One of the darkest chapters in the history of the Olympic Club was nearly complete. There was still the matter of the civil case filed by William Scholl against Bernard Klotz, Sr., to contend with.[36] That matter would probably not be adjudicated until the following year, but for the present at least New Orleans, William Scholl, and the Olympic Club could put the entire ugly incident behind them.

Down for the Count

Just 12 days after their most recent anti-prize fighting editorial,[37] the *Daily Picayune* reported on the death of John A. Geraghty, a 14-year-old who was killed in a neighborhood boxing match in the yard behind Henry Turner's bakery at 198 Bienville Street. His opponent was Turner's 16-year-old son Edward. The fatal blow was to the chest of the younger boy, just below his heart. Along with the pivot punch, this blow is specifically prohibited in professional boxing.[38] This tragic accident provided additional fuel for the anti-boxing faction's bonfire: if even children could kill each other when boxing then just imagine what grown men could do to each other, intentionally or unintentionally.

"Shadow" Maber versus Charles Johnson

The Olympic Club announced in late November that they had arranged for Charley Johnson to meet Australian William "Shadow" Maber in December. As previously described, Johnson was the same unseemly pug involved in the horrible early morning drunken brawl in the courtyard of a tallow factory in St. Bernard Parish back in 1892 against Alphonse Garcia. His reputation did nothing to attract any more than a few of the estimated 1,700 spectators who watched two second-rate fighters paw at each other between obvious and egregious fouls from both men. John Duffy officiated the bout with uncharacteristic detachment, seemingly unwilling or unable to tell a blatant foul from a side of beef, and uncharacteristically drawing more than his share of heckling and hoots for the first time in his career as a referee. In a fracas that more often resembled a wrestling match,[39] interrupted more frequently by the verbal abuse the fighters exchanged with each other and, at times, the jeering crowd than in any effective exchange of punches, there was little "science" exhibited by either man.[40] After 25 rounds not even Duffy could decide on a winner, reluctantly and halfheartedly calling the match a draw and for the $1,500 purse to be divided,[41] to which most who were present would say that the two "fighters" were overpaid by $1,400 for their efforts, or lack thereof.

What the management of the Olympic Club had thought would be an entertaining diversion for their patrons to conclude a successful 1894 boxing season turned out to be a decided flop both critically and financially. While the club had more than adequate cash reserves to stave off one poorly attended fight, they were now unexpectedly facing stiff competition from the Auditorium Athletic Club who had masterfully cobbled together their own triple event set to take place the following week. With a feeling not unlike déjà vu, the Olympic Club was once again feeling the pressure.

Auditorium Club Triple Event

The Auditorium Athletic Club's triple event began on Thursday, December 13, with a match between James Barry of Chicago and Kid Madden of New York. The following night would find Andy Bowen taking on George "Kid" Lavigne from Michigan and the event would wrap up with the current World Champion Welterweight Tommy Ryan of Chicago against the Nonpareil, Jack Dempsey.[42] This was a better than average card, one sure to draw boxing fans from across New Orleans and the region. At least that was the outcome that the club was hoping for. The day before the fight with Barry, Madden backed out, forcing the club to cancel the event with no hope of finding a suitable replacement at the last minute.[43] Tickets were refunded and Barry was paid the deposited forfeit fee plus expenses, a minor expenditure for the club, but a major opportunity loss nonetheless. An anxious Frank Williams and Joseph Sporl at the Auditorium Club still felt confident they would have a successful event with next two bouts.

Andy Bowen versus Kid Lavigne

Andy Bowen was one of the most popular fighters in New Orleans in the latter part of the 19th century. His early career was marked by his well-deserved reputation as a fierce competitor and as a hard scrapper with boatloads of determination. Bowen is best remembered for lasting 110 rounds with Texas Jack Burke on April 6, 1893, at the Olympic Club, a record that still stands as the longest prizefight in boxing history, spanning seven hours and 19 minutes.[44] However, his most recent performances had been deemed lackluster when he consistently failed to capitalize whenever he gained an advantage over his opponent. Such was the reaction to his Herculean effort against Burke.

Bowen returned to the Olympic Club a little over a month later, on May 31, 1893, to square off against another up-and-coming New Orleans boxer, Jack Everhardt, for the still-vacant lightweight championship of the South and a $2,000 purse. Bowen would win the match, but only once Everhardt had retired in the 85th round after the two had battled for five hours and 35 minutes.[45] His critics accused Bowen of squandering several opportunities to put Everhardt down, but his supporters saw things differently. New Orleans was the undisputed boxing Mecca of the United States, but nowhere had there never been such an exhibition of stamina and courage as that produced by Andy Bowen. Within the span of 56 days Bowen had boxed an incredible 195 rounds which lasted a combined 12 hours and 54 minutes. There are boxers whose entire careers would not last as long as Bowen had in these two back-to-back fights.

Bowen would take a well-deserved rest, returning to the ring a year later to face Stanton Abbott at the Auditorium Club in New Orleans for a 10-round match that ended in a pre-arranged draw as both men were standing at the end of the bout. His next fight was a rematch with Jimmy Carroll of San Francisco on August 8, 1894, at the Auditorium Club. This match also ended in a draw after 25 rounds.

On December 14, 1894, a beleaguered looking Bowen went toe to toe with George "The Saginaw Kid" Lavigne at the Auditorium Club in a fight billed as being for the American Lightweight title and a $3,000 purse. Lavigne had never seen Bowen fight and said that he could only

Andy Bowen was at the height of his popularity, but his boxing skills had begun to diminish when he agreed to meet George "Kid" Lavigne at the Auditorium Club on December 14, 1894.

base his strategy on what he had read. Lavigne was a seasoned fighter, having made his debut at the age of 17 against Morris McNally on September 7, 1886, at the Auditorium Club in Saginaw, Michigan, winning by a knockout in the 1st round. Like most of the boxers of his day, Lavigne had built his reputation and record fighting all comers at any available venue ranging from the "barn behind old man Putnam's roadhouse" and Boardwell's Opera House in Saginaw, to an abandoned skating rink in Dana, Illinois. He would finally ascend to athletic clubs on the west coast and in the northeast. His fight with Bowen would be his 32nd, and he was heretofore undefeated with a record of 23 wins and 9 draws/no decisions. While not necessarily looking past Bowen, Lavigne's thoughts were primarily focused on challenging Young Griffo to a rematch. They met 10 months earlier at the Second Regiment Armory in Chicago and battled to an 8-round draw which Lavigne and a number of sportswriters felt should have won on points.

The weigh-in scheduled for three o'clock on the afternoon of the fight had to be postponed because Bowen was too heavy. By the time the two men met at ringside at nine o'clock that evening, Bowen had worked down to 133 pounds and Lavigne was at 135 pounds. Professor John Duffy gathered the boxers at the scratch line, ran through the instructions both men knew almost by heart, laced up the approved gloves and sent them back to their respective corners. In Lavigne's corner were Jim Hall, Sam Fitzpatrick, and Martin Murphy. Bowen was backed by Billy McCarthy, Billy Layton, and Albert Spitzfaden. The great Jack Dempsey was also in Bowen's corner acting as his unofficial coach.

At 9:40 the bell signaled the start of the 1st round. The first minute was spent sparring, with each man watching the other's movements. A few punches were exchanged, but Bowen spent most of the round ducking Lavigne's attempts. In the middle of the round Lavigne slipped on the canvas, but regained his footing before Duffy could be tempted to begin his count. Bowen's left found Lavigne's nose, but left it intact. The usually effective left then found Lavigne's stomach, but barely raised a welt before Lavigne answered with a left upper-cut to Bowen's chin. Before the beginning of the 2nd round one of Lavigne's seconds sprinkled rosin around the canvas ring to prevent another potential slip and fall. The 2nd round began with determined action from both men, each landing a jarring blow followed by a clinch. The in-fighting went to Lavigne's advantage as did the round. The next 16 rounds were practically a mirror image of the 3rd round, with each man giving as good as he got to the head, face, stomach, and ribs. Lavigne drew first blood in the 10th round with a left hook to the eye. Bowen anointed Lavigne with a series of "rib roasters" that doubled him over in the 15th round. Bowen was staggered only once, in the 17th round, as Lavigne rained down blow after blow on every unprotected portion of Bowen's body, forcing Bowen to take a knee for a six-count. It was apparent to everyone but Bowen that the hometown boy was no longer on the ropes, but at the end of his rope.

George "Kid" Lavigne was a seasoned fighter making his 32nd fight when he met Andy Bowen at the Auditorium Athletic Club. It would be a night he would never forget (collection of the author).

The 18th round saw a surprisingly fresh Bowen bounce to the scratch line where he was quickly met with a stiff jab from Lavigne, followed by a flurry of combinations to the face and neck that spun Bowen around like a street drunk. Yet the plucky Bowen would not yield and was rewarded with further punishment that should have laid him down, but did not. Lavigne pressed his attack, throwing every conceivable combination of punches he could think of, most of which Bowen deftly ducked until Lavigne landed a left jab to Bowen's chin. As Bowen tilted his head back to dampen the blow, Lavigne threw a savage right that caught Bowen squarely on the jaw. It was said that the jarring sound of Bowen's head hitting the canvas floor could have been "heard a block away." The fight was stopped long enough for referee Duffy to quickly count Bowen out, and his seconds immediately jumped into the ring, worried that the blow had broken Bowen's neck. A doctor was summoned into the ring and the crowd feared the worst for their favorite. It took five anxious minutes before the doctor signaled that Bowen was breathing, but still unconscious.[46] Bowen was carried out of the ring and brought to his dressing room to be examined more thoroughly. No one seemed to anticipate that his injuries might prove fatal. The *Daily Picayune* compared Bowen's injury to those suffered by Jim Hall at the hands of Bob Fitzsimmons the previous year. Hall recovered after 45 tense minutes and was actually seconding Lavigne for the Bowen fight. The newspaper also mentioned that the Australian boxer Young Griffo experienced a similar head injury and was unconscious for nearly four hours before coming to.

As he lay unconscious and unmoving in his dressing room, Bowen suddenly vomited a meal of undigested peas and was administered whiskey to raise his pulse rate. This was considered a hopeful sign. An ambulance was summoned, but instead of taking him to Charity Hospital, Bowen was brought to his home at 132 Thalia Street between Magazine and Constance Streets. There he was examined by Dr. James Finney until the family physician, Dr. E. Denegre Martin arrived around 2:30 in the morning. Bowen was made as comfortable as possible and lingered until four o'clock in the morning when his breathing became labored, his pulse became erratic, and he began to decline slowly. With his mother and his wife Mathilde at his bedside, he died at quarter after seven the following morning having never regained consciousness.[47]

On December 15 Lavigne and his seconds were arrested along with referee John Duffy. They were all booked at the Third Precinct Station, Lavigne being charged with murder and the others as accessories. They were arraigned in the Second Recorder's Court before Judge Aucoin who set bond for each defendant. Following a coroner's inquest and arraignment the afternoon of December 27, all parties were exonerated when it was determined that the blow that felled Bowen was delivered to his jaw, while the concussion produced by his fall was declared to be the cause of death. Coroner Lawrason (Layrisson) found that Bowen's stomach was still loaded with undigested food and further concluded that Bowen's "improper condition was in great measure responsible for his death."[48] Mrs. Bowen told reporters that her husband was "in no condition to go into the ring." His workouts were listless and short lived. He would start on the punching bag, but stopped after less than 45 seconds of halfhearted work. He did not maintain his training regimen and his weight began to climb. The week before the fight he tipped the scales at 142 pounds.[49]

A crowd of more than 2,000 stood vigil outside the white picket fence at Bowen's home and followed his casket for the three-block walk to St. Teresa's Church on Erato and Camp Streets. Representatives from across the boxing pantheon, from Jack

Dempsey and Jim Hall to Jack Everhardt and Clarence Husbands, were on hand to pay their respects. There were also representatives from the Olympic Club and other athletic clubs where Bowen had boxed. Pallbearers included John H. Duffy, William A. Scholl, William "Shadow" Maber, Thomas C. Anderson, Albert Spitzfaden, Henry Allen, William Layton, Daniel Flemings, Vincent Del Valle, and Charles Spitzfaden. Interment was in St. Patrick's Cemetery No. 1 near the foot of Canal Street. Duffy lamented, "Now I'm awful blue about this. Really I don't think I could find words to say just how badly I feel, first for Andy and then for the women he leaves down here behind him." He was also reported to remark, "Ever since the sad affair happened I am literally all broke up."[50]

A fierce debate raged across the city over what actually caused Bowen's death. Outside of those opposed to boxing itself, the discussion would inevitably be distilled down to two sides: those who believed that Lavigne's punch was the culprit and those who believed it was the unpadded ring that was to blame. Those who had seen Bowen fight in the past and who were familiar with his remarkable ability to take and recover from a beating held that it had to be the unpadded pine floor that caused the concussion from which Bowen could not recover. In time this became the prevailing opinion, although there were also those who believed that it was Duffy's fault for not stopping the fight sooner. Duffy agreed that the fight should have ended sooner, but stated that Bowen's seconds should have "thrown up the sponge," and that he had no power to tell them to do so.[51] The Auditorium Club's ring was found to be nothing more than raw canvas stretched over hard pine planks with no padding of any sort beneath the canvas. It was noted that since a similar incident during the Fitzsimmons–Hall fight there had been an inch of felt padding under the canvas.[52] It was later reported that Bowen had visited the club the day prior to the fight and, when the lack of padding was pointed out to him, thought it insignificant.

In an all too brief career spanning just seven years, Bowen compiled a record of 16 wins (7 by knockout), 4 losses, and 5 draws/no contests for a .593 winning percentage. He was the reigning Lightweight Champion of the South at the time of his death.[53]

The inevitable diatribe against boxing now had its most powerful precedent upon which to argue its case. "The killing of Andrew Bowen in a prize fight in this city Friday night should sound the death knell here of that bloody brutality misnamed 'sport,'" the *Daily Picayune* declared. "The fistic carnival is over. It ended in a murder."[54] Newspapers now devoted as much column space to condemning boxing as they did in covering its high profile fights for their readers.

Some months earlier the Louisiana Attorney General M.J. Cunningham sued the Olympic Club, but lost the case both in civil district court and on appeal in state Supreme Court. However, the state argued that expert testimony had been improperly presented to the Supreme Court and a new trial in the lower court was scheduled. Before the new trial could be held, the Bowen–Lavigne fight resulted in Bowen's death. Cunningham immediately corresponded with both William Scholl of the Olympic Club and Frank Williams of the Auditorium Club, briefly reiterating his opposition to prizefighting in any form or fashion and strongly suggesting that all fights at the Auditorium Club, as well as the Olympic Club, be cancelled until the outcome of the lawsuit against the Olympic Club was resolved.[55] As expected, there was a renewed clamor to stamp out boxing altogether. In the boxing world, opinion on the reaction to Bowen's death and the pending lawsuit was divided. In New York, Richard K. Fox, publisher of the *Police Gazette* opined that "Prize fighting will get a temporary set-back probably, but that common sense view of the sport would prevail in the end."[56]

Charles E. "Parson" Davies, noted Chicago sporting man and frequent backer and manager of boxers John L. Sullivan, Peter Jackson and Joe Choynski among others, stated that "the accident will give the sport a set-back, but I do not believe that it will kill the sport. Not at all. It merely gives the preachers and cranks a chance to limber up their thunder machines and lubricate the wheels of wrath that are set a-turning with every accident, whether it happens on the football field or in the prize ring."[57] He went on to fault New Orleans Mayor John Fitzpatrick as spineless for refusing to issue the requisite permits to hold fights under the existing laws. Mayor Fitzpatrick was an ardent boxing supporter, having served as the referee for the Sullivan–Kilrain bout in Richburg, Mississippi in 1889, and frequently attended boxing events in New Orleans. He was present at the Bowen–Lavigne fight and was shocked to learn of Bowen's death. He summarized his position by saying that "if death was caused by the blow which Lavigne struck, then the sport is fatal, but if death resulted from Bowen's head striking the floor, then the death was attributable to a circumstance that can be avoided, and the sport is not fatal."[58] Spoken like a true politician.

Heavyweight champion James Corbett was in Dallas touring with his vaudeville show "Gentlemen Jack" when he was informed about Bowen's death. He candidly said that "it will hurt pugilism and makes me more eager than ever to get out of the business."[59] Bob Fitzsimmons was interviewed in Louisville, Kentucky, but refused to comment on the death of Bowen except to offer financial assistance to his widow.[60] Whether their comments were intended to describe the fate of boxing in Louisiana specifically or in America as a whole, it was clear to most that boxing in Louisiana had been dealt a fatal blow. Therefore it came as no surprise to anyone when the state filed a supplemental and amended petition in their injunction against the Olympic Club claiming that the Olympic Club had "aided, abetted, and assisted, and conducted and promoted other prize fights than those mentioned in the petition."[61]

While the future of the Olympic Club certainly looked forlorn, the death knell for the Auditorium Club had already been sounded. The Bowen–Lavigne fight was the second of their triple event bouts and the final match between Jack Dempsey and Tommy Ryan was understandably cancelled. The club lost money on the first two events—with the first match having been cancelled, thereby making the club responsible for both the fighters' expenses plus the cost of arranging and promoting the fight, and with only 1,500 tickets sold at an average price of $1.50 for the second fight, the club would just barely be able to cover the cover the $3,000 purse much less expenses. Now they were on the hook for Dempsey and Ryan's expenses for the third, cancelled event. When all was said and done the club stood to lose between $2,500 and $3,000 with no possible hope of reopening at any time in the foreseeable future. While awaiting the decision of the state Supreme Court, the Olympic Club pressed ahead with plans for a benefit for Bowen's widow scheduled to take place on January 2, 1895.[62]

Seven

1895 to 1897

"If the ring has fallen low it is not in the main the fault of the men who have done the fighting, but it lies at the door of the ring-side parasites and ruffians, who are as far below the honest pugilist as the welsher and the blackleg are below the noble race horse which serves them as a protest for their villainies."[1]

—Richard K. Fox

Two of Bowen's most intimate friends, Thomas C. Anderson and Vincent Del Valle, were in charge of arranging the program for the benefit for Andy Bowen's widow, Mathilde. The originally scheduled date of January 2 had to be briefly postponed until the 5th, but came off without a hitch. At approximately seven o'clock in the evening, James Corbett, with a heavy heart, sparred four rounds with John McVey, followed by a four-round exhibition between two black boxers, Louis Gray and Ed Brooks. Local lightweights Clarence Husbands and George Pierce were followed by Jack Everhardt and Billy McCarthy. The highlight of the evening may well have been the novelty bout between Professor Collins and a kangaroo which drew great applause from the sparse crowd of 400.[2]

For the reigning Heavyweight Champion of the World to break off a successful and financially significant theatrical engagement to travel to New Orleans at his own expense to participate in a benefit honoring Andy Bowen speaks volumes about how highly regarded Bowen was in the pugilistic community. Additionally, it was no secret that Corbett and Olympic Club president William Scholl did not care for each other, ostensibly a holdover from circumstances and events dating back to the original Fistic Carnival. Nevertheless, both men set aside their personal animosity on this special night. Corbett was originally scheduled to spar with his usual training partner, Steve O'Donnell, with whom he appeared nightly on stage. However, O'Donnell sprained his ankle during a performance of "Gentleman Jack," requiring Corbett to go against Big John McVey, someone with whom he had trained in the past. No one expected to see anything other than a friendly exhibition, but it appears that no one told McVey. Better known as a wrestler, the awkward McVey rushed at Corbett trying to land punches with both hands, sometimes windmill-style, sometimes throwing a left and a right simultaneously. The crowd perked up, as did Corbett, who thrashed McVey, sending him down in a heap with a quick right to the jaw. While some thought this to be part of the stage act put on for effect, others noticed that McVey remained unconscious and prostrate on the canvas. The curtain was dropped and after several minutes McVey was resuscitated when restoratives were administered. However well intentioned, one could only imagine the anguish that Bowen's family felt watching Andy's friends boxing in the ring, particularly seeing an unconscious McVey. The benefit was not as well attended as the occasion merited or the beneficiary warranted.

Six days later William A. Scholl unexpectedly tendered his resignation as president of the Olympic Club during a routine board meeting, stating that his current employment required his full attention. The board lost no time in tapping one of the club's founding members, Edward J. Koffskey, to serve as interim-president until elections could be held the following week. Later in the meeting, Charles Dickson and former Mayor J.V. Guillotte were named to the board and Dickson lost no time in announcing his candidacy to replace Scholl.[3] He was subsequently confirmed as the club's new president on February 4, without any serious opposition. In years past the presidency of the Olympic Club was a considered to be a coveted honor, contested almost as enthusiastically as running for public office. But few men offered themselves for what was assumed to be an arduous road ahead for the Olympic Club.

Legal matters resurfaced during February. First, former Olympic Club member Bernard Klotz, Jr., filed a motion for a new trial that was set to be heard on February 9 before Judge James C. Moise, but the motion had to be continued. The Olympic Club case that had been remanded to a lower court for retrial was also postponed overnight owing to the absence of several key witnesses. Everyone was present in Judge N.H. Rightor's court the following day when attorneys for both sides informed the court that they had agreed to submit the case as previously outlined, presenting their briefs to Judge Rightor, who expressed his hope to render a decision as soon as it was feasible.[4] As they awaited the court's decision, the Olympic Club held a small reception on Saturday, February 23, in honor of Charles Dickson's election as president. Not only was the pending legal decision on everyone's lips, but the rifle club's narrow loss in a contest with the Southern Rifle Club was also a popular topic of conversation. Held at the Olympic Club's indoor range under electric light, the hotly-contested ten-point loss stirred up a routine call for a rematch to allow the Olympic Club an opportunity to reclaim their honor.

The club's traditional Mardi Gras carnival ball took place two days later, with their clubhouse being adorned in purple, green, and gold from floor to ceiling. There was music and dancing to accompany the bountiful refreshments. While putting on a brave face, most felt it was only the calm before the inevitable approaching storm.

On Monday, March 11, Judge Rightor handed down his decision in the Olympic Club case. To the absolute shock and utter amazement of most people, his decision was in favor of the Olympic Club. The citizens of New Orleans, both those in favor of boxing and those against it, had watched as this case was hammered through the court system all the way to the state Supreme Court and back again. In rendering his decision Judge Rightor let it be known that he was as frustrated as anyone with the "evasive, baffling, and impossible statute under which the club maintains its defiance of the laws of humanity and decency." He went on to say that he found that "a prize fight is a glove contest, without gloves, and that a glove contest is a prizefight with gloves. In each case there is a duel with fists, and there is a prize. In each case there is the same danger to limb and life, the same maiming and shedding of blood, the same brutality."[5] His carefully worded decision laid the blame squarely at the feet of the state legislature for their failure to address the statute under which athletic clubs were allowed to operate. In what had become an all too familiar response, state Attorney General Cunningham announced the state's intent to appeal the lower court's decision. He apologized for his own lack of influence on the result, citing his recent personal involvement in numerous judicial-related conferences related to the recent resumption of rioting along the Mississippi River between the dockworkers and the shipping companies. Confident that their charter was secure and that the outcome of the state's appeal would once again be in their favor, the Olympic Club resumed their effort to promote boxing events. Their first announcement was strictly for effect: the club submitted a $25,000 bid on the pending fight between James Corbett and Bob Fitzsimmons.[6] There were rumors that the club might go as high as $50,000 if pressed, but most observers realized that this too was merely a thinly veiled attempt to influence the prevailing opinion regarding boxing in New Orleans. However, given Corbett's negative posture regarding Scholl and the Olympic Club, no one seriously believed that the Olympic Club's offer would be accepted, even though Scholl was no longer part of the club's management team. It would, however, send a clear signal to the boxing world that they were back in business.

Following the death of Andy Bowen, and with what appeared to be the never ending, ongoing legal uncertainty, the Olympic Club had been unable to enter into serious negotiations with a fighter of any caliber. The Fitzsimmons–Corbett fight was supposed to take place in Jacksonville, Florida, but the governor had publicly stated his intent to once again block any boxing event from happening in his state. There were also persistent rumors that the lead bidder from Florida, the Florida Athletic Club, did not have the financial resources to make good on their bid, much less to challenge the governor in court as was the case in 1894 with the Corbett–Mitchell bout. No one, especially Fitzsimmons, wanted a repeat of the Crescent City Athletic Club's financial failure. Understandably, no one was willing to make any commitment to the Olympic Club until their legal battles were resolved one way or another.

On Thursday, March 28, the Olympic Club entertained nearly 2,000 members and guests at an informal smoker featuring beer and sandwiches and a wide variety of amusing entertainment.[7] An impromptu band consisting of an accordion, a guitar, and an upright bass struggled comically through a number of popular tunes, eventually giving way to a series of singers, "some with sweet voices and others with no voices." Next on the program were humorous recitations, which tickled the audience to no end, particularly the "pathetic poems." Master of Ceremonies T.B. Lawrence introduced each act with a tone of seriousness that did little to prepare the audience for the revelry to follow. The members welcomed the diversion, but the beleaguered board in particular needed an evening of lighthearted distraction and were well rewarded for their efforts.

Arguments before the Louisiana State Supreme Court were to have been heard in mid–April, but were postponed by mutual agreement until the 27th. When the parties reconvened to rehear arguments, the proceedings began with a reading of Judge N.H. Rightor's recent decision in favor of the Olympic Club, delivered with the same satirical bent as Judge Rightor intended, characterizing "glove contests and prize fighting as a domestic industry and a legitimate occupation," further stating that the state statute was "a bit of fraudulent and mendacious legislation." The present trial, however, was granted because expert testimony was excluded from the briefs submitted to Judge Rightor for his decision. The state's case would be argued by Colonel B.R. Forman, E. Howard McCaleb, Jr., and Charles Forman. The defense team was comprised of Henry P. Dart, Judge Charles H. Luzenberg, and Frank Zengel.

Central to the defense's case was that it was not the province of the Supreme Court to determine the intent of the legislature in its prohibition of prize fighting and that the language of the law must be construed as it reads. Colonel Forman described the distinction between glove contests and prize fighting as "hair-splitting," and that they were in truth one and the same thing, regardless of the venue. Before Henry Dart could respond he was interrupted by Justice Henry C. Miller, who inquired the reasoning that the case was being heard yet again. Justice Samuel D. McEnery remarked that he had "forgotten the object of the suit." Henry Dart responded to the remarkably ill-informed and poorly-prepared justices that the state's appeal was not based on any new evidence, but based on an old transcript of the case which the state claimed omitted expert testimony. He offered the testimony of Colonel Soule and other gentlemen who had testified that "glove contests were not prizefights, but were proper exhibitions of the manly art." Justice Miller then asserted that the court could not rely on anyone's opinion on the matter, but had to rely on the facts at hand. It was at this point that Dart read to the court portions of the previous trial testimony which contained the witnesses' descriptions of prize fights and glove contests they had attended, contrasting the two events with the usual distinctions—London Prize Ring Rules versus Marquis of Queensbury Rules, bare knuckle versus gloved fists, disorderly mobs versus orderly crowds, open air versus athletic clubs, and so on. He was incredulous that the witnesses in the prior trial had been allowed to present such nonsense under the guise of testimony before the court. For more than two hours the justices posed questions and the finer points of the case were argued. Finally, a frustrated and vehement Colonel Foreman delivered his final appeal, during which he reminded the three justices of their long years of preparation in studying and practicing the law before they could be elevated to the "highest and most honored position in the State," for which they were paid $5,000 per year for their professional expertise. He then informed the court that the Olympic Club "gave a negro $7,500 for knocking a white man into a state of insensibility in an hour." He then rattled off the ever-increasing purses for the Sullivan–Corbett fight and the Fitzsimmons–Hall fight, all for the purpose and privilege of watching a man "pounding [another man] into a comatose state, unconscious, and insensible, in a little over an hour." Foreman then eloquently posed the following rhetorical questions "What is the effect on the youth of the land? Is this not an abuse of the corporate franchise?" Impassioned summations followed, with Colonel Foreman closing with the statement referring to the witnesses in the prior trial, that "it is not possible that so many respectable gentlemen could deliberately testify that the contests before the Olympic Club were scientific exhibitions if they were only vulgar, coarse, or brutal onslaughts of man upon man."[8] With this, Chief Justice Francis T. Nicholls, the former anti-boxing governor of Louisiana, adjourned the proceedings. With the case now in the hands of the court, there was no shortage of furrowed brows among both the members of the defense team and their clients. All they could do was to wait for the court's decision and hope that once again the past success of their defensive strategy would bear up, this time from the ingenious onslaught of Colonel B.R. Foreman. Foreman's argument deftly appealed to the justice's personal economic sensibilities, and he was relying on their individual attitude toward boxing to influence their decision. He was hoping that with their decision the justices would provide a clear roadmap to the legislature. At least he had planted the seeds. He, like the others involved in the case, would have to wait to learn how his argument was received.

It was an uncharacteristically subdued 12th anniversary celebration at the Olympic Club on Saturday evening, May 3, consisting of mostly older members with a few invited guests.[9] The club had recently experienced a number of resignations from more recent members who no longer wished to be a part of what they perceived to be a tarnished and waning institution. Nevertheless, those who remained were treated to an evening of "sweet music," with dancing accomplished in a temporary dancehall erected on the lawn adjoining the club. Those who wished to rest their weary feet could enjoy a wide variety of refreshments that could be found throughout the various rooms of the clubhouse, which was festooned with flags and bunting, palms and decorative accent lighting. Festivities lasted well into the wee hours and provided a welcome respite from the arduous days ahead.

On Monday, May 6, the state Supreme Court's verdict against the Olympic Club was announced. Speaking for the majority, Justice Samuel D. McEnery delivered a lengthy dissertation on Act 25 of 1890 in which he abolished any distinction between prize fighting and glove contests, and further disposed of the contentious proviso in the act which allowed glove contests to take place within athletic clubs.[10] Their decision stated that "glove contests in athletic clubs, or elsewhere, such as we have described, have no semblance to prizefights without gloves. To hold that such glove contests as are permitted in the arena by the defendant club are ordinary contests for scientific boxing would be as absurd as to say that fencing with pointed foil, merely for the pricking of blood, would be a fencing bout to decide superior points in sword exercise. The proviso, therefore, is without meaning as it is in no way related to the enacting clause, and is totally irrelevant thereto. It has been held that where the proviso is irrelevant it has been rejected. We conclude that the glove contests in athletic clubs, or elsewhere, when the object is only for a display of the art of boxing, as generally understood and practiced, without the prerequisites of challenge and training, and the attendant circumstances of a prize fight, are not what is commonly known as prize fights, and, therefore, the proviso has no relation to or connection with the offense denounced by the statute."

Swallowing hard and putting on a brave face, the Olympic Club said they respectfully disagreed with the court's decision, as all previous decisions in their favor were based on the same arguments and evidence. Nonetheless they would comply with the court's decision for the time being until it was time for them to file for an appeal, which the club's lawyers wasted no time in filing.[11] They also indicated that they intended to test the new law and began talks with Texas heavyweight Herman Bernau to come fight in New Orleans.[12] News of the club's intent to file an appeal was vilified across the state. The *Monroe News* applauded the demise of prize fighting as a continuation of the social reform that had "bounced" the state lottery. The *Alexandria Democrat* applauded the court's clarification of the statute's eternally confusing distinction between prize fighting and glove contests.[13] It all became a moot point when the court declined the Olympic Club's petition for a new trial on Monday, June 4, thus ending the ability of athletic clubs to promote prize fights and ending the city's reign at the forefront of American boxing.[14]

A weary and stressed Charles Dickson almost reluctantly agreed to stand for re-election as president of the Olympic Club, faced with a steady stream of resigning members and new lawsuits now filed by the club's own attorneys Henry Dart, Charles H. Luzenberg, and Frank Zengel to force payment for their $9,000 in outstanding legal fees.[15] No one, least of all the lawyers involved, wanted a repeat of the Metropolitan Club and Crescent City Athletic Club liquidations. New Orleanians had just learned that the Auditorium Athletic Club would demolish their arena. The building that had hosted numerous prize fights of note, meetings for presidential candidate William McKinley, theatrical productions and wild animal shows would now make way for residential development.[16]

On July 6 the Olympic Club announced that Dickson had been re-elected president, albeit with no opposition, and a new panel of officers and directors had been named to chart the future course of the once fabled institution.[17] To the astonishment of those who read the announcement, the club further revealed that a match had been made between Herman Bernau and Billy McCarthy to fight a 10 round "scientific glove exhibition" as part of a series of exhibitions designed to be strictly within the law.

Monthly Subscription Entertainment Series

In what many observers believed to be an ill-advised maneuver to test the legal climate in the city, the directors of the Olympic Club, determined to find a silver lining, devised a monthly subscription series of athletic entertainment to include wrestling and boxing exhibitions. Most significantly, no purse would be offered for the boxing exhibitions.

The first of these subscription entertainment series took place on Wednesday evening, September 4, 1895, and featured four boxing exhibitions and one wrestling match. To some it appeared as if the glory days of the Olympic Club had returned—lines of carriages and hacks filled the street in front of the Olympic Club, streetcars carried the less affluent with equal enthusiasm, and crowds gathered both inside and outside the last remaining great boxing arena. Granted the crowds were smaller than people remembered. It is estimated that there were only between 1,000 and 1,200 assembled, but the prevailing mood was one of euphoria: once again there was to be boxing at the Olympic Club.

The first event was introduced by Ed Curtis, serving as the Master of Ceremonies for the evening. It was a 4-round exhibition between Professor Duffy's "Pair of Kids," being billed only as "Freckles" versus "Mexican." Little is known about the true identity of these "kids" other than that "Mexican," also known as "Mexican Joe," was in fact a light-skinned black teenager. As they had in past appearances, the good professor's protégés provided a credible exhibition of all of the typical feints, dodging, ducking, sparring, and the other tactics of their adult counterparts for approximately 15 minutes to warm up the crowd. They were pelted with silver coins by the appreciative crowd.

The second bout featured William Crawford against "Knuckles," whose was real name was Louis Knoechel. The pair were well known locally and, from the opening bell, they went at each other for five "lively rounds," meaning that gloved fists were flying freely, with little to remind the observer of "the sweet science." The crowd felt that Knuckles had the better of it, as evidenced by Crawford's bloody and bloated left eye, and the fact that Knuckles put his opponent on the mat at least twice, but referee Professor John Duffy ultimately declined to name one man or the other the winner.

The third bout was a 6-round exhibition between two locals, Louis Guillebeau and George Pierce, who were also well known in local fight circles and who had something of a rivalry brewing from their past encounters. Guillebeau was the more skillful fighter that evening, pressing Pierce on the ropes at different times and on the verge of a knockout more than once during their 6-round bout. Guillebeau was clearly the winner on points and was declared so by Duffy, with the keen approval of the crowd.

Olympic Club president Charles Dickson and several of his fellow officers and fellow members scanned the crowd to gauge their reaction. From all appearances, the program of shorter events, irrespective of quality, appeared to be something the crowd enjoyed. It was fast and exciting. Perhaps the new subscription series could be a viable format moving forward. The next event was a wrestling match for a best two out of three falls match between Dan Fox and Mike Maestri of the Young Men's Gymnastic Club. Maestri was the larger and stronger of the two, but that did not stop Fox from tossing Maestri nearly clean out of the ring in the 1st round, or from lifting Maestri above his head in the 2nd round before dropping him to the floor, a fall that somehow Duffy missed. Ultimately, in the 1st round, Maestri had Fox on the mat within two minutes after his close encounter with the ropes, and repeated the feat within four minutes of being slammed in the 2nd round. While the standard of wrestling was only borderline, the audience seemed engaged in watching the two men grip and grapple. Again, the entire match had lasted less than ten minutes, with Maestri prevailing.

The main event of the evening was the 10-round exhibition between heavyweights Herman Bernau from Texas and Billy McCarthy from Australia, who the crowd remembered from his tiff with Jack Everhardt during the benefit for Andy Bowen's widow back in January. The Texan was the taller of the two and appeared to be in better condition than the shorter, stockier Australian. No sooner had the bell sounded for the 1st round than the two men dispensed with the typical initial exploratory sparring and got right into trading heated combinations. During one such exchange, Bernau caught McCarthy with his right to the chin, sending McCarthy face down onto the canvas. When McCarthy didn't move, in an abundance of caution Duffy forgot the count and signaled for Dr. Maylie to examine the downed man. McCarthy was rolled over and got to his feet, but the battle was over almost before it had begun.[18]

On balance, the club was satisfied with their noble new experiment, although not necessarily with the proceeds from the affair. They were used to the larger, more profitable gate receipts, but those heady days of net profits in the tens of thousands of dollars were most certainly behind them now, at least until, by some strange alignment of the planets, their legal team could once again successfully reverse the decision of the state supreme court. With a flash of outward optimism, tempered with a harsh inward dose of pragmatic, realistic acceptance of their position, the Olympic Club prepared for their next event in the monthly subscription entertainment series.

In October, as the Olympic Club was finalizing matches for their next event, reform-minded Democratic Governor Murphy Foster announced plans to end boxing once and for all during the next legislative session, along with instructions to Attorney General M.J. Cunningham to bring the full weight of the state to bear on anyone who attempted to stage prize fighting in any form or fashion.[19] It was now evident that the oft-repeated challenge to the legislature from the courts to clean up the language in the statutes had been accepted. With this news in mind, the second subscription series was held on Thursday, October 24, and offered only two events. There were at least ten policemen under the command of Captains John Journee and Richard Walsh spread out among the diverse crowd of nearly 3,000, not knowing quite what to expect. To their relief, throughout the early evening the crowd was well behaved. The principal topic of discussion was not the fight card for the evening, but rather the news that James Corbett had announced his retirement from the ring now that his match with Fitzsimmons in Florida had been cancelled. Many also learned for the first time that the great Jack Dempsey was dying of tuberculosis in Portland, Oregon, his days said to be in rapid decline.[20] At nine o'clock the first event was introduced—a best two out of three fall wrestling match between Professor Lloyd Gearhart, the despised boxing referee who was representing the Southern Athletic Club, and Mike Maestri of the Young Men's Gymnastic Club for a purse of $500 and a side bet of $500. The crowd was with Maestri, remembering Gearhardt's questionable handling of boxers at the Olympic Club in the past was still stuck in the craw of many present. For the next three hours, the crowd watched Maestri try to corner Gearhardt, occasionally getting the smaller man in his grips only to let him slip away. The crowd was getting restless, and while Gearhardt and Maestri were both exhausted, tangled in a motionless knot on the mat, they both told Professor John Duffy that they agreed to call the match a draw. Realizing that the match had gone on well beyond being tedious, the club quickly agreed. They had expected a brief wrestling match as a warm-up to the boxing match. Their decision was met with scattered applause from the crowd and a brief ten-minute intermission ensued during which a brass band played a selection of popular tunes to keep the tense throng happy and in their seats.

The combatants for the second event of the evening entered the ring to the cheers of the crowd. Local product Jack Everhardt was accompanied by his brother, Charles, Professor Robertson, and Ed McCune. A few moments later Owen Zeigler of Philadelphia and his seconds, Charles Salder and Hugh Kennedy, joined the party. The swarthy Everhardt appeared to be shorter when he stood near the taller, paler Philadelphian at the scratch line. For 25 rounds the two men fought, with the consensus opinion that Ziegler had the better of it. Ziegler had Everhardt on the cusp of defeat on several occasions and proved to be the more clever fighter. In the 11th round Ziegler injured his left hand and was forced to rely solely on his right. Everhardt, as per his reputation, got away with a couple of obvious fouls and looked no better than he had against Billy McCarthy and Stanton Abbott. Mercifully the match was declared a draw as both men were standing at the conclusion of the scheduled 25 rounds, but the crowd sided with

Ziegler as they filed out of the arena.[21] With two mediocre and protracted bouts, the second subscription series was a complete departure from the fast-paced first series, and as a result the event was neither a critical nor a financial success, despite any objection by or interference from the authorities to the Olympic Club's new format.

Hoping for a holiday miracle, on Monday, December 23, the third subscription series of "entertainment" was presented. Once again Edward Curtis served as the Master of Ceremonies and Professor John Duffy as the referee. The first bout was a three-round exhibition between lightweights Mickey Finn and William Crawford, who entertained the spectators with their speed and agility, their clever footwork, and their stiff and clean punching. The match was predictably declared to be a draw, but the decision drew no admonition from the onlookers.

The second bout also went three rounds, this time between Alphonse Garcia and Louis Knuckles (Knoechel). Those who recognized Garcia's name reminded those seated around them of his part in the drunken, tawdry fight held in the wee hours of a Sunday morning back in February of 1892 against Charlie Johnson at a tallow factory in St. Bernard. Here was a well-worn mug posing as a boxer against a fellow who was no more than a third-rate sparring partner. As the bell rang for the 1st round, no one present expected to see much from either man. They were not disappointed as what followed was a truly uninspiring effort. When the judges announced that Knuckles had their decision on points, the crowd erupted in laughter before referee Duffy could express his opinion. Clearly everyone present had just witnessed two men hell-bent on avoiding victory as fervently as they would defeat. Instead of an amuse bouche, the crowd was offered an over-salted ordure appetizer. Perhaps one of the remaining two matches would salvage the evening and the price of admission.

The third match of the evening pitted Louis Guillebeau against Jess Clark in a 4-round affair. The sparring was a bit more heated, but once again there was no science to be seen in the style of either man. Clark staggered Guillebeau with a right hook that drew blood and was rewarded with a powerful right cross to the jaw that left him groggy for the remainder of the bout. In the 3rd round Clark was soundly beaten by Guillebeau, who broke his right hand in the process. Clark was saved by the bell and managed to last through the 4th and final round without giving or receiving further damage. Guillebeau earned a unanimous decision and both men were warmly cheered as they exited the ring.

Before the final event on the card began, John Duffy announced to the crowd that Andy Bowen's widow wanted to express her thanks for Kid Lavigne's recent gift of $50, and that former New Orleans police detective Dominick O'Malley would make the first donation of the evening of $5, encouraging those assembled to open up their hearts and wallets for Mrs. Bowen's benefit. Within five minutes another $136 was collected.

Just after 9:30, the fourth and final match of the evening between featherweights Solly Smith of Los Angeles and "Torpedo" Billy Murphy from New Zealand was set to begin. This was supposed to be the feature bout of the evening and the participants lost little time in sparring, preferring to get right into the melee. Brief exchanges broken up by cautious jabbing marked the limited action in the 1st round. The next three rounds proved to be no different from the first, with light body punches interrupted by the occasional wild upper-cut missing its intended target. The 5th round began with each man engaging in "hammer and tongs fashion," being a clinch following a missed punch. It did lead to some hot in-fighting. The action picked up in the 6th round when Smith landed a solid left to Murphy's face. Despite a furious campaign of left jabs thrown by Murphy, Smith broke through his defense and landed a solid combination as the round came to a conclusion. The 7th and 8th rounds were punctuated by more in-fighting, with Smith flooring Murphy for an eight-count in the 8th round. Murphy was wearing down, getting sent to the mat in the 9th round for a five-count. The next four rounds were spent awkwardly avoiding a devastating blow, frequent clinches, and both men sparring to recover their wind. The doughty Smith took control in the 14th round, dazing this opponent with a left upper-cut to the chin. He stalked the New Zealander for a scant few moments before delivering another left that sent Murphy down for the first time, Murphy staggered to his feet and was promptly greeted with a right to the neck that sent him down for the second time. Gamely rising, Murphy was pelted by Smith, who was using a blistering succession of lefts and rights to pound Murphy's face into something resembling a map of Africa. When it became apparent that Murphy was indeed defenseless, Duffy stepped in to stop the fight just as Captain John Journee was parting the ropes to do the same. Smith was declared the winner by a technical knockout.[22] The crowd came alive in this final round and cheered both fighters as they exited the arena.

Newspaper coverage, particularly that of "Bantam" in the *Daily Picayune*, was critical of the wrestling match as "the most miserable affair" and expressed their hope that "years would pass before the club managers ever inflict another such show on the sporting public."[23] The boxing was only touched on in the most cursory manner with the reader's attention being drawn to the non-stop talk about the improbable probabilities remaining for a Corbett–Fitzsimmons contest.

Stinging from the poor reaction and attendance to the third monthly subscription series, the Olympic Club redoubled their efforts to cobble together a fight card that would turn their fortunes around. They quickly approached Johnny Murphy, a featherweight boxer from Boston who had faced off against Billy Plimmer at the Olympic Club in September of 1894 when the fight was declared a draw. Murphy had made it widely known that he wanted a chance at either Pedlar Palmer or Jimmy Barry. Charles Dickson was quick to offer him a match. Discussions began with Jimmy Barry, who had dismantled Jimmy Gorman at the Olympic Club in June of 1894, but fizzled out when Barry decided to remain in Chicago for his next four fights.

Meanwhile, the Olympic Club Rifle Team placed second in the Louisiana State Rifle League championships at the Broadway Rifle Club range on North Broad near St. Phillip Street. The Olympic squad was led by Charles Boucher and Louis Gerties, both with a score of 299, followed by Vic Lambou at 297. The entire eight-shoot series was characterized by a distinct lack of disputed decisions and argumentative competition that had detracted from prior meetings.

While arrangements were being made for the Olympic Club to broadcast the telegraphic bulletins of the fight between Jim Hall and Joe Choynski from Long Island, New York, on January 20, the Olympic Club was also trying to lure welterweight champion Tommy Ryan back to New Orleans with a match against Kid McCoy for a $2,000 purse. His fight with Dempsey at the Auditorium Club in 1894 had been cancelled following the death of Andy Bowen, but that had been for a $5,000 purse. Given the current circumstances, Ryan declined the offer.[24] Also in the works were matches between bantams Jimmy Gorman and Al Allen for late February and lightweights Horace Leeds and Jack Everhardt on the next available date in March.[25] No one could accuse the Olympic Club of not trying, but they were clearly struggling against a powerful combination of an adversarial legal and political climate, higher purses being offered in other states, and a general decline in local interest.

Try as they might, the Olympic Club could not attract patrons to their fourth subscription series, scheduled for March 11, 1896. On the bill was a four-round exhibition between two local lightweights, followed by a Greco–Roman wrestling match, and finally the telegraphic broadcast of the fight between Kid Lavigne and Jack McAuliffe. Ticket prices were lowered to 50 cents for general admission, 75 cents for reserved seats and $1 for box seats in the hopes of filling the arena as they had in years past. However, deep down the management of the club knew that the card was only marginally attractive and were prepared for the worst. Their intuition was spot-on as there were less than 200 on hand to watch lightweights Louis Guillebeau and Clarence Husbands of Algiers. Referee Hugh Keough had hardly finished his monotonous drone of all too familiar admonitions during the preliminaries when the two fighters laid into each other. Guillebeau was the better boxer by far, but he was up against a subpar opponent. Both men were frequent participants in the Olympic Club exhibitions, but neither man's career had progressed beyond that. Tonight would be no exception as the sparse crowd had to endure Husbands' wild, roundhouse punches reminiscent of a schoolyard brawl which Guillebeau easily sidestepped, striking Husbands at will. Despite this, Keough declared the bout a draw. The crowd did not put up much of a protest as they were happy to see both fighters exit the ring.

This was followed by a ten-round exhibition between two bantamweights, Canadian D.A. McClelland and Peter Shea from Chicago. McClelland provided an unusual spectacle in the ring as, being a wrestler, he clearly knew nothing about boxing. The crowd seemed to enjoy the goings-on, perhaps an over-reaction to the previous match. For the better part of 20 minutes McClelland gave Shea a game if not amusing tussle, but it was obvious that both men were in less than peak fighting condition. The fight was stopped in the 7th round and awarded to Shea on points.

The final event of the evening was a Greco–Roman wrestling match between Young Bibby and James Bardell, won by Bibby even though Bardell had thrown Bibby twice within the first 30 minutes of the match. He had boasted before the contest that he would throw Bibby three times within 30 minutes or forfeit the prize money.[26]

With fewer than 200 spectators present, the fourth subscription series was a colossal failure. The talent of the fighters and wrestlers was mediocre at best, simply not in keeping with what people had come to expect from the Olympic Club, even in recent years. Less than 18 months ago many of them had attended the title defense between world champion Bob Fitzsimmons and challenger Dan Creedon. Now they were offered a seemingly endless parade of palookas just like those they had seen at every other one of the club's "entertainments." With the Guillebeau–Husbands bout, patrons were subjected to two ordinary men dressed up in fighting costumes rather than bona fide boxers. Neither man seemed to be able to gin up enough courage to do any real damage to his opponent.

The board of the Olympic Club met not long after this last subscription series was finished and the proceeds tallied. It was painfully clear that the club was hemorrhaging money. President Charles Dickson reluctantly recommended the liquidation of the club and the board reluctantly agreed.[27] A special meeting of the shareholders was called for April 2, 1896, to formally vote on the matter. That afternoon only 20 members bothered to show up. Nonetheless a requisite vote was called and Dickson announced that he held proxies that, combined with the present vote, revealed that nearly three quarters of the members, 193 out of 267, had voted for liquidation.[28] A committee of liquidation was appointed and the meeting adjourned.

News of the liquidation of the once-vaunted Olympic Club was carried in newspapers from coast to coast. Headlines touted the decline in pugilism as the primary factor, which was a contributory cause. The state supreme court's decision is only mentioned in a handful of stories.[29] Interestingly enough, the story was ignored completely in the San Francisco papers, probably in fear that their readers would confuse their local Olympic Club with the embattled New Orleans club. The committee of liquidation filed for and received a judicial order of liquidation in Civil District Court. Beginning on May 1, 1896, the club began advertising the systematic liquidation of the Olympic Club.[30] An auction was scheduled for Tuesday, June 2, at the Auction Exchange on Common Street, during which the club proposed to auction the real estate and buildings consisting of ten lots within the Royal Street–Montegut Street–Chartres Street–Clouet Street square.

Separately the club held an auction on Monday, May 11, to liquidate the furnishings and fixtures contained in these ten buildings—from grand pianos to salad forks, crystal chandeliers to gymnasium equipment.[31] Everything was subject to auctioneer Jim Brennan's gavel. St. Mary's Catholic Club purchased the entire inventory of gymnastic equipment,[32] while the Young Men's Gymnastic Club purchased the scales that had weighed every fighter to appear at the Olympic Club, along with a plaster cast of John L. Sullivan's right arm.[33] To all observers, the Olympic Club was down for the count. On June 3 a brief but "spirited" auction of the club's land and buildings, purchased for $10,000 by Adam Gambel on behalf of the Olympic Hall Association, Limited—a group that consisted of Gambel and Frank Zengel.[34] The echo of the auctioneer's gavel had hardly faded when Joseph J. Russell announced that he was reorganizing the Olympic Club. Purportedly the new club already had 200 members.[35] No word was given about what the new organization proposed to do for furniture or fixtures, or where it might locate their clubhouse.

Further downriver, the Olympic Rifle Club, which had always enjoyed a number of common members, but which also existed and operated independently from the Olympic Club itself, announced the opening of their tournament at their grounds on Poland Avenue and Royal Street. This was at the rear of the property owned by the Lambou & Noel Lumber Mill which was controlled by Victor Lambou and Charles Noel. Six clubs were scheduled to compete over two rounds of shooting, one in the morning and another in the afternoon. The evening was reserved for a *soiree dansante* for all participants and their guests.[36] After six rounds of shooting, the Volunteer Rifle Club barely edged out the Olympic Rifle Club to claim the victory. The Olympic Rifle Club would continue to compete successfully, capturing the championship of the Louisiana State Rifle League later that year.[37]

The new year began with a glimmer of hope among several former Olympic Club members led by Joseph J. Russell and the ever-present Frank Zengel who first proposed reorganizing the Olympic Club back in July.[38] They established a new clubhouse of 547 Royal Street, between Montegut and St. Ferdinand streets.[39] Officers elected were Russell as President with Robert L. Curry as Secretary. As manager of their new club, the Board selected William B. Rewnolds (Reynolds), formerly of New York. Plans were quickly developed for the new club to stage a boxing exhibition.

In the meantime, Professor John Duffy embarked on his next notable venture in 1897 with a match between Joe Green, the same black bricklayer who was involved in the deadly 1893 fight at Duffy's saloon, and a fighter labeled the "Terrible Swede." Due to the prevailing city ordinances against prize fighting, the match more closely resembled a covert military operation than a sporting event. The *Mabel Comeaux*, a riverboat packed with nearly a hundred eager fight fans that paid $5 apiece, set out from New Orleans, stopping first in Jefferson Parish upriver from the city. The local sheriff would not allow the fight to take place there, so the vessel and its passengers spent their idle time eating and drinking almost everything on board the riverboat. Eventually the riverboat set off upriver once again, this time pulling in at Morgan's Landing in St. Charles Parish. There, on the banks of the Mississippi River, without the benefit of even a rudimentary ring, the two combatants shook hands and began to exchange punches. A resident of St. Charles Parish named Henry Long, who had not made the trip upriver by boat, came upon the fight somewhere in the 3rd round and caused quite a stir, heatedly remarking about a black man fighting a white man and the possible ramifications of Joe Green beating the Terrible Swede. He worked the crowd into something of a frenzy sufficient to stop the fight altogether. An angry and disappointed boatload of passengers returned to New Orleans.[40]

On February 10, 1897, a delegation from the newly formed Olympic Club led by Frank Zengel called on Mayor Walter C. Flower, during which they applied for a permit to hold a permissible boxing exhibition on the old club grounds.[41] The mayor deliberated for some time before pragmatically granting the club's permit. While he believed that there was still a general disapproval of boxing following the death of Andy Bowen, and he personally "was opposed to this species of amusement," state law still permitted glove contests provided that there was an appropriate tax ranging from $50 to $500 levied. Mayor Flower felt he had no recourse but to grant their request, stating that the maximum tax of $500 to be paid.[42] The "tax" levied was, in fact, nothing more than a charitable contribution which the mayor could direct at his pleasure. This practice began under the administration of Mayor Shakspeare as a means of supporting the Shakspeare Almshouse. Representatives from the Olympic Club blanched at the $500 tax as being onerous, which was exactly what the mayor intended. The club informed the mayor that if he granted this one request at the usual $50 rate that they would implement resolutions that would prohibit the club from organizing "any more contests of this character" in the future.[43]

While the once famous arena was no longer available as a venue, having been leased to a theatre company, a white canvas circus-style tent was erected in a vacant lot nearby. To the older club members, the scene was reminiscent of the very first Olympic Club boxing exhibition back in July of 1890, although this time around they exhibited far less confidence in the potential of their venture. Their gut instinct was prophetic.

There was a meager audience estimated to be from 500 to 600 assembled on the evening of February 25, 1897, mostly visiting turfmen in town for the Winter Meeting at the Fair Grounds. Also present were a number of "little boys in knickerbockers." They were greeted by Professor John Duffy, who introduced the first event of the evening between two of his students, "Freckles" and "Mexican Joe," a three-round bout which proved to be the highlight of the night. Although the exhibition was supposed to be an imitation of a professional contest, the youngsters so cleverly presented their talents that the crowd could not discern the ruse. They were followed by a three-round sparring match between two boxers identified as Fernandez and Cornu, who "displayed considerably more earnestness than science."

The main event was between perennial lightweights Louis Guillebeau and Clarence Husbands, two local fighters whose pugilistic talents had never progressed any further than the sparring or exhibition stage. On this night neither of them appeared to be in anything close to fighting trim, especially Husbands. The encounter started off in fairly routine fashion through the first three rounds, with each man landing a few solid punches, leaving the two men nonetheless winded from their meager exertions. The next three rounds were fought from long range like shadow boxers in the bright light, followed by a slow deterioration that only faintly resembled boxing. Several dozen patrons left the arena disappointed. At one point during the 8th round when the two "bruisers" had once again declared another total cessation of hostilities, Professor John Duffy threatened to resign if the two men would not at least make an effort to finish the fight. It was generally believed that after the first three rounds the two fighters quickly abandoned any pretext of engaging in actual combat, preferring to cruise through the remainder of the bout in the hope of earning a split of the $500 purse. By the 12th round Captain McCabe of the New Orleans Police stepped into the ring to stop the "fight" and quell the growing unrest among the few remaining fans.[44] No one imagined it at the time, but this sad farce was to be the final boxing match under the auspices of the Olympic Club.

The rumor mill churned out stories designed to keep the hope of boxing alive. Charles Genslinger, formerly of the Olympic Club and the Metropolitan Club, was now managing Kid Lavigne. Perhaps he could be persuaded to make a triumphant return to New Orleans. Charles Noel, described as being "the best known man that was ever connected with a fighting club, with the possible exception of Lord Lonsdale and the Marquis of Queensbury," was supposedly negotiating with the Tulane Club to organize matches for their club. There was talk of a match between Billy Plimmer and Sammy Kelly, but by this time most fighters and their managers were dead set against even considering the New Orleans market and had begun looking elsewhere, mostly out west. With a financial and critical disaster on their hands, and no other options remaining, the new Olympic Club fared no better than its predecessor and their creditors obtained a court order to liquidate the club's few remaining assets at public auction.[45] This last inglorious event was concluded on Monday, June 14, 1897.

The former Olympic Club arena and clubhouse had been purchased in June of 1896 by the Olympic Hall Association, whose principals were Adam Gambel and Frank

Zengel. The clubhouse leased rooms to a variety of benevolent groups such as the Washington Lodge No. 75 of the Knights of Pythias, the Orion Lodge of the Knights of Honor, the Third District Benevolent Association, and the Ladies' Violet Benevolent Association.[46] The former prizefighting arena was leased to the Klimt–Hearne theatrical production company who operated the facility as the Olympic Theatre.

On Monday, December 6, 1897, a small fire broke out in one of the lower dressing rooms in the Olympic Theatre at around five o'clock in the afternoon. Despite the efforts of James Corcoran, the theatre manager, and three employees to fight the blaze with fire extinguishers, the fire quickly spread throughout the lower section of the theatre. Corcoran and his employees were forced from the building to avoid suffocation from the billowing black smoke. Although an alarm had immediately been raised, the old wooden structure provided too much ready fuel for the growing inferno. By 6:30 a general alarm was sounded, bringing several additional fire companies to the scene, but at this point all they could do was to try to contain the fire. A squad of policemen from various precincts established a perimeter with ropes to hold back the growing crowd who gazed into the very heart of Hades, shrieking in fear and amazement as the splendid cupola of the once-famous arena collapsed upon the conflagration, blanketing the neighborhood with sparks and ash, and spreading the firestorm to the adjoining buildings. Within two hours, the theatre which occupied the once-famous boxing arena, the magnificent old four story clubhouse, and nine nearby cottages were completely consumed by fire, collapsing one after another as thick smoke chased away most of the curious bystanders.

The former clubhouse building, owned by the Olympic Hall Association was valued at $25,000 and the old arena at $12,000 at cost. The theatrical company lost $3,500 worth of costumes and scenery and a team of Japanese acrobats touring with the theatrical company lost $500 of material. Within the clubhouse, the uninsured renters lost their furnishings, fixtures, and documents valued between $250 and $1,000 each. Total estimated losses would exceed $60,000 of which only a fraction was insured. The neighboring buildings damaged or destroyed would bring the total loss to over $100,000 (approximately $2.6 million today).

The Klimt–Hearn company had only just staged its debut performance the previous Sunday afternoon with their production of an old melodrama, "Shadows of a Great City," which they reprised that night, Among the crowd for the evening performance were a pair of ruffians whose drunken behavior interrupted the performance and intimidated the audience.

BIG FIRE IN THE THIRD

Olympic Club and Eight Houses Burned.

New Orleans awoke on December 7, 1897, to learn that the once heralded Olympic Club and its massive wooden arena, along with several other buildings, had been destroyed by a fire thought to be the work of arsonists (*New Orleans Times-Democrat*).

Ushers were compelled to escort them bodily from the theatre. The theatre's press agent, John V. McStea (McShea), informed authorities that the theatre had received a postal card the day of the fire which read, "Mr. George Klimt, Olympic Theatre—Look out for a big surprise today or tomorrow." An investigation revealed the probability of arson based on a distinct odor detected in the smoldering ash heap the following morning. Although the two drunken louts who had been thrown out of a performance days earlier were prime suspects as they certainly had motive and perhaps even opportunity, they could not be identified and no arrests were ever made in the case.

Coverage of the fire was reported briefly in newspapers nationwide, meriting one or two sentences as a sad postscript to the demise of boxing in general.[47] Although building owners Adam Gambel and Frank Zengel announced a campaign to rebuild, nothing ever materialized and the property was eventually cleared, leveled, and redeveloped into conventional residential lots.[48] Today all that remains of the once world famous Olympic Club complex is a single section of brick wall that runs between two houses in the 600 block of Clouet Street. It is remarkable to consider that the Olympic Club constructed their massive wooden arena beginning in 1890 and, through gradual expansion that continued through 1892, erected a building that could comfortably accommodate nearly 11,000 spectators, with amenities such as a retractable roof, incandescent and carbon arc electric lighting, and telephone and telegraph service. For a brief period of time, New Orleans could boast three such edifices. In addition to the Olympic Club's arena there was the arena build by Charles Genslinger and the Metropolitan Club (1891–1894), and Charles Noel's colossal Crescent City Athletic Club arena, which was later renamed the Auditorium Athletic Club (1893–1895) that could hold well over 13,000 people.

By 1897, all three structures were gone, razed and redeveloped into residential neighborhoods.

Epilogue

The Olympic Club sponsored a grand total of a hundred fights between July 2, 1889, and February 25, 1897. Seventy of these were exhibitions which ranged from the most basic three-round sparring matches to 14-round contests. There were also 30 regulation bouts, 13 of which were for world, national or regional titles and championships. For a brief four-year span between 1891 and 1894, the Olympic Club was the grandest world championship boxing venue anywhere in the country, perhaps even the world. The greatest names in the pugilistic pantheon of the time came to New Orleans to compete in the Olympic Club's massive arena, including (in alphabetical order):

Jimmy Barry (59–0–9) was a durable bantamweight who fought at the Olympic Club in 1894 and would claim the world title later that year. He retired undefeated from the ring in 1899 and died at the age of 73 in 1943. He was inducted into the International Boxing Hall of Fame in 2000.

Jimmy Carroll (4–4–3) the on-again, off-again manager/trainer for Bob Fitzsimmons, was active in boxing circles in New Orleans and San Francisco until he retired from boxing in 1897. He died in San Francisco at the ripe old age of 69 in 1922.

Joe Choynski (50–14–6) was perhaps the hardest puncher of his era and one of the many boxers from San Francisco who passed through New Orleans. Oddly enough he only made a single appearance at the Olympic Club in a benefit exhibition for Jimmy Carroll in 1892. He died in 1943 at the age of 75 and was inducted into the *Ring Magazine* Hall of Fame in 1960 and the International Boxing Hall of Fame in 1998.

James Corbett (11–4–3) would only participate in seven matches following his victory against Sullivan at the Olympic Club in 1892—two wins, a draw, and four losses. Gentlemen Jim's entire career from 1886 through 1903 consisted of only 18 bouts. He died at the age of 66 in 1933 in New York City. He was inducted into the *Ring Magazine* Hall of Fame in 1954 and the International Boxing Hall of Fame in 1990.

Jack "The Nonpareil" Dempsey (50–3–8) only had three fights after his defeat by Bob Fitzsimmons at the Olympic Club in 1891. Few people at the time knew that he had been stricken with tuberculosis, from which he died at the age of 32 in 1895. He was inducted into the *Ring Magazine* Hall of Fame in 1954 and the International Boxing Hall of Fame in 1992.

George Dixon (50–26–44) returned to Boston after the Fistic Carnival and steadfastly refused to fight in the South again, the single exception being a brief four-round victory over Charles Slusher in Louisville, Kentucky, in 1896. He had his final fight in

1906 against Monk the Newsboy. Dixon died destitute in New York City in 1908 at the age of 37. He was inducted into Canada's Sports Hall of Fame in 1955, the *Ring Magazine* Hall of Fame in 1956 and the International Boxing Hall of Fame in 1990.

Bob Fitzsimmons (74–8–3) would become the first man to win world titles in three different weight classes—the middleweight title won in New Orleans from Jack Dempsey in 1891, the heavyweight title from James Corbett in Carson City, Nevada in 1897, and the light heavyweight title from George Gardiner in 1903 at the age of 40. He continued to fight and perform in vaudeville shows until 1914 and died of pneumonia in 1917. Fitzsimmons was elected to the *Ring Magazine* Hall of Fame in 1954 and the International Boxing Hall of Fame in 1990.

Young Griffo (63–9–37) appeared at the Olympic Club in 1894 in a preliminary bout before the Everhardt–Abbott match. One of dozens of Australian fighters who found steady work and fame in the United States, he died penniless in New York in 1927. He was inducted into the *Ring Magazine* Hall of Fame in 1981 and the International Boxing Hall of Fame in 1991.

Peter Maher (135–21–4) was an Irish heavyweight boxer who won the middleweight championship of Ireland in 1888 and the heavyweight championship of Ireland in 1890. He was beaten by Bob Fitzsimmons at the Olympic Club in 1892 as a middleweight and again in 1896 in Mexico as a heavyweight. He was inducted into the *Ring Magazine* Hall of Fame in 1978.

Jack McAuliffe (30–0–5) was a durable lightweight who got his start during the bare-knuckle era and successfully transitioned to the Queensbury era, one of only 12 world champions to retire undefeated, having held the lightweight title for 12 years from 1885 through 1897. His was the first fight in the fabled Fistic Carnival, beating Billy Myer in 1892. He died in 1937. McAuliffe was inducted into the *Ring Magazine* Hall of Fame in 1954 and the International Boxing Hall of Fame in 1995.

Charlie Mitchell (31–3–12) was an English-born fighter who was considered to be one of the best pure punchers in the game. He fought only once at the Olympic Club as part of the undercard for the Fitzsimmons–Maher bout in 1892. Mitchell died in Hove, England in 1918. He was inducted into the *Ring Magazine* Hall of Fame in 1957 and the International Boxing Hall of Fame in 2002.

John L. Sullivan (26–1–3) was one of the pioneers of boxing who was a worldwide celebrity when he lost his heavyweight title at the Olympic Club to James Corbett in 1892 as part of the Fistic Carnival. It would be his last prize fight. Sullivan died in 1918 at the age of 60. He was inducted into the *Ring Magazine* Hall of Fame in 1954 and the International Boxing Hall of Fame in 1990.

There were many boxers who fought in and around New Orleans and who acted as seconds or who were frequent patrons of the events at the Olympic Club, but who never actually had a bout there.

Jake Kilrain (18–6–12) trained in New Orleans for his match with John L. Sullivan that ultimately took place in Richbourg, Mississippi, becoming the last bare knuckle championship fight in America. He later lost to James L. Corbett at the Southern Athletic Club in New Orleans pushing Corbett into the national spotlight as a heavyweight contender. Kilrain died in 1937 in Quincy, Massachusetts. He was inducted into the *Ring Magazine* Hall of Fame in 1965 and the International Boxing Hall of Fame in 2012.

George "Kid" Lavigne (37–9–12) made his professional debut in 1886 and was active until 1909. He was involved in the fatal fight against Andy Bowen at the Audubon Athletic Club that helped to swing public opinion against boxing. Lavigne passed away in 1928 at the age of 56. He was inducted into the *Ring Magazine* Hall of Fame in 1959 and the International Boxing Hall of Fame in 1998.

Jem Mace was a light heavyweight who had his first professional fight in 1855 and toured the world as a boxing instructor and an occasional combatant. As the self-proclaimed world champion, he arrived in America and met Tom Allen in New Orleans in 1870 in what is believed to be the first world championship prizefight. Mace discovered Bob Fitzsimmons during his 1882 tour of New Zealand. He died at the ripe old age of 79 on November 30, 1910, in England. He was inducted into the *Ring Magazine* Hall of Fame in 1954 and the International Boxing Hall of Fame in 1990.

Paddy Ryan was an Irish-American boxer and the reigning World Heavyweight Champion in 1882 when he met the up-and-coming John L. Sullivan in Mississippi City (Gulfport), losing in the ninth round. Ryan retired from the ring in 1887 and passed away in New York in 1900. He was inducted into the *Ring Magazine* Hall of Fame in 1973.

Tommy Ryan (86–3–6) was scheduled to take part in the second triple event at the Olympic Club in 1893, but fell ill and his match was postponed and never rescheduled. He was the reigning welterweight champion of the world when he was scheduled to meet Jack Dempsey at the Auditorium Club in 1894, but the death of Andy Bowen cancelled this match. Ryan died in 1948 at the age of 78. He was inducted into the *Ring Magazine* Hall of Fame in 1958 and the International Boxing Hall of Fame in 1991.

Members of the Olympic Club who made significant contributions to the development of the institution include the following.

Thomas C. "Tom" Anderson, the staunch financial backer and friend of Andy Bowen, was also a former bookkeeper with the Louisiana State Lottery Company. Anderson went into the restaurant business in 1892 on North Rampart Street before going into the saloon and brothel business with Josie Arlington (Josie Lobrano). One of the most colorful characters in New Orleans, Anderson would become known as the "Mayor of Storyville" as well as a successful oilman and a Louisiana state legislator.

Charles Dickson remained with the Olympic Club until the very end. He was a member of the board from 1891 through 1895 and was President in 1893 and 1895. He owned the Brook Tarpaulin Company and was also a City Councilman from 1892 through 1896. He died in 1912 from Bright's Disease at the age of 60.

John H. Duffy would not live long enough to see the sport he so loved become part of the fabric of America. In July of 1898 he fell ill and was confined to bed rest at his home on Julia Street. For six weeks he lingered, tended to by his friend, Captain Lee of Fire Company No. 5. It was all slipping away from Duffy—his wife Kate had died of tuberculosis three months earlier, his four children were now consigned to St. Michael's Convent, and he was dying of cirrhosis of the liver. A substantial number of his friends were planning a benefit for him, but he passed away on August 18, 1898, at the age of 34. The benefit was later held for his children. Former New Orleans mayor John Fitzpatrick, who had led the movement to abolish boxing in New Orleans following the death of Andy Bowen in 1894, served as one the pallbearers.

Charles Genslinger was a successful businessman, having established the printing firm of Hunter & Genslinger in 1883. He was a member of the Louisiana Sugar Exchange, the New Orleans Bicycle Club, and was involved with the Lone Star Base Ball Club as a player and manager. Genslinger eventually became a principal shareholder and Treasurer of the Pelican Base Ball Club, President of the Sportsman's Park Association, and President of the Southern League. He left New Orleans in 1893 following the collapse of the Metropolitan Club. He attempted to replicate the success of the Olympic Club by opening athletic clubs in New York, Illinois, and Missouri, but none of these ventures achieved the level of success he so desperately desired.

Bernard Klotz, Sr., never spent a day in jail for his part in the attempted murder of William A. Scholl. He continued to own and operate Klotz Manufacturing until he sold his interest in the business in July of 1912. Within weeks of that sale Klotz opened the Snowflake Cracker Factory at 543 Magazine Street between Poydras and Lafayette streets. He passed away on March 6, 1920, at the age of 77.

Charles Noel owned and operated the Jackson Saw Mill and the Lambou and Noel Sawmill in the Third District. He was a member of the Olympic Club's Board of Directors from 1889 through 1892 and was president from 1891 through 1892. He resigned to establish the Crescent City Athletic Club which went bankrupt in 1893. Noel served on the New Orleans City Council from 1892 through 1896. He died in 1924 at the age of 65.

Joseph L. Sporl was an officer and director of the Olympic Club from 1885 through 1892 when he resigned along with Charles Noel to form the Crescent City Athletic Club. He was later involved with the Auditorium Club in 1894. An original investor in the Third District Building Association, he served as secretary of that organization until he was forced to resign after defaulting on a $39,000 personal loan. Sporl died in 1916 at the age of 60.

Frank Williams was a native of New Orleans who sold his mercantile business in Livingston Parish in 1890 and returned to New Orleans where he became involved with the Olympic Club for two years before resigning to help Charles Noel establish the Crescent City Athletic Club in 1893. The following year he was instrumental in establishing the Auditorium Club. He died unexpectedly at the age of 43 in 1895.

Frank Zengel, the ever-present attorney and real estate developer, survived his association with the Olympic Club, the Crescent City Athletic Club, and the Auditorium Athletic Club. Like his brother, he became active in politics, first in 1894 as Chairman of the Citizen's Protective Association, then as Public Administrator for Orleans Parish the following year. In 1903 Zengel was elected to the New Orleans City Council and also became a director of the Germaniz Insurance Company. Zengel died unexpectedly at the age of 44 on October 22, 1909.

Appendix
The Olympic Club Fight Record

Date	Winner	Loser	Result	Purse	Referee	Attendance
07/02/1889 (1)	John Duffy	Pat Kendrick	SPAR for 3	None	None	< 100
07/02/1889 (1)	James Kendrick	Mike Lambour	SPAR for 3	None	None	< 100
07/02/1889 (1)	Paddy Airey	Thomas Casey	SPAR for 3	None	None	< 100
07/20/1889 (2)	Peter Crawford	Louis Knoechel	SPAR for 5	None	None	< 100
07/20/1889 (2)	John Duffy	Tom Doling	SPAR for 5	None	None	< 100
09/14/1889 (3)	John Duffy	James Kendrick	SPAR for 3	None	M.A. Sporl	500–600
09/14/1889 (3)	Andy Bowen	Charles Wilson	SPAR for 3	None	John Duffy	500–600
09/14/1889 (3)	Tom Kelly	William Phillips	SPAR for 3	None	John Duffy	
09/14/1889 (3)	Peter Crawford	Louis Knoechel	DRAW in 8	$1,000	"9th Ward Resident"	500–600
07/11/1890	Charles Wilson	Tommy Ward	KO in 8	$400	John Duffy	2,000
09/16/1890	Jimmy Carroll †	Andy Bowen	KO in 21	$3,000	John Duffy	4,000–5,000
01/14/1891	Bob Fitzsimmons *	Jack Dempsey	RTD in 13	$12,000	Alexander Brewster	4,000–5,000
02/06/1891 (4)	Joe Fielden	John Cash	DRAW in 3		James Kendrick	300–450
02/06/1891 (4)	Bob Fitzsimmons	Felix Vacquelin	SPAR for 3			300–450
02/06/1891 (4)	Patsey Doodey	Charles Wilson	PTS in 3			300–450
02/06/1891 (4)	Andy Bowen	Billy McMillan	SPAR for 3			300–450
02/06/1891 (4)	Mike Smith	Tom Casey	SPAR for 3			300–450
02/06/1891 (4)	Bob Fitzsimmons	Joe Fielden	SPAR for 3			300–450
02/09/1891 (5)	Bob Fitzsimmons	John Cash	(Cancelled)	$250		None
05/19/1891	Andy Bowen	Billy Myer	DRAW in 24	$3,000	Alexander Brewster	3,000
08/25/1891 (6)	Joe Oliver	Joseph Dingemann	KO in 2	None	John Duffy	5,000
08/25/1891 (6)	George Siddons	Owen Harvey	DRAW in 10	None	John Duffy	5,000
08/25/1891 (6)	Walter O'Brien	"Mexican Joe"	DRAW in 3	None	John Duffy	5,000
08/25/1891 (6)	Otto Meyers	Bob Curry	DRAW in 3	None	John Duffy	5,000
09/22/1891	Cal McCarthy	Tommy Warren	KO in 21	$1,500	John Duffy	1,500
10/06/1891 (7)	Charles Porter	Charles Fox		None	John Duffy	700
10/06/1891 (7)	O'Brien	Tolavo		None	John Duffy	700
10/06/1891 (7)	Andy Bowen	Dave Bowen		None	John Duffy	700
10/06/1891 (7)	Dutch Neil	Charles Porter	SPAR for 3	None	John Duffy	700
10/06/1891 (7)	Albert Spruce	Joseph Suarez		None	John Duffy	700
10/06/1891 (7)	Tommy Warren	George Siddons	SPAR for 4	None	John Duffy	700
11/18/1891	Johnny Griffin †	Jimmy Larkin	KO in 4	$2,500	John Duffy	< 3,200
12/21/1891 (8)	Jack Burke	Arthur Flint		None	George Scott	2,000+
12/21/1891 (8)	(Duffy's kids)	(Duffy's kids)		None	George Scott	2,000+
12/21/1891 (8)	James Daley	Dave Bowen		None	George Scott	2,000+

Date	Winner	Loser	Result	Purse	Referee	Attendance
12/21/1891 (8)	*Frank Knell*	*Charles Johnson*		*None*	*George Scott*	*2,000+*
12/21/1891 (8)	*George Siddons*	*Charles Fox*		*None*	*George Scott*	*2,000+*
12/21/1891 (8)	*Jake Wambsgans*	*Joe Everhardt*		*None*	*George Scott*	*2,000+*
12/21/1891 (8)	*Charles Fernandez*	*Ed McCue*		*None*	*George Scott*	*2,000+*
12/21/1891 (8)	*Bob Fitzsimmons*	*Felix Vacquelin*		*None*	*George Scott*	*2,000+*
12/22/1891	Jimmy Carroll †	Billy Myer	KO in 43	$5,000	John Duffy	3,000
01/27/1892	Cal McCarthy	Tom Callaghan	KO in 14	$2,000	John Duffy	2,000+
02/28/1892 (9)	*Johnny Van Heest*	*Dutch Neil*		*None*	*John Duffy*	
02/28/1892 (9)	*Joe Choynski*	*Alex Greggins*		*None*	*John Duffy*	
02/28/1892 (9)	*Bob Fitzsimmons*	*Felix Vaquelin*		*None*	*John Duffy*	
02/28/1892 (9)	*Ned Cullen*	*Doc Brown*		*None*	*John Duffy*	
03/02/1892	Charlie Mitchell	Arthur Upham	PTS in 4		John Duffy	5,000
03/02/1892	Paddy Slavin	Felix Vacquelin	NC in 3		John Duffy	5,000
03/02/1892	Paddy Slavin	Charlie Mitchell	NC in 3		John Duffy	5,000
03/02/1892	Bob Fitzsimmons *	Peter Maher	RTD in 12	$10,000	John Duffy	5,000–8,000
09/05/1892	Jack McAuliffe *	Billy Myer	KO in 15	$9,000	John Duffy	6,500+
09/06/1892	George Dixon *	Jack Skelly	KO in 8	$7,500	John Duffy	8,500+
09/07/1892	James Corbett *	John L. Sullivan	KO in 21	$25,000	John Duffy	10,000+
03/01/1893	George Dawson	Tommy Ryan	Postponed			
03/02/1893	Billy McMillan	Billy Hinds	KO in 5	$800	John Duffy	1,500
03/03/1893	*George Dawson*	*Eddie Greeney*	*SPAR for 3*	*None*	*John Duffy*	*3,000*
03/03/1893	Denver Ed Smith	Joe Goddard	KO in 18	$10,000	John Duffy	3,000
04/06/1893	Andy Bowen †	Jack Burke	NC in 110 **	$2,500	John Duffy	8,500
05/31/1893	Andy Bowen †	Jack Everhardt	RTD in 85	$2,000	Lloyd Gearhardt	6,000–8,000
09/20/1893	Johnny Van Heest	Hughie Napier	KO in 28	$2,000	John Duffy	4,000
10/17/1893	Jimmy Gorman †	Jack Levy	KO in 8	$1,000	John Duffy	2,500
10/17/1893	Jack Everhardt	George Pierce	KO in 2		John Duffy	2,500
05/26/1894	Jack Everhardt	Jack Burke	KO in 15	$1,000	Lloyd Gearhardt	~3,000
06/02/1894	Jimmy Barry	Jimmy Gorman	KO in 10	$7,000	Lloyd Gearhardt	~3,000
06/14/1894	Johnny Connors	Jack Levy	DQ in 5	$1,000	Lloyd Gearhardt	~3,000
07/09/1894 (10)	*Burkhardt*	*Steadman*	*SPAR for 3*	*None*	*George Queen*	*~500*
07/09/1894 (10)	*Maroney*	*Piper*	*SPAR for 3*	*None*	*George Queen*	*~500*
07/09/1894 (10)	*Clarence Husbands*	*Jimmy Downs*	*SPAR for 3*	*None*	*George Queen*	*~500*
07/09/1894 (10)	*Laine*	*Alphonse Garcia*	*SPAR for 3*	*None*	*George Queen*	*~500*
07/09/1894 (10)	*Walker*	*Harry Black*	*SPAR for 3*	*None*	*George Queen*	*~500*
07/09/1894 (10)	*Andy Bowen*	*Billy Campbell*	*SPAR for 2*	*None*	*George Queen*	*~500*
07/09/1894 (10)	*Andy Bowen*	*George Pierce*	*SPAR for 2*	*None*	*George Queen*	*~500*
07/09/1894 (10)	*"Mexican Joe"*	*Schultz*	*SPAR for 3*	*None*	*George Queen*	*~500*
07/09/1894 (10)	*Tom Kennedy*	*John Cash*	*SPAR for 3*	*None*	*George Queen*	*~500*
07/09/1894 (10)	*Billy McCarthy*	*Tom Green*	*SPAR for 3*	*None*	*George Queen*	*~500*
07/09/1894 (10)	*Hill*	*Cole*	*SPAR for 3*	*None*	*George Queen*	*~500*
07/09/1894 (10)	*John Duffy*	*Pat Allen*	*SPAR for 3*	*None*	*George Queen*	*~500*
08/21/1894	Jack Everhardt †	Stanton Abbott	KO in 25	$1,500	Lloyd Gearhardt	7,000
09/24/1894	Billy Plimmer	Johnny Murphy	DRAW in 25	$2,500	John Eckhardt	4,000
09/25/1894	Young Griffo	Mickey Dunn	SPAR for 6	None	John Eckhardt	5,000
09/25/1894	Jack Everhardt	Stanton Abbott	DRAW in 25	$1,500	John Duffy	5,000
09/26/1894	Bob Fitzsimmons *	Dan Creedon	KO in 2	$5,000	John Duffy	6,000+
12/06/1894	Charley Johnson	Shadow Maber	DRAW in 25	$1,500	John Duffy	1,700
01/06/1895 (11)	*James Corbett*	*John McVey*		*None*	*John Duffy*	*400*
01/06/1895 (11)	*Louis Gray*	*Ed Brooks*		*None*	*John Duffy*	*400*
01/06/1895 (11)	*George Pierce*	*Clarence Husbands*		*None*	*John Duffy*	*400*

The Olympic Club Fight Record

Date	Winner	Loser	Result	Purse	Referee	Attendance
01/06/1895 (11)	Jack Everhardt	Billy McCarthy		None	John Duffy	400
09/04/1895 (12)	"Freckles"	"Mexican Joe"	PTS in 4	None	John Duffy	1,200
09/04/1895 (12)	William Crawford	Louis Knuckles	DRAW in 5	None	John Duffy	1,200
09/04/1895 (12)	Louis Guillebeau	George Pierce	PTS in 6	None	John Duffy	1,200
09/04/1895 (12)	Herman Bernau	Billy McCarthy	KO in 4	None	John Duffy	1,200
10/24/1895 (13)	Jack Everhardt	Owen Ziegler	PTS in 25	None	John Duffy	3,000
12/23/1895 (14)	Mickey Finn	William Crawford	DRAW in 3	None	John Duffy	1,000
12/23/1895 (14)	Louis Knuckles	Alphonse Garcia	PTS in 3	None	John Duffy	1,000
12/23/1895 (14)	Louis Guillebeau	Jess Clark	PTS in 4	None	John Duffy	1,000
12/23/1895 (14)	Solly Smith	Billy Murphy	TKO in 14	None	John Duffy	1,000
03/11/1896 (15)	Louis Guillebeau	Clarence Husbands	DRAW in 4	None	Hugh M. Keogh	~200
03/11/1896 (15)	Peter Shea	D.A. McClellan	PTS in 7	None	Hugh M. Keogh	~200
02/25/1897 (16)	"Freckles"	"Mexican Joe"	DRAW in 3	None	John Duffy	500–600
02/25/1897 (16)	Fernandez	Joseph Cornu	DRAW in 3	None	John Duffy	500–600
02/25/1897 (16)	Louis Guillebeau	Clarence Husbands	NC in 12	$500	John Duffy	500–600

Italic events indicate exhibition bouts.

* Indicates a world championship title match.
† Indicates another level title match—either regional or national.
** Indicates a world record.

EVENT KEY
(1)—(07/02/1889) Impromptu exhibitions for Mike Donovan and guests
(2)—(07/20/1889) This was an event for members of the Olympic Club only
(3)—(09/14/1889) Benefit for John Duffy
(4)—(02/06/1891) Exhibition—60% of gate to Fitzsimmons, 40% to Olympic Club
(5)—(02/09/1891) This was intended to be a benefit, but Fitzsimmons did not show up.
(6)—(08/25/1891) This was an event for members of the Olympic Club only.
(7)—(10/06/1891) Benefit for Tommy Warren
(8)—(12/21/1891) Benefit for John Duffy
(9)—(02/28/1892) Benefit for Jimmy Carroll
(10)—(07/09/1894) Benefit for William D. Ross
(11)—(01/06/1895) Benefit for the widow of Andy Bowen
(12)—(09/04/1895) First subscription series
(13)—(10/24/1895) Second subscription series
(14)—(12/23/1895) Third subscription series
(15)—(03/11/1896) Fourth and final subscription series
(16)—(02/25/1897) First and only exhibitions presented by the New Olympic Club

"Mexican" was also known as "Mexican Joe," but was in fact a black teenager. "Knuckles" more than likely refers to Louis Knoechel who was also a student of John Duffy.

After the closure and liquidation of the original Olympic Club in 1896, the club was reorganized on a smaller scale in 1897 and presented a single event. The next registered fights under the name "Olympic Athletic Club" did not occur until 1913 when three fights were held in April and May.

Chapter Notes

Introduction

1. Edwin L. Jewell, ed., *Jewell's Crescent City Illustrated* (New Orleans: Edwin L. Jewell, 1874), p. 15. It is estimated that there were 8,001 free persons of color and at least as many slaves out of a total population of 24,552.
2. J. Chandler Gregg, *Life in the Army, in the Departments of Virginia, and the Gulf, Including Observations in New Orleans, With an Account of the Author's Life and Experience in the Ministry* (Philadelphia: Perkin Pine & Higgins, 1868), p. 157.
3. U.S. Department of Commerce, Bureau of the Census, *Historical Statistics of the 1850 United States Census*.
4. James S. Zacherie, *New Orleans Guide* (New Orleans: F.F. Hansel & Bro., 1893), pp. 242–243.
5. *Daily Picayune*, April 18, 1887.
6. U.S. Department of Commerce, Bureau of the Census, *Historical Statistics of the 1850 United States Census*.
7. Henry Rightor, *Standard History of New Orleans, Louisiana* (Chicago: The Lewis Publishing Company, 1900; Henry C. Brown, *Report on the Drainage, Sewerage, and Health of the City of New Orleans* (New Orleans, 1879).
8. Thomas Ewing Dabney, *One Hundred Great Years: The Story of the Times-Picayune* (Baton Rouge: Louisiana State University Press, 1944.
9. *Daily Picayune*, January 23, 1844.
10. *Ibid.*, May 19, 1854; November 8, 1855; August 31, 1865.
11. *Ibid.*, October 16, 1891; August 18, 1895.
12. *New Orleans Crescent*, January 29, 1869.
13. *Daily Picayune*, September 23, 1837; September 25, 1841; August 23, November 15, December 14, December 22, 1843.
14. *Ibid.*, December 25, 1840.
15. *Ibid.*, January 23, 1853.
16. *Ibid.*, July 15, 1845; February 18, 1848.
17. *Ibid.*, July 9, 1845; July 15, 1845; March 23, 1857; November 18, 1866.
18. *Spirit of the Times* XXII (January 8, 1853); XXIII (February 26, 1853).
19. Joseph R. Conlin, *The American Past: A Survey of American History—Volume I* (Boston: Wadsworth Publishing, 1984), p. 260; James M. Volo and Dorothy D. Volo, *Family Life in 19th Century America* (Santa Barbara: Greenwood, 2007), p 138.
20. *Daily Picayune*, December 26, 1857.
21. *Ibid.*, January 14, 1844; July 10, 1859.
22. John Hope Franklin, *The Militant South, 1800–1861* (Urbana: University of Illinois Press, 2002).
23. Captain C.A. Stevens, *Berdan's United States Sharpshooters in the Army of the Potomac* (St. Paul, MN, 1892).
24. *Daily Picayune*, October 26, 1874.
25. *Ibid.*, June 26, 1876.
26. *Ibid.*, June 21, 1870; January 24, 1876.
27. *Daily Picayune*, October 13, October 14, 1876; *New York Times*, October 13, 1876.
28. *Daily Picayune*, October 6, 1876.
29. *Ibid.*, June 26, 1884.
30. *Ibid.*, July 26, August 16, October 7, 1886.
31. *The Times-Democrat*, July 26, 1886.
32. *Daily Picayune*, August 30, October 10, 1886.
33. *Ibid.*, December 18, 1877; December 23, 1879; December 23, 1883; March 28, 1886.
34. Charles L. Dufour, *Ten Flags in the Wind: The Story of Louisiana* (New York: Harper & Row, 1967).
35. *New Orleans Times*, January 16, 1866; October 11, 1875.
36. *Daily Picayune*, September 22, 1837.
37. *Ibid.*, September 12, 1852.
38. *Ibid.*, November 20, 1853.
39. *Ibid.*, December 16, 1860.
40. *Ibid.*, January 9, 1853.
41. *Ibid.*, December 26, 1857.
42. *Ibid.*, May 19, May 28, October 28, November 11, 1873.
43. *Ibid.*, December 5, 1857.
44. *Ibid.*, December 16, 1860.
45. Robert Froeschle, *Official Rule Book for All Pocket & Carom Billiard Games* (Chicago: Billiard Congress of America, 1971).
46. Clarence D. Long, *Wages and Earnings in the United States, 1860–1890* (Princeton: Princeton University Press, 1960); Richard White, *Railroaded* (New York: W.W. Norton, 2011).
47. *Daily Picayune*, May 6, 1837.

48. *New Orleans Times*, August 9, 1869; May 11, 1870.
49. V.G. Dowling, *Fistiana or the Oracle of the Ring* (London: Wm. Clement, 1841), p. 29.
50. *Ibid.*, pp. 63, 273; William Edwards, *The Art and Science of Boxing* (New York: Excelsior Publishing House, 1888), pp. 103–107.
51. V.G. Dowling, *Fistiana or the Oracle of the Ring* (London: Wm. Clement, 1841), pp. 63–66.
52. William Edwards, *The Art and Science of Boxing* (New York: Excelsior Publishing House, 1888), p. 108.
53. *Daily Picayune*, May 11, 1870.
54. *Times-Democrat*, February 9, 1882; *Daily Picayune*, July 9, 1889.
55. *Ibid.*, June 16, June 29, July 28, August 2, 1884.
56. *Ibid.*, January 12, February 23, March 13, March 20, March 26, 1885.
57. *Ibid.*, May 20, June 17, August 5, December 23, 1889.
58. *Ibid.*, June 4, 1890.
59. Louisiana *Senate Journal*, 1890, p. 45.
60. Louisiana *Acts*, 1890, p. 19.

Chapter One

1. *Daily Picayune*, March 24, 1882; *Times-Democrat*, March 28, 1882; *Daily Picayune*, May 5, 1882.
2. Herbert S. Fairall, *The World Industrial and Cotton Centennial Exposition* (Iowa City: Republican Publishing Company, 1885).
3. Joy J. Jackson, *New Orleans in the Gilded Age: Politics and Urban Progress 1880–1896* (Baton Rouge, LA: Louisiana State University Press, 1969), p. 38.
4. Rubert Boyce, *Yellow Fever Prophylaxis in New Orleans* (London: Williams & Norgate, 1905), p. 1.
5. U.S. Department of Commerce, Bureau of the Census, *Historical Statistics of the United States*.
6. *Times-Picayune*, March 16, 1998. The columnist, Clarence Page, references a PBS documentary *Long Journey Home: The Irish in America* (1998).
7. Tim Pat Coogan, *Wherever Green Is Worn: The Story of the Irish Diaspora* (New York: Palgrave/St. Martin's Press, 2000), p. 315.
8. U.S. Department of Commerce, Bureau of the Census, *Historical Statistics of the 1850 United States Census*.
9. Katherine Adrienne Luck, "Finding Margaret Haughery: The Forgotten and Remembered Lives of New Orleans's 'Bread Woman' in the Nineteenth and Twentieth Centuries," University of New Orleans Theses and Dissertations, Paper 1821 (2014).
10. Mary Gehman and Nancy Ries, *Women and New Orleans—A History* (New Orleans: Margaret Media, 1996).
11. The term *faubourg* was a French word often used to describe a "suburb," but which in New Orleans more accurately described a "neighborhood" or an expansion beyond the established city limits.
12. Richard Campanella, "The Turbulent History Behind the Seven New Orleans Municipal Districts," *Times-Picayune*, October 9, 2013; updated March 7, 2016.
13. Will H. Coleman, *Historical Sketch Book and Guide to New Orleans and Environs* (New York: Will H. Coleman, 1885).
14. *Daily Picayune*, May 6, 1883.
15. *Ibid.*, July 9, 1884. This represented the old street numbering system as the current numbering system adopted in the early 1890s would place the building at 2217 Royal Street.
16. *The Times-Democrat*, February 7, 1886. This would be present-day 3044 Royal Street.
17. *Sanborn Insurance Maps for New Orleans, LA—Volume Two* (New York: Sanborn Map Publishing Company, 1885), Plate 494.
18. *Ibid.*
19. *Daily Picayune*, April 17, 1887.
20. *Ibid.*, May 1, 1887.
21. *Times-Democrat*, January 20, 1889.
22. *Ibid.*, January 20, 1889.
23. *Daily Picayune*, April 29, 1889.
24. *Ibid.*, May 5, 1889.
25. *Ibid.*, May 20, 1889.
26. James B. Roberts and Alexander G. Skutt, *The Boxing Register: International Boxing Hall of Fame Official Record Book* (Ithaca: McBooks Press, 2006).
27. *Times-Democrat*, April 15, 1884.
28. *Daily Picayune*, July 6, 1889.
29. *Ibid.*, July 9, 1889.
30. *Ibid.*, June 28, 1889.
31. *New York Times*, February 8, 1882; Michael T. Isenberg, *John L. Sullivan and His America* (Urbana: University of Illinois Press, 1994), p. 106; Dale Ann Somers, *The Rise of Sports in New Orleans: 1850–1900* (New Orleans: Pelican, 1972), p. 165.
32. *Times-Democrat*, February 9, 1882.
33. Michael T. Isenberg, *John L. Sullivan and His America* (Urbana: University of Illinois Press, 1994), p. 106.
34. *Ibid.*, pp. 387–389.
35. *Times-Democrat*, February 5, 1882; *Daily Picayune*, February 8, February 23, 1882.
36. *Daily Picayune*, July 9, 1889; *New York Times*, July 9, 1889.
37. George Siler, *Inside Facts on Pugilism* (Chicago: Laird & Lee Publishers, 1907), p. 159
38. *New York Times*, July 12, 1889.
39. *Ibid.*, March 25, 1890.
40. *Ibid.*, January 12, February 23, March 13, March 20, March 26, 1885; January 17, 1887; May 20, June 17, 1889.
41. *Ibid.*, August 11, 1889; *Times-Democrat*, September 1, 1889.
42. *Daily Picayune*, September 15, 1889; *Times-Democrat*, September 15, 1889.
43. *Daily Picayune*, September 15, 1889..
44. *Ibid.*, November 5, 1889

45. *Ibid.*, January 16, 1890; June 28, 1891. There were also several members of the Olympic Club who did not resign, but who also joined the Metropolitan Club.
46. *Ibid.*, December 31, 1889.

Chapter Two

1. *Daily Picayune*, November 4, 1880.
2. *Ibid.*, November 16, 1880; December 15, 1880.
3. Joy J. Jackson, *New Orleans in the Gilded Age: Politics and Urban Progress 1880–1896* (Baton Rouge: Louisiana State University Press, 1969), pp. 39, 42; *Daily Picayune*, June 15, 1882.
4. *Daily Picayune*, February 13, 1887.
5. Joy J. Jackson, *New Orleans in the Gilded Age: Politics and Urban Progress 1880–1896* (Baton Rouge: Louisiana State University Press, 1969), p. 41.
6. *Daily Picayune*, April 8, 1888.
7. *Ibid.*, April 20, 1888.
8. *Ibid.*, June 13, 1888.
9. *Ibid.*, January 1, 1890.
10. *Ibid.*, December 2, 1889.
11. *Ibid.*, December 23, 1889.
12. *Ibid.*, October 25, 1889.
13. *Ibid.*, January 1, 1890.
14. *Times-Democrat*, January 10, 1890.
15. U.S. Department of Commerce, Bureau of the Census, *Historical Statistics of the 1890 United States Census*.
16. *Times-Democrat*, January 13, 1890.
17. *Daily Picayune*, February 12–13, 1890.
18. *Ibid.*, January 27, 1890.
19. *Ibid.*, February 1, 1890.
20. *Ibid.*, February 3, 1890.
21. *Daily Picayune*, February 3, 1890.
22. *Times-Democrat*, February 7, 1890.
23. *Times-Democrat*, February 18, 1890; *Daily Picayune*, February 18, 1890.
24. *Times-Democrat*, March 2, 1890.
25. *Daily Picayune*, March 13, 1890.
26. *Ibid.*, March 18, 1890.
27. *Ibid.*, April 8, 1890.
28. *Ibid.*, March 15, March 16, March 17, March 18, 1890; *Times-Democrat*, March 15, 1890.
29. John Smith Kendall, *History of New Orleans—Volume II* (Chicago: The Lewis Publishing Company, 1922), p. 488
30. *New York Times*, May 27, 1895.
31. Joy J. Jackson, *New Orleans in the Gilded Age: Politics and Urban Progress 1880–1896* (Baton Rouge: Louisiana State University Press, 1969), p. 40.
32. Berthold C. Alwes, "The History of the Louisiana State Lottery Company," *Louisiana Historical Quarterly* XXVII (October 1944).
33. Joy J. Jackson, *New Orleans in the Gilded Age: Politics and Urban Progress 1880–1896* (Baton Rouge: Louisiana State University Press, 1969), p. 40.
34. *Daily Picayune*, March 16, May 13, 1890; *Times-Democrat*, May 13, 1890; *Official Report of the Proceedings of the Anti-Lottery Democratic Convention* (New Orleans: Anti-Lottery League of Louisiana, August 1890).
35. *Daily Picayune*, April 7, 1890.
36. *Ibid.*, April 14, 1890.
37. *Ibid.*, May 4, 1890; *Times-Democrat*, May 4, 1890.
38. *Ibid.*, May 9, 1890.
39. *Ibid.*, June 24, 1890.
40. *Times-Democrat*, January 15, 1891.
41. *Ibid.*, July 12, 1890.
42. *Daily Picayune*, July 29, 1890; *Times-Democrat*, July 29, 1890.
43. *Times-Democrat*, July 25, 1890.
44. *Ibid.*, August 12, 1890.
45. *Daily Picayune*, September 15, 1889; July 12, 1890; January 11, 1891.
46. *Daily Picayune*, September 17, 1890.
47. *Ibid.*, September 28, 1890.
48. *Ibid.*, October 16, 1890; *Times-Democrat*, October 16, 1890.
49. *Daily Picayune*, October 17, 1890; *Times-Democrat*, October 17, 1890.
50. *Daily Picayune*, October 22, 1890.
51. *Times-Democrat*, September 1, 1890.
52. *Daily Picayune*, October 27, 1890.
53. *Ibid.*, May 1, 1887.
54. *Ibid.*, July 30, October 1, November 11, 1890.
55. *Times-Democrat*, December 31, 1890.

Chapter Three

1. James B. Roberts and Alexander G. Skutt, *The Boxing Register: International Boxing Hall of Fame Official Record Book* (Ithaca: McBooks Press, 1999).
2. *Daily Picayune*, March 20, 1885.
3. Gilbert E. Odd, *The Fighting Blacksmith: The Story of Bob Fitzsimmons* (London: Pelham Books, 1976).
4. W.W. Naughton, *Kings of the Queensbury Realm* (Chicago: The Continental Publishing Company, 1902).
5. *Times-Democrat*, July 29, 1890.
6. *Daily Picayune*, November 29, 1891.
7. *Ibid.*, January 10, 1891.
8. *Chicago Daily Tribune*, January 15, 1891; *Pittsburgh Daily Post*, January 15, 1891.
9. *Chicago Tribune*, January 15, 1891; *Detroit Free Press*, January 15, 1891; *Los Angeles Herald*, January 15, 1891; *St. Louis Post-Dispatch*, January 15, 1891; *The New York Sun*, January 15, 1891; *Daily Picayune*, January 15, 1891; *Times-Democrat*, January 15, 1891.
10. *Atlanta Constitution*, January 15, 1891.
11. *Daily Picayune*, February 5, 1891.
12. *Ibid.*, February 7, 1891.
13. *Times-Democrat*, February 10, 1891.
14. *Daily Picayune*, February 28, 1891.
15. *Daily States*, October 17, 1890.
16. Richard Gambino, *Vendetta: A True Story*

of the Worst Lynching in America, the Mass Murder of Italian-Americans in New Orleans in 1891 (New York: Doubleday, 1977), p. 76.

17. *Daily Picayune*, March 12, 1891; *Times-Democrat*, March 13, 1891.

18. *Daily Picayune*, March 14, 1891.

19. Richard Gambino, *Vendetta: A True Story of the Worst Lynching in America, the Mass Murder of Italian-Americans in New Orleans in 1891* (New York: Doubleday, 1977), p. 157.

20. No direct evidence had been introduced against either Matranga or Incardona, prompting the directed verdict.

21. *Times-Democrat*, March 15, 1891; *Daily Picayune*, March 15, 1891; *Chicago Tribune*, March 15, 1891; *New York Times*, March 15, 1891; *San Francisco Chronicle*, March 15, 1891.

22. *St. Louis Post-Dispatch*, March 17, 1891.

23. Richard Gambino, *Vendetta: A True Story of the Worst Lynching in America, the Mass Murder of Italian-Americans in New Orleans in 1891* (New York: Doubleday, 1977), pp. 126–127.

24. Joseph Masseli and Dominic Caldeloro, *Italians in New Orleans* (Charleston, SC: Arcadia Publishing, 2004), p. 7.

25. *Daily Picayune*, April 13, April 20, 1891.

26. *Ibid.*, May 24, 1891.

27. Victor Zarnowitz, *Business Cycles: Theory, History, Indicators, and Forecasting* (Chicago: University of Chicago Press, 1996), pp. 226–229.

28. *Times-Democrat*, May 4, 1891.

29. *Daily Picayune*, May 31, 1891.

30. *Saint Paul Globe*, May 21, 1891; *Atchison Daily Champion*, May 20, 1891; *Los Angeles Times*, May 20, 1891; *Chicago Tribune*, May 20, 1891.

31. *Times-Democrat*, May 20, May 21, 1891; *Cincinnati Enquirer*, May 21, 1891; *Fort Worth Daily Gazette*, May 21, 1891; *St. Louis Post-Dispatch*, May 21, 1891.

32. *Daily Picayune*, January 7, 1891.

33. *Ibid.*, March 8, 1891.

34. *Ibid.*, July 26, 1891.

35. *Ibid.*, August 1, 1891.

36. *Ibid.*, July 8, 1891.

37. *Ibid.*, July 17, July 19, 1891.

38. *Ibid.*, July 22, 1891.

39. *Ibid.*

40. *St. Paul Globe*, February 11, February 18, 1891; *Great Falls Tribune*, April 25, 1891. There may have been more than 28 fights between Minneapolis and St. Paul, but these are the only fights reported.

41. *Times-Democrat*, July 25, 1891.

42. *Daily Picayune*, July 31, 1891.

43. *Ibid.*

44. *Daily Nevada State Journal*, May 21, 1891.

45. *Daily Picayune*, September 18, 1891.

46. *Times-Democrat*, September 19, 1891.

47. *Ibid.*, September 20, 1891.

48. *Daily Picayune*, September 23, 1891.

49. *Daily Picayune*, September 30, 1891.

50. *Times-Democrat*, October 7, 1891.

51. *Daily Picayune*, October 14, 1891.

52. *Daily Picayune*, October 20, 1891.

53. *Ibid.*, November 8, 1891.

54. *Ibid.*, November 20, 1891.

55. *Ibid.*, November 17, November 22, 1891

56. *Times-Democrat*, December 22, 1891.

57. *Daily Picayune*, September 17, 1890.

58. *Ibid.*, May 23, 1890; May 21, 1891.

59. *Daily Illinois State Register*, February 14, 1889.

60. *Daily Picayune*, December 23, 1891.

61. *Ibid.*, December 30, 1891.

Chapter Four

1. *Daily Picayune*, January 22, 1892; *Times-Democrat*, January 22, 1892.

2. *Daily Picayune*, January 21, 1892.

3. *Ibid.*, January 28, 1892.

4. *Ibid.*, November 8, December 30, 1891.

5. *Ibid.*, June 28, 1891.

6. *Times-Democrat*, February 22, 1892.

7. *Daily Picayune*, February 23, 1892.

8. *Ibid.*, February 29, 1892; *Times-Democrat*, February 29, 1892.

9. *Daily Picayune*, January 6, January 22, January 29,1892.

10. *Ibid.*, January 12, January 16, January 18, 1892.

11. *Ibid.*, January 22, 1892.

12. *Ibid.*, January 17, 1892.

13. Charles Tobin, *Fitzsimmons: Boxing's First Triple World Champion* (Timaru, New Zealand: David A. Jack and Christopher P. Tobin, 1984).

14. *Saint Paul Globe*, May 2, 1891.

15. Matt Donnellon, *The Irish Champion Peter Maher* (Bloomington: Trafford, 2008).

16. *Daily Picayune*, January 21, 1892.

17. *Ibid.*, March 2, 1892.

18. *Ibid.*, February 24, 1892.

19. *Times-Democrat*, February 25, 1892.

20. *Daily Picayune*, January 28, February 29, 1892.

21. Michael Donovan, *The Science of Boxing* (New York: Dick & Fitzgerald, 1893).

22. *New York Times*, March 3, 1892; *Daily Picayune*, March 3, 1892; *Times-Democrat*, March 3, 1892.

23. *Daily Picayune*, March 2, 1892.

24. *Ibid.*, March 9, 1892.

25. *Times-Democrat*, March 13, 1892.

26. *Daily Picayune*, March 17, 1892.

27. *Ibid.*, March 22, 1892.

28. *Ibid.*, April 14, 1892.

29. *Ibid.*, April 28, 1892.

30. *Ibid.*, May 3, 1892.

31. *Ibid.*, May 15, May 23, 1892.

32. *Times-Democrat*, June 10, 1892.

33. *Daily Picayune*, May 30, June 6, June 13, July 18, 1892.

34. *Ibid.*, March 6, 1892; *Boston Post*, September 5, 1892.

35. *Times-Democrat*, May 29, 1892.

36. *Daily Picayune*, July 11, August 15, 1892.

37. *Ibid.*, August 3, 1892.
38. *Ibid.*, May 7, 1892.
39. *The Times* (Philadelphia), August 27, 1892; *Pittsburgh Daily Dispatch*, September 1, 1892.
40. *Daily Picayune*, September 5, 1892.
41. *New York Times*, August 26, August 30, September 1, September 3, 1892.
42. *Chicago Tribune*, February 24, 1889.
43. *Boston Post*, September 6, 1892; *Chicago Daily Tribune*, September 6, 1892; *St. Louis Post-Dispatch*, September 6, 1892; *Atlanta Constitution*, September 6, 1892; *San Francisco Call*, September 6, 1892; *New York World*, September 6, 1892; *Times-Democrat*, September 6, 1892; *Daily Picayune*, September 6, 1892.
44. Bellocq would become famous for his extensive body of work photographing the prostitutes of Storyville which were published posthumously.
45. *Times-Democrat*, September 7, 1892; *Detroit Free Press*, September 7, 1892.
46. *Boston Post*, September 7, 1892.
47. *Detroit Free Press*, September 7, 1892.
48. *Ibid.*; *San Francisco Chronicle*, September 7, 1892; *Atlanta Constitution*, September 7, 1892; *Cincinnati Enquirer*, September 7, 1892; *Times-Democrat*, September 7, 1892; *Daily Picayune*, September 7, 1892
49. *Louisville Courier-Journal*, May 10, 1896; Richard K. Fox, ed., *The Police Gazette* (New York: Richard K. Fox, 1896), p. 160.
50. *San Francisco Chronicle*, September 7, 1892; *St. Louis Post-Dispatch*, September 7, 1892; *New York World*, September 7, 1892.
51. *Boston Post*, September 7, 1892.
52. Richard K. Fox, ed., *The Police Gazette* (New York: Richard K. Fox, 1896), pp. 140–141.
53. *Times-Democrat*, October 31, 1891.
54. *Daily Picayune*, February 10, 1892.
55. Richard K. Fox, ed., *The Police Gazette* (New York: Richard K. Fox, 1896), p. 138.
56. *Boston Post*, August 29, September 5–7, 1892; *The World* (New York), August 28, September 6, 1892
57. *Times-Democrat*, March 9, 1892.
58. *Boston Post*, September 8, 1892; *Chicago Daily Tribune*, September 8, 1892; *Los Angeles Herald*, September 8, 1892; *New York Tribune*, September 8, 1892; *New York Times*, September 8, 1892; *San Francisco Chronicle*, September 8, 1892; *St. Louis Post-Dispatch*, September 8, 1892; *Atlanta Constitution*, September 8, 1892; *Brooklyn Daily Eagle*, September 8, 1892; *Times-Democrat*, September 8, 1892; *Daily Picayune*, September 8, 1892.
59. *American Settler* (London), September 24, 1892.
60. *Chicago Tribune*, September 9, 1892; *Times-Democrat*, September 9, 1892.
61. *Evening Star* (Washington, D.C.), September 8, 1892.
62. *Daily Picayune*, September 9, 1892.
63. *Ibid.*, September 19, 1892.
64. *Times-Democrat*, September 25, 1892; *New York Times*, September 26, 1892.
65. *Evening Star* (Washington, D.C.), September 8, 1892; *Pittsburgh Dispatch*, September 8, 1892, *Chicago Tribune*, September 9, 1892.
66. *Times-Democrat*, October 6, 1892.
67. *New York Times*, October 2, 1892; *Democrat and Chronicle* (New York), October 3, 1892.
68. *Daily Picayune*, October 4, 1892; *Times-Democrat*, October 4, 1892.
69. *Daily Picayune*, October 31, November 29, 1892. They were also joined by Frank Williams, Frank Zengel, Reuben M. Frank, William North, and Nathaniel H. Cloutman, all of whom were former officers of the Olympic Club.
70. *Times-Democrat*, October 31, 1892; *Chicago Tribune*, October 31, 1892; *The World* (New York), October 31, 1892; *New York Sun*, October 31, 1892.
71. *Atlanta Constitution*, November 14, 1892; *Philadelphia Inquirer*, November 14, 1892.
72. *Daily Picayune*, March 5, 1893.
73. *Ibid.*, November 17, 1892.
74. *New York Times*, December 7, 1892.
75. Lyle Saxon, *Fabulous New Orleans* (Gretna, LA: Pelican, 1928), p. 185.

Chapter Five

1. $9,000 for the McAuliffe–Myer fight; $7,500 for the Dixon–Skelly fight; and $25,000 for the Sullivan–Corbett fight. The $41,500 was just the prize money and did not include any fight-related expenses.
2. *Daily Picayune*, December 15, 1892.
3. *Times-Democrat*, January 20, 1893.
4. *Daily Picayune*, January 6, 1893.
5. *Times-Democrat*, February 22, 1892; *Daily Picayune*, February 23, 1892.
6. *Times-Democrat*, February 4, 1893.
7. *Daily Picayune*, February 5, 1893.
8. *Ibid.*, March 1, 1893.
9. *Ibid.*, February 21, 1893.
10. *Ibid.*, February 25, 1893.
11. *New York Times*, March 3, 1893; *Daily Picayune*, March 3, 1893.
12. *Daily Picayune*, March 4, 1893.
13. Gilbert E. Odd, *The Fighting Blacksmith: The Story of Bob Fitzsimmons* (London: Pelham Books, 1976).
14. *Boston Post*, August 9, 1892.
15. *Daily Picayune*, November 1, 1892.
16. *Ibid.*, March 10, 1893.
17. *Times-Democrat*, January 20, 1893.
18. *Ibid.*, January 24, 1893.
19. *Daily Picayune*, March 9, 1893; *New York Times*, March 9, 1893; *Times-Democrat*, March 9, 1893.
20. *New York Times*, March 9, March 10, 1893.
21. *New York Times*, July 30, September 7, 1893.
22. *Daily Picayune*, October 18, 1893.
23. *Ibid.*, March 5, 1893.
24. *Ibid.*, March 11, 1893.
25. *Ibid.*, November 6, 1893.
26. *Times-Democrat*, August 8, 1889.

27. *Ibid.*, December 24, 1889.
28. *Daily Picayune*, September 17, 1890.
29. *Ibid.*, March 2, 1892; *Times-Democrat*, March 2, 1892.
30. *Daily Picayune*, April 7, 1893; *New York Times*, April 8, 1893.
31. *Daily Picayune*, May 19, 1893.
32. *Ibid.*, June 1, 1893.
33. *Times-Democrat*, June 9, 1893.
34. *New York Times*, July 31, 1893.
35. *Daily Picayune*, September 7, 1892.
36. *Ibid.*, September 28, 1893.
37. *Ibid.*, October 11, October 18, October 20, October 25, 1893.
38. The Southern Improvement Company, Ltd., was a newly formed entity whose principal owner was Frank Zengel, prominent member of both the Olympic Club and the Crescent City Athletic Club.
39. *Daily Picayune*, September 21, 1893.
40. *Times-Democrat*, June 7, 1893; *Daily Picayune*, June 8, 1893.
41. *Daily Picayune*, June 12, 1893.
42. *Times-Democrat*, July 13, 1893.
43. *Ibid.*, August 17, 1893.
44. *Daily Picayune*, October 20, 1894.
45. *Ibid.*, August 13, 1893.
46. *Times-Democrat*, October 24, 1894.
47. Katherine Adrienne Luck, "Finding Margaret Haughery: The Forgotten and Remembered Lives of New Orleans's 'Bread Woman' in the Nineteenth and Twentieth Centuries," University of New Orleans Theses and Dissertations, Paper 1821 (2014).
48. *Daily Picayune*, August 23, 1882.
49. *Ibid.*, August 11, August 16, 1882.
50. *Ibid.*, August 30, 1882.
51. *Ibid.*, September 5, 1882.
52. *Ibid.*, September 5, September 25, 1882.
53. *Ibid.*, May 26, 1883.
54. *Ibid.*, March 24, 1887.
55. *Ibid.*, April 17, May 29, 1887.
56. *Ibid.*, August 17, 1884; December 4, 1888.
57. *Ibid.*, December 12, 1888.
58. *Ibid.*
59. *Ibid.*, May 27, 1888.
60. *Times Democrat*, November 26, 1888.
61. *New York Times*, March 9, 1891; *Daily Picayune*, April 29, 1891.
62. *Daily Picayune*, November 11, 1890.
63. *Ibid.*, January 9, 1891.
64. *Ibid.*, April 15, 1891.
65. *Ibid.*, April 18, 1891.
66. Karen Clampitt, "Margaret Haughery and the Klotz Cracker Factor," *Times-Picayune*, August 26, 2011; updated September 1, 2011. Clampitt is the great-great-granddaughter of Bernard Klotz, Sr., and refers to his gambling loss on the Sullivan–Corbett fight.
67. *Daily Picayune*, June 14, 1893.
68. *Ibid.*, September 7, 1893.
69. *Ibid.*, September 1, 1893; *New York Times*, September 8, 1893.
70. *Times-Democrat*, September 4, 1892; September 8, 1893.
71. *Daily Picayune*, September 21, 1893.
72. *Ibid.*, September 28, 1893.
73. The United States did not start naming hurricanes until 1953.
74. *Times-Democrat*, October 5, 1893. The unnamed Category Four hurricane is still the third deadliest in United States history as of this writing. By comparison, Hurricane Katrina in 2005 ranks fourth, killing more than 1,500 people.
75. *Ibid.*, October 17, 1898; October 18, 1893.
76. *Ibid.*, October 16, 1893; *New York Times*, October 19, 1893.
77. *Daily Picayune*, October 26, 1893; *The Times-Democrat*, November 10, 1893.
78. *The Times-Democrat*, October 18, 1893; *Daily Picayune*, October 18, 1893.
79. *Daily Huronite*, January 26, 1894.
80. *Daily Picayune*, November 11, 1893.
81. *Ibid.*, December 16, 1893.
82. *Ibid.*, December 17, 1893; *Times-Democrat*, December 16, December 17, 1893.
83. *Daily Picayune*, December 16, 1893.
84. *Ibid.*, December 16, 1893.
85. *Ibid.*
86. *Atlanta Constitution*, January 7, 1894.

Chapter Six

1. *New York Times*, February 11, 1894; John Smith Kendall, *History of New Orleans—Volume II* (Chicago: The Lewis Publishing Company, 1922), pp. 486–500.
2. *The Times-Democrat*, January 1, January 5, 1894; John Smith Kendall, *History of New Orleans—Volume II* (Chicago: The Lewis Publishing Company, 1922), p. 500.
3. *Times-Democrat*, January 5, 1894; *Daily Picayune*, January 6, January 7, 1894.
4. *Daily Picayune*, January 13, 1894.
5. *Ibid.*, January 22, 1894.
6. *Times-Democrat*, January 24, 1894.
7. *Daily Picayune*, April 24, 1894.
8. *Ibid.*, May 1, 1894.
9. *Times-Democrat*, May 15, 1894.
10. *Ibid.*, May 8, 1894.
11. *Daily Picayune*, March 3, 1894.
12. *Ibid.*, May 6, 1894.
13. *Ibid.*, May 8, 1894.
14. *Ibid.*, May 18, May 22, 1894.
15. *Times-Democrat*, May 27, 1894; *Daily Picayune*, May 28, 1894.
16. *Daily Picayune*, June 3, 1894.
17. *Times-Democrat*, June 15, 1894.
18. *Daily Picayune*, June 6, 1894.
19. *Ibid.*, June 19, 1894.
20. *Boston Post*, June 19, 1894.
21. *Ibid.*, July 9, 1894.
22. *Ibid.*, July 20, July 22, 1894.
23. *Ibid.*, July 25, 1894; *Times-Democrat*, July 26, 1894.

24. *Daily Picayune*, August 9, 1894; *Times-Democrat*, August 9, 1894.
25. *Daily Picayune*, August 10, 1894; *Times-Democrat*, August 11, 1894.
26. Library of Congress Motion Picture, Broadcasting and Recorded Sound Division, Washington, D.C.
27. *Daily Picayune*, September 9, 1894.
28. *Times-Democrat*, September 6, 1894.
29. *Daily Picayune*, August 22, 1894.
30. *Ibid.*, September 25, 1894.
31. *Ibid.*, September 26, 1894.
32. *Times-Democrat*, September 27, 1894.
33. *Ibid.*, October 24–25, 1894.
34. *Daily Picayune*, April 11, April 28, July 31, September 7, 1894.
35. *Ibid.*, October 25, 1894; *Times-Democrat*, October 25, 1894.
36. *Times-Democrat*, August 30, 1894.
37. *Daily Picayune*, September 27, 1894.
38. *Ibid.*, October 8, 1894.
39. *Evening World* (New York), December 7, 1894.
40. *Los Angeles Times*, December 7, 1894.
41. *Daily Picayune*, December 7, 1894.
42. *Ibid.*, December 11, 1894.
43. *St. Louis Post-Dispatch*, December 13, 1894.
44. *Daily Picayune*, April 8, 1893; *The Times* (Philadelphia), April 8, 1894; *Chicago Daily Tribune*, April 8, 1893.
45. *Daily Picayune*, June 1, 1893.
46. *Ibid.*, December 15, 1894
47. *St. Louis Post-Dispatch*, December 15, 1894; *Evening World* (New York), December 15, 1894; *Daily Picayune*, December 16, 1894. It is often erroneously reported that Bowen died in the hospital and that he had regained consciousness before he died.
48. *Daily Picayune*, December 28, 1894.
49. *Ibid.*, December 16, 1894.
50. *Ibid.*
51. *Ibid.*
52. *Ibid.*, December 15, 1894.
53. As compiled by Tracy Callis, historian for the International Boxing Research Organization.
54. *Daily Picayune*, December 16, 1894.
55. *Ibid.*
56. *Ibid.*
57. *Ibid.*, December 17, 1894.
58. *Louisville Courier-Journal*, December 16, 1894.
59. *St. Louis Post-Dispatch*, December 16, 1894.
60. *Chicago Daily Tribune*, December 16, 1894.
61. *Daily Picayune*, December 20, 1894.
62. *Times-Democrat*, December 30, 1894.

Chapter Seven

1. Richard K. Fox, ed., *The Police Gazette* (New York: Richard K. Fox, 1896).
2. *Daily Picayune*, January 6, 1895.
3. *Ibid.*, January 12, January 17, 1895.
4. *Ibid.*, February 10, February 14, 1895.
5. *Times-Democrat*, March 12, 1895.
6. *Ibid.*, March 16, 1895.
7. *Daily Picayune*, March 29, 1895.
8. *Ibid.*, April 28, 1895.
9. *Ibid.*, May 4, 1895.
10. *Ibid.*, May 7, 1895.
11. *Ibid.*, May 12, 1895.
12. *Times-Democrat*, May 29, 1895.
13. As reported in the *Daily Picayune*, May 13 and May 20, 1895, respectively.
14. *Times-Democrat*, June 4, 1895.
15. *Daily Picayune*, June 29, 1895; *Times-Democrat*, July 10, 1895.
16. *Times-Democrat*, July 14, 1895.
17. *Ibid.*, July 6, 1895.
18. *Daily Picayune*, September 5, 1895.
19. *Ibid.*, October 2, 1895.
20. *Times-Democrat*, October 22, 1895.
21. *Ibid.*, October 23, October 27, 1895.
22. *Ibid.*, December 22, December 24, 1895; *Times-Democrat*, December 22, 1895.
23. *Daily Picayune*, October 27, 1895.
24. *Ibid.*, January 23, 1896.
25. *Ibid.*, February 6, February 17, 1896.
26. *Ibid.*, March 12, 1896.
27. *Ibid.*, March 23, 1896.
28. *Ibid.*, April 3, 1896; *Times-Democrat*, April 4, 1896.
29. *Evening Times*, April 4, 1896; *Louisville Courier-Journal*, April 4, 1896; *The Inter-Ocean* (Chicago), April 4, 1896; *Galveston Daily News*, April 5, 1896; *Houston Post*, April 5, 1896; *Fort Worth Daily Gazette*, April 5, 1896; *Salt Lake Herald*, April 12, 1896.
30. *Daily Picayune*, May 1, 1896.
31. *Ibid.*, May 10, 1896.
32. *Ibid.*, May 13, 1896.
33. *Ibid.*, May 22, 1896.
34. *Ibid.*, June 3, 1896.
35. *Ibid.*, July 1, 1896.
36. *Ibid.*, July 26, 1896.
37. *Ibid.*, November 8, 1896.
38. *Ibid.*, July 1, 1896.
39. New Orleans Public Library, *Underwriter's Inspection Bureau of New Orleans Street Rate Slips*, 1897. This address today would be 2725 Royal Street.
40. *Times-Democrat*, January 25, 1897; *Daily Picayune*, January 25, 1897.
41. *Times-Democrat*, February 11, 1897.
42. *Daily Picayune*, February 11, 1897.
43. *Ibid.*, February 16, 1897.
44. *Ibid.*, February 26, 1897.
45. *Ibid.*, June 9, 1897.
46. *Ibid.*, June 3, August 7, 1896; December 7, 1897.
47. *Los Angeles Herald*, December 7, 1897; *Pittsburgh Press*, December 7, 1897; *Morning Post*, December 7, 1897; *El Paso Herald*, December 7, 1897; *The Tennessean*, December 7, 1897; *Salt Lake Herald*, December 7, 1897.
48. *Daily Picayune*, December 7, 1897.

Bibliography

Books

Biographical and Historical Memoirs of Louisiana—Volume I. Chicago: The Goodspeed Publishing Company, 1892.
Boyce, Rupert William. *Yellow Fever Prophylaxis in New Orleans, 1905.* London: Committee of the Liverpool School of Tropical Medicine by Williams & Norgate, 1906.
Brown, Henry C. *Report on the Drainage, Sewerage, and Health of the City of New Orleans.* New Orleans, 1879.
Carter, Hodding, ed. *The Past as Prelude: New Orleans, 1718–1968.* New Orleans, 1968.
Coleman, Will H. *Historical Sketch Book and Guide to New Orleans and Environs.* New York: W.H. Coleman, 1885.
Conlin, Joseph R. *The American Past: A Survey of American History—Volume I.* Boston: Wadsworth, 1984.
Coogan, Tim Pat. *Wherever Green Is Worn: The Story of the Irish Diaspora.* New York: Palgrave/St. Martin's Press, 2000.
Dabney, Thomas Ewing. *One Hundred Great Years: The Story of the Times-Picayune.* Baton Rouge: Louisiana State University Press, 1944.
Donnellon, Matt. *The Irish Champion Peter Maher.* Bloomington: Trafford, 2008.
Donovan, Michael J. *The Science of Boxing.* New York: Dick & Fitzgerald, 1893.
Dowling, V.G. *Fistiana or the Oracle of the Ring.* London: Wm. Clement, 1841.
Dufour, Charles L. *Ten Flags in the Wind: The Story of Louisiana.* New York: Harper & Row, 1967.
Edwards, William. *The Art and Science of Boxing.* New York: Excelsior Publishing House, 1888.
English, Andrew P. *Ringside at Richburg.* Baltimore: Gateway Press, 2008.
Fairall, Herbert S. *The World Industrial and Cotton Centennial Exposition.* Iowa City: Republican Publishing Company, 1885.
Fleischer, Nat, and Sam Andre. *An Illustrated History of Boxing—Sixth Edition.* New York: Kensington, 2001.
Fox, Richard K. *Life & Battles of James J. Corbett.* New York: Richard K. Fox, 1892.
Fox, Richard K., ed. *The Police Gazette.* New York: Richard K. Fox, 1896.
Franklin, John Hope. *The Militant South, 1800–1861.* Urbana: University of Illinois Press, 2002.
Froeschle, Robert L. *Official Rule Book for All Pocket & Carom Billiard Games.* Chicago: Billiard Congress of America, 1971.
Gambino, Richard. *Vendetta: A True Story of the Worst Lynching in America, the Mass Murder of Italian-Americans in New Orleans in 1891.* New York: Doubleday, 1977.
Gayarre, Charles. *The History of Louisiana—The French Domination—Volume I.* New York: Redfield, 1854.
Gehman, Mary, and Nancy Ries. *Women and New Orleans—A History.* New Orleans: Margaret Media, 1996.
Gregg, J. Chandler. *Life in the Army, in the Departments of Virginia, and the Gulf, Including Observations in New Orleans, With an Account of the Author's Life and Experience in the Ministry.* Philadelphia: Perkin Pine & Higgins, 1868.
Harding, William E. *Life & Battles of Jake Kilrain.* New York: Richard K. Fox, 1888.
Howe, William W. *Municipal History of New Orleans—Seventh Series IV.* Baltimore: John Hopkins University, 1889.
Huber, Leonard Victor. *New Orleans: A Pictorial History.* New Orleans: Pelican, 1971.

Irvine, L.H. *Our Jim—The World's Champion*. San Francisco: Crown, 1892.
Isenberg, Michael T. *John L. Sullivan and His America*. Urbana: University of Illinois Press, 1994.
Jackson, Joy J. *New Orleans in the Gilded Age: Politics and Urban Progress 1880–1896*. Baton Rouge: Louisiana State University Press, 1969.
Jewell, Edwin L., ed. *Jewell's Crescent City Illustrated*. New Orleans: Edwin L. Jewell, 1874.
Kendall, John Smith. *History of New Orleans—Volume II*. Chicago: The Lewis Publishing Company, 1922.
King, Grace Elizabeth. *New Orleans—The Place and the People*. New York: Macmillan, 1917.
Laffoley, Steven. *Shadowboxing: The Rise and Fall of George Dixon*. Nova Scotia: Pottersfield Press, 2012.
Long, Clarence D. *Wages and Earnings in the United States, 1860–1980*. Princeton: Princeton University Press, 1960.
Lynch, Bohun. *Knuckles and Gloves*. London: W. Collins Sons & Company, 1922.
Masseli, Joseph, and Dominic Caldeloro. *Italians in New Orleans*. Charleston, SC: Arcadia Publishing, 2004.
McGinty, Garnie William. *Louisiana Redeemed: The Overthrow of Carpet-Bag Rule, 1876–1880*. New Orleans: Pelican, 1998.
Morrison, Andrew. *The Industries of New Orleans*. New Orleans: The World Industrial & Cotton Centennial Exposition, 1885.
Naughton, W.W. *Kings of the Queensbury Realm*. Chicago: The Continental Publishing Company, 1902.
Norman, B.M. *Norman's New Orleans and Environs: Containing a Brief Historical Sketch of the Territory and State of Louisiana and the City of New Orleans*. New Orleans: B.M. Norman, 1845.
Odd, Gilbert E. *The Fighting Blacksmith: The Story of Bob Fitzsimmons*. London: Pelham Books, 1976.
O'Hara, Barratt. *From Figg to Johnson*. Chicago: The Blossom Book House, 1909.
O'Reilly, John Boyle. *Athletics and Manly Sport*. Boston: Cashman, Keating & Company, 1890.
Perkins, Daniel W. *Practical Common Sense Guidebook Through the World Industrial and Cotton Centennial at New Orleans*. Harrisburg, PA: Lane S. Hart, 1895.
Richey, Emma C., and Elvina P. Kean. *The New Orleans Book*. New Orleans: The L. Graham Co., 1915.
Rightor, Henry. *Standard History of New Orleans, Louisiana*. Chicago: The Lewis Publishing Company, 1900.
Ripley, Eliza. *Social Life in Old New Orleans*. New York: D. Appleton, 1912.
Roberts, James B., and Alexander G. Skutt. *The Boxing Register: International Boxing Hall of Fame Official Record Book*. Ithaca: McBooks Press, 1999.
Saxon, Lyle. *Fabulous New Orleans*. Gretna, LA: Pelican, 1928.
Siler, George. *Inside Facts on Pugilism*. Chicago: Laird & Lee Publishers, 1907.
Somers, Dale Alan. *The Rise of Sports in New Orleans: 1850–1900*. New Orleans: Pelican, 1972.
Stillman, Marshall. *Mike Donovan—The Making of a Man*. New York: Moffat, Yard & Company, 1918.
Sullivan, John Lawrence, and Dudley Allen Sargent. *Life and Reminiscences of a 19th Century Gladiator*. Boston: Jas. A. Hearn & Company, 1892.
Tobin, Chris. *Fitzsimmons: Boxing's First Triple World Champion*. Timaru, New Zealand: David A. Jack and Christopher P. Tobin, 1984.
Twain, Mark, and Charles Dudley Warner. *The Gilded Age: A Tale of Today*. New York: New American Library, 1969.
Volo, James M., and Dorothy D. Volo. *Family Life in 19th Century America*. Santa Barbara: Greenwood, 2007.
White, Richard. *Railroaded*. New York: W.W. Norton, 2011.
Zacherie, James S. *New Orleans Guide*. New Orleans: F.F. Hansel & Bro., 1893.
Zarnowitz, Victor. *Business Cycles: Theory, History, Indicators, and Forecasting*. Chicago: University of Chicago Press, 1996.

Government Publications

Official Report of the Proceedings of the Anti-Lottery Democratic Convention. New Orleans: Anti-Lottery League of Louisiana, August 1890.
State of Louisiana *Acts*, 1890.
State of Louisiana *Senate Journal*, 1890.
U.S. Department of Commerce, Bureau of the Census
Historical Statistics of the 1840 U.S. Census
Historical Statistics of the 1850 U.S. Census
Historical Statistics of the 1860 U.S. Census
Historical Statistics of the 1870 U.S. Census
Historical Statistics of the 1880 U.S. Census

Newspapers

American Settler (London) 1892
Atchison Daily Champion 1891
Atlanta Constitution 1891–1894
Boston Post 1892–1894
Brooklyn Daily Eagle 1892
Chicago Daily Tribune 1891–1892
Cincinnati Enquirer 1891–1892
Daily Huronite 1894
Daily Illinois State Register 1889
Detroit Free Press 1891
El Paso Herald 1897
Evening Star (Washington, D.C.) 1892
Evening Times (Washington, D.C.) 1896
Fort Wayne News 1896
Fort Worth Daily Gazette 1891–1896
Galveston Daily News 1896
Great Falls Tribune 1891
Houston Post 1896
The Inter-Ocean (Chicago) 1896
Los Angeles Herald 1891–1897
Louisville Courier-Journal 1896–1897
New Orleans Crescent 1869
New Orleans Daily Picayune 1837–1896
New Orleans Daily States 1890
New Orleans Times 1866–1875
New Orleans Times-Democrat 1882–1896
New Orleans Times-Picayune 1923–1998
New York Democrat and Chronicle 1892
New York Sun 1891–1897
New York Times 1876–1895
New York Tribune 1892
New York World 1892
Philadelphia Times 1892
Pittsburgh Daily Dispatch 1892
Pittsburgh Daily Post 1891
Pittsburgh Press 1897
St. Louis Post-Dispatch 1891–1892
St. Paul Globe 1891
Salt Lake City Herald 1896–1897
San Francisco Call 1892
San Francisco Chronicle 1892
The Tennessean 1897
Wilkes Spirit of the Times 1853

Academic Works

Coman, Seth J. "The Golden Age of Boxing in New Orleans, 1880–1895." University of New Orleans Theses and Dissertations, 1995.
Eagleson, Dorothy Rose. "Some Aspects of the Social Life of the New Orleans Negro in the 1880's." Tulane University Theses and Dissertations, 1961.
Luck, Katherine Adrienne. "Finding Margaret Haughery: The Forgotten and Remembered Lives of New Orleans' 'Bread Woman' in the Nineteenth and Twentieth Centuries." University of New Orleans Theses and Dissertations, Paper 1821, 2014.
Madden, Ann. "Popular Sports in New Orleans, 1890–1900." Tulane University Theses and Dissertations, 1956.

Articles

Adams, William H. "New Orleans as the National Center of Boxing," *Louisiana Historical Quarterly* XXIX (January 1956).
Alwes, Berthold C. "The History of the Louisiana State Lottery Company." *Louisiana Historical Quarterly* XXVII (October 1944).
Campanella, Richard. "The Turbulent History Behind the Seven New Orleans Municipal Districts." *The Times-Picayune*, October 9, 2013; updated March 7, 2016.
Clampitt, Karen. "Margaret Haughery and the Klotz Cracker Factor." *The Times-Picayune*, August 26, 2011; updated September 1, 2011.
Dunstan, Roger. "Gambling in California." California Research Bureau, California State Library (January 1997).

Ephemera

Chase, John C. *Frenchman, Desire, Good Children.* Gretna, LA: Pelican, 1949–1988.
The Creole Tourist's Guide and Sketch Book to the City of New Orleans. New Orleans: The Creole Publishing Company, 1911.
Federal Writer's Project of the Works Progress Administration. *New Orleans City Guide.* Boston: Houghton Mifflin, 1938.
Genslinger, Charles H. *Athletic Clubs of America.* Buffalo: Charles H. Genslinger, 1915.

Bibliography

Names of Streets in the City of New Orleans and the Assessment Districts in Which They Are Located. New Orleans: Weed & Kelly, 1871.

New Orleans Progressive Union. *A Standard Guide to the City of New Orleans Illustrated.* New Orleans, 1911.

New Orleans Public Library. *Underwriter's Inspection Bureau of New Orleans Street Rate Slips—1897.*

New Orleans Public Library. *Ward Changes—1805 to 1847.*

Old Street Names of New Orleans. New Orleans: S.P. Lafaye, 1912.

Picayune Publishing Company. *A Little Guide to New Orleans.* New Orleans: Nicholson & Company, 1892.

Picayune Publishing Company. *The Picayune's Guide to New Orleans.* New Orleans: Nicholson & Company, 1896.

Picayune Publishing Company. *The Picayune's Guide to New Orleans.* New Orleans: T. Fitzwilliam & Company, 1897.

Pickings from the Picayune. Philadelphia: T.B. Peterson & Bro., 1846.

Sanborn Insurance Maps for New Orleans, LA—Volume Two. New York: Sanborn Map Publishing Company, 1885.

Soards' Guide Book and Street Guide of New Orleans. New Orleans: L. Soards, 1884.

Soards' Guide Book and Street Guide of New Orleans. New Orleans: L. Soards, 1885.

Street Railway Guide to the City of New Orleans and its Suburbs. New Orleans: Fountain & Christian, 1884.

Waldo, J. Curtis. *Illustrated Visitor's Guide to New Orleans.* New Orleans: J. Curtis Waldo, 1879.

Witteman, A. *Picturesque New Orleans.* New Orleans: F.F. Hansel & Bro., 1900.

Index

Abbott, Stanton 149, 154–158, 163, 175, 185, 190; Everhardt versus 154–157, 156–157
Abingdon, Squire 123
Adams, Lionel 159–160
Ahrens, Charles 66
Algiers 10, 14, 178
The Algiers Bull 14
Allen & Hille 11
Allen, Al 178
Allen, Henry 166
Allen, Pat 149, 190
Allen, Tom 17, 186
American Biscuit Company 134, 137–138, 159
Anderson, Thomas C. 49, 127, 166, 168
Arms, Major William 12
Arthur, Chester Allen 88
Ashton, Jack 46
Athletic Club League 45, 52
Athletic Clubs 8–9, 13, 18–19, 27, 30, 36–37, 40–43, 45–48, 52, 54 56, 59, 61, 66–69, 74, 77–79, 81, 87, 93, 95, 99–100, 107–113, 115–116, 120–127, 129–131, 140–149, 152, 158, 162–166, 170–173, 175, 183, 185–187; Auditorium 144, 148–149, 152–153, 158, 162–163, 165, 166–167, 173, 183, 186–187; Audubon 43; Bench Athletic & Pleasure Club 50; Boulevard Club 115; Columbia 19, 45; Metropolitan Club 2, 38, 45, 72–73, 75, 77–78, 80–82, 85, 87–88, 90, 108, 110, 112–113, 115–116, 126–127, 140, 143, 173, 181, 183, 187, 194; New Orleans 19, 40, 100; Southern 9, 18, 36, 40, 42–43, 45, 52, 61, 99–100, 127, 144–145, 175, 185; West End 19, 36, 42, 44, 48, 66, 74, 93
Atlantic Press Yard 28
Auditorium Athletic Club 144, 148–149, 152–153, 158, 162–163, 166–167, 173, 183, 186–187; Bowen versus Lavigne 162–163; Triple Event 162
Audubon Athletic Association 43
Audubon Athletic Club 43
Audubon Park 21, 115

Babbitt, A.D. 12
Bachemin Rifle Club 12
Bagnetto, Antonio 64
Baker, Judge Joshua G. 61, 64
Bardell, James 178
Barnes & Uhjohn 13
Barnes Hotel 32
Barnett, Jerry 121
Barrett, Capt. William 49, 94, 102, 141, 144
Barry, James (Jimmy) 150,162, 177, 184, 190; versus Gorman 150
baseball 2, 5–6, 10, 15, 18, 37, 45, 52, 88, 105, 108
The Bayou Lafourche Mule 14
Beauregard, Gen. P.G.T. 44
Behan, William J. 21
Behan Rifle Club 11
Bellocq, Ernest J. 96, 196
Belou, John 131
Bench Athletic & Pleasure Club 50
Bernard Klotz & Company 133, 135–136, 138–139, 160
Bernau, Herman 172–174, 191
Bertus, Paul 16
Bezeneh, Louis 18, 42
Bienville 7
billiards 2, 10, 13–15, 132; see also pool
Bitterwolf, Officer 133
Bixamos, Charles 54
Black Hand 52; see also Mafia
Bloom, Dr. J.D. 51–52
Boardwell's Opera House (MI) 163

Bonck, Harry (Bouck) 66
Booth, Capt. John 44, 132
Boston Club 8, 15, 43
Bosworth, Frank 117, 123
Boudro's Garden 37, 54, 131
Boulevard Club 115
Bourg, Horace 46
Bowden, James Edward Theodore "J.E.T" 145–146
Bowen, Andy "The Louisiana Tornado" 18, 40, 42, 48–49, 57, 59, 66, 73–76, 78, 93, 105, 113, 119, 127–130, 140, 142, 149–150, 152, 162–170, 174, 176, 178, 180, 186, 189–191; versus Burke 127–130; versus Carrol 48–50; versus Everhardt 130–131; versus Fielden 113; versus Gibbons 75; versus Lavigne 162–166; versus Myer 66, 76
Bowen, Mathilde 165, 168
boxing 1–3, 6, 9–10, 15–19, 30–34, 36–37, 40–43, 45–47, 53–54, 57, 65–69, 72–74, 77, 79, 82–83, 86–89, 91, 93, 95–97, 99, 102, 104–107, 109–111, 113–119, 121–123, 126–127, 130, 140, 142–153, 156, 158, 161–163, 165–167, 169–173, 175, 177–178, 180–186; city ordinances 6, 18, 36, 40–43, 46, 67, 71, 101, 123, 180; Louisiana state statutes 19, 31, 47, 81, 101, 143, 146, 148, 169–175; see also prizefighting
Boylan Protective Police 50, 145
Brady, William A. 69, 152
Brakenridge Lumber Company 135
Breaux, Justice Joseph A. 147
Brewster, Alexander 34, 57, 66–67, 74, 189
British 6, 12, 17, 99, 117
Broadway Rifle Club 153, 177

Index

Brooks, Ed 168, 190
Broughton, Jack 16
Bruns, J.H. 43
Buffalo Bill 13
Burke, Edward 21
Burke, Jack 82, 127–128, 148, 150, 162, 189–190; Bowen versus 127–130; Everhardt versus 150; versus Needham 85, 110
Burke, James "Deaf" 15
Burke, Nicholas 135
Bush, Charles 34
Busha, Isidore 41
Butler, Dennis 30
Butler, Gen. Benjamin F. 24

Calamity Jane 13
Caldwell, James H. 7
California Athletic Club 54, 56, 67–68, 95
Callaghan, Tommy 77–78, 110, 190; McCarthy versus 77–78, 110
Camera Club 8, 96
Caminada, Francisco 142
Camors, J.B. 137
Campbell, Billy 190
Campbell, J.C. 145
Carambat, Frank 127
Cardenas, Phil 50
Carey, John D. 27, 131
Carradine, Reverend Beverly 44
Carroll, Jimmy 47, 49, 54, 57, 59–60, 68, 74–76, 78, 81, 89, 93, 96, 127, 152, 163, 184, 189–191; versus Bowen 48–50; versus Myer 73–76
Carrollton, City of 21, 26, 32, 66, 140
Caruso, James 63–64
Casey, Phil 102
Casey, Tom 46, 59, 189
Cash, John 59, 189–190
Charity Hospital 44, 51–52, 135–134, 140, 165
Cheniere Caminada 142
chess 2–3, 8, 10, 29–30
Chess, Checkers and Whist Club 8, 31, 36
Chevalier, Fernand 18
Choynski, Joe 89, 96, 99, 117, 120–121, 148, 151, 167, 177, 184, 190
City Park 11, 21
Civil War 5–6, 8, 11, 22–24, 39, 43, 101, 116, 135, 138
Clark, Jess 176, 191
Cleary, Michael 34, 42–43
Cleveland, Grover 88, 99
Cloutman, Nathaniel H. 28, 38, 196

cockfights 5, 8
Collins, Professor 168
Columbia Athletic Club 19, 45
Colvine, Jimmy 57
Comitz, Loretto 64
Commercial Rifle Club 12
Committee of Fifty 52, 61
Coney Island Athletic Club (NY) 95, 121, 141, 146
Conley, Eddie 54, 57, 59
Connors, Johnny 151; versus Levy 151
Cooper, A.B. 28, 38
Coos, Capt. John M. 44, 73
Corbett, James J. 1, 36, 43, 57, 68–69, 86–88, 92, 96–106, 110–112, 116, 122, 124, 127, 139, 141, 143–149, 151–152, 154, 157, 167–168, 170–171, 175, 177, 184–185, 190, 196–197, 199; Sullivan versus 97–105, 110
Corbett, Patrick J. 78
Corcoran, James 182
Cormier, Louis E. 43
Cornu, Joseph 149, 181, 191
Costello, Thomas 34
Coughle, Abe 82
Courtain, George E. 139, 160
Coyle, P.R. 131
craps 26
Crassons, E. 53
Crawford, Peter 37, 189
Crawford, William 174, 176, 191
Creedon, Dan 152–154, 157–158, 178, 190; Fitzsimmons versus 157–158
Creoles 4–5, 8, 21, 26–28, 90, 109
Crescent City Athletic Club 2, 107–108, 110, 112–113, 115, 119–127, 130–131, 140–144, 148, 170, 173, 183, 187, 197; Bowen versus Fielden 113; Fitzsimmons versus Hall 120, 122–126; Gibbons versus Daly 120
Crescent City Jockey Club 68
Crescent City Rifle Club 11–12
cricket 3
Crittenden, W.J. 57
Cullen, John 133
Cunningham, M.J. 142, 144, 146, 149, 166, 170, 175
Curry, Robert L. 180, 189
Curtis, Ed 173, 176
Cushing, Jack 152

Daly, Jim 102, 120, 130–131
Daly, Mike 120; Gibbons versus 120

Daly, Corporal 133
Danforth, Tommy 46–47
DaPonta, L.B. 12
Dardis, M. 28
Dart, Henry P. 144–145, 147, 171, 175
Davey, Judge Robert 40
Davies, Charles E. "Parson" 167
Davis, Jefferson 36, 52
Davos, Joe 128
Davis, Warden Lemuel 62
Dawson, George 115–116, 118–119, 190
deCross, Harvey 82
Delaney, Bill 102
Del Valle, Vincent 166, 168
Dempsey, Jack "Nonpareil" 47, 53–59, 65–66, 74, 76, 81–83, 86, 93, 96, 112, 123, 151, 153, 156–157, 162, 164, 166–167, 175, 177, 184–186, 189; Fitzsimmons versus 54–60, 76
Denegre, Walter 61, 165
Dickson, Charles 67, 109, 119, 128–129, 131, 169, 173–174, 177, 179, 186
Dixon, Bruce 48
Dixon, George "Little Chocolate" 77–78, 92, 95–97, 101, 110, 141, 184–185, 190, 196, 200; versus Skelly 95–97, 110
Dodd, Charles W. 139
Doherty, George 105
Donaldson, Prof. John 102, 149
Donnegan, Ed 133
Donnelly, Capt. E.J. 128
Donovan, Michael (Mike) 30, 34, 42, 99–100, 102–104, 191, 195, 199–200
Doody, Patsey 57
Douglas, W.H. 67
Driscoll, Emmett 105
Drolla, Charles P. 28, 38, 71, 106
Drysdale, Dr. John 27, 67
dueling 10–11, 107, 109, 169
Duffy, Prof. John 18, 30, 37, 42, 46–49, 57, 63, 73–76, 85, 87, 90, 94, 96, 102, 105, 113–116, 118–119, 123–124, 128–129, 141, 143, 149, 152–153, 156, 158, 161, 163–166, 173–177, 180–181, 186, 189–191
Duffy, Patrick 33
Dufreche, F. 131
Dunn, Arthur 71, 134
Dunn, Jere 54
Dunn, John 10

Index

Duson, Professor 149
Duval & Favrot 73
Duvall Athletic Club (FL) 143–144, 146

Eagle Rifle Club 12
Early, Gen. Jubal 44
Earp, Wyatt 30
Eckhardt, John 149, 156, 190
Eckhardt, Johnnie 143, 149
Edison Kinetoscope Company 152
Eicke, Herman 131
Eicke Rifle Club 12
Einseidel, Dietrich 80, 112
Endeavor Rifle Club 12
Enterprise Rifle Club 12
Evans, W.L. 71, 134
Everhardt, Jack 115, 130, 142–143, 148–150, 154–158, 162, 166, 168, 174–175, 178, 185, 190–191; Bowen versus 130–131; versus Abbott 154–15, 156–157; versus Burke 150; versus Pierce 142
exhibition events 2, 15, 18–19, 30, 36–37, 39–43, 46, 50, 59–60, 69, 71–73, 75–76, 81–82, 87, 98, 113–114, 118, 125, 144, 147–149, 151–152, 156–157, 163, 168, 171, 173–174, 176, 178, 180–181, 184, 191
Expectation Rifle Club 12, 65
Eyrich, R.G. 12

Farrell, Bob 66
Faubourg Marigny 1, 26
Faubourg Ste. Marie 26
Faubourg Washington 26–27
fencing 3, 9, 172
Ferguson, Judge J.H. 92
Fernandez, Joe 72, 181, 191
Fielden, Joseph (Joe) 59, 113, 189; Bowen versus 113
Finn, Mickey 176, 191
Finney, Dr. James 165
Finney, John J. 31, 36, 159–160
Fitzpatrick, Hugh 139
Fitzpatrick, John 34, 36, 115, 153, 167, 186
Fitzpatrick, Sam 164
Fitzsimmons, Bob "Ruby Robert" 46–47, 49, 53–60, 65–68, 73–74, 76–77, 81–89, 92–93, 96, 98, 110, 112–113, 117–118, 120–126, 130–131, 140–142, 144–145, 148, 151–154, 156–158, 165–167, 170–171, 175, 177–178, 184–186, 189–191, 200; versus Creedon 157–158; versus Dempsey 54–60, 76; versus Hall 120, 122–126; versus Maher 81–85, 110
Flemings, Daniel 166
Florida Athletic Club 170
Flower, Walter C. 180
Foley, William 14
Forman, Col. B.R. 144
Forman, Charles 171
Foster, Murphy J. 44, 175
Fox, Charles 72–73, 78, 189–190
Fox, Dan 174
Fox, Richard K. 152–153, 167–168, 196, 198–199
Frank, Leon 132
Frank, Reuben M. 67–68, 92, 196
"Freckles" 72, 173, 181, 191
French 1, 3–8, 14, 25–26, 34, 80, 90, 115, 142, 149, 193, 199
French Quarter 3, 5, 7–8, 14, 26, 34, 101, 122
Frogmoor 11–12
Fulsom & Company 10

Gambel, Adam 179, 181, 183
gambling 6, 8, 15, 21, 23, 26, 34, 39, 44, 66, 79, 122, 139, 143, 197, 201
Garcia, Alphonse 79, 114, 161, 176, 190–191
Garcia, Joseph Suarez 79, 189
Gasser, Chief D.M. 159
Gearhardt, Lloyd 130, 150–151, 154–156, 175, 190
Genslinger, Charles H. 28–29, 36–38, 45, 72–73, 75–79, 82, 85, 87–88, 90, 108, 110, 126, 181, 183, 187, 201
Geraci, Rocco 64
Geraghty, John A. 161
Germans 4–6, 25–26, 83, 117
Gerteis, Louis 11
Gibbons, Austin 75, 78, 120; versus Daly 120
Gilmore, Thomas 135–136
Glynn, Colonel John 12
Goddard, Joe 116, 118–119, 190; Smith versus 118–119
Godfrey, George 121
Goodrich, George 114–115
Gorman, James (Jimmy) 150, 177–178, 190; versus Levy 143
Gorman, Johnny "The Lilliputian Lord" 143
Goss, Joe 98
Gossip & Company 10
Granite Athletic Club (NJ) 67
Gray, Louis 168, 190
Green, Joe 114, 180
Grevenig, Louis 125
Griffin, John 73, 76, 78, 189; versus Larkin 73, 76
Griffiths, Albert "Young Griffo" 156–157, 163, 165, 185, 190
Guillebeau, Louis 174, 176, 178, 181, 191
Guillotte, J.V. 37, 57, 94, 102, 169
gymnastics 2, 10

Hall, Jim 55, 67–68, 81, 85–86, 89, 112, 119–126, 130, 154, 164–166, 170–171, 177; Fitzsimmons versus 120, 122–126
Hammel, John 66
Harding, William E. 30, 199
Harmony Club 8
Harney, Owen 130, 149
Harper, Dr. 52
Harrison, Barker 34
Harrison, Benjamin 64, 88, 99
Haughery, Margaret 24–25, 135–139, 193, 197, 201
Hayne, Franklin B. 61
Heard, W.W. 45
Hennessy, David 40, 50–52, 60–64, 66; murder 50, 52, 60, 63, 195, 199; riot 61–65; trial 52, 60–61
Henry, Joseph 45
Hickory, James 134
Hill, A.M. 144
Hinds, Billy 116–118, 190; McMillan versus 116–117
Hodgkins, Howe 54
Hogan, Kid 121
Holscher, Benjamin G. 27–28, 38
horse racing 3, 8, 34
Howard, Charles T. 44
Howe, Dr. George 12
Hubbard & Bowers 10
Hughes, David 139
Hughes, N.D. 131
Hughes, W.L. 107
Husbands, Clarence 166, 168, 178, 181, 190–191

illustrations 22, 24, 25, 30, 31, 32, 33, 35, 40, 49, 49, 51, 55, 56, 62, 63, 69, 74, 78, 82, 83, 84, 86, 91, 93, 95, 98, 99, 100, 101, 107, 108, 118, 122, 125, 127, 128, 132, 134, 154, 157, 158, 163, 164, 182
Imperial Rifle Club 153
Incardona, Bastiano 64, 195
Irish 4, 6, 11–12, 15–16, 23–25, 31, 33, 54, 57, 77–78, 81–82, 92–93, 97–98, 105,

116–117, 149, 185–186, 193, 195, 199
Italian 6, 16, 26, 50, 52, 62–65, 195, 199–200

Jackson Rifle Club 11, 153
Jackson Sawmill 111, 187
Jaeger & Depass 137
James, Frank 32
James, Jesse 32
Janvry, Jules 106
Jefferson, City of 26–27
Jefferson Parish 37, 180
Johnson, Charles (Charley, Charlie) 43, 79, 102, 114, 161, 176, 190; versus Maber 161
Johnson, Charles 105
Johnson, Fred 95
Journee, Capt. John 175, 177
Joyce, P.A. 135, 139
J.P. Arnoult Rifle Club 12, 29, 45, 52, 65–66, 131
Julian, Martin 117, 123, 125
Julier, Conrad C. 38, 131–132

Kammer, Charley 121
Kantz, Joseph 131
Kelliher, Denny 68
Kellogg, William Pitt 22
Kelly, John Edward *see* Dempsey, Jack
Kelly, Sammy 181
Kelly, "Smiling" Jack 105
Kelly, Tom 189
Kemmick, Charles 68
Kennard, J.H. 71
Kennedy, Charles 127
Kennedy, Hugh 175
Kennedy, John 105
Kennedy, Tom 190
Kennedy, Willis 18
Keough, Hugh 178
Kernaghan, William 10
Killion, Larry 105
Kilrain, Jake 17–18, 30, 33–36, 42–43, 57, 66, 68, 71, 87, 98–99, 145, 156, 167, 185, 199
Klein, L.H. 105, 123
Klimt, George 182–183
Klimt-Hearn Company 182
Klotz, Bernard, Jr. "Buddy" 132–134, 147–148, 158–161, 169; trial 159–161
Klotz, Bernard, Sr. 132–148, 158–161, 187; trial 159–161
Knoechel, Louis "Knuckles" 37, 149, 174, 176, 189, 191
Koffskey, Edward A. 27–28, 131, 169

Labatut, Henry P. 147
LaBlanche, George "The Marine" 127–128, 130

Lafayette, City of 24, 26–27
Lambou, Henry 28, 53
Lambou, Victor 28, 53, 131, 177, 179
Lambou & Noel 53, 111, 179, 187
Langster, Steve 18
Lannon, Harry 41–42
Lannon, Joe 102–103
Larkin, James (Jimmy) 73, 76, 78, 189; Griffin versus 73, 76
Lavigne, George "Kid" 162–167, 176, 178, 181, 186; Bowen versus 162–166
Law, John 25
Lawrason, Coroner (Layrisson) 165
Lawrence, T.B. 170
Lawson Rifle Club 13
Layton, Billy 164, 166
Lazarus, Judge Henry L. 125
Leonard, Mike 152
Leonhard, Charles P. 28, 38
Leonhard, Louis P. 28
Levy, Jack 143, 150–151, 190; Connors versus 151; Gorman versus 143
Lewis, Evan "Strangler" 116–117
Lilly, Chris (Lillie) 16
Logan, Dr. Samuel 52
Long, Henry 180
London Prize Ring Rules 17, 32–34, 36, 71, 87, 105, 144, 171
Loose, Jacob 138
Louisiana Club 8
Louisiana Greys 11
Louisiana Rifle Club 12–13
Louisiana State Lottery 8, 44, 8, 147, 186, 194, 201
Louisiana Supreme Court 19, 90, 136, 146–149, 166–167, 169–172, 175, 179
Lowenthal Johann 29
Lowry, Robert 36
Luzenberg, Charles H. 60, 71–72, 144, 147, 171, 173
Lynch, Alphonse 46
Lyons, Adolph "Dolly" 121

Maber, William "Shadow" 161, 166, 190; Johnson versus 161
Mace, Jem 17
Macheca, Joseph P. 62, 64
Mackenzie, Capt. George Henry 29
Macready, Charles 135–138
Madden, Kid 162
Maestri, Mike 174–175
Mafia 52, 62, 64; *see also* Black Hand
Magnolia Garden 29

Maher, Peter 81–85, 87–88, 92, 96, 98, 110, 120–121, 123, 144–145, 151–152, 157, 185, 190, 195, 199; Fitzsimmons versus 81–85, 110
Mandeville, Dr. W.R. 144
Marchesi, Antonio 63–64
Marchesi, Asperi 63–64
Mardi Gras 8, 29, 68, 77, 82–83, 101, 109, 145, 169
Margaret Haughery & Company 135–138
Margaret's Steam and Mechanical Bakery 25, 136, 138–139
Marigny, Bernard 26
Marion Rifles 11
Marmouget, Andrew P. 131
Marquis of Queensbury Rules 17–18, 36, 57, 71, 105, 144, 171, 181
Marr, Judge Robert H. 71–72, 143
Martin, Dr. E. Denegre 165
Martin, Harris "The Black Pearl" 68, 82
Masterson, Bat 34, 93, 102, 105, 120, 123–124
Matranga, Charles 50, 60, 64, 195
Maylie, Dr. 174
McAuliffe, Jack 54, 57, 59, 74–75, 81, 87, 92–96, 101–102, 105, 110, 119, 123–124, 151, 178, 185, 190, 196; versus Myer 92–95, 110
McCain, J.M. 45
McCaleb, Edwin Howard 126, 144, 171
McCarthy, Cal 69–71, 76–78, 95, 110, 189–190; versus Callaghan 77–78, 110; versus Warren 70–72, 76
McCarthy, William (Billy) 130, 143–144, 153, 164, 168, 173–175, 190–191
McClelland, D.A. 174
McCoy, Kid 177
McCoy, Thomas 16
McCune, Ed 72, 79, 175
McEnery, Harry "Bantam" 68–69
McEnery, Samuel D. 31–32, 159, 171–172
McGraw, Mike 139
McGregory, Lem "St. Joe Kid" 40
McHale, Jimmy 30, 40, 127
McKinley, William 173
McLaughlin, Major Frank 56–57, 85, 120
McMillan, Duncan 117
McMillan, William 59, 116–

Index

117, 189–190; versus Hinds 116–117
McNally, Morris 163
McNeely, Capt. H.P. 66
McNeely, Lem 66
McShea (McStea), John V. 183
McVey, John 168–169, 190
Meister, Herman 38
Merriam, William Rush 67
Metropolitan Club 2, 38, 45, 72–73, 75, 77–78, 80–82, 85, 87–88, 90, 108, 110, 112–113, 115–116, 126–127, 140, 143, 173, 181, 183, 187, 194 154, 170, 185, 190; Burke versus Needham 85, 110; Gibbons versus Bowen 75; Siddons versus Warren 110; Van Heest versus Siddons 110
Metropolitan Rifle Club 13, 65
"Mexican Joe" 173, 181, 189–191
Meyer, Cassius 108
Miller, G.H. 41
Miller, Henry C. 152, 171
Miller, M.M. 14
Miller, Pete 152
Milneburg 37, 52, 131
Mississippi Company 25
Mitchell, Charles (Charlie) 33–34, 69, 81, 83, 86–87, 98, 110, 120, 123–124, 141, 143, 145–147, 154, 170, 185, 190; Slavin versus 110; versus Upham 110
Moise, Judge James C. 159–160, 169
Monasterio, Pietro 61, 63
Montgomery Guard 11
Moore, David 41, 152
Morgan, Frank 102
Morphy, Paul 29–30
Morris, John 44, 147
Muldoon, William "Iron Duke" 33–34, 36, 57
Mumford, William 24
Murphy, A.J. 136
Murphy, Billy "Torpedo" 176–177, 191
Murphy, "Handsome" Dan 34
Murphy, Johnny (Johnnie) 34, 155–156, 190; Plimmer versus 155–156
Murphy, Martin 164
Myer, Billy "The Streator Cyclone" 48, 57, 66, 68, 74–76, 78, 81, 87–88, 92–96, 105, 110, 149, 185, 189–190, 196; Bowen versus 66, 76; Carroll versus 74–76; McAuliffe versus 92–95, 110
Myles, Dr. Albert B. 134

Napier, Hugh 140–141, 190; Van Heest versus 140–141
Needham, Danny 68, 82, 85, 110, 127; Burke versus 85, 110
Neil, Frank "Dutch" 79, 189–190
New Basin Canal 23, 135
New Orleans Athletic Club 19, 40, 100
New Orleans Baseball Park 37
New Orleans Camera Club 95
New Orleans Pelicans 6, 88, 108
New Orleans Rifle Club 10–12
New York Athletic Club 30
Newsom, H.C. 45
Newton, Judge 121, 146
Nicholls, Francis T. 19, 31, 34, 44, 148, 171
Nicholson, Eliza Jane 8
Noel, Charles 28, 38, 53, 67, 83, 88, 92, 101, 106–109, 111–113, 115, 119–122, 124–126, 128, 130–131, 144, 179, 181, 183, 187
North, William 27, 38, 196
Nuñez, José Vicente 3

Oakley, Annie 13
O'Connell, William "Doc" 47, 54, 56
O'Conner, William "Billy" J. 50–51
O'Donnell, Steve 168
Oliver, Joe 42, 115, 189
Olympic Club Anniversaries 26, 45, 65, 130, 148, 172; arena 1–2, 46–48, 53, 56–57, 65, 78, 80, 83, 89–90, 100, 180–183; benefit events 37, 72–76, 106, 113, 151, 167–169, 174, 176, 184, 186, 191; clubhouse 27–28, 45–46, 65, 67, 79–81, 89, 94, 101–102, 132, 151–152, 169, 172, 179–182; exhibition events 2, 15, 18–19, 30, 36–37, 39–43, 46, 50, 59–60, 69, 71–73, 75–76, 81–82, 87, 98, 113–114, 118, 125, 144, 147–149, 151–152, 156–157, 163, 168, 171, 173–174, 176, 178, 180–181, 184, 191; fire 182–183; membership 1, 28, 45, 65, 67, 131–132, 170, 173, 179; officers 27–28, 37, 53, 71, 131, 173, 180
Olympic Guards 43–44
Olympic Hall Association 179, 181–182
Olympic Rifle Club 13–14, 28–29, 37, 45, 52–53, 65–66, 88, 153, 179

O'Malley, Dominick 50, 61, 123, 176
Oriental Club 67
Orleans Rifle Club 13
O'Rourke, Sean 15

Packard, Stephen B. 31
Palmer, Pedlar 177
Parkerson, William S. 61, 64
Patorno, Anthony 52
Patton, Isaac 39
Patton's Tallow Factory 79, 114
Pelican Club 14–15
Pelican Rifle Club 13
Peters, Henry 131
Peterson, Theodore 38, 45–46, 53, 106, 152
Peterson & Janvry 38, 106
Peyton, James C. 133, 151
Pickwick Club 8
Pierce, Eddie 121
Pierce, George 142–143, 149, 168, 174, 190–191; Everhardt versus 142
Pinchback, P.B.S. 22
Pipes, Dr. D.W. 45
Plessy, Homer A. 90–92
Plimmer, Billy 121, 155–156, 177, 180, 190; versus Murphy 155–156
Pokegama Athletic and Sportsman's Association (MI) 68
Pokorny, Michael 119
Police Gazette 30, 33, 100, 152–153, 167, 196, 198–199
Polizzi, Emmanuele 61, 64
pool 2, 10, 13, 15, 38, 41, 80, 41, 80, 106, 132–133, 152, 159 (see also Billiards)
Porter, Charles (Charlie) 72, 79, 189
prizefighting 2, 6, 16, 19, 30–31, 33, 36, 40–41, 69–72, 83–84, 88–89, 95, 106, 109, 114, 139, 142–145, 147, 162, 166, 169, 171–172, 182, 186 (see also Boxing)
Pujol, Jules 18
Puritan Club (NY) 55

Queen, George 46, 190
Quintero, Lamar C. 195

Rathery, Herbert 72
Reconstruction 6, 22–23, 59, 88
Redon, Marsh 100
Reiss, J.J. 137
Renaud, John K. 12
Renaud, P.A. "Bud" 33–34, 124

Index

Reynolds, Ed "Big Gas House Man" 18
Reynolds, William B. (Rewnolds) 180
Rich, Co. Charles W. 34
Richbourg (MS) 17, 34, 145, 167, 185, 199
rifle clubs 9–13, 28–29, 37, 45, 52–53, 65–66, 88, 131, 153, 169, 177, 179; Bachemin 12; Behan 11; Broadway 153, 177; Commercial 12; Crescent City 11–12; Eagle 12; Eicke 12; Endeavor 12; Enterprise 12; Expectation 12, 65; Imperial 153; Jackson 11, 153; J.P. Arnoult 12, 29, 45, 52, 65–66, 131; Lawson 13; Louisiana 12–13; Metropolitan 13, 65; New Orleans 10–12; Olympic 13–14, 28–29, 37, 45, 52–53, 65–66, 88, 153, 179; Orleans 13; Pelican 13; Southern 13, 65, 169; Unexpected 13; Volunteer 13, 153, 179; Washington Artillery 11; *see also* target shooting
Rillieux, Norbert 21
Robertson, Professor 175
Roche, Dick 105
Roeber, Ernest 116–117
Rogers, Isiah 16
Romero, Frank "Nine Fingered Frank" 64
Roper, Jim 9, 11
Ross, William D. 53, 106–107, 131, 151, 191
Routh, Clarence 134, 147, 159, 161
Royal Street 3, 27–29, 43, 61, 67, 78–80, 89–90, 92, 94, 101, 108, 132–133, 154, 179–180, 193, 198
Russell, John 50
Russell, Joseph J. 179–180
Ruty, E. 131
Ryan, John 134
Ryan, Paddy 31, 31–34, 57, 66, 68, 186
Ryan, Tommy 68, 82, 115–116, 119, 127, 162, 167, 177–178, 186, 190

St. Bernard Parish 27, 37, 41, 79, 114, 160, 176
St. Charles Avenue 11, 14, 21, 114–115, 119
St. Charles Hotel 14, 25, 100
St. Louis Hotel 14
Salder, Charles 177
Sambola, Judge Anthony 44, 116
Scaffedi, Antonio 61
Schenck, Charles H. 137
Scholl, William 131–135, 139–140, 142–143, 147–148, 151–153, 155, 158–161, 166, 168–170, 187
Schooler Bulls-Eye Trophy 12
Schwabacher (J&M) 139–140
Scott, George 189–190
Scully, Jim 68
Seeman, Dr. Charles L. 71, 132
Seenan, John 68
Seiferth, Herman J. 144
Seligman, Jacob M. 61
Selph, Dudley 12
Shakspeare, Joseph A. 18, 39–40, 42–44, 51–52, 61, 64, 82, 180
Shakspeare Almshouse 39, 180
Shanssey, John 30
Shea, Mike 59–60
Shea, Peter 178, 191
Shields, B.C. 71
Siddons, George 72–73, 77–78, 87, 90, 110, 121, 140, 189–190; versus Van Heest 110; versus Warren 110
Siefcar, Lucas 149
Skelly, "Handsome" Jack 54, 92, 95–97, 110, 141, 190, 196; Dixon versus 95–97, 110
Slavin, Frank "Paddy" 67–69, 81, 83, 86–87, 98, 110, 152, 190; Mitchell 110; versus Vacquelin 110
Smith, "Denver" Ed 116, 118–119, 190; versus Goddard 118–119
Smith, J.L. 18
Smith, Mike 43, 59, 189
Smith, "Mysterious" Billy 116
Smith, Solly 176–177, 191
Soto, John A. 34
Soule, Col. George (Professor) 73, 171
Southern Athletic Club 9, 18, 36, 40, 42–43, 45, 52, 61, 99–100, 127, 144–145, 175, 185
Southern Gymnastic Club 18
Southern Improvement Company 131, 197
Southern League 37, 88, 108, 187
Southern Park *see* Magnolia Garden
Southern Rifle Club 13, 65, 169
Southern Yacht Club 8, 66
Spanish 1, 3–6, 48, 142
Spanish Fort 5
Spitzfaden, Albert 49, 127, 164, 166
Spitzfaden, Charles 166
Sporl, Joseph L. 28, 67, 69, 106–107, 113, 162, 187
Sportsman's Park 6, 18, 37, 42, 54, 187
Sullivan, Jim 121
Sullivan, John A. 128
Sullivan, John L. 1, 17–18, 30–36, 54, 57, 60, 66–69, 71, 81, 86–88, 92, 96–106, 110, 112, 116, 121–122, 127, 139, 144–145, 167, 171, 179, 184–186, 190, 193, 196–197, 200; versus Corbett 97–105, 110
Sullivan, "Yank" 105
Sweeney, James 46
swimming 2, 10

Tanney, Joe 41–42, 114
target shooting 2, 10–11, 37; *see also* rifle clubs
Tarleton, Ed 152
Tarleton, Marc 152
Taylor, Walter T. 53
Taylor & Churchill 10
"The Terrible Swede" 180
Third District 1, 12, 26–28, 38, 92, 101, 105, 111, 114, 122, 130, 142, 187
Third District Benevolent Association 182
Third District Building Association 28, 43, 53, 111, 187
Thoele, Henry 28
Tissot, Judge Aristice Louis (A.L.) 135–136
Tito, Peter 45
Tobin, William 14
Tourgee, Judge Albion W. 91
Traina, Charles 64
Travis, John 9, 11
Turner, Edward 161
Turner, Henry 161
Tuthall, Gus 57
Twin City Athletic Club (MN) 68, 116

Unexpected Rifle Club 13
Upham, Arthur 46, 55–56, 79, 83, 190; Mitchell versus 110

Vacquelin, Felix 36, 40, 42–43, 46, 59, 73, 83, 110, 189–190
Vance, John C. 45
Van Heest, Johnny 140–141, 190; versus Napier 140–141; versus Siddons 110
Vincent & Company 134
Volunteer Rifle Club 13, 153, 179

Index

Walsh, Capt. Richard 175
Ward, Tommy 46, 189; Wilson versus 46
Warmoth, Henry Clay 22
Warren, Tommy 69–73, 76–78, 110, 143–144, 189, 191; McCarthy versus 70–72, 76; Siddons versus 110
Washington Artillery Rifle Club 11
Washington Guard 16
Watkins, Justice Lynn B. 148
Welch, Billy 98
West End 5, 32, 42
West End Athletic Club 19, 36, 42, 44, 48, 66, 74, 93
West End Hotel 32
Whalen, Officer 133

Wickliffe, John C. 61
Wilkinson, James 79
Williams, Ed 79
Williams, Frank 67, 77, 81, 87, 92, 109, 120–121, 125–126, 148, 162, 166, 187, 196
Williams, William H. 71
Willis, Abe 95
Wilson, Charles "Kid" 46, 59, 189; versus Ward 46
Woods, Billy 59
World Industrial and Cotton Centennial Exposition 21, 23, 193, 199–200
Wren, G.L.P. 45
wrestling 2, 10, 16–17, 32, 37, 73, 109, 116–117, 161, 173–175, 177–178

Wright, Walter J. 28, 38, 53, 131
Wright, William H. 27, 53
Wyman's Gardens 140

Yellow Fever 4, 6, 23, 193, 199
Young Bibby 178
Young Men's Democratic Association 38, 40
Young Men's Gymnastic Club 8–9, 19, 36, 40, 61, 174–175, 179

Zeigler, Owen 175
Zengel, Frank 38, 67, 131, 144, 147–149, 171, 173, 179–180, 182–183, 187, 196–197

www.ingramcontent.com/pod-product-compliance
Lightning Source LLC
Chambersburg PA
CBHW081556300426
44116CB00015B/2904